Lone Stars of David

COMPILED AND EDITED BY

HOLLACE AVA WEINER AND

KENNETH D. ROSEMAN

Lone Stars of David The Jews of Texas

BRANDEIS UNIVERSITY PRESS

Waltham, Massachusetts

In Association with the Texas Jewish Historical Society

Published by University Press of New England

Hanover and London

Brandeis University Press
Published by University Press of New England,
One Court Street, Lebanon, NH 03766
In association with the Texas Jewish Historical Society
www.upne.com
© 2007 by The Texas Jewish Historical Society
Printed in the United States of America

5 4 3 2

Publication of this volume is made possible in part by a grant from the
Texas Jewish Historical Society.

Halftitle page: Perry Kallison among his Polled Herefords. Photo courtesy
of Southwest Collection/Special Collections Library, Texas Tech
University, Lubbock, Texas, Frank Reeves Photographic Collection.

Page ii: Ahavath Sholom, Fort Worth. Photo by Carolyn Cruz.

Library of Congress Cataloging-in-Publication Data
Lone stars of David : the Jews of Texas / compiled and edited by Hollace
Ava Weiner and Kenneth D. Roseman.
    p. cm.—(Brandeis Series in American Jewish History, Culture, and Life)
Includes bibliographical references and index.
ISBN-13: 978–1–58465–622–7 (cloth : alk. paper)
ISBN-10: 1–58465–622–0 (cloth : alk. paper)
1. Jews—Texas—History.   I. Weiner, Hollace Ava, 1946–
II. Roseman, Kenneth.
F395.J5L66 2007
976.400492'4—dc22   2006024834

 University Press of New England is a member of the
Green Press Initiative. The paper used in this book
meets their minimum requirement for recycled paper.

The editors gratefully acknowledge permission to reproduce the following:

Parts of the chapter "Home on the Range" in the present work appeared
in *Halff of Texas: Merchant Rancher of the Old West* (Austin: Eakin Press, 2000),
by Patrick Dearen. Parts of the chapter "'The Man Who Stayed in Texas'"
in the present work appeared in *Kindler of Souls: Rabbi Henry Cohen of Texas*
(Austin: University of Texas Press, 2007), by Henry Cohen II; and in
"A Forgotten Tzaddik," *CCAR Journal: A Reform Jewish Quarterly* 53 (Winter
2006), by Henry Cohen II. Parts of the chapter "East Texas Oil Boom"
appeared in *Raisins and Almonds . . . and Texas Oil! Jewish Life in the Great
East Texas Oil Field* (Austin: Sunbelt Eakin Press, 2004). Parts of the
chapter "Neiman-Marcus" appeared in "'Al' Neiman: The Princely
Pauper," by Hollace Weiner, © *Fort Worth Star-Telegram*, August 24, 1986.
Parts of the chapter "Minority Report" appeared in "Houston's a better
place, thanks to 'Dr. Ray' Daily," by Lynwood Abram, May 23, 2005,
© 2005 Houston Chronicle Publishing Company reprinted with
permission, All Rights Reserved.

Endleaves: Jewish cartographer Jacob De Cordova's 1849 map of Texas
received the endorsement of the state's top elected officials, whose
signatures appear at left. They include then-Senator Sam Houston and
Congressman David S. Kaufman, who was of Jewish descent. Pictured
here, as a reverse transparency, is the lower third of the map, which
altogether measures 40 by 33 inches. Detail, courtesy Special Collections,
The University of Texas at Arlington Library, Arlington, Texas

For the complete list of books in this series, please see www.upne.com and www.upne.com/series/BSAJ.html

Hollace Ava Weiner and Kenneth D. Roseman, editors
Lone Stars of David: The Jews of Texas

Jack Wertheimer, editor
Jewish Education in an Age of Choice

Edward S. Shapiro
Crown Heights: Blacks: Jews, and the 1991 Brooklyn Riot

Kirsten Fermaglich
American Dreams and Nazi Nightmares: Early Holocaust Consciousness and Liberal America, 1957–1965

Andrea Greenbaum, editor
Jews of South Florida

Sylvia Barack Fishman
Double or Nothing: Jewish Families and Mixed Marriage

George M. Goodwin and Ellen Smith, editors
The Jews of Rhode Island

Shulamit Reinharz and Mark A. Raider, editors
American Jewish Women and the Zionist Enterprise

Michael E. Staub, editor
The Jewish 1960s: An American Sourcebook

Judah M. Cohen
Through the Sands of Time: A History of the Jewish Community of St. Thomas, U.S. Virgin Islands

Naomi W. Cohen
The Americanization of Zionism, 1897–1948

Seth Farber
An American Orthodox Dreamer: Rabbi Joseph B. Soloveitchik and Boston's Maimonides School

Ava F. Kahn and Marc Dollinger, editors
California Jews

Amy L. Sales and Leonard Saxe
"How Goodly Are Thy Tents": Summer Camps as Jewish Socializing Experiences

Ori Z. Soltes
Fixing the World: Jewish American Painters in the Twentieth Century

Gary P. Zola, editor
The Dynamics of American Jewish History: Jacob Rader Marcus's Essays on American Jewry

David Zurawik
The Jews of Prime Time

Ranen Omer-Sherman
Diaspora and Zionism in American Jewish Literature: Lazarus, Syrkin, Reznikoff, and Roth

Ilana Abramovitch and Seán Galvin, editors
Jews of Brooklyn

Pamela S. Nadell and Jonathan D. Sarna, editors
Women and American Judaism: Historical Perspectives

Annelise Orleck, with photographs by Elizabeth Cooke
The Soviet Jewish Americans

Steven T. Rosenthal
Irreconcilable Differences: The Waning of the American Jewish Love Affair with Israel

Jonathan N. Barron and Eric Murphy Selinger, editors
Jewish American Poetry: Poems, Commentary, and Reflections

Barbara Kessel
Suddenly Jewish: Jews Raised as Gentiles

Naomi W. Cohen
Jacob H. Schiff: A Study in American Jewish Leadership

Roberta Rosenberg Farber and Chaim I. Waxman, editors
Jews in America: A Contemporary Reader

Murray Friedman and Albert D. Chernin, editors
A Second Exodus: The American Movement to Free Soviet Jews

Stephen J. Whitfield
In Search of American Jewish Culture

David Kaufman
Shul with a Pool: The "Synagogue-Center" in American Jewish History

Beth S. Wenger and Jeffrey Shandler, editors
Encounters with the "Holy Land": Place, Past and Future in American Jewish Culture

Joyce Antler, editor
Talking Back: Images of Jewish Women in American Popular Culture

Jack Wertheimer
A People Divided: Judaism in Contemporary America

Diane Matza, editor
Sephardic-American Voices: Two Hundred Years of a Literary Legacy

Sylvia Barack Fishman
A Breath of Life: Feminism in the American Jewish Community

TO HELEN GOLDMAN WILK,
whose persistence and confidence
turned this proposal into reality.

*"A woman of valor, who can find . . . from
afar she brings her sustenance . . . She senses that
her enterprise is good, so her light is not extinguished
at night . . . Her children rise and celebrate her; and
her husband, he praises her . . ."* —Proverbs 31

Contents

When I was asked to write a personal reminiscence of the life of a Jew in Texas as an opening essay for this volume, I was, of course, pleased and initially thought that it would be very easy to do. Once I started writing, I had to come to grips with several things that I had not thought about in many years.

To begin with, what I thought would be a simple task is really rather complicated—complicated by my own background as a small-town boy. It is further complicated by the culture of the Jewish community in Texas at the time that I was growing up. Simply put, I think that the life of someone such as me, who grew up in a small town, was totally different than the life of someone who came of age in one of the larger Texas cities. In the 1920s and 1930s, Jews who grew up in the larger cities, generally speaking, lived a rather segregated life among Jews. In small towns, Jews grew up reasonably well integrated into that community.

My family began immigrating to America in 1848 and to Texas after the Civil War. They came one at a time from Kempen, a German village in what was then Prussia. My grandfather, Leo Schwarz, came by steerage in 1872 when he was age eighteen, and I have his travel diary. His ship docked in New Orleans, where he bought some four-cent cigars to bring to his brothers in Hempstead, a railroad stop fifty miles beyond Houston. A few years later, his father, Rabbi Heinrich Schwarz, joined the family in Texas. He was the state's first ordained rabbi to lead a congregation. His sons built a backyard synagogue where their father conducted services, mainly for the extended family. As the brothers married and had children, they looked for other towns along the railroad line in which to open retail stores. My grandfather moved to Lockhart, where my mother, Edith, was born in 1887. She married Carl Strauss, a traveling piano salesman. Shortly after I was born in 1918, they moved to Stamford.

Stamford (pop. 4,000) is in West Texas. Our extended family, which included my Aunt Birdie and Uncle Louis Rosenwasser and their four children, were the only Jews in that town. Interestingly, the fact that I was Jewish was not paramount in my thinking—although my mother certainly saw to it that we knew that we were Jewish. It really was not of tremendous importance—I was Jewish, and I knew it. While we never saw a rabbi in Stamford and had no formal religious training, my mother created a very strong impression on my brother Ted and me that we were Jewish and how significant that was. In some mystical way, my mother managed to convince my brother and me that we were "God's chosen people." I used to tell my friends—laughingly, after I got to college—that I would walk around Stamford somewhat embarrassed at being one of "God's chosen people," something I could not really talk about because "they" would not understand.

My one real connection with Judaism came on the High Holy Days when we would drive more than 150 miles from Stamford to Fort Worth to attend services with my grandparents on either Yom Kippur or Rosh Hashanah—rarely both. We closed the store for the Jewish holidays, which usually seemed to fall on a Saturday. That sort of aggravated my father. Saturdays were busiest in the fall when the cotton was picked and the workers had been paid. The cotton would come in, and our store would be closed.

We did not have a problem with anti-Semitism. People were not "anti" our family—we were the only Jewish family in town, and we were obviously not numerous enough,

Bob Strauss stands on the bumper of the family Model T Ford with his cousins and baby brother in his hometown, Stamford, Texas. Perched on the car, left to right, are Helen Rosenwasser, Berniece Rosenwasser, and Bob Strauss. Standing in front of the Model T is Felicia Siegel holding Ted Strauss. Family Photo Collection of Sydney Levine.

nor threatening enough, for many people to dislike us. As a matter of fact, I think that my father and my uncle were two of the most popular people in the town by sheer dint of their personalities and their basic generosity with people less fortunate. My Uncle Louis, for example, was elected president of the local Chamber of Commerce. My father and my uncle, between them, played poker, golf, and in general socialized on a broad scale.

Yet they did not go out at night to social affairs because, as I look back, they probably weren't invited. Even in that small community, my parents and my aunt and uncle had limited social interaction with others—particularly after dark. I never thought much about it at the time, but in retrospect, obviously, it did have something to do with our faith. My recollection is very clear that on most nights, my aunt and uncle came to our house after work, or we went to their house. During the day, each had dry goods stores, and they competed with each other. My uncle, who had a much larger store, was a far better businessman than my father, who preferred to play the piano. He was a marvelous musician.

As I was preparing to leave Stamford to go to the University of Texas in the fall of 1935, it never occurred to me that when I got to Austin my social life would be limited to the Jewish community on campus, which I found exceedingly uncomfortable. Frankly, my brother Ted and I each joined Jewish fraternities because the other fraternities were not open to us. Our parents were pleased that we joined Jewish fraternities because, in their minds, this gave us exposure to a culture that they felt was important and about which we knew little. We resented this limitation because it was based on our religion. Yet belonging to a fraternity enlarged our lives on the entire campus as we each became deeply involved in campus politics and the broader social life available. At the University of Texas, while my grades were certainly not impressive, my ability to emerge as one of the campus leaders stood me in good stead.

Strangely, although I resented the designation of Jewish and non-Jewish fraternities, I think that the fraternity experience in Austin, my sudden awareness that Jewish people were steered to a slightly different track, served me very well as I was preparing to figure out my life in the larger community. In the larger world, there were very definite social distinctions for those of us in the Jewish faith.

During my senior year in law school at the University of Texas, as war was breaking out around the world, a senior official with the Federal Bureau of Investigation in Washington was visiting a number of law schools to recruit up to three seniors in each graduating class to join the FBI. As I recall, about half of our class went through the interview process. A couple were selected, one of which was me. I was really more than impressed—I was shocked that I had done so well in my interview with the FBI. It led to four years as an FBI agent, from 1941 to 1945, moving around the nation from place to place. It was a tremendous experience, particularly maturing for me.

After my FBI service, in the fall of 1945 I moved to Dallas, my wife Helen's hometown, and began the practice of law. It's sort of strange, but I became active in Jewish community affairs. I worked with the Jewish Federation and the American Jewish Committee, and I served as synagogue president at Temple Emanu-El. I was on the committee that selected my synagogue's rabbi in 1949. Years later, I recommended that the governor appoint the rabbi to the University of Texas Board of Regents, which he did. I invited another rabbi from my Dallas synagogue to give invocations before Democratic National Committee meetings and luncheons. Someone asked me once, "Why him?" I responded, "He's my rabbi. I did not pick him through the democratic process. It was a unilateral decision!" When I was U.S. ambassador in Moscow in 1992, I hosted at the American embassy a Passover Seder that was conducted in Russian, English, and Yiddish.

I have had a significant career, including political success and a diplomatic life. With another FBI agent, I founded a law firm that has become of one of the larger, more successful firms in the country, with a significant international practice and with offices in Europe and Russia.

The point of this list of accomplishments is not to impress anyone with my career. It is to attribute such success to the lessons that I learned and the experiences that I had

Diplomat Robert Strauss visits with Israeli Foreign Minister Moshe Dayan and Rahel Dayan in 1980, the era of the Camp David accords. Strauss was Middle East Peace Envoy for President Jimmy Carter. Family Photo Collection of Sydney Levine.

growing up in the only Jewish family in a small West Texas town and, later, to my positive law school and FBI experiences.

Let me conclude by saying that there may have been times that I thought myself handicapped by coming from a small, narrow West Texas town and being of the Jewish faith. As I look back, at eighty-seven years of age, I see the strengths that I developed and the lessons that I learned both in Stamford and at the University of Texas. I realize that those things that I once thought handicapped me actually served, in some way, to be the bedrock of what I became—for better or worse.

I would be remiss if I did not also include my most cherished achievement: that of having a successful family life. Helen and I were very happily married for nearly sixty-six years, and I have three grown children who are also happily married, seven grandchildren, and five great-grandchildren. We remain close with our extended family, including the cousins who grew up with me in Stamford. My family has always been a source of pride and joy, through good times and bad, and I strongly feel that the culture of growing up Jewish in a small community shaped my relationship with my wife and children and my colleagues.   ✴

Acknowledgments

In the beginning, Jonathan Sarna, editor of this series on American Jews in different geographic locales, gave my name to Phyllis Deutsch at University Press of New England. She contacted me in the fall of 2002, asking that I compile an anthology about the Jews of Texas. Flattered and flabbergasted, I mulled over the offer for a year, weighing pros and cons. Helen Wilk—a past president of the Texas Jewish Historical Society (TJHS) and my cohort in many a project—was the chief proponent for embarking on this anthology. She connected me with Ken Roseman, then the interim rabbi in Corpus Christi. He agreed to collaborate as co-editor and began conceptualizing the themes and chapter topics that provided a framework for the anthology. The next step was a formal proposal to the Texas Jewish Historical Society, which for years had talked about sponsoring a new book on the Jews of Texas. The society's first book, *Deep in the Heart: The Lives and Legends of Texas Jews* (Eakin Press, 1989), a handsome, ground-breaking volume, was out of print. The board had voted several times to embark on a second book reflecting the latest scholarship. This is that book. Ruthe Winegarten, lead author of the earlier volume, spoke with me by phone and corresponded via e-mail in the months before her death in 2004. She reviewed this book's proposed table of contents, suggested additional topics, and recommended bringing on board two writers—Cathy Schechter (co-author of *Deep in the Heart*) and Jan Statman.

Rough drafts from more than a dozen authors arrived in January 2005. Three months later, the TJHS hosted a Texas Jewish History symposium at the University of Texas Austin campus in collaboration with UT's Center for American History and the Texas State Historical Association. Helen Wilk coordinated the enriching, daylong seminar. Gladys Leff, of blessed memory, treated the crowd to a retrospective on the battle for women's rights in Texas, the subject of her chapter. Immediately after the symposium, Bryan Stone, a participant and assistant professor at Del Mar College in Corpus Christi, spent five hours with me over dinner, dissecting every presentation, every rough draft, and every aspect of the book. He stayed the course and became this book's unofficial associate editor.

During the gestation of this book, the TJHS has had four presidents: Jack Gerrick, Charles Hart, Marvin Rich, and Vickie Vogel. They provided encouragement, leadership, insight, friendship, and underwriting. Board members pitched in without fail. Ben Pfeffer, the TJHS's longtime treasurer, was a Rock of Gibraltar. Alan Livingston took time from his global oil deals to phone and write, especially when the road was bumpy. He sent contact numbers for people in the "awl bidness," and he peer-reviewed chapters in his line of expertise. The architectural team of David and Binnie Hoffman not only peer reviewed the chapter on little synagogues, they took photos of Beaumont's restored Temple Emanuel and scanned documents from their personal trove of memorabilia. At the last minute, Davie Lou Solka supplied photos from Corpus Christi. In San Antonio, peer-reviewer Lenore Karp double-checked information by looking through old city directories and microfilmed newspapers. Lenore's lasting contribution to future research efforts are the indexes she has compiled listing San Antonio and Bexar County references in the city's three early Jewish community newspapers. The indexed files are in the Texana/Genealogy Department of the San Antonio Public Library. Among the most important advisors from the TJHS were Howard and Annette Lackman. Howard, history professor emeritus from the University of Texas at Arlington, peer reviewed the almost-final drafts. He counseled, consoled, and became a confidant guiding me through each last-minute crisis. In the calm of the Lackman home, we discussed syntax and scholarship. He and Annette even phoned from their vacation in Florida.

A popular history book is not only ideas and words but also pictures and illustrations. My gratitude extends to the libraries and archives that preserve images of the past. At the Dallas Jewish Archives, my colleague Leslie Wagner went beyond the call of duty and tracked down photos from private collections, from the Dallas Holocaust Museum, and from Dallas City Hall, then she asked if she could do anything further.

At the University of Texas in El Paso, imagine my surprise when the archivist on the other end of the phone, Susan Schwartz Novick, identified herself as the great-granddaughter of Olga Kohlberg, who is profiled in this book. Novick proofread the manuscripts on El Paso and recommended photos from UTEP's remarkable Special Collections Department. Also in El Paso, Mary Ann Plaut, the Jewish community's archivist, filled in multiple gaps, corrected misspellings, and researched footnote citations. Victor Mirelles, the gifted photographer who works with the El Paso Museum and Holocaust Center, selected and scanned images from the museum archives.

Assisting in San Antonio was Bunny Gardner, archivist at San Antonio's Beth-El Congregation. She connected me with Alex Halff, who loaned me priceless family photos for use in this volume. At San Antonio's Institute of Texan Cultures, Library Programs Coordinator Patrick Lemelle provided images from his institution's vast collection.

At my alma mater, the University of Texas at Arlington, it was old home week when I returned to the Special Collections section of the campus library. Brenda McClurkin, my "lab partner" during two semesters of archives classes, provided VIP treatment. Cathy Spitzenberger found, conserved, and unfolded Jacob de Cordova's 1849 map of Texas. Gary Spurr knew exactly where to find the photo of Martin Frost wearing a cowboy hat, although the Frost papers had not yet been processed. Blanca Smith located National Council of Jewish Women pictures from the *Star-Telegram* collection.

At UT's Center for American History in Austin, Assistant Director Brenda Gunn and Image Assets Coordinator Steven Dale Williams supplied several dozen photographs, some on deadline. Also in Austin, Mike Widener, head of special collections at UT's Tarlton Law Library, helped research Justice Rose Spector's legal opinions and located a photo of her in judicial robes. In Waco, Ellen K. Brown combed The Texas Collection at Baylor University for illustrations. Bill Buckner, in the Genealogy Division of the Waco-McLennan County Library, pulled up microfilm from 1916 at a moment's notice.

At Cincinnati's Jacob Rader Marcus Center of the American Jewish Archives, Kevin Proffitt and Camille Servizzi supplied documents, photos, and quick answers to historical questions. Anya Roos at Austin's Bob Bullock Texas State History Museum suggested a document to illustrate the Galveston Movement, and Lyn Slome at the American Jewish Historical Society in New York quickly supplied it. Amy Hooker, at Midland's Petroleum Museum, researched oil field images. I am also grateful to Franzas Cupp, director of Sweetwater's Pioneer City-County Museum, for preserving small-town memorabilia, from motel brochures to newspaper ads. Thanks to Aaron Kornblum, archivist at Berkeley's Western Jewish History Center of the Judah L. Magnes Museum, for scanning the only known photo of Rabbi Jacob Voorsanger. Thanks also to Sarah Jackson, Harris County archivist, who scanned a picture from a 1911 newspaper and pointed out that it was taken by Joe Litterst. Bruce Cammack, at Texas Tech University's Southwest Collection/Special Collections Library, provided images of the Kallison Ranch and photos from the Hermine Tobolowsky papers. Kerry Hoffman and Greg Tucker at Houston's Beth Israel remained on call.

Special thanks go to my friends in Fort Worth who shared their time and professional expertise, especially the volunteers at the Beth-El Congregation Archives. Rosanne Margolis, an insatiable reader, dependable colleague, and loyal friend, proofread the manuscript, discovered that one chapter mentioned her grandmother (the second Mrs. Max Stool), and dug up a priceless photo for the book. Laurie Barker James peer reviewed, selected photos, wrote captions, and used her sociology, grant-writing, and government background to co-author the book's political essay. She and Gary Whitfield assisted with the antebellum Jewish census of Texas conducted with the help of archivists at the Fort Worth Public Library's Genealogy/Local History Room. When legal assistance was needed, I contacted Tom Williams, a first-amendment attorney who always found time to counsel me. Another attorney, Roger Simon, a legal-writing professor at the Texas Wesleyan University School of Law, proofread the manuscript, with a dictionary and the *Chicago Manual of Style* by his side. Photojournalist Carolyn Bauman Cruz, a colleague from my *Star-Telegram* days, went on the road again with me to Hebrew Rest Cemetery in Fort Worth, to Burleson, and to Austin. Ellen Appel, a professional photographer, snapped photos and brainstormed about the cover. Scott Barker and Morris Madson connected Barry Shlachter and me with Ridgmar Oil & Gas Co., where comptroller Linda Baird pulled snapshots of gushers from business and family files.

As deadline neared, among the editorial cadre working over Thanksgiving, Christmas, Chanukah, and New Year's were Lauraine Miller, Howard Lackman, Annette Lackman, Gary Whitfield, Bryan Stone, and my daughter, Dawn, an editor with Fox Radio News, who provided the insightful suggestions of an inside/outsider. Jonathan Sarna also worked through the holidays, reading the book's introduction on a plane en route to Israel.

Once the manuscript was at the publisher's, photographer Ellen Appel got to work on the book jacket. On a legal pad, she sketched a cowboy boot accented with Jewish stars. Larry Nelson, vice-president of manufacturing for Justin Brands, Inc., took that drawing to the El Paso workshop of Jesus Campos, his company's top boot designer. Campos refined the sketch, cut out leather inlays, and crafted a prototype boot before making the final pair. From start to finish, it took four months to create the priceless *Magen David* cowboy boots that grace the book jacket. The vintage wagon wheel came from Philip Murrin's River Ranch. The setting, replete with hay and horseshoe, is Park Ridge Riding Stables in Benbrook. I thank one and all for their collaboration.

Last but not least, now and forever, I thank my husband Bruce, a master speller and communicator who not only proofreads but also shares the highs and the lows, shops and cooks on the home front, listens in times of crisis and indecision, and has weathered every deadline since my college journalism days.

—Hollace Ava Weiner

Sergeant David Levi Kokernot, ca. 1861, in the only published photograph of a Texas Jewish Confederate in uniform.
UT Institute of Texan Cultures at San Antonio, No. 072-0100, courtesy Miss Clifton Mc Neel.

The Formative Years   Forging a Dual Identity

I

Introduction "I Caught the Contagion of Bragging . . ."

HOLLACE AVA WEINER

The stereotypical Texan stands legs apart, hands on hips, and brashly proclaims that everything is bigger (and, therefore, better) in Texas. Texas abounds in stereotypes—some that celebrate Lone Star mythology, some that denigrate it. Jews, too, are often perceived stereotypically—in positive ways as being scholarly and studious, and negatively as being weak and miserly. When Jewish identity cross-pollinates with the Texas persona, the weakling becomes strong; the Shylock turns into a generous spender with an unlimited charge account at Neiman-Marcus. Beaumont's Rabbi Samuel Rosinger, who moved to Texas in 1910, when oil wells were gushing 75,000 gallons of crude a day, noted the change in himself: "I caught the contagion of bragging about . . . my great state."[1] The Jewish Texan who revels most in the intersection of these stereotypes is Kinky Friedman, the self-proclaimed "Texas Jewboy," a country singer-songwriter, mystery novelist, and would-be governor. Friedman embodies the image of the vaudevillian Jew and the self-promoting Texan. His antics inform the world that Texans can be Jewish and that Jews most certainly live in Texas—131,000 of them, or six-tenths of one percent of the state's population.

Friedman's antics aside, what he celebrates is a frontier image, which persists, of independence, nonconformity, expansiveness, muscle, and grit.[2] This embrace of frontier attributes can be ascribed not only to Texas's early Jewish settlers, but to other Jewish pioneers who ventured to America's West. They deliberately left behind large concentrations of coreligionists in the urban Northeast. In newly settled Diaspora regions, acculturation—blending in without becoming absorbed—became the key to survival and Jewish continuity. "We no longer live in the Ghetto world of our own," Rabbi David Rosenbaum observed as he adjusted to Austin in 1911.[3] Accommodations and adaptations had to be made. And so, Rabbi Solomon Greenberg, a farmer and *shochet*, smoked his kosher turkeys in a manner similar to the way that his neighbors in Tyler, Texas, smoked their hams.[4] In the Texas Hill Country, Helena Landa made matzos by spinning a spur across the flat dough, because that was the best implement at hand.[5]

Jews like Landa, who were among the early waves of Texas settlers, found that what mattered more than religion or nationality was mettle and industriousness. The frontier welcomed newcomers, for their numbers helped guarantee safety against Indians, outlaws, and the challenges of nature. By dint of hard work and adaptability, Jews fit in. The first clergyman appointed to the University of Texas Board of Regents, for example, was a rabbi—Maurice Faber. (The certificate formalizing the appointment, however, identified him as "Father Faber," rather than "rabbi.")[6] In 1873, German immigrant David Hirsch of Corpus Christi buried his wife, Jeannette Weil Hirsch, in the closest Jewish cemetery, 140 miles away in Gonzales. When his friend, Captain Richard King, founder

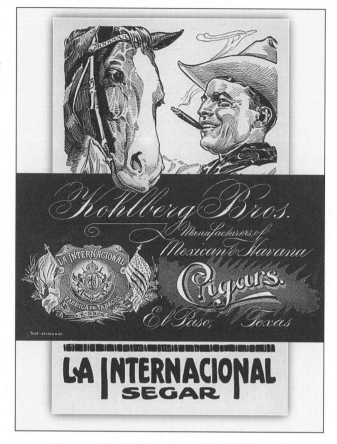

Have a "segar." The Kohlberg brothers, German-Jewish immigrants, were the Southwest's first cigar manufacturers. Their turn-of-the-century advertisements capitalized on the macho image of the Texas cowboy. University of Texas at El Paso Library, Special Collections Department, Kohlberg Family Papers MS 369.

of the legendary King Ranch, learned about Jewish burial customs, he donated land in Corpus Christi for a Hebrew cemetery, the city's first Jewish landmark.[7] In Palestine, an East Texas city, a Jew is credited with luring the first railroad line to the town. One local resident wrote the *American Israelite* in 1873, "[We] constitute the bone and sinew of the county."[8] These Jewish pioneers saw themselves as individuals contributing to the commonweal, rather than as members of a ghettoized group. As Seth Wolitz notes in *Jewries at the Frontier*, Jewish people came to Texas individually, not en masse, while the first Jews to arrive in New York confronted Governor Pieter Stuyvesant as a group: "The New York Jewish experience . . . starts off with a clash of wills . . . They came as a group and have maintained and functioned over the centuries with highly organized group-consciousness and solidarity. Texas Jewry has a different history and therefore a different mentality."[9] Even the Galveston Movement, which brought ten thousand Jews to the Texas Gulf Coast over a seven-year period between 1907 and 1914, dispersed the immigrants into fifteen states and dozens of cities throughout the Midwest and Far West.

Texas, while similar to the American West and to the Deep South, distinguishes itself from the rest of the nation. Its history harks to 1836 and a war for independence from Mexico, not from Great Britain. For a decade, Texas was a nation with its own flag, establishing a strong sense of place. During the Civil War, Texas was the only Confederate state unscathed by major land battles. Yet battlefronts helped define Texas. Indian raids continued through 1875. Mexican border incursions flared until 1916. The "reverberations of this warfare . . . affect[ed] both attitudes and organization," observed Texas historian T. R. Fehrenbach. People had to be judged on their ability, not caste or class or creed, as often happened in the more status-conscious Deep South. Texans came to prize

Kinky Friedman, June 1975, Texas
singer-songwriter and would-be
governor. Friedman represents the
cross-pollination of Jewish identity
with the Texas stereotype. Center for
American History, University of
Texas at Austin, CN Number 04628,
Texas Music Poster Collection.

eccentricity and to mistrust conformity. The state constitution vests less power in its
elected officials than any other state except California.[10]

Texas is big, with the largest landmass among the lower forty-eight states. It stretches
801 miles from north to south (from the environs of Amarillo's B'nai Israel to Brownsville's Temple Beth El) and 795 miles from east to west (from Texarkana's Mount Sinai and
Marshall's erstwhile Moses Montefiore Congregation to El Paso's B'nai Zion). Texas's
wide-open spaces, undeveloped terrain, and embryonic institutions proved an attraction
for nineteenth-century Jews of diverse backgrounds who were confident enough to strike
out on their own in search of economic opportunities. Some failed and went back East or
returned to Europe. Those who succeeded had traits often found among settlers in frontier
environments. Studying the evolution of Texas Jewish communities can lead to analysis of
patterns common not only to Jews but also among other ethnic groups drawn to the frontier or to boomtowns, small towns, and early industries that followed the frontier epic.

There is a common supposition that the first Jews to come to Texas—like those who went
to Oklahoma and Wyoming and California—were soldiers of fortune, true Lone Stars,
mavericks who yearned to strike out on their own, leave Jewish institutions behind, and

Rabbi or priest? When Tyler's Rabbi Maurice Faber was appointed to the University of Texas Board of Regents, state officials were so unfamiliar with Jews that they inscribed the certificate to "Father" M. Faber. Collection of Hollace Weiner.

embrace the raw frontier. Unlike Jews immigrating through Ellis Island and remaining in New York, these settlers were not directly fleeing pogroms and anti-Semitism but were lured by raw, rugged opportunity.

The accuracy of this composite Texas-Jewish pioneer depends on the definition of "first" (not to mention the definition of *Jew*, which can be even harder). When did the "first" Jews arrive in what is now Texas? Was it in the 1820s, when Texas was part of Mexico? Or did the first Jews arrive in the 1500s with the conquistadors? The Marranos—a.k.a. *conversos* and crypto-Jews of Spain—were seeking religious freedom and fleeing the oppression of the Spanish Inquisition. The phenomenon of the crypto-Jew in the Southwest has spawned much mythology. Yes, Spanish Jews who were converted forcibly to Catholicism came to the Southwest. In "Jews Without Judaism" (chapter 2), Bryan Stone contends that *conversos* do not figure in the history of Texas Jewry. They are of negligible significance, if any, in the development of Jewish life in the Lone Star State. They did not create Jewish communities or institutions. They did not settle and most likely did not travel within the boundaries of present-day Texas. Certainly, stories abound among Hispanics along the Texas-Mexican border of families with Semitic customs. There is anecdotal evidence aplenty. No scholarly historical or anthropological study documents this in present-day Texas. Moreover, this seems more a latter-day phenomenon of recovered memory. It has been refuted by folklorist Judith Neulander, who terms crypto-Jews an "imagined community."[11]

The first researcher to document Texas-Jewish history was Henry Cohen, a scholar, linguist, and rabbi. He came to Galveston's pulpit at B'nai Israel in 1888—only fifty-two years after the fall of the Alamo and Texas independence.[12] His research, published in the early issues of the venerable *Publications of the American Jewish Historical Society* and in the Jewish encyclopedias of his time, makes no mention of Marranos peopling the Southwest during the Age of Exploration. Rather, Cohen makes a strong argument that the first Jews to reach Texas are bound up in the pantheon of Anglo-Texas heroes. Cohen paints the earliest Jews in Texas as pioneers who surveyed the terrain, publicized its potential, and brought settlers aplenty to this new Promised Land.

The Jewish Davy Crockett was A. Wolf, who brandished a sword at the Alamo and lost his life. Wolf's name is among those inscribed on a monument on the grounds of the Texas state capitol. The Jewish Sam Houston was David S. Kaufman, a Princeton University graduate and a member of Texas's first U.S. congressional delegation. Kaufman is the namesake of a city and a county. Evidence as to whether he was Jewish is conflicting. Natalie Ornish's *Pioneer Jewish Texans*, the first contemporary study of its kind, reports in a footnote that a penciled remark on Kaufman's Princeton University records states, "Hebrew extraction."[13] (Martin Frost, who served in the U.S. House of Representatives from 1979 to 2005 and considers himself the state's first and only Jewish congressman, researched Kaufman and concluded that Representative Kaufman had a non-Jewish burial in a congressional cemetery.)[14] Rabbi Cohen also describes men who were the Jewish equivalent of Stephen F. Austin. These include Samuel Isaacks, who settled one of empresario Stephen Austin's original three hundred tracts of land. Another was Henri Castro, who "sent to Texas . . . 5,000 emigrants from the Rhenish provinces of Germany, the first organized emigration to Texas."[15]

In "Jews Without Judaism," Bryan Stone questions some of Cohen's assumptions. Isaacks, he concludes, may have been distantly descended from Jews, but even this is conjecture. Castro's family had not practiced Judaism for more than two centuries. None of the colonists in Castroville, a buffer settlement that protected San Antonio from Comanche raids, was Jewish. Stone debunks an oft-repeated legend that Henri Castro put on *tefillin* and *davened* in the woods—for there are few woods in the arid South Texas terrain surrounding Castroville.

A number of the Jewish pioneers heralded by Cohen and other researchers were figures like Simon Wiess—a Polish-Jewish seafarer and cotton shipper who married a Presbyterian. His offspring, who did not follow Judaism, were among the founders of the Humble Oil and Refining Company. Jews would like to claim them, and some writers have. The Wiess family, as well as David Kaufman, who had Jewish antecedents, did not involve themselves with Jewish community or continuity. To paraphrase Seth Wolitz, they nonetheless helped legitimize a Jewish role in the founding of the Texas Republic by imparting a sense of rootedness.[16] Indeed, it could be argued in more than philosophical ways that every Jew—and, indeed, every hybrid-Jew—is an important side of Judaic history.

Not all of the Jewish pioneers deserted the tribe of Israel. The Sanger brothers, profiled in "Confederates Stories" (chapter 3), may not have practiced Judaism when they first opened trading posts in the antebellum Texas frontier. Yet they kept in touch with extended family and utilized their Jewish network of relatives and friends to find brides who, unbelievably, came to Texas. Furthermore, the Sangers and other Jews who fought in and survived the Civil War returned home with greater commitment to their Jewish identity. Researcher Gary Whitfield documents how these veterans were involved in forming B'nai B'rith lodges and congregations. War was a maturing experience that reinforced their identity as both Jews and as Texans. Ultimately, the more formal development of the Texas-Jewish community lies with those like the Sanger brothers, who helped start Jewish institutions in Dallas and Waco. It lies with those who balanced their dual identities—not with the crypto-Jews and their romantic stories, not with the Jews who intermarried, no matter how much oil they drilled or how prominent their offspring may have become.

Another example of a pioneer Texan who remained committed to Jewish continuity—even as he transformed himself into an authentic cowboy—was Mayer Halff, who is profiled by Patrick Dearen in "Home on the Range" (chapter 4). Wearing leather-tooled boots and a ten-gallon hat, Halff herded cattle from the Pecos River north to Montana. His biography is titled *Halff of Texas*, a fitting pun because his cattle grazed on a large percentage of the state. Mayer Halff was also among the founders and benefactors of San Antonio's first congregation, Beth-El, in 1874. When Halff first opened a dry goods store in Liberty, Texas, some customers paid him with cattle instead of cash. Comfortable dealing in basic, raw commodities, he herded the cattle to market.

Mayer Halff was not the only Jewish retailer to go into ranching and leave his mark on the land. Among other notable Lone Star Jewish ranchers were the Weils of Corpus Christi and the Kallisons of San Antonio. Charles Weil, an Alsatian immigrant, opened a general store in Corpus Christi in 1869, selling supplies to area ranchers. When the railroad line to Mexico was completed, his retail business dried up, and he became a full-time rancher. His son, Jonas Weil, was the subject of columns written by newspaperman Fred Gipson, author of the novel *Old Yeller*.

Nathan Kallison and his son Perry became well known among ranchers in the environs of San Antonio. The father, a Chicago saddlemaker, moved to San Antonio in 1899 for his wife's health. In Texas, his leatherwork was far more prized. From a small workshop, he expanded his saddlery into a block-long farm-and-ranch store. With the profits from the retail business, he invested in a ranch on which his son Perry raised cham-

Back at the ranch. Saddlemaker Nathan Kallison moved his family from Chicago to San Antonio, where he opened a workshop that grew into a farm-and-ranch store. With the profits he bought a cattle ranch in 1899 and built this sturdy entrance. Photo courtesy of Southwest Collection/ Special Collections Library, Texas Tech University, Lubbock, Texas, Frank Reeves Photographic Collection.

Meat on the hoof. When Perry Kallison took over operations at the ranch, he raised Polled Herefords. "Polled" means that the fast-growing, beefy crossbreeds did not have horns. Texas Polled Hereford Association Directory, circa 1960s.

pionship cattle, sowed experimental crops, and made a name for himself with a daily radio show.[17] First-generation immigrants, forbidden to own land in the Old Country, eagerly bought property in the New World. In Texas, the property most prized was ranchland.

The bane of Texas ranching was drought. Regardless of a person's beliefs, during years without rainfall ranchers were likely to give in to superstition and voodoo science. Both Jonas Weil and Perry Kallison were active in Texas's regional rainmaking efforts—as was the non-Jewish Charles W. Post of the Post cereal empire. Kallison's rainmaking attempt, which involved seeding the clouds with silver iodide, failed to bring a drop. Weil's effort—which entailed exploding a hot air balloon filled with sulfuric acid and iron shavings—was followed by a downpour.[18]

Ranching was largely a masculine endeavor. Pioneer Jewish women who balanced home, community service, and religion created other role models for women of the West. Olga Kohlberg, a cultured, Westphalia-born bride, moved in 1884 to the wilds of El Paso, a lawless place of cowboys and renegades. Kohlberg, profiled in "Clubwomen Create Communal Institutions" (chapter 5), helped civilize her space by introducing kindergartens and starting a baby hospital. She was among the founders of her synagogue, Temple Mount Sinai, and an organizer of the Jewish Welfare Association of El Paso. Anna Hertzberg, a New Yorker who came to San Antonio as a bride, started a music club,

Rancher and rainmaker. When drought hit the South Texas ranching industry, Jonas Weil helped explode balloons filled with sulfuric acid into the atmosphere. Rain began before nightfall. The Cattleman, September 1940 and October 1951, Southwestern Cattle Raisers Museum Library, Fort Worth. Photos by Carolyn Cruz.

then launched a section of the Council of Jewish Women. By example, Hertzberg and Kohlberg showed Jewish women how to better the civic realm and how to build a Jewish community. These women followed a pattern established by Philadelphia's Rebecca Gratz. With her mother and sisters, Gratz was a charter member of a secular social service society. Subsequently, in 1819, the Gratz women started Philadelphia's Female Hebrew Benevolent Society. Later, Rebecca Gratz launched the first Jewish Sunday school in America. Like Gratz, the pioneer Jewish women leaders in Texas balanced general social service with Jewish community building.[19]

A recurring theme in Texas Jewish history is that of balancing and blending dual identities. The Marshall Sisterhood in East Texas sold hot tamales to raise money for the social hall at Congregation Moses Montefiore. The National Council of Jewish Women in Beaumont sold ham-salad sandwiches at the Jefferson County Fair. Clubwomen and professional women asserted themselves among Jews and gentiles with values of *tikkun olam*, repairing the world. Those profiled in this volume include attorney Hermine Tobolowsky, mother of the Texas Equal Legal Rights Amendment (Gladys Leff's "Opening Legal Doors for Women," chapter 18); Justice Rose B. Spector, elected to the Texas Supreme Court, and State Senator Florence Shapiro ("Most Politics Is Local," chapter 16); and Dr. Ray K. Daily, a physician who stirred controversy on the Houston School Board (Lynwood Abram's "Minority Report," chapter 17). Unlike the frontiersmen, clubwomen and professional women were not often entrepreneurs, but rather crusaders patiently yet forcefully spreading Jewish values of equal justice and equal opportunity.

Another role model for Jewish continuity is the small-town entrepreneur who, owing to commercial success and civic prestige, created and led a Jewish community. Abe Levy of Sweetwater, profiled in Jane Guzman's "West of Neiman's" (chapter 13), purchased a Torah and called to worship Jews scattered within a hundred-mile radius for High Holy Day services and Passover Seders. The Riskind family in Eagle Pass hosted services in the apartment above their store. In Brownsville, Sam Perl functioned as lay rabbi for more than fifty years. Lea Donosky, whose relatives, the Stools of Del Rio, are profiled in Doug Braudaway's "On the Border: A Deck of Cards Led to Del Rio" (chapter 10), recalls that "being Jewish in a small Southern town meant hitting the road for the holidays." She writes:

"Scattered through small towns in a kind of economic Diaspora, Jews . . . drove to the nearest synagogue for services. (Orthodox Jews made the drive before sundown of the holiday.) In more isolated areas, where there weren't enough Jews to support a synagogue, they would drive to a central point for services held in a makeshift synagogue, perhaps a room above a shoe store or just someone's living room. These days were special not just because of their religious significance . . . For us, like any other minority seeking out and finding its own, there is a feeling of comfort and ease in those few hours in which we exist as a majority. The sense of separateness that minorities live with daily seems to nourish this need to gather."[20]

Balancing and blending dual identities. El Paso's Temple Mount Sinai Church League athletes displayed Jewish stars on their uniforms while embracing Texas's "mainstream" religion— athletics. Collection of Hollace Weiner.

Kallah of Texas Rabbis, 1947. Being in remote Texas meant traveling great distances to be among Jewish peers. The Kallah, inaugurated in 1927, gave rabbis a chance to mingle, present scholarly papers, and discuss common congregational problems. In 1937 the rabbis met at Corpus Christi's Temple Beth El. Sidney Wolf, the host rabbi, stands in the first row, holding a toddler. Center for American History, UT-Austin, DI 02478, Texas Jewish Historical Society.

Affiliation with Hebrew congregations and organizations tends to be high among Texas Jews. As Elaine Maas, a historian of Houston Jewry, has observed, with regard to congregational affiliation,

> Houston is still unlike the large Eastern cities but is similar to the smaller Southern communities in that most Jews feel it important to belong to a synagogue or temple. This circumstance may perhaps be explained by [Jews'] proportionately smaller numbers and their desire to affiliate for sake of identity.[21]

It also may be explained geographically by Texas's location in the Bible Belt—a circumstance that manifests itself in relatively high rates of church attendance among gentiles. Among Jews, religious affiliation has become an aspect of acculturation.

A common stereotype about Texas—and Southern—Jews is that, by and large, they were anti-Zionist in the years leading up to Israel's establishment. Historian Stephen J. Whitfield assumed that a 1910 classified advertisement from a Beaumont congregation looking for a rabbi who was a "good mixer" was a "disparagement of Zionism before 1948."[22] (On the contrary, the rabbi hired from the ad, Samuel Rosinger, was an outspoken Zionist.) Suppositions of anti-Zionism were reinforced by the "Beth Israel revolt," during which the leadership at Texas's oldest congregation issued a set of Basic Principles disavowing Zionism and many traditional Jewish religious practices.[23] The congregation split. Bitter memories linger.[24]

Historian Stuart Rockoff, who grew up in that congregation, chose to research Zionism and anti-Zionism in Texas. He uncovered so much grassroots Zionist activity in Texas that his essay, "Zionism: Deep in the Heart of Palestine" (chapter 7), disproves the stereotype. The Texas Zionist Association was a model for other statewide Zionist confederations. Zionist conferences were front-page news. In Austin, the mayor and governor spoke at a Zionist conference that convened at the statehouse.

Networking among teens. The teens wearing "Head Honcho" hats, seated in the first row, are leaders from Houston's Temple Emanu El Federation of Temple Youth who organized this eight-day regional summer conclave in 1979 at UAHC Greene Family Camp. The teens and their advisors, from Reform congregations in Oklahoma and Texas, gathered in the chapel at the 160-acre camp, founded in 1976 in Bruceville, Texas. Courtesy, Beth-El Congregation Archives, Fort Worth.

WANTED, RABBI,
(REFORM)
By CONGREGATION EMANUEL,
Of BEAUMONT, TEXAS.

Young man, a native of America or England, that is a good lecturer who can make himself agreeable with either Orthodox or Reform Congregation. In other words, we want a MIXER. We pay $1,500.00 a year. Address

H. A. PEARLSTEIN,
Pres't of Emanuel Congregation, Beaumont, Tex.

Wanted. The classified ad in the American Israelite, April 7, 1910, seeking a "mixer," expressed the need, acute in small towns, for a rabbi to bridge differences among Orthodox, Conservative, and Reform Jews and to be ambassador to the larger community. The ad lured Rabbi Samuel Rosinger to Beaumont's Temple Emanuel. Collection of Hollace Weiner.

Most Jews gravitated to the state's larger cities (chapter 15, "Six-Tenths of a Percent of Texas," by Rabbi Kenneth D. Roseman); however, the small-town experience looms large. What transpired in Texas's small towns is similar to small-town experiences across the United States. The Texas experiences are crystallized in "Little Synagogues Across Texas" (chapter 14, co-authored by Hollace Weiner and Lauraine Miller), an examination of a dozen Jewish communities where synagogues are still standing, although not necessarily utilized for Jewish worship. Demographic historian Lee Shai Weissbach notes that prior to World War I, Jews often gravitated to small towns:

[S]mall communities have always been fundamental features in the American Jewish landscape. These communities played a crucial role in American Jewish settlement and mobility patterns . . . [T]he vast majority of the country's individual Jewish communities were, in fact, smaller ones in less prominent cities and towns.[25]

In Texas, hospitality toward Jews manifested itself again during the World War II era when Nazi-era refugees began trickling into El Paso ("The Wild West Welcomes Holocaust Survivors," chapter 19). Sometimes Jews settled in a small town by chance—as with Max Stool in Del Rio. Sometimes it was due to a sudden economic boom, like the California gold rush or a gusher of oil, as explored by writer Jan Statman in "East Texas Oil Boom: From New Jersey Farm Boy to Scrap Metal King" (chapter 9). Jews, and others, rushed to fill a mercantile niche or vacuum. The Zale Jewelry Corporation, profiled by Lauraine Miller in "Diamonds for the Rough" (chapter 11), is a byproduct of the boomtown phenomenon. The Zale brothers' uncle, jeweler Sam Kruger, moved to Wichita Falls with a Hamilton watch franchise, ready to sell timepieces and diamonds to people enriched from oil discoveries. While the uncle was selling to the carriage trade, his nephews marketed to workers with grease-covered clothes for a dollar down and a dollar a week. As these small towns thrived, so too did the Jewish community. When a small town went into commercial decline, the Jewish community began migrating out.

Texas history exhibits a modest degree of anti-Semitism, although in general there seems to be more ignorance and curiosity about Judaism than prejudice. Rabbi Samuel Rosinger (the "mixer" from Beaumont) blamed the religious prejudice that he evidenced on the "anti-Jewish account of the Gospel." He wrote: "Let a Christian and a Jewish child have a falling out, the first epithet the Christian child will throw at his Jewish antagonist

"We no longer live in a ghetto world of our own." Rabbi David Rosenbaum (left) preached those words to his Austin congregation. The Chicago-raised rabbi enjoys an evening out in 1911 with another Chicago lad, Fort Worth's Rabbi G. George Fox and his wife, Texan Hortense Lewis Fox. The stylized moon and stars were popular props at traveling amusement shows. Courtesy, Beth-El Congregation Archives, Fort Worth.

is, 'You are a Christ-killer.'"[26] Texas Governor James "Pa" Ferguson, the son of a Methodist preacher, was not averse to declaring that a "mob" of Israelites had "lynched the Savior."[27] In 1922, Galveston's Rabbi Cohen wrote Rabbi Rosinger that the Women's Christian Temperance Union was determined to have New Testament Bible readings in the public schools and that "probably the K.K.K. . . . is at the bottom of it."[28]

The Ku Klux Klan thrived in Texas during the early 1920s. Its venom was targeted primarily against Catholics, African-Americans, bootleggers, and womanizers. Rabbi Rosinger was part of a coalition of Catholics, Jews, and Rotarians who petitioned and marched against the Klan and its mob violence.[29] Not every rabbi stood up to the KKK. Fort Worth's Rabbi G. George Fox wrote that he knew many Klansman, for they were among the city's elected officials. He accepted a cash gift from the Klan. Many tales are told about Jewish merchants in Texas and throughout the South who sold sheets to Klansmen for uniforms. Another oft-told story is about the merchant who recognized the masked Klansmen by their shoes—which were purchased in his store.

What this suggests is that prejudice in Texas was less blatant against Jews than against racial minorities. Observes Texas historian T. R. Fehrenbach:

> Anti-Semitism was far less a Texan than a Northern American trait, which, much evidence shows, was given impetus by European immigration. No mobs in Texas ever attacked a Jew . . . The Texas violence toward blacks, which at times could be very violent, was provoked and condoned not by any desire to wipe Negroes off the earth, but to keep them conquered and in their appointed place.[30]

Former Texas Supreme Court Justice Rose Spector contends in "Most Politics is Local" (chapter 16) that being a woman poses more political challenges in Texas than being a Jew. Former Congressman Martin Frost notes that when he grew up in Fort Worth in the

1960s, Jews played first string on his high-school football team. His parents, however, did join a short-lived Jewish country club. As Rabbi Ralph Mecklenburger notes in "Comfort and Discomfort: Being Jewish in Fort Worth" (chapter 21), anti-Semitism in Texas is not overt, but subtle. Restricted clubs are evidence of the "five o'clock curtain" and lingering social separation between Jews and non-Jews. Fort Worth oilman Ted Weiner (profiled in Barry Shlachter's "West Texas Wildcatters," chapter 8) built his home and sculpture garden not in Westover Hills, the area's most exclusive enclave, but in Ridglea, a neighborhood more welcoming to Jews during the 1960s. Jewish teenagers today experience discomfort when evangelical students rally 'round the flagpole once a year in support of their faith. Although Jews adjust well to the Texas stereotype and have demonstrated since frontier days that they can herd cattle, drill for oil, boast, and build empires such as Neiman-Marcus, they know they remain different in one important aspect of identity.

This book is about some Jewish Texans. As coeditor Rabbi Kenneth D. Roseman noted in a paper read at the Texas Jewish History Symposium that served as a prelude to this anthology, this volume

> attempts to examine the main themes of the development of Texas Jewry by choosing individual examples to illustrate richer and broader realities. In this task, the book applies the ancient rabbinic principle, *miktzat kekulo*, allowing a part to represent the totality. It is, admittedly, an imperfect method, but a complete and comprehensive history will never be possible.[31]

The Texas Jewish Historical Society expects that this collection will stimulate others to record and to publish their family, community, and mercantile histories, for Texas-Jewish historical research is in its early stages. Still to be studied are Jewish farm-and-ranching families' impact on agriculture in such areas as spinach production in Crystal City, wheat in arid Bexar County, and sweet onions in the Rio Grande Valley.[32] Neiman-Marcus may be internationally known, but other sophisticated retailers such as Sakowitz in Houston deserve their due. Jewish leaders' impact on the Raza Unida party and the Civil Rights Movement in Texas have yet to be explored. Readers may think they are finished, but there is much more to tell. ✡

NOTES

1. Samuel Rosinger, "Deep in the Heart," in *Lives and Voices: A Collection of American Jewish Memoirs,* ed. Stanley F. Chyet (Philadelphia: Jewish Publication Society of America, 1972), 141.

2. See Seth L. Wolitz, "Bifocality in Jewish Identity in the Texas-Jewish Experience," in *Jewries at the Frontier: Accommodation, Identity, Conflict,* ed. Sander L. Gilman and Milton Shain (Urbana: University of Illinois Press, 1999), 185–223; Bryan Edward Stone describes Friedman as a "living caricature of the Jewish Texan," someone with "precursors in the theater." He compares him with comedian Lester Bangs and observes that acculturation "happens locally rather than nationally." Bryan Edward Stone, "'Ride 'em Jewboy': Kinky Friedman and the Texas Mystique," *Southern Jewish History* 1 (1998): 23–42.

3. David Rosenbaum, "The Rabbi as Ambassador to the Gentiles. Chips from a Rabbinical Workshop," n.d., David Rosenbaum papers, box 1, folder 1, Spertus College Archives, Chicago.

4. Hollace Weiner, "A Tale of Turkeys," *Fort Worth Star-Telegram,* November 28, 1996.

5. Harry Landa, *As I Remember* (San Antonio: Carleton, 1945), 26.

6. Hollace Ava Weiner, "The Mixers: The Role of Rabbis Deep in the Heart of Texas Jewry," *American Jewish History* 85, no. 3 (September 1997): 326.

7. Fanny Weil Alexander, "Charles and Sarah Weil," booklet distributed to descendants, July 1959, collection of author.

8. *American Israelite*, April 18, 1873.

9. Wolitz, "Bifocality in the Texas-Jewish Experience," 187.

10. Weiner, "The Mixers," 290–91; T. R. Fehrenbach, *Lone Star: A History of Texas and the Texans* (New York: Macmillan, 1968), 654.

11. Judith Neulander, "Crypto-Jews of the Southwest: An Imagined Community," *Jewish Folklore and Ethnology Review* 16, no. 1 (1994): 64–68; Judith Neulander, "The New Mexican Crypto-Jewish Canon: Choosing to be 'Chosen' in Millennial Tradition," *Jewish Folklore and Ethnology Review* 18, no. 1–2 (1996): 19–58; Barbara Ferry and Debbie Nathan, "Mistaken Identity? The Case of New Mexico's 'Hidden Jews,'" *Atlantic Monthly*, December 2000, 85–96.

12. Henry Cohen, "Settlement of the Jews in Texas," *Publications of the American Jewish Historical Society* 2 (1894): 139–56; Henry Cohen, "The Jews in Texas," *Publications of the American Jewish Historical Society* 4 (1896): 9–19; Henry Cohen, "Texas," *Jewish Encyclopedia* (New York and London, 1906), 12:121–22; Henry Cohen, "Texas," *Universal Jewish Encyclopedia* (New York, 1943), 10:205; Rabbis Henry Cohen, Ephraim Frisch, and David Lefkowitz, "One Hundred Years of Jewry in Texas, the Original Researches of Dr. Henry Cohen," booklet (Austin: Jewish Advisory Committee for the Texas Centennial Religious Program, 1936).

13. Natalie Ornish, *Pioneer Jewish Texans: Their Impact on Texas and American History for Four Hundred Years, 1590–1990* (Dallas: Texas Heritage Press, 1989), 289n3.

14. Martin Frost, telephone interview with author, December 11, 2005, notes in possession of author.

15. Cohen, "Texas," *Universal Jewish Encyclopedia*, 10:203.

16. Wolitz, "Bifocality in the Texas-Jewish Experience," 202.

17. "Nathan Kallison [obituary]," *The Cattleman* 31, no. 8 (January 1945): 90; Doug Perkins, "Meeting and Greeting at Kallison's," *The Cattleman* 61, no. 5 (October 1974): 38, 186.

18. Grady Stiler, "Rainmaking Nothing New to Texas Ranchers," *The Cattleman* 38, no. 5 (October 1951): 34–35.

19. Dianne Ashton, "Gratz, Rebecca," in *Jewish Women in America: An Historical Encyclopedia*, ed. Paula E. Hyman and Deborah Dash Moore (New York: Routledge, 1997), 1:547–50.

20. Lea Donosky, "True South, Small-town Jews, For the few and far between, holiday crowd is miles away," *Atlanta Journal-Constitution*, Dixie Living section, September 15, 1991. Reprinted in "Southern Jews," in *True South: Travel through a Land of White Columns, Black-eyed Peas and Redneck Bars*, ed. Jim Auchmutey and Lea Donosky (Athens, Ga.: Longstreet Press, 1994), 170–71.

21. Elaine H. Maas, "The Jews of Houston Today," *169 Years of Historic Houston*, http://www.houstonhistory.com/erhnic/history2jews.htm (accessed Dec. 26, 2005).

22. Stephen J. Whitfield, "Jews and Other Southerners: Counterpoint and Paradox," in *Turn to the South: Essays on Southern Jewry*, ed. Nathan M. Kaganoff and Melvin I. Urofsky (Charlottesville: University Press of Virginia with American Jewish Historical Society, 1979), 90; the original "mixer" advertisement appeared in the *American Israelite*, April 7, 1910.

23. Michael A. Meyer, *Response to Modernity: A History of the Reform Movement in Judaism* (Oxford: Oxford University Press, 1988), 465n111.

24. Malcolm H. Stern, "Role of the Rabbi in the South," in *Turn to the South*, 28.

25. Lee Shai Weissbach, *Jewish Life in Small-Town America: A History* (New Haven: Yale University Press, 2005), 4–5.

26. Samuel Rosinger, *My Life and My Message* (Beaumont: Privately published, 1958), 281–82.

27. James Ferguson, "The Cloven Foot of the Dallas Jews," *Ferguson Forum*, reprinted in *Colonel Mayfield's Weekly*, March 24, 1923.

28. Henry Cohen to Samuel Rosinger (December 7, 1922), Cohen, Henry collection, correspondence files, Center for American History, University of Texas at Austin; May Nelson Paulissen and Carl Randall McQueary, *Miriam: The Southern Belle* (Austin: Eakin Press, 1995), 111.

29. Thomas E. Kroutter, Jr., "The Ku Klux Klan in Jefferson County Texas, 1921–1924," Master's thesis, Lamar University, Beaumont, 1972, 39-41.

30. Fehrenbach, *Lone Star*, 654.

31. Kenneth D. Roseman, "Introduction," read at "Lone Stars of David: A Texas Jewish History Symposium," Austin, Texas, April 9, 2005.

32. I. L. "Buddy" Freed, "Jews in Small Texas Towns," *Texas Jewish Historical Society* newsletter, June 1999, 6-7; Sharon Katz, "The Story of Abe Katz," *Texas Jewish Historical Society* newsletter, February 2002, 13–14, 23; Harold M. Hyman, *Oleander Odyssey: The Kempners of Galveston, Texas, 1854–1980s* (College Station: Texas A&M University Press, 1990), is a business history documenting the Kempner family's enterprises including the Imperial Sugar Company of Texas.

2

On the Frontier Jews without Judaism

BRYAN EDWARD STONE

There have been Jews in Texas since the earliest years of European settlement in the state, but until the 1850s there really was no Judaism. Individuals tied to the Jewish faith by parentage or by personal belief entered the Texas frontier seeking adventure and commercial gain, but never religious opportunity. Indeed, given how strongly rooted Judaism is in communal activity and shared history, it is probably safe to say that anyone willing to enter a place as remote as frontier Texas, as far removed from active Jewish communities and resources, was by definition someone for whom Jewish religious practice was not especially important. In venturing to Texas, Jewish immigrants abandoned larger Jewish communities, most of the rituals of Jewish life, and sometimes the faith itself. Many formally converted to Christianity, most married non-Jews, and several drifted into an ambiguous ecumenicism. They may have displayed strong enough Jewish ties to be identified by later researchers but were unable (and perhaps unwilling) to live anything resembling a traditional Jewish life.

As Texas grew and changed, and particularly as it made its way from Spanish to Mexican rule, through its brief decade of independence to statehood, its Jewish population slowly increased. As modern researchers have pointed out, Jews were present throughout the state's development and participated in many of the iconic events of Texas history, including the Goliad massacre, the siege of the Alamo, and the Battle of San Jacinto. Jews involved in the independence movement and in the Texas Republic have been of special interest to historians who have delighted in spotlighting the Jewish contribution to Texas independence. For the sake of accuracy, however, it is important to remember that Jews were a miniscule minority in the Texas Republic, that they necessarily made a negligible contribution to its development, and that they neglected in this period to establish a single formal Jewish institution. While it is worth noting the involvement of Jews at these events, it is important to recognize that their participation was in no way an expression of their Jewish faith or identity. There is little reason to single them out except for our own modern wish to remember, honor, even perhaps to mythologize the memories of our ancestors. Histories that focus on the adventurous exploits of early Texas Jews mask the gradual development of actual Jewish life in the state. After statehood was achieved in 1846, many Jewish settlers arriving in Texas sought to build religious institutions that would assure Jewish survival there. They sent for faith leaders and arranged for the necessities to keep Jewish rituals and traditions intact. These are the real ancestors of today's Texas-Jewish community.

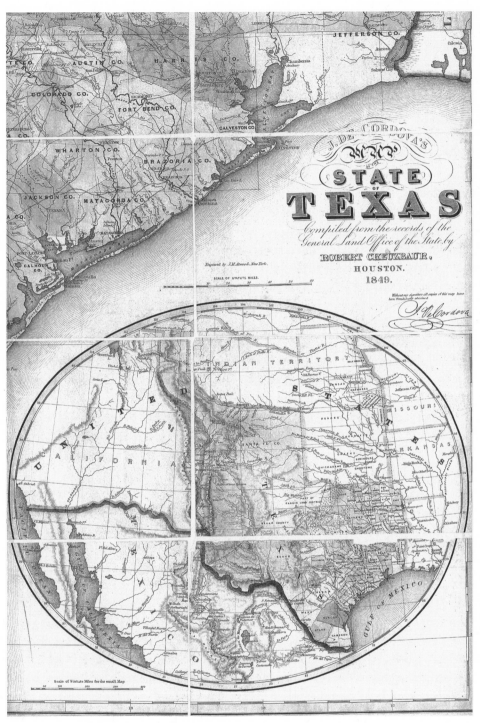

Welcome to Texas. Land promoter Jacob De Cordova's 1849 map of the twenty-eighth state was one of the first published after statehood. The oval inset shows the new state in relation to Indian lands, Mexico, California, Missouri, Arkansas, and Louisiana. De Cordova's signature is at upper right. The white lines, where the map was repeatedly folded and unfolded, show where a paper conservator has repaired the worn and torn creases. Detail courtesy, Special Collections, The University of Texas at Arlington Libraries, Arlington, Texas.

SPANISH AND MEXICAN TEXAS

According to many accounts, the first Jews to set foot in what is now Texas were Spanish refugees from the Mexican Inquisition, which brutally enforced adherence to the Roman Catholic faith in Spain's New World colonies. Before the 1492 expulsion of Jews from Iberia, tens of thousands of Spanish Jews were forced to convert to the Holy Faith rather than face imprisonment, exile, or execution. The sincerity of these forced conversions is necessarily doubtful. However, with the establishment of Spanish colonies in America, far from the watchful eyes of the Crown and the Church in Madrid, *conversos* were among the settlers. Many scholars contend that the remote and unsupervised condition of the American frontier provided a haven for crypto-Jews, *conversos* who continued to practice their forbidden religion in secret.[1] In 1571, the Crown established in Mexico City an Inquisitional authority that began investigating claims of crypto-Judaism in New Spain and held in the 1570s at least three autos-da-fé, public acts of penance that, in many cases, included burning unrepentant Jews at the stake.

While these events were occurring in Central Mexico, Texas remained a distant and unexplored Spanish frontier. In 1579, South Texas as far north as present-day San Antonio was included in a massive colonization grant issued to Luis de Carvajal y de la Cueva, a descendant of Portuguese Jews who was himself a devout and sincere Catholic. Carvajal traveled through Iberia recruiting colonists to help him settle the claim and to build it into a profitable commercial enterprise. For reasons that remain inadequately explained, Carvajal's charter neglected to include the usual requirement that every colonist provide certification of his or her descent from "Old Christians" rather than from *conversos*. Thus a number of crypto-Jews, including members of Carvajal's own extended family, were included among his settlers. Many of these were later tried and executed for their illegal practices, and Don Luis himself was imprisoned in part for his role in harboring them. Much of the research attesting to the Jewish faith of Carvajal's colonists is of questionable validity because it depends heavily, and uncritically, on Inquisitional testimony provided by defendants under torture, by informants planted in defendants' cells, and by witnesses with personal grudges. Still, scholars have been able to marshal so much detail from so many documents that if the Carvajals were not actually secret Jews, the depth of the Inquisition's fraud to paint them as such is hard to believe.[2]

But though there may have been secret Jews in the Carvajal colony, and though the colony's charter included South Texas, Texas-Jewish history does not really begin with Carvajal. While Don Luis and his colonists thoroughly explored and settled their holdings in Mexico, they do not appear to have ventured north of the Río Grande into present-day Texas. In 1590, after Carvajal's death in a Mexican prison, a follower named Gaspar Castaño de Sosa led an expedition of about 160 colonists across the Río Grande and north along the Pecos into present-day New Mexico, where they were soon arrested and returned to Mexico City. If there were crypto-Jews among them, which is quite possible, then these were the first Jews to enter present-day Texas—although it must be observed that they passed through briefly and left no physical or textual record, no settlements, and no institutions.

The crypto-Jewish past has had one striking long-term effect in Texas. There are many reports today of Hispanics in South Texas, as elsewhere in the American Southwest, discovering that they are descended from crypto-Jewish families and citing family customs such as lighting candles on Friday evenings and refraining from eating pork as proof of their Jewish ancestry. Solid scholarship, however, suggests that these traditions may have their roots not in Spanish Judaism but in more recent evangelical Protestant sects that imitated Jewish rituals.[3] While curious and compelling, then, the claim of a four-hundred-year-old crypto-Jewish heritage in Texas is probably wishful thinking on the part of researchers who want to demonstrate an ancient Jewish connection to Texas or an ancient Hispanic connection to Judaism.

Whether or not there were crypto-Jews in Spanish Texas, their Jewish lives were by definition secret, and so Texas never had an active and open Sephardic, or Spanish-Jewish, presence. Texas Jewry always has been predominantly Ashkenazic, of non-Spanish European extraction. Thus the modern Jewish community traces its origin not to Spanish Jews fleeing the Inquisition but to European Jews who started arriving in the early nineteenth century after Mexican independence, as part of a general Anglo migration into what is now Texas. Rabbi Henry Cohen of Galveston, the first historian of Texas Jewry, identified a number of these earliest Jewish settlers. Cohen was a meticulous researcher, combing through the available archives in Austin and other Texas cities and collecting information through interviews with the state's early Jews and their surviving family members. The rabbi's work provides an invaluable foundation for later research. Even more than one hundred years after the publication of his articles, they remain the starting point for further inquiry into early Texas Jewish history. He cast a wide net in his search for early Jews, however, and often erred on the side of accepting someone as a Jew even if he or she probably was not. Cohen identified every Jew in frontier Texas—and then some.

According to Cohen, a Jew was present among the original "Old 300" families that formed the Anglo colony chartered by Moses Austin and administered after his death by his son Stephen F. Austin. The Austin Colony, established in 1821, marks the quasi-mythical origin of Anglo settlement in Texas, so Cohen's effort to claim one of the Austin settlers as a Jew can be understood as an attempt to fix a Jewish presence at the modern state's very founding. Samuel Isaacks, who was born in Mississippi in 1804 and traveled to Texas seventeen years later in advance of his family, was, according to Cohen, "[t]he first Jewish settler in Texas of whom any record is preserved."[4] Indeed, an Isaacks descendant recorded in 1935 that "[t]here is . . . a tradition in my immediate family, but with no other so far as known, that some three centuries ago a family of Jews, one of whom was our ancestor, lived in Wales." This ancestor, according to the tradition, married a Christian woman and was disowned by his family, "[w]here upon he renounced Judaism and added the 'k' to his name to distinguish him from the Jews." The author claims to have accepted this story as true until his own genealogical research inclined him against it.[5] This tradition demonstrates only that the Isaacks family may have been Jewish two hundred years before arriving in Texas but not since. While more recent researchers, using Cohen as a reference, have maintained the possibility that Isaacks was a Jew, absent any further evidence Cohen's original claim seems misplaced.

The first clear presence of self-identified Jews in Texas was in the early 1830s in the seaside community of Velasco, at the mouth of the Brazos River near present-day Freeport. Abraham Cohen Labatt, a merchant active in the Jewish communities of Charleston and New Orleans, briefly moved his business to Velasco in either 1831 or 1836. There he found two other Jewish residents, Jacob Henry from England and Jacob Lyons from Charleston. That Henry and Lyons were recognizable to Labatt as fellow Jews suggests that they were self-consciously and, in some measure, openly living as Jews. Labatt himself returned to Velasco several years later, suggesting that there was enough Jewish companionship there to satisfy a man who had participated in several larger Jewish communities.[6]

Among the other Jewish individuals whom Rabbi Cohen identifies in Mexican Texas are Joseph and Hyman Hertz, who moved to Nacogdoches around 1832 and "were considered the two most thoroughly educated men in the country." Hyman died in 1833, while Joseph left Texas in 1835 and eventually returned to Europe. Simon M. Schloss settled in Texas in 1836, also in Nacogdoches, and worked in real estate before moving to New Orleans. Albert Emanuel arrived in Texas in 1834, remaining permanently in Nacogdoches "and entering upon mercantile pursuits." Sam Maas arrived in Nacogdoches in early 1836 and moved three years later to Galveston, where "he was a merchant, after which he entered the real estate business."[7] And though Cohen neglects to mention him, Samuel Schutz arrived in remote El Paso in 1854 and soon became one of the settlement's leading businessmen.

While Cohen records few Jews in Texas before independence, some patterns are clear. First, most of the people he identified were immigrants from Germany, and all passed through the United States, frequently New Orleans, before making their way into Texas. Most were engaged in either "mercantile pursuits," "real estate," or both, though Joseph Hertz was a physician. All of these men displayed great mobility, either moving around within Texas or migrating back and forth between Texas and the United States. Significantly, Cohen makes no explicit mention of these men practicing the Jewish faith: perhaps their Jewishness, if real, was lost amid the commercial opportunities of the Texas frontier.

THE TEXAS REPUBLIC AND STATEHOOD

While one historian described Labatt, Lyons, and Henry as "the Velasco Jewish Community," this description seems more wishful thinking than reality.[8] Despite the appearance of a few (possibly) Jewish individuals in Velasco, Nacogdoches, and Galveston, Mexican Texas contained no Jewish institutions or anything resembling organized Jewish communal life. Only with the establishment of the Republic of Texas in 1836, a dominant-Anglo democracy with religious freedom written into the constitution, did Jewish settlers begin to arrive in significant, if still small, numbers.

As Rabbi Cohen relates, a number of Jews were present in Texas in 1836 at the time of independence, and many participated in that struggle. David S. Kaufman, for whom Kaufman County is named, was of Jewish descent and was a prominent political figure during and after the Texas Revolution. Albert Emanuel "was one of the first to volunteer in the Texas army," and he served in the cavalry at the Battle of San Jacinto. An individual named Kohn also fought at San Jacinto and served in the Texas Spy Company. Edward J. Johnson of Cincinnati traveled to Texas to participate in the revolution, losing his life in the massacre at Goliad, at which Benjamin H. Mordecai, M. K. Moses, and Herman Ehrenberg were also present. Eugene Joseph Chiméne, who arrived in Texas in 1835, fought at San Jacinto and settled in the tiny new community of Houston; Dutch-born David Levi Kokernot of Gonzales, who later converted to Christianity, served in the Texas army and was involved in the Grass Fight of 1835; Dr. Moses Albert Levy served as surgeon-general in the Texas army and was present when the Texans captured the Alamo in 1835; and A. Wolf and his two sons were among those killed when the Mexicans recaptured it. Of all these men involved in the Texas revolution, however, the only one whom Cohen explicitly identifies as a Jew is Levi Charles Harby, a U.S. naval officer who joined the Texas cause and later served in both the Mexican War and the Civil War. When he died in Galveston, according to Cohen, "his last words [were], 'There is no God but Israel's God.'" As Cohen was writing, Harby's daughter-in-law was alive and presumably was the source for this sentiment.[9]

Of all the figures identified as Jews in Republican Texas, three have received the most attention from modern researchers beginning with Cohen, despite the fact that none was

Adolphus Sterne (18?–1852). An Indian fighter, arms smuggler, Scottish Rite Mason, legislator, and close friend of Sam Houston, Sterne converted to Catholicism yet made references in his diary to Jewish holidays. Center for American History, UT-Austin, CN Number 04606.

a practicing Jew. Henri Castro, Adolphus Sterne, and Jacob de Cordova, all of whom were *descended* from Jews, form a kind of canon of early Texas Jewry, not because of their actual religious faith, but because all three made memorable contributions to the development of the secular society. Their names often appear in non-parochial accounts of Texas history, establishing a "Jewish" contribution to the state's development and affirming that Jews were (and so are) authentic Texans. To strengthen that claim, historians consistently have exaggerated the Jewishness of these men, but ironically such historians have missed a crucial point. Religious identity in the Texas frontier—indeed, in many a frontier—was fluid and changeable as people adapted their orthodoxies to the conditions in which they lived and in which they interacted with people of a variety of faiths and cultural backgrounds. As such, the very *lack* of a clear Jewish identity in men like Castro, Sterne, and de Cordova was the most typically Texan thing about them. Researchers wishing to demonstrate that frontier-era Jews were "real" Texans might emphasize their religious ambivalence rather than struggling against fact and reason to depict them as observant Jews, a condition that would have been out of place indeed in frontier Texas.

Of the members of this triumvirate, Rabbi Cohen gives the most attention to the one who had the weakest claim on Jewish identity, Henri Castro. An Alsatian immigrant to the United States, Castro received a charter from the Republic of Texas to settle a large land grant southwest of San Antonio, where he established the town of Castroville and one of the state's most successful immigrant colonies. Of his colonists, most of whom were also Alsatian, none was Jewish. Cohen describes Castro as "descended from one of the oldest Portuguese families (the Marrano family of De Castro)." Marranos (a derogatory term, meaning swine) described Spanish and Portuguese Jewish *conversos*. Cohen's use of the term suggests that neither Henri Castro nor, more than likely, any of his recent ancestors, were self-identified Jews. The only further evidence that Cohen provides of Castro's Jewishness is an odd bit of hearsay dropped among the last sentences of the article. Here Cohen says of Castro that "[t]he instinct of the Marrano must have been strong within him, as it is related, upon the authority of a contemporary, that during his surveying tours he would leave his companions in order to retire to the forest for the purpose of binding his phylacteries (tefillin)."[10]

Cohen's decision to bury this account near the end of his article, to leave the source anonymous, and to phrase it as he did suggests that he doubted its veracity. Certainly the "spirit of the Marrano" must have been very strong indeed if it would lead Castro to such an act at least two hundred years after his family became Christian! And other questions suggest themselves. Why would a man centuries removed from Jewish tradition resort to such a specific religious ritual? How did his traveling companions know what Castro did in the privacy of the forest unless he told them—and why would he tell them after going to such trouble to be secretive? If Castro indeed spoke openly about his Jewish faith, why is there no other record of it, even in his own writings? Can we trust Cohen's source (not a Jew or the rabbi surely would have named him) to understand the significance of what he had heard about Castro and to convey it accurately some sixty years after the fact? And finally, Castro's colony was situated in the arid lands to the southwest of San Antonio: *forest*?

No other evidence of Castro's Jewishness exists, yet researchers consistently have included him in accounts of early Texas Jewry. Harold Sharfman, citing no source but Cohen, elaborated the *tefillin* story, claiming that Catholic colonists who accompanied Castro "into the backwoods . . . watched him disappear into the forest and reverently awaited his return. They knew that he retired into the privacy of those woods to pray to the God of Israel."[11] Another researcher, also citing Cohen, concluded that Castro was "a pious Jew."[12] Castro's transformation over time from "descended from Marranos" to "a pious Jew" says more about researchers' wish to strengthen a modern Jewish claim on him than it does about Castro's own religious belief.

In similar ways, historians have placed Adolphus Sterne, an early settler of Nacogdoches and friend of Sam Houston, and Jacob de Cordova, a merchant, mapmaker, globe-trotting promoter of Texas lands, and participant in the founding of Waco, at the center of early Texas Jewish history, despite clear evidence that neither was actively practicing Judaism. Sterne probably was born to Jewish parents in Germany but never practiced the religion, married a devoted Catholic, and officially converted to Catholicism in adulthood. While he makes several references in his diary to Jewish holidays, he also speaks explicitly about his regular attendance at Christian worship services, and he critically evaluates the relative abilities of Texas ministers from several denominations. As a dedicated churchgoer, he condemns the lax worship of a Jewish acquaintance in nearby San Augustine: "to day is Yom Kippur," he recorded in October of 1843. "Mr. Flatau is doing Penance, nonsense, to keep up a Religion only one day in the year."[13]

While Castro and Sterne were clearly not Jewish, the case with Jacob de Cordova is more ambiguous. Born to a Jamaican family of clear Jewish background, Jacob's half-brother Phineas was a cofounder of Austin's Congregation Beth Israel. Jacob, however, was not himself a member of any congregation, though he lived in several communities where synagogues existed, and, despite his visibility in Texas, he never participated in Jewish communal activities. Like Sterne, de Cordova married a Christian woman and, perhaps most telling, is buried in the Texas State Cemetery in Austin under a granite cross. When an effort was made in the 1950s to remove the symbol from his grave, a de Cordova family member protested, claiming that Jacob was essentially ecumenical, "a deeply religious individual" but "NOT A MEMBER OF ANY SPECIFIC CHURCH" and that "some of his family were of Jewish faith, some were of other faiths."[14] In these cases, one must observe that Mr. Flatau and Phineas de Cordova, both of whom were clearly practicing Jews but who were not friends of Sam Houston, founders of towns, or per-

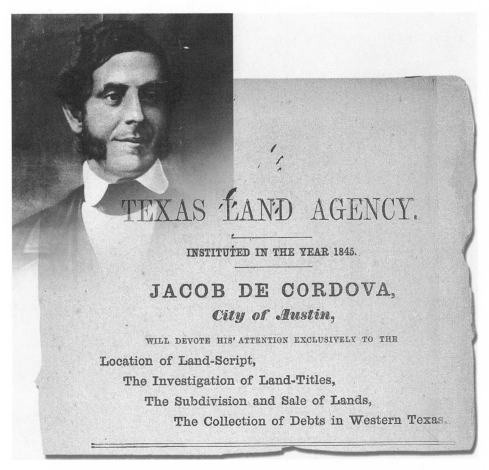

INSTITUTED IN THE YEAR 1845.

JACOB DE CORDOVA,

City of Austin,

WILL DEVOTE HIS ATTENTION EXCLUSIVELY TO THE

Location of Land-Script,

The Investigation of Land-Titles,

The Subdivision and Sale of Lands,

The Collection of Debts in Western Texas.

Jacob Raphael De Cordova (1808–1868). Texas cartographer, printer, publisher, land promoter, and legislator born in Jamaica, De Cordova was raised in England and later in Philadelphia where his father was president of Congregation Mikveh Israel. The advertisement for his Texas Land Agency was part of the frontispiece of his 1858 book, Texas: Her Resources and her Public Men. DeCordova photo from The Texas Collection, Baylor University, Waco, Texas.

manent guests in the Texas State Cemetery, have received comparatively little attention from modern Jewish historians. By 1845, there were more Jews in Texas than before, but they were still virtually invisible. Jewish religious institutions did not appear until a decade after Texas was annexed by the United States in 1846.

THE FIRST FORMAL JEWISH INSTITUTIONS

When Texas became a state, travel for Americans and Europeans became easier, and for the first time large enough numbers of Jews appeared in the state to begin to establish the institutions necessary for lasting and authentic Jewish life and religious practice. However, building the Jewish population was a long and gradual process because Jews, who were involved predominantly in mercantile professions, tended to be mobile and often passed through Texas for a time, rather than making it a permanent home. Many Texas Jews wished to increase their numbers, and they promoted their state as a destination for Jewish migration by emphasizing the state's commercial opportunities and the availability of land. And with European anti-Semitism on the rise, they presented Texas as a place where Jews would be safer than in their native lands.

In 1850, Lewis A. Levy, a founding member of Houston's Jewish community and later of Congregation Beth Israel, argued that Europe's persecuted Jews would be better off in the United States than in any other nation. "The amount of one year's tax where they are now," he claimed, "would pay for their transmigration, and then a whole continent would be open for them to settle in where they choose." Texas offered particular induce-

Lewis A. Levy (1799–1861) and Mary A. Levy (1800–1888). The Levys, who were married in England, moved to Houston in 1841, invested in land, had twenty children, and apparently hosted the state's first Jewish wedding when their eldest daughter married in 1847. Courtesy Rosanne D. Leeson.

ments, especially if the immigrants were willing to take up farming. "In our own State," he wrote, "thousands of acres of land can be bought, within the settled portions of the State, for the small sum of from 25 cents to $1 per acre; good arable, fertile land, where a man can make a living to his liking." Traveling to Texas and purchasing land there, Levy continued, would make Jews "more independent than the Autocrat of Russia or the Emperor of Austria." Levy, who had moved to Texas with his wife Mary, wrote that he "would not exchange my fifteen acre lot, with the house on it, and the garden around it, which I possess near the city of Houston for all [the] thrones and hereditary dominions of both those noted persons."[15]

Some Jews who arrived in Texas recognized the validity of observations like these and were quick to purchase land. Harris Kempner, the patriarch of one of Galveston's most prominent Jewish families, "had great faith in Texas and in Texas lands," as his son Isaac recalled. Kempner arrived in the state in 1854 from rural Poland, where land was valuable, "but those in his religious and social status could not—were not permitted to—acquire it. He had great esteem for his right in this country to acquire land."[16] Kempner is indicative, though, of a general trend among Jewish landholders: While he purchased large amounts of rural property, his life and his livelihood were urban, and Kempner lived and remained in Galveston. Despite appeals to seek their fortunes in the countryside, Texas Jewry would grow in and along with Texas cities.

Thus Houston and Galveston, sister cities that were always competitive but mutually dependent, provided the first context for what rightly can be called Jewish community in Texas. At least one Jewish merchant, Eugene Chiméne, was in Houston at its founding in

Harris Kempner (1837–1894) and the American Dream. Kempner, a Polish immigrant, started out as a door-to-door peddler in Coldspring, Texas, fought in the Civil War, and became a multi-millionaire cotton factor based in Galveston. Engraving, University of Texas Institute of Texan Cultures at San Antonio, No. 098-1026.

1836. In a booming city like Houston, Jews found opportunities as peddlers and retail merchants, providing the goods that a growing population needed. Lewis and Mary Levy, Henry Wiener, and Michael Seeligson, for example, all arrived in the city before 1840 and established businesses there. By 1850, as many as seventeen Jewish adults (eleven men and six women) were living among a white population of nearly two thousand.[17] Galveston, which was an older city with a larger population than its inland neighbor, provided the seaport for goods traded in Houston, and Jewish merchants in the area often moved easily between the two cities: the Levys, Seeligson, and others all lived for a time in both places. Others, however, settled permanently in Galveston, and by 1850 there were four Jewish families there, a total of twelve adults and fourteen children.[18]

The Dyers and Ostermans, related by marriage, formed the core of Galveston's Jewish community and initiated the first organized Jewish worship in Texas. Leon, Rosanna, and Isadore Dyer, siblings born in Dessau, Germany, immigrated to Baltimore with their parents in the late 1810s. The family soon split up, following business opportunities throughout the country. Leon, the oldest, left a family business in New Orleans to participate in the Texas Revolution and settled in Galveston. Rosanna married a jeweler, Joseph Osterman, a founding member of the Baltimore Hebrew Congregation, and the couple joined Leon in Galveston by 1838 to open a general store. Isadore followed in 1840, establishing an insurance business.

According to one source, the Dyers and Ostermans "were meticulously observant in traditional religious practice," and it is clear that they had been active in the Jewish community in Baltimore. But given the lack of organized communal life in Texas, it is not surprising that Isadore married an Episcopalian in 1841.[19] Still, when Isadore's six-year-old son died in 1852, the family secured a Jewish burial, purchasing a plot of land for a ceme- tery and arranging for Rabbi M. N. Nathan of New Orleans to travel to Galveston for the consecration ceremony. In his remarks, Nathan described the event as "the first public assemblage in a quarter so remote from the birth-place and cradle of our religion," where Jews were meeting "to lay the foundation-stone, as it may be termed, of the edi- fice of Judaism." The *Galveston Daily News* also described it as "the first [worship service] ever performed publicly by a Hebrew minister in Texas." And Rabbi Isaac Leeser, pub- lisher of the *Occident*, a Jewish newspaper in Philadelphia, reported the event as "a com- mencing step towards working unitedly for the upholding of the faith of their fathers" by "the few Israelites residing" in Galveston.[20]

Houston Jews lagged behind Galveston's by only a few years, establishing a burial ground in 1854 and a Hebrew Benevolent Society in 1855 with Lewis Levy as its first chairman. Created "for the purpose of mutual assistance and relief, as well as to render aid to all [the] poor of their church, whether in pecuniary or physical distress," the So- ciety, among its first orders of business, collected "a sufficient amount of money to build a fence around their grave-yard."[21] Although some accounts date the founding of Hous- ton's first congregation to 1854 (and its cemetery, unbelievably, to 1844), it was not until 1859 that Congregation Beth Israel was chartered officially and that its leaders advertised in the *American Israelite* for a religious leader. "The Hebrew Congregation Beth Israel (House of Israel) is desirous of engaging a gentleman who is capable to act as Chazan, Schocket, Mohel and Bangal Koray," the ad stated, referring to an all-in-one prayer leader, kosher slaughterer, circumciser, and Torah reader. The salary was a fixed one thousand dollars per year "besides perquisites, which if he be a Mohel, will reach a con- siderable amount, as there is no Mohel in the country."[22] The community's desire for someone to provide the rudiments of Jewish ritual demonstrates the presence in Hous- ton of enough tradition-minded, practicing Jews to establish and maintain lasting reli- gious institutions. Within a year, Beth Israel employed the state's first full-time rabbi, Zacharias Emmich, though Emmich does not seem to have been ordained formally.[23] In March of 1860, Beth Israel erected a wooden building downtown as a place of worship, "the front of which is used as a Synagogue, the back portion as a meeting room," and which they had "handsomely fit up."[24] This was the state's first Jewish house of worship.

Michael Seeligson of Galveston reported to the *Occident* in 1852 that "[t]here are not many Jews in the state; but still you will find a sprinkling of them in every village."[25] In- deed, as Galveston and Houston took the lead, smaller communities began establishing Jewish institutions throughout the decade before the Civil War. San Antonio Jews conse- crated a cemetery in 1854 and began holding services under the auspices of a Hebrew Benevolent Society in 1856. The *American Israelite* reported in May of that year that the city held about fifty Jews, "most of them flourishing merchants." They had "organized themselves into a congregation, purchased a lot of ground for a burial place, and will at an early date furnish a room for a temporary Synagogue."[26] Meanwhile Jews also were making homes in the developing trading towns of rural East Texas. In 1850, they may have represented as much as eight percent of the population of Jefferson, while a steady stream of Jewish migrants made its way directly from Syracuse, New York, to Marshall, Texas.[27] In 1854, Samuel Schutz arrived in El Paso, at the state's farthest western reaches, where he would become a leading retailer and a founder of that city's Temple Mount Sinai in 1898.[28] And in 1860, the Jews of Victoria, not far from Houston, held "Minyan services" in honor of the High Holidays.[29]

MAINTAINING JEWISH TRADITION

What was life like for the people involved in these earliest stages of Jewish communal activity in Texas? How did they maintain the requirements of Jewish tradition in such remote and isolated circumstances? Clearly, it was impossible to hold to most aspects of Jewish ritual. Trained religious leaders were a rarity—no ordained rabbi would settle permanently in the state until after the Civil War—depriving Texas communities of religious education, worship directors, and kosher food. The Jewish population was necessarily small, even in the larger cities, which severely limited the resources available for building and maintaining synagogues, cemeteries, and schools. And as a tiny minority within an overwhelmingly Christian society—neighbors on whom Jews depended for most of their social and business contacts—Jews had to find ways to maintain their distinctiveness without either drawing undue or prejudicial attention from gentiles or, perhaps worse, merging entirely into the gentile population.

Isaac Leeser observed in the *Occident* in 1846 that Jewry was taking hold in the American West, "where the climate is mild, and the soil new and fruitful," but he worried about the hardships of living a Jewish life in virtual isolation. "[The *Occident*] goes out to fully a hundred small places, where we have a single subscriber in each," he noted. "It may be that each of these readers is the only Israelite in the place, or that there are one or two others near him." In "the immense State of Texas," he observed, "although many Jews live scattered here and there, there is but one incipient congregation," and Texas Jews "are lost among the masses, because they are without religious instruction."[30] Leeser's fears were largely justified, but to a surprising extent Jews in frontier Texas survived as Jews, often in astonishing ways.

In 1852, for example, Galveston's Michael Seeligson wrote to the *Occident* about a member of his community who, in the absence of a *mohel*, performed his infant son's circumcision himself. "People endeavored to persuade him to wait till the child could be taken thither, or a Mohel be sent for," he wrote. "But he replied, that our Father Abraham performed this duty on the eighth day, why should he not do it also?" The *Occident* later reported about a Houston couple who, when they could not afford to bring a *mohel* to town, resolved to postpone the circumcision ceremony until one was available. The ceremony was performed *eight years* later, with "such solemnity and with such composure on the part of the boy," the *Occident* reported, "that it made a deep impression on all the by-standers"—though, one imagines, not nearly the impression it made on the boy himself.[31]

Joseph and Helena Landa were the only Jewish family in the German town of New Braunfels in the Hill Country west of Austin, but they held regular services at home, including an elaborate annual Passover Seder. "My mother would brew the sweet raisin wine which we were to drink on the occasion," Landa's son Harry remembered. The women and servants spent weeks preparing homemade matzos. "The dough consisted simply of flour and water," he wrote, "and was rolled out on a table in long thin sheets. A large tin form was used to cut them into the proper size, and several old fashioned spiked spurs with large rowels were run over them to make the air holes." The strange bread was popular, and in addition to the amount needed to feed the fifteen family members and servants, more was prepared for neighbors. "The quantity that was baked would fill one side of a room," Landa recalled. "Several barrels of flour (196 pounds each) were necessary to supply the requirements."[32]

Galveston provides a telling example of the relationship that Jews enjoyed with their gentile neighbors—generally friendly and respectful, but with undercurrents of suspi-

Helena and Joseph Landa, Hill Country pioneers. The Landas were the only Jews in New Braunfels, Texas, but they held Sabbath services at home and hosted an elaborate Passover Seder. Helena Landa put air holes into homemade matzo by running a spur across the unleavened dough. Helena Landa photo, UT Institute of Texan Cultures at San Antonio, No. 074-0423, courtesy of Mrs. Robert Murray; Joseph Landa photo, Center for American History, UT-Austin, CN Number 12112, Texas Jewish Historical Society Collection.

cion. In 1853, Galvestonians elected Michael Seeligson as their mayor. Seeligson, born in Holland, lived for a while with his family in Philadelphia and traveled to Houston in 1839. After running a store there, he moved on to Galveston, where he was elected alderman in 1840 and 1848 before serving briefly as mayor. Seeligson made no secret of his Jewishness, and in fact he declared in a letter to the *Occident* that his primary intention in running for mayor was to show that a Jew could achieve such an office. "I accepted the office," he wrote, "to thwart the Designs of a certain Clique who by the by were preaching publicly the Crusades against our Nation." Seeligson reveals, then, a certain degree of anti-Semitism in Galveston, but not enough to prevent his election. "This is certainly an Evidence," Seeligson continued, "[that] if our people would only sustain their rights and privileges in this republican country, and Demean themselves accordingly, they can be elevated to any office they aspire."[33]

The longing to remain part of the Jewish world, and to make sense of experience in a Jewish context, remained for many early Texans. These feelings would become the basis of a genuine, lasting, and distinctive Jewish experience in Texas. A final, revealing example: In 1853, Isaac Jalonick, of Belton in Central Texas, wrote to Rabbi Leeser in Philadelphia. "It will surprise you Sir to hear from such remoot part on the frontier of Texas," he began. "But it is as it shuld be, the prophicing [must] be full fild." The prophecy that the Jewish people eventually would spread across the globe indeed was being fulfilled, and early Texas Jews like Jalonick were part of that great diasporic movement. But it came at a cost. Jalonick confessed that until he had discovered Leeser's newspaper, the *Occident*, he had been ignorant of matters relating to America's Jews. He had spent years in Mexico and California before settling in Texas, far removed from Jewish life, and he hoped Leeser could help him to reconnect by sending him a Bible and a prayer book. Jalonick signed himself "a True Jew & a friend to our [cause]," but like the rest of Texas's pioneer Jews, he had put himself into a situation in which the practice of his faith was impossible.[34] ✱

NOTES

1. Seymour B. Liebman details the religious customs of Mexican crypto-Jews in *The Jews in New Spain: Faith, Flame, and the Inquisition* (Coral Gables: University of Miami Press, 1970).

2. The Carvajal family's devotion to Judaism is documented in Alfonso Toro, *The Carvajal Family*, tr. Frances Hernández (El Paso: Texas Western Press, 2002); and Richard G. Santos, *Silent Heritage: The Sephardim and the Colonization of the Spanish North American Frontier, 1492–1600* (San Antonio: New Sepharad Press, 2000).

3. Research advocating a crypto-Jewish presence in South Texas is provided by Carlos Montalvo Larralde, "Chicano Jews in South Texas," Ph.D. Dissertation, University of California at Los Angeles, 1978; and Richard G. Santos, "Chicanos of Jewish Descent in Texas," *Western States Jewish Historical Quarterly* 15 (July 1983): 327–33. Many more studies detail crypto-Jewish life in New Mexico. Persuasive (and still unrefuted) evidence of the falseness of identical claims in New Mexico is provided by Judith Neulander, "The New Mexican Crypto-Jewish Canon: Choosing to be 'Chosen' in Millennial Tradition," *Jewish Folklore and Ethnology Review* 18 (1996): 19–58.

4. Henry Cohen, "Settlement of the Jews in Texas," *Publications of the American Jewish Historical Society* (hereafter PAJHS) 2 (1894): 139.

5. S. J. Isaacks, "The Isaacks Clan in America and Texas (El Paso, 1935), rev. and ed. Gary D. Isaacks, 1995, http://www.geocities.com/astromood/ISAACKSc.html (accessed April 28, 2005).

6. "Velasco," Texas Jewish Historical Society Collection, Center for American History, University of Texas at Austin (hereafter TJHS), Box 3A173, Folder 3; Cohen, "Settlement of the Jews in Texas," 139; I. Harold Sharfman, *Jews on the Frontier* (Chicago: Henry Regnery Co., 1977), 254.

7. Cohen, "Settlement of the Jews in Texas," 143–45.

8. Sharfman, *Jews on the Frontier*, 254.

9. Cohen, "Settlement of the Jews in Texas," 144–47, 150–51.

10. Henry Cohen, "Henry Castro, Pioneer and Colonist," PAJHS 5 (1897): 39, 43.

11. Sharfman, *Jews on the Frontier*, 259.

12. Natalie Ornish, *Pioneer Jewish Texans* (Dallas: Texas Heritage Press, 1989), 57.

13. Adolphus Sterne, *Hurrah for Texas!: The Diary of Adolphus Sterne, 1838–1851*, ed. Archie P. McDonald (Waco: Texian Press, 1969), 175.

14. Mrs. J. W. (La Una de Cordova) Skinner to Texas Board of Control (March 30, 1953), TJHS, Box 3A164, Folder 4. See also Juliet George Dees, "By The Brazos And The Trinity They Hung Up Their Harps: Two Jewish Immigrants in Texas," Master's thesis, Texas Christian University, 1991, 83–84; and Henry Barnston, "The History of the Jews of Houston," n.d, Jacob Rader Marcus Center of the American Jewish Archives (hereafter AJA), SC-5244, in which Barnston, writing in the early twentieth century, states that de Cordova's family "has since unfortunately been lost of Judaism."

15. *Asmonean*, June 28, 1850.

16. Isaac Herbert Kempner, "My Memories of Father," *American Jewish Archives* 19 (April 1967): 57.

17. Elaine Maas, "Jews," in *The Ethnic Groups of Houston*, ed. Fred R. von der Mehden, (Houston: Rice University Press, 1984), 141.

18. Ruthe Winegarten and Cathy Schechter, *Deep in the Heart: The Lives and Legends of Texas Jews* (Austin: Eakin Press, 1990), 18.

19. "Trail Blazers of the Trans-Mississippi West," *American Jewish Archives* 8 (October 1856): 73–74.

20. "Ceremonial at Galveston," *Occident* 10 (August 1852): 380; "Hebrew Burial Ground," *Galveston News*, August 31, 1852; *Occident* 10 (October 1852): 365.

21. "Houston, Texas, Hebrew Benevolent Association," *Occident* 13 (July 1855): 199.

22. *American Israelite*, November 18, 1859, 159.

23. Hollace Ava Weiner, *Jewish Stars in Texas: Rabbis and Their Work* (College Station: Texas A&M University, 1999), 235n1.

24. *Occident* 15 (March 1860): 306.

25. M. Seeligson to Isaac Leeser (November 1851), AJA Ms. 197, reprinted *Occident* 10 (April 1852): 58–59.

26. *American Israelite*, May 23, 1856, 374.

27. Carol Tefteller, "The Jewish Community in Frontier Jefferson," *Texas Historian: Publication of the Junior Historians of Texas* 35 (September 1974): 5; Susanne Parker, "Shema Israel: The Reform Jewish Movement in Marshall," TJHS, Box 3A172, Folder 6; Audrey Daniels Kariel, "The Jewish Story and Memories of Marshall, Texas," *Western States Jewish Historical Quarterly* 14 (April 1982): 197.

28. Floyd S. Fierman, "Insights and Hindsights of Some El Paso Jewish Families," *El Paso Jewish Historical Review* 1 (Spring 1983): 225–28.

29. *Die Deborah*, October 12, 1860, 59.

30. It is unclear to what "incipient congregation" Leeser refers. Isaac Leeser, "The Importance of Missions," *Occident* 11 (May 1853): 85–86.

31. *Occident* 10 (April 1852): 58–59; *Occident* 18 (April 1860): 24.

32. Harry Landa, *As I Remember* (San Antonio: Carleton, 1945), 26.

33. M. Seeligson to Isaac Leeser (June 19, 1853), AJA Ms. 197, reprinted *Occident* 11 (June 1853): 188.

34. Isaac Jalonick to Isaac Leeser (May 28, 1853), AJA Ms. 197.

Confederate Stories

The Sanger Brothers of Weatherford, Dallas, and Waco

GARY P. WHITFIELD

With the drumbeat of war, the three Sanger brothers shuttered their stores and enlisted one by one in the Confederate cavalry, infantry, and state militia. The Sanger boys, immigrants from Bavaria, had journeyed separately to the American South in the 1850s, angling for profits and opportunity—not stability or Jewish identity. At the war's onset, Lehman Sanger, confident of his survival, buried three hundred dollars in gold pieces.[1] After the war, he dug up his treasure and launched a chain of stores that lured his scattered family to Texas. In a pattern common among Jewish veterans across Texas, the Sanger brothers sparked a chain migration of relatives and friends to the Lone Star State and became stalwart leaders of the state's embryonic Jewish community.

Like most Jewish pioneers who ventured into frontier Texas, Lehman and Isaac Sanger were initially fortune hunters, adventurers, and entrepreneurs who exhibited little outward concern for Judaism. Before the war, Texas had around twelve hundred Jews and but one chartered congregation, Houston's Beth Israel, founded in 1859.[2] The state had four Jewish cemeteries: Galveston's, consecrated in 1852; Houston's and San Antonio's, begun in 1854; and Victoria's, which dates to 1856. For the living, institutional religion was of little import on the frontier.

During the Civil War, more than two hundred Texas Jews enlisted on the side of the South—an indication of Jewish integration into the social and political climate. After Appomattox, these Jewish soldiers returned, sobered by war and more inclined to reflect upon religion, identity, and community. As they rebuilt their lives during the postwar decades and met with economic success, Jewish veterans—including the Sangers—spearheaded the creation of thirteen B'nai B'rith lodges, more than a dozen Jewish cemeteries, and congregations throughout the state.[3]

In San Antonio, for example, former artillery officer Samuel Mayer was a founding member of the B'nai B'rith lodge and the founding president of Temple Beth-El, serving two terms from 1874 to 1880. In Austin, Henry Hirshfeld, who received a battlefield promotion to sergeant while serving in Morgan's Cavalry Company A, became a founding member of Hill City B'nai B'rith and later the founding president of Temple Beth Israel. Daniel Dopplemayer, who fought with the Seventh Texas Infantry, was the first president of Marshall's Temple Moses Montefiore. Prussian-born Sam Schwarz, a wounded South Carolina veteran, resettled in Hempstead, Texas. Schwartz coaxed his brother, a Talmudic scholar with rabbinic ordination, to emigrate from Europe. He did and led services in a backyard synagogue built with separate entrances for men and women.

In Galveston, an island city brimming with Confederate veterans and post-war federal-

Soldiers and salesmen. Isaac Sanger (1836–1918), left, was the first Sanger brother in Texas and opened a frontier trading post in 1857. Lehman (1838–1911), right, joined him in 1859 in Weatherford. (The date of his death on this placard is off by one year.) When the Civil War began, Lehman buried gold coins that financed his postwar business venture. Philip (1841–1902), who was working in Savannah in 1861, enlisted in the 32nd Georgia State Troops and battled soldiers led by General W. T. Sherman on their march to the sea. From the collections of the Texas/Dallas History and Archives Division, Dallas Public Library.

occupation troops, Congregation B'nai Israel was chartered in 1868. Among its founding members were cavalry officer Henry Seeligson, wounded defending Texas soil; Private Harris Kempner, who had two horses shot out from under him; Private Moritz Kopperl of the state militia, and Private Jacob Frank of the First Texas Infantry, the unit with the Confederacy's longest casualty list.

THE SANGERS: TEXTBOOK EXAMPLES

Waco and Dallas bear the imprint of the Sanger brothers. Isaac Sanger (1836–1918) was the first from a family with ten siblings to come to America and ultimately to Texas. He arrived in McKinney in the late 1850s with his German-born friend Eli Baum (1830?–1867). The pair had met in New York and persuaded their employer to bankroll their Texas mercantile venture. In McKinney, a fur-trapping outpost where settlers drank from gourds, checked the time on sundials, and banded together for house-raisings, the business partners opened the Baum & Sanger store in a "rickety frame cracker-box."[4] The emporium, thirty-five miles north of Dallas, was profitable enough for them to summon Isaac's brother Lehman Sanger (1838–1911), who was working with a cousin in Savannah, Georgia. By late 1859, the trio headed for Weatherford, the county seat of Parker County, seventy-five miles to the west, a region famed for buffalo hunters, cattle drives, and Indian raids.

It was in this setting that Baum and the Sanger brothers opened a dry goods store on the Weatherford town square. For fifty-five dollars they bought a portion of a commercial lot and constructed a concrete building—unusual at a time of lumber storefronts. Both the building and the business succeeded. The Sanger store became a community

Morris Lasker (1840–1916). A future financier and Texas legislator, Lasker picked up the mail for the Sanger brothers' Weatherford store. Center for American History, UT-Austin, CN Number 12116, Texas Jewish Historical Society.

center, with the ground floor serving as a gathering area for posses and a holding pen for prisoners threatened by mobs. The upstairs served as a meeting room for the Phoenix Masonic Lodge chartered during the Civil War.

Advertising in the local paper, The White Man, the Sanger store offered bartering customers full price for pelts. Other storekeepers purchased furs for a fraction of their worth and suddenly had to scramble to compete. With business booming, Isaac and Lehman wrote their brother Philip in Savannah with news of their success. Philip, who supplied wares to peddlers, sent his brothers two eager apprentices. One of them was Morris Lasker (1840–1916), a future Galveston financier and state legislator who was put to work at odd jobs such as picking up the mail.

One day, a "wild" man followed Lasker from the post office, shouting that someone from the Sangers' address had written his wife an amorous letter. The man cursed the Sangers and threatened Lasker with a Colt revolver and a Bowie knife until the editor of The White Man, Indian fighter John Robert Baylor (1822–1894), intervened. Baylor, the nephew of Baylor University's Baptist co-founder, looked the troublemaker in the eye and vouched for all present. The fellow backed out the door.[5]

Previous researchers have attributed such harassment "presumably" to anti-Semitism and the Sangers' German-Jewish background.[6] However, autobiographical recollections of Morris Lasker and Lehman Sanger attribute the spate of nasty incidents against the Sangers mainly to the "enmity of their competitors." Lasker describes a skull and crossbones painted on Eli Baum's door with a message to get out of town. In "another attempt to annoy" the Sangers, he relates that a copy of an "abolitionist" newspaper, the New York Tribune, appeared in their mailbox. A "secret tribunal" ruled that a business competitor planted the newspaper.[7] The outcome of the tribunal, the Sangers' friendship with editor John Baylor, and the brothers' leadership within local Masonic circles are evidence of a strong level of social acceptance. Religion was oftentimes irrelevant on the frontier. As the name of the Parker County newspaper (The White Man) implies, prejudice was aimed mainly against the most visible racial minorities.

Alert for commercial opportunities, the Sanger brothers soon sent Lehman Sanger and Morris Lasker to open a branch store in Decatur, the seat of nearby Wise County.

Bored by the slow pace, Lasker put his earnings toward purchase of a horse fit "for Indian duty." His first call to arms turned out to be a ruse. Upon arriving at the site of a reported "war party," Lasker and his forty riding companions found an equally bored citizenry who had paid five Kiowa with firewater to perform a "war dance."[8]

Soon enough Lasker would find excitement.

SECESSIONIST FEVER

The election of President Abraham Lincoln in November 1860 caused heated debate in the divided state. Texans along the Gulf Coast and the Louisiana line profited from the slave-based economy and sided with the secessionist sentiment of the Deep South. Texas's northernmost counties bordered Indian Territory—land that would someday become Oklahoma. Frontier voters generally opposed secession, concerned that they would lose federal troop protection from Indians. In Wise County, where Morris Lasker and Lehman Sanger were storekeepers, the county had a slave population of 95, and secession lost by a close vote of 78 to 76. In Parker County, where Isaac Sanger and Eli Baum worked and where the census recorded 324 slaves, secession was adopted by a vote of 535 to 61.[9] Statewide, secession passed with 76 percent of the vote.

Immediately after the referendum, men began readying units for battle. In Decatur, volunteers marched around the square, many with "Dexter's best," a popular whiskey, tucked under their jackets.[10] The men formed militias—fighting units that the Confederate government, then based in Montgomery, Alabama, soon brought into organized Army divisions.

"Although neither of the three [Sanger brothers] possessed much cash or chattel of any description," Lehman Sanger wrote, "when the war began, having cast their lots with the people of the South, they considered it only their full duty to serve the land of their adoption." They were no different than scores of other Jewish men in Texas, who volunteered at a disproportionately high rate. Although many had left Europe to avoid conscription, they felt that they had a cause for which to fight once federal troops attacked the South.

These men were later praised as eager, well-disciplined soldiers. "They were all volunteers, and I know there was not a Jew conscript in [my] Legion," wrote Major General Thomas Neville Waul, who commanded a force of some two thousand Texans that formed in the countryside northwest of Houston. Praising his Jewish recruits, Waul recalled:

> Two of the infantry companies had a large number of Jews in their ranks, and the largest company in the command—120 men—was officered by Jews, and three-fourths of the rank and file were of that faith. There were also a number of Jews scattered through the command in the other companies.

Waul's remarks were published in the *Galveston Daily News* on June 10, 1894, in response to a letter to the editor disparaging the "patriotism and gallantry of the Jew as a soldier." Waul responded that he considered it an "honor to command a force composed to a considerable extent of Israelites." None were court-martialed. Few requested sick leave. "In battle, without distinction of race or religion, all were apparently willing and eager for the contest. I will say, however, I neither saw nor heard of any Jew shrinking or failing to answer to any call of duty or danger . . . I jot down these recollections that you may have the testimony of one Gentile to attest to the courage, endurance and patriotism of the Jew as a soldier."[11]

Waul's remarks were reprinted the following year in Simon Wolf's seminal book, *The American Jew As Patriot, Soldier and Citizen*. In that volume, Wolf, too, repudiates the canard that Jews were not fighters. He attempts to identify by name and unit every Jewish soldier who fought in America's wars, starting with the Revolution. In Texas he identifies 108 Civil War veterans—an incomplete list to be sure. Wolf's roster draws mainly from Jews who lived along the Gulf Coast or who had prominent friends in Galveston and Houston. Many Texas Jews—among them Daniel Dopplemayer of Marshall and David Levi Kokernot—are not mentioned. The book lists Lieutenant Henry Seeligson of Galveston, but omits his brother George and relative Louis Seeligson. Wolf identifies at most fifteen from Waul's Legion, despite the general's statement that he had approximately ninety Jewish soldiers in one company and many more spread throughout the command. Further, Wolf's book lists few soldiers from the state's interior and none—like Moritz Kopperl and Eli Baum—who served in militia regiments activated under Confederate command.[12]

None of the Sangers made the list.

Missing from the 1895 roster. Dutch-born Captain David Levi Kokernot (1805–1892) shipwrecked on the Texas coast in 1830, battled for Texas independence in 1836, fought for the Confederacy with Terry's Texas Rangers, converted to Christianity, and became a rancher in Gonzales. Simon Wolf lists him as fighting in Texas's War for Independence but not the Civil War. This is the only published photo of a Texas Jewish Confederate in uniform. UT Institute of Texan Cultures at San Antonio, No. 072-0100, courtesy Miss Clifton McNeel.

CIVIL WAR SERVICE

The Sanger stores first lost Morris Lasker to the call of war. He traded his gold watch for a dun pony in 1861 and then rode three hundred miles to San Antonio on horseback with John Baylor. Lasker was smarting for action and got plenty with the unit that formed en route—the Texas Mounted Riflemen, later called the Second Texas Cavalry. Lasker served in Company H, engaging in skirmishes on the Rio Grande, along the Sabine River, and in the mosquito-infested swamps of Louisiana. "Soldiers of the Second Texas Cavalry were made up of Western cowboys, farmers and frontiersmen," wrote a Yankee prisoner. "They were the dirtiest, worst-looking men we ever saw. They were all poorly clothed and tough in manner, but as their prisoners, we were always treated in a kind and gentlemanly manner."[13]

After Morris Lasker's departure from Decatur, Lehman Sanger shuttered the shop and moved to Weatherford. On March 3, 1862, he joined a Parker County unit, Company A of the Twenty-First Texas Infantry. Soon his outfit was dispatched to the Texas Gulf coast near Galveston, where it participated in the recapture of the island city from federal troops on January 1, 1863. The attack was precipitated by information from a Jewish spy, Isabelle Dyer, who informed the Confederate commander, Major General John Bankhead Magruder, that Union forces had been tipped off about a later attack date. The general swiftly readied his troops and attacked by surprise.

"The rest of the three years' service," Lehman Sanger wrote, "if not fighting Yankees, [I was] fighting mosquitoes at Galveston and Sabine Pass."

His unit also marched thirty-eight miles to the Louisiana line for the bloody May 1864 engagement at Calcasieu Pass. Confederate forces captured two gunboats, took 166 prisoners, and defeated the Union Navy for control of a portion of the coast. Company A took several casualties. Besides war wounds, many men succumbed to a typhoid outbreak in the Galveston hospital.

Isaac Sanger and Eli Baum had a less glamorous record of service. Their role with McCord's First Frontier District was to defend North Texas against Indian raids and track down deserters from both sides. Members armed themselves and received a monetary "bounty" for the weapons they brought to the district arsenal: a six-shooter and a rifle for Isaac Sanger and a shotgun for Eli Baum.[14] "As to arms, these militia men had every variety and caliber and kind and quality. . . . They all had one weapon in common—they all had big, huge knives."[15]

Among their ranks was Captain J. M. Luckey, initially one of the most ardent supporters of secession. As the war rolled on and Confederate money became worthless and supplies scarce, Luckey's sentiments switched. Men in the ranks accused him of treason and threatened mutiny. Isaac Sanger, who had been appointed Parker County District Clerk in 1863, rancher Oliver Loving, and former Weatherford Mayor J. A. Leach tried to keep order among the local frontier troops, but to no avail. Luckey was lynched in 1864.[16]

Meanwhile, Philip Sanger in Savannah, Georgia, became caught up in war fever. When secession was imminent, his employer and cousin, David Heller, suggested that Philip flee Savannah with him and join relatives living in Cincinnati. Philip instead enlisted on October 12, 1861, in Company E, Thirty-Second Georgia State Troops. With large numbers of men garrisoned without benefit of health and sanitation measures, illness befell soldiers on both sides at the opening of hostilities. In August 1862, Philip came down with a fever that kept him on the sick list for four months.

Philip later fought in twenty-eight engagements under General Joe Johnston, often battling Union General William Tecumseh Sherman on his march to the sea. In July 1863, the Thirty-Second helped defend Fort Wagner, a fortress off the South Carolina Coast near Charleston, then moved to northern Florida to try to stop the Union forces from cutting off Confederate beef supplies. On February 20, 1864, in an attack dubbed the Battle of Ocean Pond, Sanger's unit surprised and defeated federal troops from New York, New Hampshire, and Massachusetts. (The famed Fifty-Fourth Massachusetts, depicted in the movie *Glory*, was among them.) It was Florida's largest skirmish. More than eight hundred Confederates were wounded. Among the battle-scarred was Philip Sanger. After the fighting ended, Sherman retreated.[17]

That summer, Philip Sanger served as "acting" private secretary at General Headquarters, handling dispatches to troops fighting Sherman. When he returned to combat in December 1864, Philip and his unit evacuated citizens from his hometown of Savannah. The retreat continued for months until March 19, 1865, when the Confederates attacked federal troops at Bentonville, North Carolina. It was the South's largest final burst. Federal troops initially reeled back, but their superior firepower ruled. Philip and his comrades lay down their weapons in final surrender on April 26, 1865.

Tattered, penniless, and hungry, Philip Sanger mulled his options. Savannah had nothing left for him. He had two brothers in Texas, but he would not learn their fate for some time. He had four brothers and three sisters still in Bavaria, waiting for the war's end to emigrate. He had relatives in Cincinnati, where his cousin David Heller had fled. Unsure of his future, Philip Sanger made the trek to Cincinnati, but not for long.

POSTWAR

With the South decimated, Isaac Sanger faced financial problems. The Confederate government had assumed his debts to New York suppliers. When the Confederacy collapsed, the suppliers had yet to be paid. As defeated men trudged home, their pockets empty, their hopes dashed, creditors prepared to seize what meager assets the veterans had. In his manuscript detailing the history of the Sanger Brothers' firm, Lehman recalled, "Nobody had enough money to buy a horse, so we tramped it afoot, occasionally getting a ride on an ox-wagon. . . . We finally arrived in Weatherford, slightly disfigured."

Lehman Sanger's reason for returning to Weatherford was to retrieve the gold that he had had the forethought to hide, six feet under, in the backyard of a trusted friend and pharmacist, Dr. Desmeth. Lehman dug up his treasure and left Weatherford with little thought of staying in Texas or the South, for the postwar period was chaotic. Business prospects—indeed the future of any endeavor—appeared slim.

On the way back to Houston, however, the stagecoach stopped in Millican, a railhead eighty miles northwest of the city. It was there that Lehman was "struck with the business conditions." Postwar Millican was a rough-and-tumble place. "It was hard to tell who were the tougher: Uncle Sam's troops or the floating population, which was composed of good, bad or indifferent," he wrote. The city swarmed with people needing provisions. Lehman quickly journeyed to Houston to purchase a small selection of groceries. While there, he spotted a familiar face, an old McKinney associate who went by the name "Little Wolf." The pair agreed to become partners, with Wolf adding dry goods to the inventory. In Millican, they set up a tent-like storefront and slept on the floor to protect their merchandise. Their wares sold out in twenty-four hours.

Texans Who Went to War

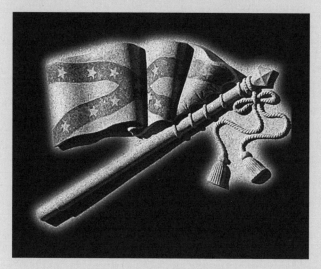

Rebel battle flag carved on Jacob Samuels's tombstone.
Flag photographed by Carolyn Cruz.

Turn-of-the-century American Jewish leader Simon Wolf, an attorney and a diplomat, researched the names and ranks of American Jewish soldiers who served in the armed forces from 1774 to 1865. His state-by-state rosters were published in 1895 under the title *The American Jew as Patriot, Soldier and Citizen* (Philadelphia: Levy-type). He listed 108 Jewish Texans who fought in the Civil War. A century later, researcher Gary Whitfield began documenting additional soldiers and increased the roster to more than 180—among them four who fought for the Union. Veterans named in Simon Wolf's book are listed below in capital letters. Soldiers documented in the latest roundup are printed in capital and lower-case letters.

1. ALEXANDER, ABRAHAM S.—Capt., 1st Texas Inf., Cmdr. Oswald's Btn.
2. Alexander, Alex—Sgt., 1st Texas Heavy Arty., Co. I
3. Alexander, Seelig—Capt., 5th Texas Inf. Co. A
4. Alexander, B.—Magruder's Trans-Mississippi Dept.
5. ANGEL, A.—5th Texas Inf., killed at Manassas
6. ASH, HENRY—5th Texas Inf. Co. C
7. AUERBACH, J.—physician, 5th Texas Inf. Co. A
8. AUERBACH, E.—5th Texas Inf. Co. B., killed at Wilderness
9. BACHARACH, WOLF—5th Texas Inf. Co. A
10. Baum, Eli—McCord's Frontier Rgt. Texas State Troops
11. Baum, S. M.
12. BENEDICT, JACOB—1st Texas Inf. Co. F, killed at Malvern Hill
13. Berliner, Bero B.—Waller's Texas Cav.
14. BILLIG, ISAAC—5th Texas Inf. Co. A
15. Block, Herman Mendelsohn—Sibley's Brig.
16. Block, Hyman—Texas 25th Texas Cav. Co. H.
17. Block, Isaac—Waul's Legion, Co. B
18. Bock, Isidore—3rd Texas Cav. State Troops, Co. B
19. Bondi, August—John Brown's 5th Kansas Cav., Union Army
20. BUCK, ROBERT—1st Arty.
21. COBMAN, LOUIS—5th Texas Inf. Co. A, wounded at Gettysburg
22. COHEN, HENRY—1st Texas Inf. Co. L
23. COHEN, S.—5th Texas Inf. Co. A, killed at Gettysburg
24. Cohn, Isaac—Griffin's Btn., Texas Inf. Co. F
25. COLEMAN, LOUIS—5th Texas Inf. Co. A, wounded at Gettysburg
26. COLEMAN, MEYER—26th Texas Inf. Co. A
27. CRAMER, A.—lt., 8th Texas Inf. Co. B, Flourney's Regt.
28. CRAMER, JOSEPH—1st Texas Inf, wounded at Gettysburg
29. DANIELS, J.—8th Texas Inf. Co. C
30. DANNENBAUM, JOSEPH—Co. C, Cook Regt.

Engraving of Simon Wolf. Courtesy Center for American History, UT-Austin, CN Number 12109, Cohen (Henry) Papers.

31. DAVIDBURG, DAVID D.—6th Texas Inf. Co. B

32. DAVIDSON, DAVID H.—6th Texas Inf. Co. B

33. DAVIDSON, HENRY—26th Texas Inf. Co. A

34. DEUTSCH, S.—6th Texas Inf. Co. C

35. DEUTSCH, SOLOMON—1st Texas Inf., wounded.

36. DOPPELMAYER, DANIEL—7th Texas Inf. Co. D

37. DREYFUS, CHARLES—26th Texas Inf. Co. A

38. DREYFUS, SAMUEL—1st Texas Inf. Co. A

39. ELSASSER, I.—5th Texas Inf. Co. A

40. Ephraim, Jacob—enlisted near Hempstead

41. Farber, Arnold—19th Texas Inf. Co. D

42. Finkelstein, Abe—bugler, flag bearer

43. FISCHEL, LEON—Wirt Adams Cav.

44. FLEISCHEL—Capt.

45. FOX, A.—Waul's Legion, Co. B

46. FOX, ALLEN—Co. C, hvy. arty.

47. Frank, Jacob—1st Texas Inf.

48. FRANK, L.—Elmore's Texas Inf. Co. A

49. FRANK. J.W.—1st Texas Inf. Co. L, killed at Sharpsburg

50. Frederick, William Calvin—7th Texas Inf. Co. E

51. FRIEDBERGER, G.—9th Texas Cav., killed at Corinth

52. FRIEDBERGER, GABRIEL—Terry's Cav.

53. FRIEDBERGER, SAMUEL—Terry's Cav.

54. FRIEDLANDER, N.—26th Texas Cav. Co. A

55. Gabert, Simon—4th Missouri Cav. (Freemont's Hussars), Union Army

56. GANS, LEON—Parson's Texas Cav. Co. A

57. Gans, Morris—Williamson Co. Bowies, Texas militia

58. GANS, SAMUEL—26th Texas Cav., wounded at Cane River

59. GLASER, WOLF—1st Texas Inf.

60. GOETZ, JULIUS—14th Texas Inf. Co. A, wounded

61. Goldsticker, Henry—Pvt., LaVaca Guards

62. GOLDSTICKER, J.—4th Texas Inf., killed at Sharpsburg

63. Haber, Abraham—Maj., Brig. Commissary

64. Halff, Solomon—Waul's Legion, Co. B, Co. F

65. Halfin, Eli—6th Texas Inf. Regt. Co. C

66. Halfin, Henry—Coastal Def., 24th Brig., Texas militia

67. Halfin, Sol—4th Texas Cav. Co. C

68. Harby, Harry J.—8th Texas Field Btry.

69. HARBY, HENRY J.—26th Texas Cav. Co. C

70. Harby, J.D.—8th Texas Field Btry.

71. Harby, Levi Charles—Commodore (Simon Wolf lists L. C. Harby with S. Car.)

72. HELLER, LOUIS—6th Texas Inf.

73. HIEF, CHARLES—6th Texas Inf. Co. B, captured

74. HINES, A.—4th Texas Inf. Co. B, lost arm at Gaines' Mill

75. HIRSCHBERG, J.—26th Texas Cav. Co. A

(continued on p. 42)

JWV emblem on grave at Fort Worth's Emanuel Hebrew Rest. Emblem photographed by Carolyn Cruz.

76. HIRSHFELD, HENRY—Parson's Brig.

77. HOLDSTEIN, ISIDORE—8th Texas Inf. Co. A

78. Honigsberger, Isaac—1st Texas Inf. Co. H

79. HYAMS, S.—26th Texas Cav. Co. A

80. Jacobs, Jacob—14th Texas Inf. Co. A.

81. Jacobs, James M.—18th Texas Inf. Co. D

82. JACOBY, MAX—1st Texas Inf. Co. A, lost leg at Frazier's Farm

83. Kahn, Emanuel—3rd Texas Cav. Co. A

84. Kahn, Lionel—Union Army

85. Karpeles, Emil

86. Karpeles, Leopold—46th Mass. Inf., Union Army, Medal of Honor recipient

87. KAUFMAN, C.

88. KAUFMAN, EDWARD—1st Texas Inf.

89. KAUFMAN, K.

90. KELLER, THEODORE—Col., 2nd Texas Inf., wounded at Corinth

91. KEMPNER, HARRIS—1st Texas Inf.

92. KLOPMAN, L.—8th Texas Inf. Co. A., killed at Jenkins' Ferry

93. KOHLMAN, M.—26th Texas Cav. Co. A

94. Kokernot, David Levi—Sgt. Maj., Terry's Texas Rangers

95. Kopperl, Moritz—1st Texas State Troop, Co. B

96. LACHMAN, E.—5th Texas Inf. Co. D, wounded at Manassas

97. Lang (or Long), Samuel Dist Texas Hvy. Arty., Co. C

98. LASKER, MORRIS—2nd Cav.

99. LAZARUS, B.—4th Texas Inf. Co. E

100. LAZARUS, S. S.—1st Texas Inf. Co. L, wounded at Chickamauga

101. LEAVE, R.B.—1st Texas Inf. Co. B, wounded at Malvern Hill

102. Leavitt, Gus—18th Texas Inf.

103. LEOPOLD, W.—1st Hvy. Arty.

104. Levey, Michael

105. LEVISON, A.—Waul's Legion, Co. B

106. LEVISON, PAUL—Waul's Legion, Co. B

107. LEVY, ISAAC—Light Arty. Co. B

108. Levy, M. C.—14th Texas Field Btry.

109. Levy Maurice L.—Mounted Coast Guards, Graham's Co., Texas State Troops

110. Levy, Meyer—24th Brig., Texas State Troops (blockade runner)

111. LEVY, ROBERT—5th Texas Inf. Co. A

112. LEWIS, ISAAC—5th Texas Inf. Co. C

113. Lichtenstein, Moritz—Sibley's Brig.

114. London, Max—6th Texas Inf. Co. A

115. MAAS, LOUIS—5th Texas Inf. Co. D, killed at Manassas

116. Maas, Max—2nd Lt., 4th Texas Inf. Btn. (Oswald's) Co. B

117. Marx, Samuel—Texas 24th Cav. Brig. Co. B, Texas State Troops

118. MAYER, LEO E.—captured

119. Mayer, Samuel—Maj., CSA, Texas Arty.

120. Melasky, Bennet—36th Texas Cav. Co A

121. MELASKY, J.—26th Texas Cav. Co. A

122. MEYER, JOSEPH—Hvy. Arty. Co. C

123. MICHEL, HENRY—15th Texas Inf.

124. MORRIS, LEHMAN—Sgt., 1st Texas Inf. Co. D, killed at Gettysburg

125. Nathusius, Otto—Maj., Waul's Legion, attached to Mississippi unit (Simon Wolf lists Nathusius with Miss.)

126. Ney, Joseph—3rd Texas Cav. Co. B

127. Ney, Julius—19th Texas Cav. Co. G

128. Nussbaum, J.—Cpt., W. H. Duke's Vols., Jefferson

129. Oppenheim, Julius—Bauvinghauser's Reserve Corp

130. OPPENHEIMER, A.—22nd Texas Inf.

131. OPPENHEIMER, BENJAMIN—22nd Texas Inf.

132. OPPENHEIMER, DANIEL—Capt., 3rd Cav.

133. OPPENHEIMER, J.—2nd Texas Inf.

134. OPPENHEIMER, S.—22nd Texas Inf.

135. PEPPER, L. S.—8th Texas Inf. Co. A

136. PEPPER, SAMUEL—8th Texas Inf. Co. A

137. PICKARD, H.—5th Texas Inf. Co. H

138. Pinski, Mark—Capt., W. H. Duke's Vols., Jefferson

139. POHALSKI, G. D.—11th Texas Inf. Co. G

140. POHALSKI, P.—11th Texas Inf. Co. G

141. RICH, LOUIS M.—Cook's Texas Cav. Co. C

142. Rose, Abraham—3rd Texas Cav. Co. B

143. Rosenbaum, H.—21st Texas Inf. Co. A and F

144. Rosenberger, Henry—4th Texas Inf. Co. C

145. ROSENFIELD, ALEXANDER—26th Texas Cav. Co. A

146. ROSENFIELD, HENRY—26th Texas Cav. Co. A

147. ROSENFIELD, MICHAEL—26th Texas Cav. Co. A

148. SAMPSON, E. J.—4th Texas Inf., buried at Richmond's Jewish Cemetery

149. Sampson, Samuel

150. Samuels, Jacob—Waller's Texas Cav. Co. F

151. SAMUSH, J.

152. Sanger, Isaac—McCord's Frontier Regt., Texas State Troops

153. Sanger, Lehman—21st Texas Inf. Co. A

154. Seeligson, Edward—Waller's Cav. Regt. Co. E

155. SEELIGSON, HENRY—Lt., Cavalry

156. Seeligson, George—Waller's Cav. Regt. Co. E

157. Seeligson, Louis—Benavides Cav. Regt. Co. G

158. Senechal, Alexander—2nd Texas Inf. Co. B

159. Senechal, Louis—1st Hvy. Arty. Co. G

160. SHOWLSKI, CHARLES—5th Texas Inf. Co. E

161. SIEGEL, JOSEPH—8th Texas Inf.

162. SILBERBERG, GEORGE—9th Texas Inf. Co. B

163. Simon, Alexander—Cpl., 15th Texas Cav.

164. SOLOMON, JOSEPH A.—11th Texas Inf. Co. G

165. Spring, M. L.—4th Texas Inf. Co. A

166. Stein, Henry—Waul's Legion, Co. C

167. STEIN, ISAAC—Marshall's Regt.

168. STEINER, VICTOR—Texas Rangers

169. Stern, Jacob—CSA Qm., Jefferson

170. TEAH, ABRAHAM—8th Texas Inf.

171. TEAH, ABRAHAM—22nd Texas Inf.

172. Wagner, Louis—Bexar Guards, 30th Brig., Texas State Troops

173. WALKER, A.—1st Texas Inf. Co. K

174. Weil, Solomon—Navarro City 16th Brig., Texas State Troops

175. WEIS, ALBERT—2nd Texas Cav.

176. WEIS, LEOPOLD—2nd Texas Cav.

177. Weltman, James—1st Lt., 12th Texas Inf. Co. C

178. Wertheimer, Abraham—Bee Co. Home Guards, Texas Militia

179. Wertheimer, William—6th Texas Inf. Co. B

180. Wertheimer, Charles—Waller's Texas Cav. Co. A, Lavaca

181. WETMORE, JAMES—8th Texas Inf. Co. C

182. WIENER, SOLOMON—Terry's Scouts

183. WOLF, A.—5th Texas Inf., wounded

184. WOLF, A. F.—5th Inf. Co. A, killed at Sharpsburg

185. WOLF, BENJAMIN—5th Texas Inf. Co. A

186. WOLF, SIMON—4th Texas Inf. Co. F, killed at Manassas

By the fall of 1865, Lehman Sanger and Little Wolf had dissolved their partnership. Older brother Isaac Sanger arrived to help with business. Morris Lasker reunited with the Sangers and came on board for a spell. As the need for vigilant protection passed, the Sanger brothers wrote relatives in Cincinnati, urging them to move to Texas and help expand the business. Future railroad lines would extend north to the small towns of Bryan, Hearne, Calvert, Bremond, Kosse, Groesbeck, and Corsicana. Isaac and Lehman envisioned a Sanger store at every terminus of the Houston & Texas Central Railroad. Their brother, Philip Sanger, the Georgia veteran, was the first to join them in Texas, followed by a cousin, August J. Rosenfield, from Cincinnati, and Asher Mandelbaum, a cousin from the North.

JEWISH CONNECTIONS

Lehman Sanger's expansion plans were put on hold late in 1865 when, on a buying trip to Houston, he came down with dengue fever, a mosquito-borne tropical virus. Bedridden, he was nursed back to health in the home of Zacharias Emmich and his wife Cecilia.[18] Emmich (1817–1901), a part-time rabbi, had befriended Lehman during the war while visiting Jewish troops at nearby Camp Lubbock. A native of Baden, Germany,

Emmich was the state's first Jewish spiritual leader. He had come to Texas from La-fayette, Indiana, in 1860 after Houston's Congregation Beth Israel advertised for a spiri-tual leader, *shochet* (kosher meat slaughterer), and *mohel* (to circumcise newborn boys). He served Beth Israel for two years, then left full-time religious work for retailing. He still participated in the life of the Jewish community as a teacher, pulpit substitute, and chaplain.[19]

Lehman Sanger's relationship with the Emmichs, whom he characterized as "my dear old friends," indicates a deeper Jewish connection than evidenced in his autobiographi-cal writings, which mention no religious observances. There is no reference to Jewish holiday closings in extant business records from Sanger stores in McKinney, Weather-ford, Decatur, or Millican. Nonetheless, the family's religious connection was strong. Lehman engaged in philosophical discourse with at least one fellow soldier who later reminisced about their discussions comparing Judaism with Christianity.[20] Lehman's younger brother Sam (1843–1918), who immigrated to the United States in 1866, had studied at seminaries in Wurzburg and Berlin and was an ordained rabbi. He taught He-brew in Cincinnati and Philadelphia, where he led a small congregation, before opening a shoe store in New York. Sam Sanger once remarked, "When I am among theologians, they compliment me as being the best merchant among them, and when I am among merchants, they give me credit for being the best theologian in the crowd."[21] The Sanger brothers also exhibited what Lasker called "a loyalty to each other" and to their extended family. They stayed in contact with relatives in the United States, Canada, and Bavaria. Most indicative of their strong Jewish identity is the fact that the Sanger siblings and their business associates all married Jewish partners, many of them cousins.[22]

In Europe, the Sangers had been rural winemakers and weavers from Obenbreit am Main. They joined other Jewish tradespeople selling wares at Sunday country fairs. When eldest son Isaac turned sixteen in 1852, he left Bavaria for New Haven, where his uncle, David Heller, lived. When the next two brothers turned sixteen, they too immigrated to New Haven in 1854 and 1856. A year after the war, in 1866, two more brothers—Jake and Alex—immigrated to Cincinnati. Later that year, the older brothers sent for their par-ents, who initially settled in Cincinnati with their five remaining children: Sam, David, Sophie, Bertha, and Ada.

BACK TO BUSINESS

In 1867, two of the younger Sanger brothers—Dave, age sixteen, and Jake, twenty-two—came to Millican and helped with the pending move to the next railroad terminus twenty miles north in Bryan. Yellow fever struck both towns, and work ceased. Because Dave and Jake "were not acclimated," Lehman wrote, "our first great misfortune befell us." The brothers died four days apart in October 1867, "casting a gloom . . . over us." The epidemic also killed the family's longtime business associate, Eli Baum, and his wife. The Baums were laid to rest in Galveston.[23] The younger Sanger brothers were buried at the Jewish cemetery in Houston.

Following the epidemic, the Sangers closed shop in Millican and focused on Bryan, the railroad's new northern terminus. To keep prices down and goods in stock, oldest brother Isaac began buying merchandise at auctions in Galveston and New Orleans. In 1868, he took up permanent residence in New York and opened a purchasing office. Over the next five years, the rest of the Sanger brothers worked and settled in Texas, following the rails

Bryan, Texas, late 1860s. The Sanger store in Bryan was the first to use the family name. From the collections of the Texas/Dallas History and Archives Division, Dallas Public Library.

and installing a brother, a cousin, or an in-law to operate a branch store at every stop. The last brother to join the enterprise was Alex (1847–1925), a Cincinnati bookkeeper, who in 1871 began his apprenticeship in Corsicana, a county seat fifty-five miles south of Dallas.

The railroad's next terminus was Dallas. Unlike cities elsewhere on the rail route, Dallas was destined to enjoy long-term growth because an east-west rail line was to intersect there. In advance of the railroad, Lehman and Philip Sanger traveled to Dallas by buggy, rented space on the courthouse square, and advertised in the *Dallas Herald*. They were already widely known, with their stores drawing customers from a three-hundred-mile radius. When they applied for loans, credit investigators with R.G. Dun & Company wrote, "This house stands high here . . . Char[acter], hab[its] and cap[acity] good for Jews."[24] The older brothers departed from Dallas and left the opening of the next store to younger brother Alex and cousin August J. Rosenfield.

The pair immediately became acquainted with the city's other leading Jewish retailers. On July 1, 1872, two weeks before the H&T Central Railroad reached Dallas, Sanger and Rosenfield were among eleven businessmen to organize the Dallas Hebrew Benevolent Association, the region's first Jewish institution. Alex Sanger was elected vice-president and Rosenfield, secretary. The group's formation apparently was triggered by the death of a Jewish man described as "a stranger in our midst." The society purchased land for a cemetery and underwrote the cost of the young man's burial. The next order of business was to erect a fence around the cemetery, separating it from the adjacent Masonic graveyard. By September, the group was organizing the city's first High Holy Day services. To lead services, they selected another businessman, Aaron Miller, whose descendants would remain in Dallas for generations. A Purim ball followed in March. A B'nai B'rith lodge formed in November 1873, with Philip Sanger, Alex Sanger, and A. J. Rosenfield among its charter members. At mid-year, Alex Sanger began a one-year term as president of the Dallas Hebrew Benevolent Association. On the civic front, Alex ran successfully for city alderman. His dual role, as leader in the Jewish and secular commu-

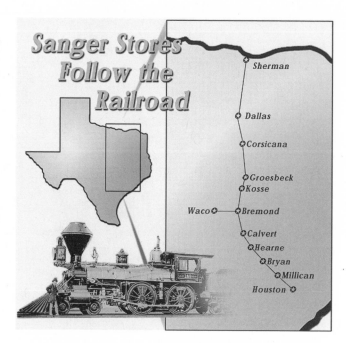

Sanger stores follow the railroad. The Houston & Texas Central Railroad laid track from Houston north, building depots at regular intervals so that steam-powered engines could be replenished with water. The Sangers followed the rail lines and opened a store at almost every stop. The map follows the progression of Sanger Brothers' stores that opened between 1865 and 1873. When the Santa Fe Railroad built east-west tracks in 1887, the company founded a town north of Dallas and named it Sanger after the mercantile family. Map by Garry Harman, The Artworks.

nities, was typical of the city's successful Jewish entrepreneurs. Their visibility helped integrate the Jewish community into the growth of the city.

The next step for the city's Jews was to form a congregation. Local Jewish women put this on their agenda in January 1875, when they formed a Ladies Hebrew Benevolent Association that advocated weekly worship services and religious instruction for children. The women raised money to purchase land for a synagogue and persuaded the men to follow through. On September 30, 1875, fifty-one men founded Congregation Emanu-El and elected Philip and Alex Sanger to the executive board.[25]

The next order of business was to engage a rabbi. Two clergymen applied. Coincidentally—or perhaps by design—one of the candidates was Rabbi Aron Suhler, a childhood friend of the Sangers and a seminary classmate of Sam Sanger.[26] Suhler, a widower who had served an Akron congregation, landed the Dallas pulpit and served for four years. Later, Philip Sanger was elected temple president from 1889 to 1894, and Alex was president from 1899 to 1901.

Meanwhile, one hundred miles southwest, a cluster of Sanger relatives was becoming involved in another emerging Jewish community. In February 1873, the H&T Central Railroad completed a spur to Waco—a Brazos River city that had long served as a crossroads for cattle, cowboys, and western pioneers. Located at the confluence of two rivers and named for an ancient tribe of Indians, Waco was in the heart of a cotton-growing and sheep-farming region. After the Civil War, thousands of longhorn cattle forded the river as cowboys herded them toward the Chisholm Trail, the route to Midwest beef markets. When a suspension bridge was built across the Brazos in 1870, Waco's population grew to three thousand. On February 4, 1873, the H&T Central began daily service to Waco from tiny Bremond. Since the railroad was going to Waco, so were the Sanger brothers. Philip and Lehman Sanger summoned their brother Sam to Waco. Sam, who had been operating a New York shoe store, closed his business and traveled by ship to Galveston and by rail to Waco. On his arrival on March 4, the Waco branch of Sanger Brothers opened for business stocked with eighteen hundred dollars in merchandise. The first year, sales tallied thirteen thousand dollars, a fraction of the Dallas branch's volume of more than five hundred thousand dollars.[27] Waco was secondary to Dallas, yet it was more profitable than Bremond, where cousin Asher Mandelbaum worked, than Calvert, where Sophie's spouse Lippman Emanuel was in charge, Corsicana, where Philip was working, or Bryan, where Lehman oversaw operations. Gradually, the Sangers closed stores in those faltering towns. At various times, they had operated in fourteen Texas cities. By 1876, only Waco and Dallas were left of the chain, but how they flourished.

Lehman joined Sam in Waco. Unlike Dallas, Waco already had a Jewish cemetery and a Hebrew Benevolent Association that dated to 1869. The benevolent society also had a Torah. Shortly after Sam Sanger's arrival, the Jewish community, which included twenty "young men" plus sixteen families, staged its first Purim ball. Late in the fall, on November 9, 1873, the Sangers were instrumental in starting a B'nai B'rith lodge. (It was no accident that the Dallas and Waco B'nai B'rith lodges were chartered only four days apart.) In January 1879, the Waco lodge "resolved to organize a formal congregation" to be named Congregation Rodef Sholom. Lodge members pledged money to construct an edifice.

The Sanger store in Waco often filled with veterans who migrated from the Deep South to farmlands just north of Waco. Throughout the 1870s, many of the store's customers were bearded Confederate veterans from Alabama and Georgia who had left their devastated homesteads for the promise of cheap land and a fresh start on the Texas frontier. Many had served with Philip Sanger at the last Confederate charge in Bentonville. In the Sanger store, these veterans reminisced.

There are streets, schools, buildings, and even a Texas town named after the much-admired Sangers. Their stores in Weatherford, Waco, and Dallas were community landmarks utilized for more than just shopping. In the commercial world, the Sangers are

Honoring Johnny Reb. Confederate veterans' monument at the Parker County Courthouse, Weatherford, Texas, faces toward the site of the store that Isaac Sanger, Lehman Sanger, and Eli Baum opened in the late 1850s. The store, a concrete building among a row of lumber storefronts, became a community meeting place. Photo by Gary P. Whitfield.

remembered as the first in Texas to install elevators, escalators, and gas and electric lights. They instituted a night school for employees. Their Dallas and Waco stores set the pace for several decades until 1926, when the family sold the chain. The Jewish institutions that the Sangers helped found in Dallas and Waco still flourish. During Waco's annual Veterans' Day Parade, the Waco Sons of Confederate Veterans lower the Lone Star flag at Fourth and Austin streets, paying homage at the former site of a Sanger landmark store. ✦

ACKNOWLEDGMENTS

The author would like to thank the following for assisting with the Jewish veterans roster: Ellen K. Brown, The Texas Collection, Baylor University; Bill D. Buckner, Genealogy Division of the Waco-McLennan County Library; Barbara Gilbert; Charles Hart; Ann Heinrich; Peggy Kornreich, Eva Long; Robert Marcus; Brenda McClurkin, Special Collections University of Texas at Arlington Libraries; Bruce Mercer, Masonic Grand Lodge Library of Texas, Waco; Greg Meyer, Texas Jewish Historical Society (TJHS); Susan Pritchett, Tarrant County Historical Commission; Robert Rosen, Charleston, South Carolina; Lynna Kay Shuffield; Charles Spurlin; Donald Teter, Baytown, TJHS; Teri Tillman, Natchez, Mississippi; David and Vickie Vogel, Schulenburg, TJHS; and Bob Weltman, Dallas. *Texas Confederate Home Roster.* Compiled by Katherine Hooper Davis, Linda, Ericson Devereaux, and Carolyn Reeves Ericson. Nacogdoches, Texas: Ericson Books, 2003.

NOTES

1. Lehman Sanger, "History of the Firm," p. 42, Box 3A168, "Merchants: Sanger" folder, Texas Jewish Historical Society Collection, Center for American History, University of Texas at Austin (hereafter TJHS).

2. The antebellum population estimate of 1,200 Jews in Texas, out of 604,000 total residents, is based on a study of 1860 U.S. Census records by Gary Whitfield, Hollace Weiner, and Laurie James, notes in possession of Weiner. The estimate is the same proportion of Jews that lived in the state in 1877 when the *American Jewish Year Book* estimates that approximately 3,300 Jews resided in the Texas, which then had a total population of 1.59 million, or two-tenths of a percent.

3. See Robert Rosen, *The Jewish Confederates* (Columbia: University of South Carolina Press, 2000), for further discussion of the high percentage of Jews who fought for the Confederacy.

4. Gerry Cristol, *A Light in the Prairie: Temple Emanu-El of Dallas, 1872–1997* (Fort Worth: Texas Christian University Press, 1998), 8; J. Lee and Lillian J. Stambaugh, *History of Collin County, Texas* (Austin: Texas State Historical Association, 1958), 33.

5. "Letter of Morris Lasker to Mr. Alex Sanger, Galveston, Texas, Jan. 1, 1909," pp. 17–18, Sanger Brothers Collection, The Texas Collection, Baylor University, Waco, Texas.

6. Leon Joseph Rosenberg, *Sangers': Pioneer Texas Merchants* (Austin: Texas State Historical Association, 1978), 9–11.

7. Lasker to Alex Sanger, January 1, 1909.

8. Ibid.

9. Randolph Campbell, *An Empire for Slavery, The Peculiar Institution in Texas, 1821–1865* (Baton Rouge: Louisiana State University Press, 1989), 266; Alwyn Barr, *Black Texans: A History of the Negro in Texas, 1528–1971* (Austin: Jenkins Pub. Co., Pemberton Press, 1973), 17.

10. Cliff D. Cates, *A Pioneer History of Wise County* (Decatur: Old Settlers Association, 1907), 120–26.

11. T. N. Waul to Leo N. Levi, May 16, 1894, reprinted in *Galveston Daily News*, June 10, 1894.

12. Simon Wolf, *The American Jew as Patriot, Soldier and Citizen* (Philadelphia: Levy-type, 1895), 100–101; Wolf's list was based upon a call for submissions, rather than state-by-state investigation; Carolyn Gray LeMaster, in *A Corner of the Tapestry: A History of the Jewish Experience in Arkansas, 1820s–1990s* (Fayetteville: University of Arkansas Press, 1994), 46, notes that "well over seventy Jewish Arkansans fought on the Confederate side," while Wolf puts the Arkansas total at fifty-two.

13. Confederate Military Service of Alfred Louis and John Wesley Dochery, p. 107, Regimental Records, 2nd Texas Cavalry, Confederate Research Center, Hill College, Hillsborough, Texas (hereafter CRC).

14. Personnel Records, Texas State Archives, Austin, Texas.

15. Regimental Records, 21st Texas Infantry, CRC.

16. Lehman Sanger, "History of the Firm," 48.

17. Regimental History Packets, 32nd Georgia Infantry, p. 864, CRC; Michael Morgan, "Surprise at Ocean Pond," *America's Civil War*, March 2005, 47–52; Service Records, General Reference Branch (NNRG-P), National Archives and Records Administration, Washington, D.C.

18. Rosenberg, *Sangers'*, 16; Lehman Sanger, "History of the Firm," 42.

19. *American Israelite*, November 18, 1859; *Occident*, March 15, 1860, 306; *Houston City Directory of 1866*, xiii, quoted in Helena Frenkil Schlam, "The Early Jews of Houston," Master's thesis, Ohio State University, 1971; Ruthe Winegarten and Cathy Schechter, *Deep in the Heart: The Lives and Legends of Texas Jews* (Austin: Eakin Press, 1990), 21; Hollace Weiner, "The Mixers: The Role of Rabbis Deep in the Heart of Texas," *American Jewish History* 85 (September 1997): 299.

20. Lee Ettelson, "To my grandchildren," p. 62, referring to January 12, 1902 Letter to Editor in Waco newspaper, Box 2B565, Sanger Brothers Collection, The Texas Collection, Baylor University.

21. Lasker to Alex Sanger, p. 23.

22. Sam married an American, Hannah Heller, of Cincinnati. Lehman married Canadian-born cousin Isabella Wenk (1848–1923) whom he met while working as a cigar-roller in Canada. Philip wed Cornelia Mandelbaum, whose brother, Asher Mandelbaum, became manager of a Sanger store. Sophie Sanger married Lippman Emanuel, another relative who managed the Sanger's chain store in Calvert. Alex married Fannie Fetchenbach. Bertha Sanger wed Joseph Lehman. Ada Sanger married Jacob Newberger.

23. The ages of the Baums at the time of death are unclear due to discrepancies between U.S. Census records for 1860 and burial records from 1867. The 1860 Census lists E. Baum in Weatherford, age twenty, and E. Baum in Decatur, age thirty-three. The 1867 burial records from Galveston list "E. Baum, 9/17/1867, age 25," according to Gertrude M. and Donald L. Teter, *Texas Jewish Burials* (Baytown: Texas Jewish Historical Society, 1997), 20. The mortuary report printed in the *Galveston Daily News*, September 18, 1867, p. 3, col. 2, lists "E. Baum, 35, died at Millican, & was brought here for Interment." The Baums listed on the 1860 census would have been twenty-seven and thirty in 1867.

24. "Dallas County, Nov. 28 1872, July 1873," as listed in Texas, Vol. 8, p. 45, R.G. Dun & Co. Collection, Baker Library, Harvard Business School, Boston, Mass.

25. Cristol, *A Light in the Prairie*, 7–16, 24–27.

26. "Half a Century of Wedded Life," *Waco Tribune*, March n.d., 1917, 33, reprinted, Sanger Brothers Collection, The Texas Collection, Baylor University, Waco.

27. Rosenberg, *Sangers'*, 41.

REFERENCES

Texas Confederate Home Roster. Compiled by Katherine Hooper Davis, Linda Ericson Devereaux, and Carolyn Reeves Ericson. Nacogdoches, Texas: Ericson Books, 2003.

Galveston Deaths; Obituaries and Tombstones of Confederate Veterans Buried in Broadway Cemeteries. Compiled by Bertha Ellen Beall, Norma Dunten, and Joyce Newman, introduction by Rose Mary Fritz. Vol. I, n.d.

Texas Jewish Historical Society Newsletters.

Reform Advocate, 1914, compilation of articles on Texas.

Rockdale Cemetery Website, www.rootsweb.com/~usgenweb/tx/milam/cemph/jewish/jewish.htm.

4

Home on the Range Mayer Halff's Cattle Empire

PATRICK DEAREN

It was a November evening in 1905, and aged cattleman and merchant Mayer Halff scanned the San Antonio banquet room and the eager faces of his young employees. A man of vision and enormous energy, he could appreciate their dedication to making this rush season a success for his San Antonio dry goods firm, M. Halff & Brother. As he rose to pay them tribute, he suddenly was overcome by emotion.

He knew his health was failing and that his days were nearing an end, but theirs were only beginning—and the road before them was filled not only with promise, but temptation. With the insight of a self-made man, he proceeded to challenge them to live by the ideals so dear to him: integrity, honesty, economy, industry, and courtesy.

"Character and standing," he said with choked voice, "can never be taken away from you . . . In my life I have succeeded beyond my expectations. I only wish for each of my boys that he will follow in my footsteps."

Mayer Halff's steps had cut a trace that few could equal, for it stretched from France to Texas to several other present-day states spanning fifteen hundred miles of western country. Rarely was a man so equally at ease in a plush banquet hall, a dusty cow camp, or in the company of a rabbi.

Mayer was born February 7, 1836, in Lauterbourg, France, to Jewish parents, Henry Halff III and his wife Eve. Until the late 1700s, Jews had been prohibited from residing in the larger French cities, and many still chose a rural life there in the province of Alsace, where persecution was less likely. The livestock industry ruled Mayer's boyhood, for he came from a line of cattle traders. Indeed, Jews had long dominated all aspects of the Alsatian cattle industry. Non-Jewish demand for beef was considerable, but cattlemen also ensured Jewish use of the meat by slaughtering in accordance with religious ritual. Merchandising, as well, was in Mayer's blood; two uncles were storekeepers, and his great-grandfather had been a peddler.

As with all Jewish boys in Alsace, Mayer pursued synagogue studies that included instruction in Hebrew, Torah, and Jewish law. At age thirteen, his Bar Mitzvah in the local synagogue entitled him to all the privileges and responsibilities of an adult Jewish male.

Soon afterward, economic depression and political unrest set the stage for Mayer's future. Not only did little financial opportunity exist for a boy suddenly turned man, but France and Germany both claimed Alsace, and war threatened. Furthermore, conscription in the French army of Louis Napoleon Bonaparte was virtually assured for any Alsatian male.

Mayer's cousin, Adolphe Halff, had faced a similar dilemma and had immigrated to Texas, a state with strong ties to France dating from its days as the Republic of Texas. Only a teenager himself, Adolphe evidently wrote home to Lauterbourg and convinced Mayer to join him in a peddling enterprise.

Rancher and gentleman. Mayer Halff (1836–1905), born in Lauterbourg, Alsace, at one time controlled almost one million acres of ranchland in Texas. Collection of Alex H. Halff.

In 1851, fifteen-year-old Mayer bid adieu to his family, including his thirteen-year-old brother Solomon, and boarded a ship for America. Already, he was exhibiting the initiative and boldness of a person destined for success. Disembarking at New Orleans on November 4, he eventually joined Adolphe in Galveston, a thriving seaport on the Texas Gulf Coast.

As a peddler for the next several years, Mayer likely traveled a circuit through plantations and towns that included Liberty, situated at the head of the navigable Trinity River fifty miles north of Galveston. Only twenty miles inland, Liberty was a vital port that connected the area with the world's shipping lanes. No point in the state offered greater opportunity, and in 1856 Mayer and Adolphe decided to become resident merchants in the city.

"Our motto being 'Cheap for Cash,' we will not be undersold by any store in the place," the cousins proclaimed in an April 28, 1856, newspaper ad in the *Liberty Gazette*.

M. Halff & Brother's letterhead. The elaborately drawn letterhead stationery of the Halffs' Peña Colorado and Pecos ranches features what appear to be four crossbreed cattle and brands used on livestock. Collection of Alex H. Halff.

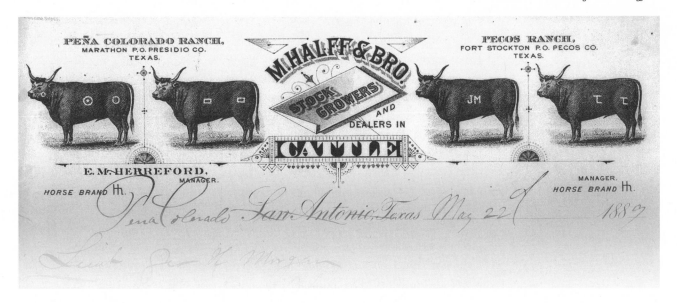

Mayer Halff's ad in Liberty Gazette, April 1, 1859. Halff's dry goods store featured "fancy groceries," perfume, "ready-made clothing," gloves in every size and color, and notions "too tedious to mention." Collection of Alex H. Halff.

Business was brisk on into summer, and on August 8 Adolphe sailed from Galveston on the steamer *Nautilus* in search of goods in distant manufacturing centers. On board were twenty-nine other passengers, none of whom could have anticipated the deadly hurricane that waited beyond the horizon. That night, the tide rose to unusual heights, and when the *Nautilus* failed to arrive in New Orleans, authorities feared the worst. Soon, a steamer embarked from New Orleans to Galveston and found one hundred miles of coast strewn with wreckage and livestock carcasses. The *Nautilus* had foundered, carrying Adolphe to a watery grave. The only survivor was a man buoyed by a cotton bale.

The blow to Mayer must have been overwhelming, for he had lost not only a cousin, a countryman, and a friend, but also his mentor and business partner.

While Mayer was experiencing tragedy, another cousin from Lauterbourg stepped in to assist. Felix Halff, whose expertise paralleled Adolphe's, had carved his own niche in the merchandising world. After immigrating to Louisiana in 1851, Felix Halff peddled for a period before establishing a mercantile operation. On the heels of Adolphe's death, he relocated to Liberty and entered into business with Mayer. Their association was not to endure, however, and it was still another Halff from Alsace whose destiny would be enmeshed with Mayer's.

In 1857, nineteen-year-old Solomon Halff abandoned plans to teach in Europe and joined his brother in Liberty. Initially, Solomon served only as Mayer's bookkeeper, but

French connection. Felix Halff emigrated from Lauterbourg, Alsace, and joined his cousin Mayer after another cousin perished in a shipwreck in the Gulf of Mexico. Collection of Alex H. Halff.

it was the beginning of a business relationship that would flourish during the next four and a half decades. Vital to their empire's growth was Mayer's early decision to accept cotton, hides, and cattle in lieu of cash.

In Liberty County Court on May 3, 1860, Mayer renounced his allegiance to France and became a United States citizen. Only weeks later, he sold his mercantile operation to Alphonse Dreyfus, who was married to Felix Halff's sister Julie. The Dreyfuses had immigrated to Louisiana in 1856 and had lived in Louisiana before relocating to Liberty, where they shared a residence with Felix at the time of the 1860 census.

Mayer, free of the responsibilities of operating a store, turned his energy to his burgeoning cattle business. Already, thousands of East Texas cattle had beaten a trail through mosquito-infested swamps to New Orleans, and by May 1861 Mayer was Louisiana-bound at the point of his own herd. A trail outfit of the day was usually small; Mayer was probably joined by two other drovers who relied on packhorses for supplies.

Just how many herds Mayer pushed to the New Orleans area is unclear, but he had discovered in the flinty hooves and mossy horns a passion that would only grow stronger.

A United States citizen for less than a year when the Civil War broke out, Mayer evidently was not interested in participating in the conflict. He moved from Liberty County sometime after August 1862, but his exact whereabouts for much of the war is not clear. For a while, he apparently engaged in cotton trading in South Texas and northern Mexico. When Yankee soldiers neared a small Confederate garrison at Fort Brown in Brownsville in November 1863, the rebels burned the post and thirty-eight hundred pounds of cotton supplied by Mayer. By early 1865, he was living in Matamoras, Mexico, but when the war ended a few months later, he rejoined Solomon in Texas.

Solomon, meanwhile, had faced different experiences in the Confederacy. Though he was still a French citizen, the Confederate Army drafted him on December 29, 1862. Refusing to report for duty, he was jailed by authorities until January 15, when he filed a statement claiming exemption from the draft because he was a subject "of the Emperor Napoleon."

Although details are clouded, records in the Texas State Archives show that Solomon nevertheless served for an indeterminate period in Company B, Infantry, Waul's Legion. The duration of his commitment in this volunteer unit was to be "3 years or [duration of] War unless sooner discharged." Organized by Thomas Neville Waul, the legion had a significant concentration of Jewish soldiers. It consisted of ten infantry companies, five cavalry companies, and two artillery companies. Recalled General Waul on May 17, 1894:

> Two of the infantry companies had a large number of Jews in their ranks, and the largest company in the command, 120 men, was officered by Jews, and three-fourths of the rank and the file were of that faith. There was also a number of Jews scattered through the command in the other companies.

By war's end in 1865, San Antonio was the dominant city in Texas and had a growing reputation as a cattle center. The Halff brothers and Abraham Levy, who was married to Felix Halff's sister Esther, soon established a San Antonio haberdashery that grew into a one-hundred-thousand-dollar operation within three years.

On September 2, 1866, Mayer married twenty-year-old Rachel Hart in Detroit. The daughter of British-born Isaac Hart and the former Julia Cohen, Rachel had grown up in New Orleans, a city that Mayer may have frequented on business. Earlier in 1866, Rachel's father, a shirt manufacturer, had moved his family to Detroit. Possibly, a Jewish matchmaker arranged the marriage of Rachel and Mayer, a common practice among Alsatian Jews.

On a pair of trips to Europe during the next four years, Solomon had brushes with military officials. The first came in the spring of 1867, when French military orders demanding his conscription caught up with him. Although he escaped the obligation, perhaps by paying three thousand francs, he found himself facing the draft again during another visit to Alsace in 1870. Ordered on May 17 to report for duty, he avoided service once more and returned to Texas.

Rachel Hart Halff (1845–1919), twenty-six. Rachel Hart grew up in New Orleans and married Mayer Halff in 1866. Collection of Alex H. Halff.

M. Halff & Bro.

Cor. East Commerce and Rusk Streets

San Antonio, Texas

Manufacturers

"Ranger" Brand Goods

Wholesalers--Dry Goods, Notions, Furnishing Goods, Clothing, and Ladies' Ready-to-Wear

Visit Us In Our New Big Establishment
WATCH US GROW---GROW WITH US

Mayer Halff's San Antonio wholesale dry goods store ran this ad in a special edition of the Reform Advocate, a national Jewish weekly that in 1914 published a series of front-page articles on Texas Jewish communities. Collection of Hollace Weiner.

In 1872, Mayer and Solomon ended their partnership with Abraham Levy and organized their own merchandising venture in San Antonio. By 1873, M. Halff & Brother had a stock of twenty thousand dollars and was on its way to becoming one of the Southwest's leading dry goods and wholesale operations.

As his resources grew, Mayer again heeded the summons of thundering hooves. Millions of longhorns ranged free in Texas, and to the north lay not only tall-grass prairies perfect for maturing cattle, but railroads ready to carry Texas beef to a hungry nation. In 1877, Mayer joined other Texas cattlemen in driving thousands of longhorns up the trail to Dodge City, Kansas. Thereafter, Mayer generally would defer to his brother on dry goods matters and concentrate on cattle interests, sometimes independent of Solomon but usually under the banner of M. Halff & Brother.

By the early 1880s, intercontinental railroads linked Texas with distant markets, encouraging the brothers to acquire vast breeding grounds in their adopted state. The Peña Colorado Ranch, which began to come under Halff control in March 1882, comprised forty-four deeded square miles and seventy-five thousand leased acres near present Marathon in the Big Bend. Eventually, twenty-five thousand cattle bearing a Circle Dot brand would graze the complex of craggy mountains, Chihuahuan Desert, and snaking watercourses. A hundred miles to the northeast, Mayer and Solomon burned their brand on fifty square miles of mountainous Pecos River country that history would know as the Pecos Ranch or JM outfit. Ultimately, the brothers leased hundreds of thousands of acres adjacent to the river.

In acquiring the two spreads, Mayer once more exhibited the courage that had carried him halfway across the world as a mere lad. The Big Bend was still wild in the early 1880s; the continued garrisoning of Camp Peña Colorado on Circle Dot land testified to the U.S. Army's conviction that Indian raids remained a threat. The Pecos region, in its own way,

Halff of Texas, a play on words and the title of a book about the Halff family's far-flung ranching interests, is an apt description of the lands on which the family's cattle grazed. Map by Garry Harman, The Artworks.

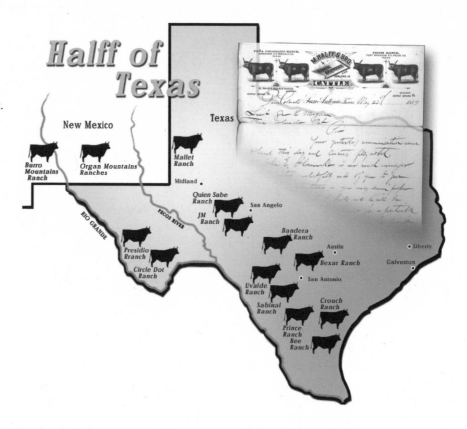

Halff of Texas, a play on words and the title of a book about the Halff family's far-flung ranching interests, is an apt description of the lands on which the family's cattle grazed. Map by Garry Harman, The Artworks.

was no less treacherous, for the river was synonymous with hell in the eyes of many frontiersmen. A moat with currents as swift as a racehorse, the Pecos was notorious for sheer banks, quicksand, and alkalinity. An animal might wander its coils for hours without finding a place to gain access to the waters. Only a cattleman with Mayer's vision could look beyond the pitfalls of these two ranches and see the possibilities inherent in the nutritious grasses.

Longhorns were ideally suited for such a rugged land, but they were lean and sinewy, while Herefords and shorthorns carried much more meat on their frames. Mayer was wise enough to realize that the infusion of high-grade bulls into his herd would increase the weight of each future steer by 150 to 200 pounds, thereby magnifying his monetary return at market. As he proceeded to import scores of Hereford and shorthorn bulls to West Texas in 1883, he told the *Texas Live Stock Journal* that he considered the bovines the best that Texas had ever seen.

Mayer also paid careful attention to range management, a striking emphasis in an era in which overstocking was the norm. Indeed, the *San Antonio Stockman* hailed his prudence as "another reason for Mr. Halff's success in the cattle business." Furthermore, he was among the first Pecos ranchers to make extensive use of windmills to draw water to the surface of the arid pastureland. The first mill tower went up on the JM as early as 1883, and by 1900 fifty-one windmills whirred in the JM winds, expanding the effective grazing range to the ranch's outer boundaries.

From his earliest days as a rancher, Mayer was a hands-on owner, keeping a base of operations in San Antonio but regularly frequenting his ranges, which eventually dotted New Mexico Territory, Indian Territory, Kansas, Colorado, Wyoming, and Dakota Territory. In Texas alone, he ultimately controlled almost a million acres, a total that dwarfed Rhode Island and was one-third the size of Connecticut.

Like other West Texas ranchers of the 1880s, Mayer had to contend with the inscrutable forces of nature. The "Big Drift" in the winter of 1884–1885 brought tens of thousands of South Plains cattle marching southward, driven by a relentless blizzard. When they reached the impassable Pecos, on the JM and elsewhere, the animals flooded the range and stripped it of winter forage. Soon, the east side of the river was little more than dust and cattle carcasses. That spring, outfits from the Panhandle and the Pecos pushed an incredible 120 to 150 thousand cattle back toward their home ranges, leaving the JM devastated.

Still, Mayer's woes were only beginning. Within weeks of the roundup, drought strangled the region. By the next year, the Pecos was a dusty hell of sun-baked alkali all the way up through Fort Sumner, New Mexico. "From the Pecos River for 100 miles below and 200 miles above the Texas and Pacific Railroad [a stretch that included the JM]," reported the May 25, 1886 *Texas Live Stock Journal*, "cattle are reported as dying daily by the . . . thousands." Searing conditions persisted on into 1887, when cowhand M. L. Liles found the JM a wasteland. "They hadn't had enough rain to wet a man's shirt sleeve for eighteen months," he recalled many years later.

In mid-June, the Big Dry of 1885 to 1887 finally relented, but half the cattle that had grazed along the Pecos two years before were now rotting carcasses.

The strength of character that saw Mayer through such trials spilled over into his home life. Despite his frequent absences, he was so committed to his wife Rachel and their four children who lived past infancy that a newspaper referred to him as an "affectionate man in his family circle." Their San Antonio home was a cultural and social center, testimony to his rare ability to wander freely through both a cowboy's world and that of a cosmopolitan gentleman. He was a patron of the arts and supported many charitable causes and civic activities in San Antonio, which he once described as "*the* town" for him.

A small number of Jewish ranching families made important contributions to the early livestock industry in Texas, and two of the most prominent were joined in the 1890s when Mayer's older son, Alex, and younger daughter, Lillie, married into the Oppenheimer family. The parallels between Mayer and patriarch Dan Oppenheimer were notable. Both were born in Europe in 1836 and immigrated to Texas through Galveston in the 1850s. Each entered the mercantile business, with Dan and his brother Anton partnering in a store in Rusk, Texas, in 1858. Unlike the Halffs, both Oppenheimer brothers readily enlisted in the Confederate Army. Soon after the Civil War, both Mayer and the Oppenheimers relocated to San Antonio, where each party eventually established a haberdashery and bank. Like Mayer, the Oppenheimers became smitten by beef-on-the-hoof, spurring them to amass one hundred thousand acres of ranch land in South Texas.

The 1898 wedding of Lillie Halff and Jesse Oppenheimer in San Antonio illustrates the continuity of Jewish heritage amid adaptation to a new world. The March 25, 1898, *San Antonio Daily Express*, while acknowledging each family's prominence in Jewish circles, also hailed the Halffs and Oppenheimers as "social leaders." The Temple Beth-El ceremony, at which Rabbi Samuel Marks officiated, was followed by a banquet adjacent to the Alamo at the Menger Hotel, the city's preeminent lodging establishment. The menu for the evening included non-kosher items such as tenderloin, blue point oysters, and game partridge.

*Marriage alliance. The wedding of
Jesse D. Oppenheimer and Lillie Halff,
March 24, 1898, united two of
San Antonio's leading business,
ranching, and civic-minded families.
Courtesy of the Historic Menger Hotel,
San Antonio, TX.*

*Wedding feast. Guests were wined and
dined at a five-course dinner of Gulf
oysters, tenderloin with truffles, game,
assorted desserts, and Roquefort cheese.
The menu is indicative of the families'
sophisticated tastes, exposure to travel,
and Classical Reform Jewish diet.
Courtesy Historic Menger Hotel,
San Antonio, TX.*

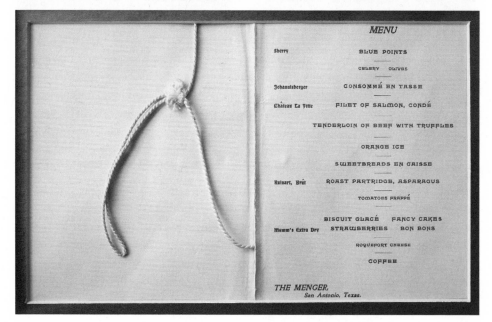

Over the years, Mayer relied on both rail transport and drives to deliver cattle to distant locales. After a hard winter on his West Texas range in 1892–1893, he dispatched twenty-six hundred two-year-old steers up the Goodnight-Loving Trail to a buyer in Colorado or Wyoming. Herds from other ranches also were on the move, spaced ten to fifty miles apart along the Pecos. On a treeless flat just past Fort Sumner, New Mexico, Mayer's cattle marched straight into a storm from hell. As a black cloud swooped down, hard, white rocks began to pummel animals and men alike.

The cowhands frantically stripped the saddles from their mounts and cowered beneath the stout leather. Still, they took a terrible beating. When the hailstorm finally

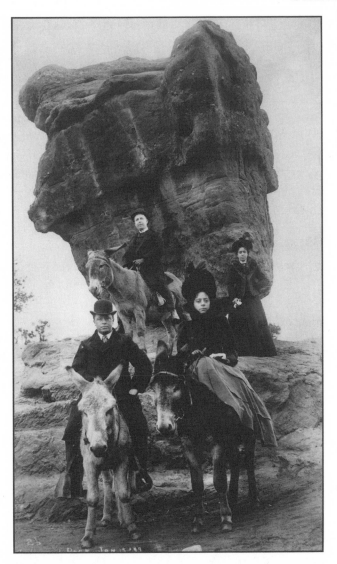

Honeymooning in Colorado. Alex and Alma Oppenheimer Halff, front, spent their 1899 honeymoon in Colorado Springs, where they rode burros to Balanced Rock in the Garden of the Gods. Behind the newlyweds are friends Dave and Ida Straus.
UT Institute of Texan Cultures at San Antonio, No. 073-1140, Courtesy of Mrs. Harry Halff.

abated, the bruised men found themselves amid cattle carcasses that sprawled as far as they could see against a plain white with ice. Six hundred cattle had perished, along with virtually every horse in the outfit.

A rider started back down the three-hundred-mile trail to Texas to enlist Mayer's help; without horses, the drovers stood no chance of delivering the surviving cattle. Mayer met the man in Toyah, on the Texas and Pacific railroad, and listened to his story in stunned silence.

"Was there no more cattle in this country but Halff's herd?" Mayer finally asked.

"Yes," said the rider, "four, five more herds along there on the trail pretty close together."

"And the hail didn't kill any cows for them?"

"No, it didn't hit them, this hail storm didn't."

"Well, I can't understand it," Mayer declared. "What's the matter with God Almighty? Does he kill the old Jew's cattle and not bother the gentiles'?"

Throughout his life, Mayer paid homage to his Jewish heritage. In San Antonio on May 31, 1874, he attended a Hebrew Benevolent Society meeting at which Temple Beth-El was founded. Three years earlier, the Society had purchased property for a future synagogue. During an 1874 fund-raising campaign for its construction, Mayer and Solomon each contributed one thousand dollars, a sum matched by only one other founder. In later years, Mayer remembered the Jewish indigent in Alsace with monetary gifts at Hanukkah through an old friend, L. Fromenthal of Lauterbourg.

Nevertheless, Jewish rituals seldom were observed at Mayer's ranches, and anti-Semitism apparently was not a problem. His two most trusted ranch managers, Rufe Moore and Barnes Tullous, occasionally did refer to him as "that old Jew peddler," but they intended no disrespect. Indeed, the two cowmen had the highest regard for Mayer, a man of unquestioned character. "The humblest Negro porter in the big wholesale establishment and the wildest cowboy on his ranches each felt that he had in Mr. Halff a friend who would listen sympathetically and deal justly," noted the December 24, 1905, *San Antonio Daily Express*.

On one occasion, however, Mayer's Jewish background created a problem. When ranch manager Rufe Moore traded twenty-seven hundred beeves for tons of bacon, Mayer decided that his general manager had lost his mind.

"What in the name of God would a Jew do with a train load of hog meat?" Mayer complained.

Moore, however, went ahead with his plan, storing the bacon over the winter and waiting for prices to rise. The next spring, he sold it at a sizable profit, leading Mayer to praise Moore as "the smartest man I've ever seen."

In 1896, the Halff brothers acquired two additional sweeping ranches, the 144-square mile Mallet southwest of Lubbock, and the Quien Sabe, an outfit whose very name was the stuff of legend. First known as the Two Moon, the Quien Sabe had ranged cattle along the Rio Grande and Pecos before relocating to the Staked Plains, eighteen to twenty-five miles south of Midland. Its unusual brand, two half circles that almost interlocked, once led a stranger to ask what it represented. "*Quien sabe?*" a cowhand replied, Spanish for "Who knows?" And so the outfit would be known.

Along with a lease on almost one hundred Quien Sabe sections, the equivalent of one hundred square miles, Mayer and Solomon assumed ownership of eleven thousand Herefords and Hereford crossbreds. Ultimately, their herd would graze five hundred to six hundred square miles in the Midland country.

Not long after purchasing the Quien Sabe, Mayer introduced his younger son Henry to the West Texas range. Almost immediately, Henry developed a love for the western life.

"Henry, when quite a lad, would come to the ranch and ask me to let him ride my horse—many times at night to stand my guard and let me sleep," recalled Quien Sabe cowhand Bob Beverly. "And, of course, I never objected if the herd was broke in and the weather was good."

As Henry grew in experience, he took a Halff herd north by trail through brutal country and reached a pivotal moment in his life. After nurturing the cattle for months, he finally sat poised in the saddle to push them across one last river in Kansas. Beyond, the tall-grass prairie looked like the Promised Land to the young Jewish drover. It turned out to be a place of tragedy. As soon as the animals swam the river, they dropped to the ground, killed by the cold water.

"He couldn't believe it," recalled Henry's son, Albert Halff. "Dad said he lost his religion—he couldn't believe that there would be a God who would do that. He was never religious after that."

Even as Mayer groomed his younger son for the cattle business, the Halff brothers continued to shape their ranching kingdom. On a single day in December 1898, they sold their Big Bend ranch and enlarged the already-sprawling JM by the purchase of twelve square miles of land. Eventually, only one other ranch would lie in what otherwise would have been ninety-three contiguous miles of Halff country across West Texas.

On December 7, 1900, M. Halff & Brother and a new partner, Charles Schreiner, jointly acquired ninety-one South Texas sections, the last great spread to bear Mayer's brand. Schreiner, a non-Jew born in France, had moved to San Antonio in 1852 and had entered the livestock business in 1857. By the time of his partnership with the Halffs, Schreiner was a cattle magnate, owning more than six hundred thousand contiguous acres in the Texas Hill Country.

The Schreiner and Halff outfit comprised choice land on both sides of the Frio River and quickly became Mayer's most profitable ranch. Still, he hadn't forgotten his West Texas holdings. When Mayer and Solomon had a falling out and bitterly ended their forty-four-year business relationship in December 1901, it paved the way for a ranching partnership between father and son. For $190,000, Mayer conveyed to Henry an undivided one-half interest in his West Texas properties, as well as in Colorado. They were to split profits or losses equally and consult one another before making any acquisition or investment.

In early 1905, Henry married twenty-one-year-old Rosa Wechsler of New York City, who would later convert from Judaism to Christian Science. He soon brought her to the Quien Sabe, an environment to which she quickly adapted, despite her urban roots. Although her trousseau included a habit for use on a sidesaddle, the wild Quien Sabe broncs demanded that she ride astride.

"Henry brought me a pair of Levi's," Rosa recalled, "and in the morning at six o'clock he would bring me a cup of coffee and he would say to me, 'Come on, the old man will catch you.' And when I said, 'Who is the old man?' he said, 'The sun.' We used to ride and ride and ride all day every day."

By that fall, Rosa was close to delivering their first child, so Henry took her to his parents' home in San Antonio. But now there was a crisis: Mayer was fading swiftly, gripped by what doctors termed an "abscess of the prostate."

Mayer's "Any Boy May Win" speech, delivered to loyal employees of his dry goods operation that November, served as a fitting conclusion to his five and a half decades in the business world.

"Talking about success, I have a message for you each," he told the thirty-four young men. "Don't tell me opportunity is for the rich, boys—it is for you young men who are grappling with the hard facts of life, for you whose soul is in the struggle."

His remarks had a powerful impact. "Probably no sermon preached in San Antonio in many a day has had more appreciation," reported the *San Antonio Express.*

Soon confined to his bed, Mayer clung to life long enough to become a grandfather; Rosa gave birth under his very roof to little Mayer Henry on December 12. Three days later, Mayer summoned Rufe Moore and dictated his wishes for a simple funeral. Not only was his request in accordance with Jewish tradition; it also reflected his humility in the face of riches and his lofty standing in the community.

On December 23, Mayer died peacefully, a man wealthier in family and friends than in material possessions.

"We honor him for his one great quality, towering above all his others—modesty and unostentatious goodness," eulogized Rabbi Samuel Marks of Temple Beth-El at unpre-

Rosa Wechsler Halff, 1883–1973. Rosa Wechsler, a New York socialite, married Henry Halff in 1905 and fell in love with ranch life. Courtesy Henry Mayer Halff.

Rabbi Samuel Marks of San Antonio's Temple Beth-El. Marks was the Halff family's rabbi and friend. UT Institute of Texan Cultures at San Antonio, No. 068-2514, Courtesy of Temple Beth-El.

62

tentious services two days later. "He descends to his grave with a crown upon his brow and an unsullied name, and he leaves behind the gratitude of the entire community."

In a life spanning portions of two centuries, Mayer had risen from humble beginnings as a foot peddler to build a mercantile business of giant proportions. From a mere boy tending his father's cows in Alsace, he had become ruler of a cattle empire that stretched across several states and territories. He had lived the American Dream in a way that few men ever would, building on a foundation of honor and determination to achieve not only success, but respect.

"He was the kind that made this the greatest republic the world has ever known," onetime Quien Sabe cowhand Bob Beverly observed in 1944. "I say, 'Peace to his ashes.' I take my hat off to him and his kind."   ✱

REFERENCES

This chapter is drawn primarily from the same source material as the author's comprehensive biography of Mayer Halff, *Halff of Texas: Merchant Rancher of the Old West* (Austin: Eakin Press, 2000), which in turn is based partially on materials in the Halff Family Collection of Alex H. Halff of San Antonio. The collection includes personal, ranching, and business items. A significant portion of the collection is on microfilm at the Panhandle-Plains Historical Museum, Canyon, Texas. Also consulted were dozens of interviews (such as M. L. Liles to J. Evetts Haley, Kenna, New Mexico, August 4, 1937, Nita Stewart Haley Library, Midland, Texas), census records, county tax rolls, livestock magazines, letters, scores of secondary volumes, and more than twenty contemporary Texas and Kansas newspapers ranging from the *Rio Grande Republican* (1885–1893) to the *Dodge City Times* (1883–1884). For general background information on the region where Mayer Halff had ranch holdings, see *Crossing Rio Pecos, A Cowboy of the Pecos, The Last of the Old-Time Cowboys,* and *Saddling Up Anyway* by the same author.

5

"These One-Sex Organizations"
Clubwomen Create Communal Institutions

HOLLACE AVA WEINER

"The Jewess has no mission apart from the Jew," declared Rabbi Jacob Voorsanger, one of the foremost Jewish leaders in the American West. His admonition was reprinted and rebuked during the Gay Nineties in *The American Jewess*, the Lilith magazine of its day. At that time, Jewish women had started flirting with secular women's clubs, a trend that undermined traditional Jewish gender lines. Only Jewish men routinely mixed with gentiles, and that was to earn a livelihood. Rabbis such as Jacob Voorsanger argued that Jewish women needed to be at home, protecting their families from melting into the mainstream. "These one-sex organizations have a tendency to widen the breach that already exists between the sexes," the rabbi warned.[1]

In Texas, one or two Jewish women in every major city defied Rabbi Voorsanger's dictum. The cleric was a figure well known among Lone Star Jews, for he had led Houston's Beth Israel Congregation, the state's pioneer synagogue, and his views were widely publicized. Among those who challenged the rabbi's words by their actions was Jeannette Miriam Goldberg (1875–1935), a "new woman," so called because she was a college graduate who transformed her women's club work into a paying career. Another defiant high-profile Jewish clubwoman was Olga Kohlberg (1864–1935). She launched the state's first public kindergarten, an accomplishment that posthumously propelled her into the El Paso Hall of Honor. In San Antonio, Anna Hertzberg (1862–1937) organized the city's Tuesday Musical Club, creating a power base from which she was instrumental in the founding of the first San Antonio symphony orchestra. Hertzberg also hosted annual Christmas parties and Easter egg rolls that were among the social events of the season.[2] Rabbi Voorsanger feared, as did others familiar with the impact of immigration and the frontier on traditional institutions, that such Jewish clubwomen would assimilate into the Bible Belt and leave Judaism behind. Far from it, they learned lessons about leadership in the larger world and applied them to the smaller Jewish universe. In an era when women took a back seat to men in Jewish affairs, Olga Kohlberg was among the founders of El Paso's first Jewish congregation. As for Goldberg and Hertzberg, with their leadership skills and influence they launched local sections of the National Council of Jewish Women and led their more timid Jewish sisters into the civic arena.

Most Jewish women felt conflicting impulses about whether to step into the mainstream or to hold back and preserve their heritage. Among Texas-Jewish women, there was no apparent clamor to join the nonsectarian club network, otherwise many of Goldberg's, Kohlberg's, and Hertzberg's relatives and friends would have followed them there. Most Jewish women feared the proselytization of which the rabbis warned. To be

The ever-quotable Jacob Voorsanger.
Rabbi Voorsanger (1852–1908),
pictured in San Francisco in the late
1890s, warned that Jewish women who
socialized or worked outside the home
might assimilate into the mainstream.
In some ways, he was right. Courtesy of
Western Jewish History Center, Judah L.
Magnes Museum (Jacob Voorsanger
collection: 1969.010).

sure, not every woman's club welcomed Jews. The Women's Christian Temperance Union made that clear by its name. Some elite clubs, such as the Junior League founded in New York in 1901, were restricted to white Anglo-Saxon Protestant women.[3]

The Council of Jewish Women, organized like a "new woman's" nonsectarian club, provided Jews with a structure identifiable to outsiders and a comfort zone from within. It was self-consciously part of the broader Progressive movement, emphasizing social and urban reforms. The Council mobilized Jewish women to perform mitzvot both within and beyond their congregations, quickly giving them an identifiable role in shaping their communities. Once they collectively stepped into the secular realm, Jewish clubwomen across Texas exerted a marked influence on civic improvements and cultural growth, underscoring the impact of their emergence into the mainstream.

The National Council of Jewish Women, controversial at its founding, began in 1893, an outgrowth of the Chicago World's Fair. The Windy City exposition included a Jewish Women's Congress organized by Hannah Greenebaum Solomon (1858–1941), one of the first Jews recruited into the Chicago Women's Club, which pressed for urban reforms. Solomon's search for a geographic cross section of delegates to the Jewish Women's Congress attracted ninety-three representatives from twenty-nine large cities. The dele-

From generation to generation. The Council of Jewish Women, founded in 1893, gave Jewish women leadership opportunities otherwise unavailable. As members parlayed skills into employment and membership in secular organizations, the council became a victim of its decades of success. National Council of Jewish Women, Collections of the Manuscript Division, Library of Congress.

gates included one Texan, Ada Chapman, the spouse of a Dallas rabbi. To nurture and expand this network of committed Jews, Solomon and her cohorts decided that a byproduct of the Jewish Women's Congress would be a permanent organization—the National Council of Jewish Women (NCJW). This new group would have Judaic study as one pillar and social service as the other. Yet its existence was controversial. "The National Council should never have been organized," carped Rabbi Voorsanger. "It is contrary to social instinct." Rabbi Kaufmann Kohler, a leading Reform Jewish leader and eventually President of Hebrew Union College, chastised the Council for its "morbid craving after non-Jewish speakers." Answering such critics, *The American Jewess* responded: "New conditions have arisen and Progressive people are trying to adapt . . . It will not be possible for the Jewess of the future to live the restricted life of her mother."[4]

JEANNETTE MIRIAM GOLDBERG

At the NCJW's first triennial in 1896, the board appointed Jeannette Miriam Goldberg to serve as vice-president for Texas. A passionate educator, Goldberg (1875–1935) had grown up in the post–Civil War era when college doors and caring professions (such as teaching, nursing, and social work) began opening for women. Goldberg's hometown of Jefferson, located on a river near the Louisiana line, was past its commercial prime, its population in decline. The fourth of five children, Goldberg left home to enroll in Vassar College's preparatory division and received an A.B. degree from New York's Rutgers Female Institute. Goldberg returned to Texas, working as Sabbath School superintendent in Jefferson and in Houston. She remained single and pursued a career, teaching literature at schools in Dallas, Waco, and Sherman as well as in Birmingham, Alabama. While teaching at Waco Female College, she sang in the choir at Congregation Rodef Sholom. Goldberg found women's club work stimulating. As chairman of the Texas Woman's Council, part of the Texas Federation of Women's Clubs (TFWC), she wrote articles on

tainly have the co-operation and confidence of every
member of the Conference.

If, In your Drive or Campaign to help aid the College
in its financial straits, I shall be very happy to do
anything I can to assist you. You know, I am an H.U.C.
woman first and always and it was my distinction of
being the only women who worked with Dr. Krauskopf in
response to his S. O. S. call he made when he was en-
deavoring to raise the fund of the I. M. Wise Endowment
Fund.

With kind regards to you, I am

Sincerely yours,

Jeannette Miriam Goldberg

Sincerely yours. Jeannette Miriam Goldberg (1875–1935) turned her love of Judaism and communal organizing into a career as executive secretary of the Jewish Chautauqua Society. In this letter of September 15, 1927, to Rabbi Hyman Enelow, she discusses fund raising for Hebrew Union College. Courtesy of the Jacob Rader Marcus Center of the American Jewish Archives, Cincinnati, Ohio.

educational issues, such as clubwomen's push for literacy, libraries, kindergartens, and conservation of wildlife. When the TFWC met in Jefferson, she delivered a lecture on civics. When she learned about the creation of the Council of Jewish Women, she traveled to New York for its first national convention. Her twin priorities were advancement of women through self-study and cultural clubs and a return to Judaism by those drifting toward assimilation.[5] In 1898, with a core group of seven women, Goldberg organized Texas's first Council of Jewish Women "section" in Tyler, a larger Jewish community near Jefferson.[6] Tyler, a fashionable and prosperous county seat, had a Jewish congregation that dated back to 1887 and a Ladies Hebrew Benevolent Society that focused on one-on-one charity. The Council of Jewish Women's intent was broader—to strengthen Jewish life within the city and to create professional social service programs that benefited large numbers of people. Tyler's Council of Jewish Women took charge of hiring Sabbath School teachers for Congregation Beth El, encouraged families to celebrate Jewish holidays, and helped immigrants learn English. What these women most enjoyed was the novelty of getting together. "The social hour is a drawing-card and seems to make 'Council Day' the 'red-letter' day of the month," President Mrs. Jacob Lipstate wrote in her annual report.[7]

Also in 1898, Goldberg assisted Dallas women forming Texas's second NCJW section. In Dallas, the organizing spark came from the city's new rabbi, George Alexander Kohut, whose stepmother, Rebekah Kohut, was president of New York City's NCJW. The Dallas women immediately coalesced with the pre-existing club network. In 1899, they and their rabbi served on committees formed to launch a public library. They planted trees on acreage set aside by the city's federation of women's clubs for a memorial grove. For their daughters, the Jewish women started a Junior Council in 1901. The next year, two of the women's spouses, identified as "Mr. Sanger and Mr. Kahn," were one-hundred-dollar patrons helping underwrite the NCJW's triennial convention in Baltimore. For reasons still unclear, the Dallas Council fell apart over the next three years. It was reestablished in 1913 when the NCJW's executive secretary, the charismatic Sadie American, made an organizing tour through Texas.[8]

In the spring of 1901, Jeannette Goldberg visited Beaumont, then the state's oil capital, and launched a Council section there with twenty-seven women. In the vestry of Temple Emanuel, the women established a library stocked with three hundred books.

Goldberg next announced plans through the Jewish press to organize a Council section in Fort Worth. Two Jewish women, Sarah Carb and Sophie Brann, who already were involved in the local club network, mailed out one hundred postcards, one to each Jewish household, announcing an organizing meeting in the parlor of the Delaware Hotel. Twenty-two women attended. Within four years, these women had opened a night school for immigrants. They appointed a representative to the city board of charities. They became a "patroness" of the city's free kindergarten. When Fort Worth's Reform congregation, Beth-El, disintegrated in 1903, six months after forty-seven men had chartered the institution, the Council of Jewish Women had the wherewithal to revive it. The group's early president, Polly Mack, wrote in one of her annual reports: "Jew and Gentile in Ft. Worth look up to our Section for inspiration."[9]

Jeannette Miriam Goldberg's efforts across Texas led to her election in 1902 to the Council of Jewish Women's national executive board. She carved out a role as field sec-

Under Polly Mack's leadership, the Fort Worth Council of Jewish Women revived the Reform congregation that had collapsed in 1903 and opened a night school for immigrants in 1907. Courtesy, Beth-El Congregation Archives, Fort Worth.

retary. In that capacity, she traveled cross-country organizing chapters and motivating coreligionists who had grown indifferent toward Judaism. "We have had enough lullaby and slumber in religious life," she exhorted. "[W]e now need wakefulness and spirit, to revivify the dry bones of American Judaism."[10]

In 1905, the Jewish Chautauqua Society, headquartered in Philadelphia, hired Goldberg as its field secretary, a position similar to her volunteer role with the Council. Under Goldberg's leadership, the Chautauqua Society launched study circles, assemblies, and a national correspondence school to train Sabbath School teachers. In her travels throughout the United States, Goldberg helped organize congregations and recruit rabbis to lead them. The Society opened religious schools in the Dakotas and in south New Jersey farm colonies started with Baron De Hirsch funds. The Chautauqua Society also initiated a university lecture circuit—still in operation in 2006—featuring rabbis who speak to non-Jewish audiences.

Rabbi Julian Feibelman, who became acquainted with Goldberg when he was a Mississippi boy taking Chautauqua correspondence classes, maintained that she "kept her hand on the pulse of virtually every congregation" in the nation. She was "instrumental in helping many rabbis to advancement in pulpits." He lauded Goldberg as "one of the two Jewish women in America capable of addressing an audience on Jewish subjects—the other was Sadie American." When Goldberg died on February 28, 1935, she was eulogized in the *Philadelphia Exponent* as "a modern Miriam" and a "high priestess" of Judaism. By pursuing the life of a single career woman, she had a greater impact on Judaism than the disapproving Rabbi Jacob Voorsanger might have imagined. A century later, she might have become a Reform rabbi.

OLGA KOHLBERG

When Olga Bernstein Kohlberg moved to El Paso as a twenty-year-old bride in 1884, she found herself marooned in a frontier border town. Texas's western-most city had dirt streets and one trolley pulled by a mule. It was a quintessential Wild West town where cowboys on horseback galloped into saloons and bandits roamed with bravado. Pat Garrett, the lawman who killed Billy the Kid, was the turn-of-the-century customs collector. Kohlberg was widowed in 1910 when a drunken gambler, who was ensnared in a lawsuit over debts to her husband, barged into his cigar store and shot him to death.

The resilient Olga Kohlberg, who had grown up in Elberfield, Westphalia, spent her adult life trying to civilize her surroundings. "Olga lost no time in seeking companions with whom she could share a semblance of what she had left in Germany," writes historian Natalie Ornish in *Pioneer Jewish Texans*. Gathering a cluster of genteel women, Kohlberg started a Child Culture Study Circle to learn about kindergartens, which had been introduced in Germany in 1837. The study circle recruited an educator from Missouri, purchased teaching materials, and in 1893 started its own kindergarten. The next year, the study circle convinced the El Paso Board of Education to establish the state's first public kindergarten, using the teacher and the materials that the women had brought to the city. The study circle, the forerunner of the El Paso Woman's Club, changed its name and mission several times. It opened the town's first hospital. It financed and operated the public library until the city took it over. It was instrumental in creating a children's sanatorium, dubbed the "Baby San," in 1911 in nearby Cloudcroft, New Mexico, where infants suffering from the desert heat recuperated in cooler climes at an elevation of nine thousand feet. Kohlberg, a mother of four children, twice served as president of the El

Olga Bernstein Kohlberg, late 1880s.
Kohlberg (1864–1935) is credited with
establishing Texas's first public
kindergarten and helping to open
El Paso's first hospital and library.
University of Texas at El Paso Library,
Special Collections Department,
Kohlberg Family Papers MS 369.

Paso Woman's Club and also became first vice-president of the Texas Federation of Women's Clubs.[11]

Women's club work gave Kohlberg the clout and the administrative experience to help the city's fledgling Jewish community organize. In 1898, she and her husband, Ernst, were among the founders of Temple Mount Sinai, the city's Reform congregation. She helped organize the Jewish Welfare Association in El Paso, the forerunner of the El Paso Jewish Federation, which serves as an umbrella organization for Jewish causes at home and overseas. When the Council of Jewish Women came to El Paso in 1917, it carried on the work Kohlberg had begun by providing volunteers for many of the institutions that she and her study circle had founded.

Olga Kohlberg sowed the seeds for civilizing the border region. Although her husband was a pioneer who served on the City Council, started an electric company, and opened the region's first cigar manufacturing plant, posterity has deemed her contributions more significant. In 1972, the El Paso County Historical Society inducted her into the El Paso Hall of Honor. A public school was named for her in 1997. At the city's Olga B. Kohlberg Elementary, students study her legacy and contribute to an Internet site about her life and times. A contemporary researcher, Debbie M. Pazos, summed up Kohlberg's life during a B'nai Zion Sisterhood program in 2005 by concluding, "A true pioneer, she spent fifty years driving changes in El Paso that moved it from a frontier town to a modern city serving its citizens' educational, social, and religious needs. Described as dignified, tolerant and courageous, Mrs. Kohlberg was a wife, a mother and a Lady."[12]

ANNA HERTZBERG

Classical music was what Anna Goodman Hertzberg missed most when she moved to San Antonio as a bride in 1882. A talented pianist, she had attended the New York Conservatory of Music. Her husband, jeweler Eli Hertzberg, a Russian immigrant, had been in Texas since 1865 and was twenty-two years her senior. The family was well off, and the Hertzbergs raised their only child, Harry, in comfortable circumstances and persuaded Anna's parents, brother, and sister to move to San Antonio. Family was not enough for Anna Hertzberg, who felt stifled in the so-called "domestic sphere." She pushed the limits.

In 1898, she became a charter member of the Woman's Club of San Antonio and discovered a route to activism. If she perceived an unmet need or problem, she organized a club to remedy it. With five other women, including her sister Jenny Sachs, in 1901 she organized the Tuesday Musical Club, a performing club similar to men's "singing societies." Members played for one another's enjoyment and at benefits to raise money for the city's free kindergarten and to put a new roof on the Alamo. The Musical Club invited guest artists to San Antonio, then struggled "to get its booted, hell-for-leather citizenry to hear them."[13] Concert proceeds went into scholarships for budding musicians.[14]

In the spring of 1907, a woman visiting San Antonio from Cleveland told Hertzberg and Rabbi Samuel Marks of Temple Beth-El about the Council of Jewish Women and what it was accomplishing in Ohio. At that time, the only active Texas sections of the NCJW were in Tyler and Fort Worth. The chapters in Dallas, Beaumont, and Waco had disintegrated, though they later would be revived. Hertzberg, the experienced organizer, was impressed with the notion of bringing "our" Jewish women "into closer relationship" to work toward "the highest order of philanthropy." She called an organizing meeting. Eighty-two women (including a handful of out-of-towners from Seguin, a nearby cotton community, Mexico City, and Freemont, Oklahoma) attended the first meeting of the San Antonio Council of Jewish Women, electing Hertzberg president. By year's end, membership exceeded one hundred. According to Hertzberg's first annual report, the Council spawned dozens of activities, from a sewing circle that fashioned "garments . . . for the needy" to Bible classes led by a college professor.[15]

Anna Hertzberg (1862–1937). Musician, politician, and clubwoman, Hertzberg founded San Antonio's Tuesday Musical Club and was elected to the city school board before women could vote. UT Institute of Texan Cultures at San Antonio, No. 074-0422, Courtesy of Judge Walter Loughridge.

Anna Hertzberg, national vice-president. Hertzberg's name is among those in the program at the Council of Jewish Women's eighth convention, held in Chicago. Courtesy, Beth-El Congregation Archives, Fort Worth.

Council of Jewish Women

Eighth Triennial Convention

CHICAGO, ILL., NOVEMBER FIFTH TO ELEVENTH

PROGRAM

GENERAL SUBJECT: Twenty-Five Years of Progress

NATIONAL OFFICERS

HONORARY VICE-PRESIDENTS

Mrs. Jacob Schiff	New York City	Mrs. Solomon Hirsch	Portland, Ore.
Mrs. A. N. Cohen	New York City	Mrs. M. C. Sloss	San Francisco
Mrs. Hugo Rosenberg	Pittsburgh, Pa.	Mrs. Caesar Misch	Providence, R. I.
	Mrs. Isidore Newman	New Orleans, La.	

1914-1917

President—Janet Simons Harris (Mrs. Nathaniel E.)
114 South Avenue, Bradford, Pa.

Recording Secretary—Edna K. Glicksman (Mrs. Harry)
103 Avon Street, New Haven, Conn.

First Vice-President—Anna Hertzberg (Mrs. Eli)
521 W. Euclid Ave., San Antonio, Tex.

Treasurer—Jenny K. Herz (Mrs. Leo. H.)
45 Sheldon Terrace, New Haven, Conn.

Second Vice-President—Rose Brenner (Miss)
252 Carroll Street, Brooklyn, N. Y.

Executive Secretary—Ernestine B. Dreyfus (Mrs.)
3437 The Paseo, Kansas City, Mo.

The San Antonio section's activities reflected the city and the times. The Council passed a resolution "condemning the caricaturing of the Jew on the stage," a reference to touring vaudeville acts that depicted Jews kissing money. San Antonio's sunny climate drew people recovering from respiratory diseases. The Council raised money for the Montefiore Society that cared for poor, sickly Jewish men "wintering in our midst." San Antonio was also a magnet for political exiles and migrant workers from Mexico. Hertzberg was proudest when the Council opened the city's first "Night School for Immigrants." It taught "spelling, reading, writing and composition work in English," making "it possible for the deserving immigrants to . . . secure more profitable positions."[16] The start of the night school in 1907 coincided with the first boatloads of Jewish immigrants docking in Galveston under the Galveston Plan. Over the next seven years, the movement would bring to the Texas Gulf Coast port ten thousand Eastern European Jews who had few English-language or job skills. From 1907 to 1913, San Antonio received 184 of these immigrants.[17]

A stitch in time. The Dallas NCJW offered sewing classes to young women, circa 1915. Volunteer teachers from the council stand in the back, far right. Frank Rogers Commercial Photographs. From the National Council of Jewish Women, Dallas Section Records, Dallas Jewish Historical Society archives.

Americanization School, 1940. The National Council of Jewish Women's Americanization School in Fort Worth helped immigrants learn English and pass U.S. citizenship tests. Instructors, standing, are long-time director Amelia Rosenstein and volunteer Janet Teter, far right. These students are from Poland, Austria, Germany, and Russia. Courtesy, Fort Worth Star-Telegram Photograph Collection, Special Collections, The University of Texas at Arlington Libraries, Arlington, Texas.

Hertzberg saw to it that the NCJW provided a bridge to the rest of the city's women's organizations. In its first year, the NCJW affiliated with the San Antonio City Federation of Women's Clubs and the Free Kindergarten Association. Hertzberg served as state president of the Texas Federation of Women's Clubs from 1911 to 1913. During her term, women's clubs statewide lobbied for laws protecting married women's property rights. Clubwomen also championed the poll tax because the proceeds were earmarked for the state's fledgling public school systems. Concern over public education led Hertzberg to run successfully for the San Antonio school board in 1909—this before women had the right to the ballot box. (While Hertzberg favored women's suffrage, the issue was too divisive to become part of the Council of Jewish Women's agenda, locally or nationally. Women like Hertzberg and Hannah Solomon, who were committed to voting rights for women, generally worked with single-issue organizations focused on that cause.) Although women could not vote, Hertzberg demonstrated their influence. In her correspondence, she exhorted each clubwoman to convince "all the male voters of . . . her own family" and "as many more as she can reach" to vote for issues benefiting women and children.[18] "The organized womanhood of Texas has been a most potent factor in improving the educational system of Texas," she wrote the *Waco Morning News* on June 15, 1913. She characterized Texas clubwomen as "the power behind the throne."

LEAPING FORWARD

Throughout the first sixty years of the twentieth century, the National Council of Jewish women served as a veritable bridge, providing Texas women with an avenue back and forth from the Jewish community to volunteer positions in the larger realm. It was a safe, yet somewhat daring way to interact with the outside world. In Dallas, for example, the Council started the city's first free milk fund and provided students with "penny lunches"

in the years before schools had cafeterias. In Waco, never shy of controversy, the Council pushed for birth control education and in 1939 organized the Maternal Health Center, which evolved into the city's Planned Parenthood organization.

Collectively, the Council of Jewish Women coalesced with broader, activist groups. In the 1920s, Texas sections allied with the Association of Southern Women Against Lynching. During the world wars, sections sold Liberty Bonds and War Bonds. Between the wars, the Council and the Texas Federation of Women's Clubs advocated a world court and other mechanisms for a lasting peace. Marguerite Marks, president of the Dallas section, was elected president of the Texas Committee on the Cause and Cure of War. In most Texas cities during the 1950s, the Council began partnering with the Junior League (which was closed to Jews) and together spearheaded cutting-edge programs.

These were years when relatively few Jewish women in Texas attended or completed college, decades when females were not expected to do much beyond care for their homes and families. Jewish women, through the NCJW, proved themselves leaders and social activists. Participation in the NCJW gave them intellectual stimulation, leadership training, and self-confidence. Indeed, Annette Strauss, who became mayor of Dallas in 1987, recalled that her first volunteer experience in Dallas was addressing envelopes for the Council of Jewish Women.

From 1898 to 1967, Council sections formed in twenty-two Texas locales, yet only four remained viable into the twenty-first century. Those remaining chapters are in the metropolitan areas with the greatest concentrations of Jews: Dallas and Houston, with more than forty-two thousand Jews each in their metropolitan areas; Austin, the third-fastest growing Jewish community in the nation, with more than thirteen thousand Jewish residents; and San Antonio, with more than eleven thousand Jews. The most recent sections to disband were in Fort Worth and El Paso, each with around five thousand Jews. Leadership had gravitated to other institutions.

The Council's rise and decline in the Lone Star State reflects demographic and social trends among Jews in Texas and elsewhere.[19] After World War I, for example, the economy burgeoned. The Council organized in El Paso, Sherman, Austin, Corsicana, Wichita Falls, and Port Arthur. During the Great Depression, sections disbanded in Tyler, Corsicana, Wichita Falls, and Temple. After World War II, an influx of veterans and the buildup of military installations led to new sections in the Rio Grande Valley and Corpus Christi.

The Council peaked in Texas—and elsewhere in the United States—in the 1950s, when there were fifteen active Lone Star chapters (and 245 nationally). During the 1960s, the numbers began to tumble. Texas sections disbanded one after another in Galveston, Waco, Beaumont, the Rio Grande Valley, and Port Arthur. By decade's end, there were nine chapters remaining in Texas (and 193 nationally). Some, but not all, of the decline reflected movement of Jews from rural to urban areas and from cities to suburbs.

More significantly, feminism and multiculturalism were opening new avenues for Jewish women and devaluing old-fashioned volunteerism. Ripples from the Civil Rights struggle reduced discrimination against women. Barriers that once excluded Jews and restricted them to their own organizations began to dissolve. Social clubs sought to diversify and represent the total community. Among marginalized groups in Texas, Jewish women in the ranks of the NCJW were among the most visible and best trained for community endeavors. The Council's decades of success made Jewish women prime candidates for the Junior League, for bank boards, and for public office. In Fort Worth, Louise Kuehn Appleman, a vice-president of the local NCJW, became Junior League president, was elected to the junior college board, and became president of her congregation in 1987. In earlier decades, a Jewish woman in these positions would have been impossible to imagine.

The volunteer era. During the affluent post–World War II decade, the NCJW grew dramatically as stay-at-home women filled leisure hours with volunteer activities, reflected in this 1958 NCJW booklet. National Council of Jewish Women, Collections of the Manuscript Division, Library of Congress.

Within Judaism, institutions once exclusively male began to tap women for decision-making roles. Synagogues began naming women to executive board positions beyond the stereotypical recording secretary's role. Jewish social service agencies began hiring women, rather than taking them for granted as volunteers. Since the 1970s, across Texas and the nation, Jewish women have been breaking the glass ceiling—or, to use a religious metaphor, parting the *mechitzah*, the curtain separating Orthodox men from women at prayer.

When the National Council of Jewish Women was created in 1893, women's clubs were new and controversial. Women's civic activism rested on the belief in separate spheres. Women were guardians of the domestic realm. Men left the house for work in the public domain. Only by stretching the boundaries of the domestic sphere through their club work could women such as Anna Hertzberg, Olga Kohlberg, and Jeannette Goldberg participate in the larger world. The institutions that they founded and fostered, institutions that civilized and enhanced their pioneer communities, largely remain.

With the push for gender equality, the increasing number of professional women in the workforce, and the acceptance of multiculturalism in the latter twentieth century, women's clubs like the NCJW lost their initial reasons for existing. They began disbanding or scrambling to keep pace with societal shifts. The NCJW was no longer the only bridge for Jewish women seeking access into the larger universe. It is viable only in Texas cities with a large enough concentration of Jews to support multiple Jewish volunteer organizations. In medium-sized and small Jewish communities, women are often presidents of their congregations, while traditional Jewish women's groups struggle to build membership and recruit leaders.

In today's Texas, more and more Jewish women have an impact on the community, but it is individually rather than collectively. Jewish women have been elected mayor in such cities as Dallas (twice!), Plano, and Marshall. They serve on city councils and in the legislature. "While it is good that we Jews are accepted, it is not good for the Jewish community's identity," laments Fort Worth's Ellen Mack, a Jewish educator and the third generation in her extended family to serve as a local NCJW president. "We lost our collective role shaping the larger community. We are not as identifiable as Jews."[20] ✡

ACKNOWLEDGMENTS

The author thanks the Jewish Women's Archive in Boston for awarding her a research fellowship in 2002 to explore how Jewish women build communities.

NOTES

1 *American Jewess* (April 1896); 379–81.

2. Marian N. Braubach, *Always on Tuesdays . . . One Hundred Years of Music: A History of the Tuesday Musical Club Inc., 1901–2001* (San Antonio: Tuesday Musical Club, 2000), x, 11, 32.

3. Janet Gordon and Diana Reische, *The Volunteer Powerhouse* (New York: Rutledge Press, 1982).

4. Kaufmann Kohler in the *Southwest* [Dallas] *Jewish Sentiment*, October 18, 1901, 1; Voorsanger, from editorial in *The American Jewess*, April 1896, 379–81.

5. Jeannette Miriam Goldberg to Rabbi Max Heller (November 9, 1878), Ms. 33, Max Heller Papers, Box 2, folder 19, Jacob Rader Marcus Center of the American Jewish Archives, Cincinnati (hereafter AJA); J. M. Goldberg to Dr. H. G. Enelow (September 15, 1927), Ms. 11, Hyman G. Enelow Papers, Box 7, folder 12, AJA.

6. Jeannette Miriam Goldberg, "Report of the Tyler (Texas) Section," *Proceedings of the Council of Jewish Women, Fourth Triennial Convention, Chicago, Illinois, December 5 to 12, 1905*, pp. 149, 351.

7. Mrs. Jacob Lipstate, "Report of Tyler Section," Proceedings of the Fifth Triennial Convention, Cincinnati, Ohio, December 1 to 10, 1908, pp. 319–20.

8. Although the Dallas section's official history states that it began in 1913, news accounts, minutes of the Dallas Federation of Women's Clubs, and NCJW triennial proceedings show the prior existence of a Dallas section. History of Dallas Federation of Women's Clubs: 1898–1936 (Dallas: Clyde C. Cockrell & Son Publishers, 1936), 166–69; Proceedings of the Council of Jewish Women Third Triennial Convention, Baltimore, Maryland December 2–9, 1902; The Dallas section's 1913 rebirth is detailed in Miriam Jaffe, National Council of Jewish Women, Greater Dallas Section, 1913–1988 (Dallas: NCJW, 1988).

9. Southwestern [Dallas] Jewish Sentiment, October 25, November 5, 1901; Mrs. Theodore [Polly] Mack, "Report of Fort Worth Section," Proceedings of the Fifth Triennial," 288–89.

10. Jeannette Miriam Goldberg, "Report of Miss Goldberg on Organizing," Proceedings of the Council of Jewish Women, Fourth Triennial, 143–49.

11. C. L. Sonnichsen, Pass of the North (El Paso: Texas Western Press, 1968), 1; Mary S. Cunningham, The Woman's Club of El Paso: Its First Thirty Years (El Paso: Texas Western Press, 1978), vii–xi, 24–34, 53–64; The Woman's Collection, Texas Woman's University, Denton Texas; Handbook of Texas Online, s.v. "Kolberg, Olga Bernstein," www.tsha.utexas.edu/handbook/online/articles/KK/fko9.html (accessed September 23, 2005); "Mrs. Olga Bernstein Kohlberg," Who's Who of the Womanhood of Texas, vol. I, (Austin: Texas Federation of Women's Clubs, 1924), 195; Ruthe Winegarten, Texas Women: A Pictorial History, from Indians to Astronauts (Austin: Eakin Press, 1896), 48.

12. The school's Web site is http://kohlberg.episd.org/; Debbie M. Pazos, "Trolley Transport Through Time: Olga Bernstein Kohlberg, Hedwig Mathias Schwartz," program booklet, Congregation B'nai Zion Sisterhood, August 28, 2005.

13. San Antonio Express, n.d., in Braubach, Always on Tuesdays, 10

14. "Mrs. Anna Hertzberg," Who's Who of Womanhood of Texas, vol. I, 87; correspondence and undated newspaper articles in "Hertzberg, Anna" file 3A173, Texas Jewish Historical Society Collection, Center for American History, University of Texas at Austin.

15. Mrs. Eli [Anna] Hertzberg, "Report of San Antonio Section," Council of Jewish Women Proceedings of the Fifth Triennial Convention, Cincinnati, Ohio, 1908, 314.

16. Ibid.

17. "Statistics of Jewish Immigrants Who Arrived at the Port of Galveston, Texas, During the Years 1907–1913, Inclusive," Ms. 263, Henry Cohen Papers, AJA.

18. Mrs. Eli Hertzberg to Mrs. Percy V. Pennybacker, July 29, 1902, Texas Federation of Women's Clubs Papers, Texas Woman's University, Denton; Mrs. Eli Hertzberg, "The State President Sends Weekly Letter," Waco Morning News, June 15, 1913.

19. Conclusions and statistics on NCJW sections are derived from the author's Master's thesis, "The Jewish Junior League: The Rise and Fall of the Fort Worth Council of Jewish Women," University of Texas at Arlington, 2004.

20. Ellen Feinknopf Mack, interview with author, August 7, 2003.

6

"The Man Who Stayed in Texas"
Galveston's Rabbi Henry Cohen, a Memoir

HENRY COHEN II

In September 1930, Rabbi Stephen Wise, spiritual leader of New York's Free Synagogue and president of the Jewish Institute of Religion, was asked to name "the ten foremost religious leaders in this country." The list, published in the *New York Times* on September 22, included nine Christian clergy and one rabbi—Henry Cohen of Galveston, Texas. The headline read, "10 LEADERS OF CHURCH LISTED BY RABBI WISE . . . One Negro Among Them." (That one Jew was among them did not impress the headline writer.) When a Jewish journalist questioned Wise as to why he chose the Galveston rabbi, he replied, "One man in the rabbinate, Henry Cohen, had come to have [such] a fine religious or spiritual influence in a large section of the country . . . that Woodrow Wilson referred to him as 'the foremost citizen of Texas.'"

Rabbi Wise went on to inform the journalist that he, along with influential investment banker and philanthropist Jacob Schiff, had urged Cohen to come to New York City to become Chaplain at Large to the Jewish Inmates of Public Institutions. Cohen had respectfully declined because of his sense of duty to the people of Galveston and the state of Texas. Wise, arguably the foremost public speaker in the American rabbinate, concluded, "Oratory is so often a cheap and easy thing, life is always so difficult and stern a thing. Henry Cohen is a soul who touches and kindles souls."

Much has been written about my grandfather—including a *Reader's Digest* portrait in 1939, a biography, *The Man Who Stayed in Texas*, by my parents in 1941, a national radio dramatization that aired in 1955, and, in the past two decades, profiles in *Pioneer Jewish Texans* and *Jewish Stars in Texas*, as well as a biography for children, *Henry Cohen: The Life of a Frontier Rabbi*. In recent years, I have written a biography that offers a perspective based on my memories, a search for the sources behind the stories told about him, and a historical analysis of how he both reflected and transcended ideologies of his time.[1] Let us begin with some memories of the man behind the myth. I grew up in Houston, but on weekends went to Galveston. There, in my grandparents' home (called "the rabbinage") at 1920 Broadway Avenue, I enjoyed listening to amazing stories about the legendary rabbi. Psychologically, it was as though I had two grandfathers named Henry Cohen, one real and one mythical. There was "Grandpa" Cohen—we never called him *zayde* because the only Yiddish I knew was "Bei Mir Bist Du Schein," as sung by the Andrews Sisters. Grandpa Cohen enjoyed saying to me such silliness as "ellipticalasiatical pantry curious nervouscordial." Grandpa Cohen belted out from Gilbert and Sullivan's *HMS Pinafore*, "For he is an Englishman, for he himself hath said it . . ." Grandpa Cohen would annoy Grandma by singing British dance hall ditties considered R-rated by Victorian standards, as in "Go away, naughty

Rabbi Henry Cohen, 1884, at a Caribbean pulpit. Rabbi Cohen, twenty-two, wore flowing ministerial robes and a top hat at his first pulpit in Kingston, Jamaica. The photo was reproduced and matted at Galveston's Morris photography studios. Photo from the personal collection of Rabbi Henry Cohen II.

boy . . ." Grandpa Cohen smoked cigars until the ashes fell and burnt holes in his black suit, further annoying Grandma. Once, a very proper lady friend spent the night at the Cohens, and in the morning she awoke to find next to her a broomstick dressed as a man. (Grandpa's idea.) Grandpa Cohen also made sure the family memorized poems he taped to the bathroom wall, so that you had to read them when you were sitting on the toilet. For sixty-five years I have been unable to get out of my head, "We had a little tea party this afternoon at three; 'twas very small three guests in all just I, myself, and me . . ."

Grandpa Cohen liked lyrics and, on occasion, liquor. After returning from his morning rounds (which he listed in pencil on his stiff white shirt cuff), he would belt down a shot of scotch. He might recall how he had provided a case of scotch for the great Scottish vaudevillian, Harry Lauder, whenever he performed in Galveston singing, "I Love a Lassie," or, for the home crowd, "The Dixie Girls Are Good Enough for Me." That was the Grandpa Cohen who, when I returned from my third year at Hebrew Union College, asked almost plaintively, "What could I teach at the College?" I answered, "Maybe you could teach the students how to be rabbis." Grandpa Cohen was a natural. By that I mean that he was the same on the pulpit as off, no deep sonorous tones. Who you saw and heard was who he was.

That was Grandpa—a playful, earthy, life-loving, unpretentious mensch, a very human being. Then, in my psyche alongside Grandpa, the mensch, was "Rabbi Cohen," supermensch! Rabbi Cohen was the almost mythic hero of many stories that I loved hearing as a child. There were stories of South Africa, and he would show the scar on his head from the wound that he received when a Zulu hit him over the head with the butt of a gun. More impressive were stories of how he intervened to help a stowaway about to be deported to Russia or a juvenile being flogged in a state institution.

But to return to my grandfather's roots: Born April 7, 1863, in London to a poor tinsmith, David Cohen, and his pious wife, Josephine, Henry was one of eight children, three boys and five girls. He was sent to Jews Hospital, a boarding school subsidized by wealthy Jews for the children of less fortunate coreligionists. There, one of his friends was Israel Zangwill, who would become a novelist and playwright and would play a key role, with Henry Cohen, in the immigration of Jews through Galveston. At age fifteen, Henry worked for the Board of Guardians, distributing bread tickets to the poor and earning enough to attend Jews College at night. There he became immersed in Jewish studies.

After three years at Jews College, Henry gave in to his brother Mark's plea that he take a break from academic work and experience a different world. With financial support from the Board of Guardians, Henry spent an adventurous two years in Africa where, because of his facility with languages, he learned the Zulu's click dialect and became an interpreter. After returning from Africa in June 1883, he resumed his Jewish studies and, upon graduation, was given the title "minister," which authorized him to perform all Jewish clerical duties (including that of *mohel* and *shochet*) except rendering decisions in Jewish law. For that, one must have *semicha*, and such ordinations were not given in England until 1896. These ministers were expected to be, in the words of the director of the college, "men of thoroughly English feelings and views, conversant with the classics of their own language as well as those of the sacred tongue . . . whose ardour and enthusiasm will . . . rouse and kindle with Shakespearean vigor and Miltonian sweetness."

After graduating in 1884, Henry was sent by England's chief rabbi, Nathan Adler, to the colonies, specifically Kingston, Jamaica, where he became the minister of the Amalgamated Congregation of Israelites, which included Ashkenazic Jews of Central and Eastern European descent and Sephardic Jews whose ancestors came from Spain and North Africa. (Years later, when I visited the synagogue that he dedicated, I saw evidence of the antagonism that later drove him to America: two *ner tamids*, or eternal lights—one for the Sephardim, one for the Ashkenazim!)

In New York, before returning to England, Henry learned of an opening for a rabbi at Congregation Beth Israel in Woodville, Mississippi. It was 1885, the year that a gathering of Reform rabbis in Pittsburgh proclaimed a "platform" that set forth the principles of Classical Reform Judaism. Perhaps influenced by those principles, perhaps because he did not wish to return to the rather authoritarian rule of the chief rabbi of England, Cohen accepted the position with Woodville's Reform congregation, although he insisted that his congregants close their stores on Saturday mornings, when Shabbat worship services were held. The consequence was that most customers waited until Saturday afternoon to come to town, so that even gentile merchants closed their stores, and many came to hear the young rabbi preach.

After three years in Woodville, Cohen became rabbi at B'nai Israel in Galveston, Texas, a thriving port, population twenty-two thousand, including about 175 Jewish families. There he remained as the *active* rabbi for almost sixty-two years (perhaps a record term of service in one synagogue) before he retired in 1950, at age eighty-seven.

Before 1900, Henry was to marry Mollie Levy, have two children, Ruth and Harry, edit one book, *Talmudic Sayings,* and write more than twenty articles or pamphlets. Among the topics were the history of the Jews of Texas and (after the Dreyfus Affair and pogroms in Russia) "National Loyalty, a Jewish Characteristic." His scholarly pursuits came to a sudden curtailment on September 8, 1900, the day that one-fourth of the population of Galveston, approximately seventy-five hundred men, women, and children, drowned in a catastrophic hurricane. As a member of the city's Central Relief Committee, Rabbi Cohen played a significant role reconstructing the morale of the citizens. In the aftermath of the storm, Henry Cohen became the rabbi of all Galvestonians.

In 1901, the rabbi delivered a lecture to the students and faculty of the University of Texas Medical School in Galveston on "The Hygiene and Medicine of the Talmud." Rabbi Cohen remained closely connected with the medical school, as he established a loan fund for students who could not afford tuition and visited the fraternities regularly, at times meeting the special needs of students (such as persuading a casino owner to donate a piano so that one student could practice).

Also in 1901, two boxers—Joe Choynski, son of Polish Jewish immigrants, and Jack Johnson, who would become the first African-American heavyweight champion—were

Henry Cohen with wife, Mollie Levy Cohen, son, Harry, left, and daughter, Ruth, circa. 1895. Mollie and the children were "B.O.I."—born on the island, a matter of pride to Galvestonians. Center for American History, UT-Austin, CN Number 12108, Cohen (Henry) Papers.

jailed for staging an illegal fight. Rabbi Cohen argued that these two men should not be incarcerated like hardened criminals. He arranged for the pair to spend nights out of jail—Johnson in his Galveston home and Choynski in a hotel. During the day, their jail cell became a gym where the boxers staged exhibition matches for local sports fans.

After the brutal Kishineff pogroms in Russia in 1903, Jacob Schiff, the successful New York investment banker and philanthropist, believed that rather than crowd the urban ghettos on the East Coast, a significant number of Jews could be settled in the Southwest and Midwest, where employment was more available. Some saw dispersion as a means of decreasing anti-Jewish sentiment, which was believed to be caused, in part, by the "embarrassing" Yiddish-speaking Jews from Russia and Poland. Schiff sought the co-operation of Rabbi Cohen's boyhood friend, Israel Zangwill, then head of the Jewish Territorial Organization (which is abbreviated ITO). The ITO's goal was to find a region where the Jews could establish an autonomous entity. Zangwill agreed to work with Schiff, perhaps because his previous attempt to establish a Jewish nation in Uganda had failed and the ITO needed to do something to help Jewish victims of persecution.

But where to send the Jews? Among the American ports suggested were Charleston, New Orleans, and Galveston. Morris Waldman, a noted social worker who investigated conditions in Charleston, concluded that the Jews there were "inhospitable" to Eastern European immigrants.[2] New Orleans was ruled out because it was so large a city that most of the immigrants might decide to stay there, contrary to the goal of dispersal. Galveston seemed ideal: too small to offer economic opportunities that would tempt immigrants to stay; railroad lines to the Midwest and Southwest; and an energetic, humanitarian rabbi, Henry Cohen.

Jacob Schiff was the sole benefactor for what became the Galveston Movement (or the Galveston Plan). He was prepared to provide five hundred thousand dollars. He wrote Zangwill in October 1906 that he would consider the plan a success if twenty thousand to twenty-five thousand Jews settled in the American hinterland, for surely others would follow. Waldman, the social worker, was sent to Galveston to become general agent of the Jewish Immigration Information Bureau (JIIB). He developed a close relationship with the rabbi, who tried to persuade him to live in the "rabbinage." Waldman compromised and had meals almost every day with the Cohen family. He later wrote about Henry Cohen,

> He was "the Rabbi" not only to his own congregation or even to the wider Jewish community, he was "the Rabbi" to the whole city. Indeed, he was "the Rabbi" to a good part of Texas and the Southwest . . . It was the day of bicycles, and as I think of the dynamic little Rabbi now, I have a picture of him flitting to and fro on his "wheel," doing his countless chores, usually errands of mercy . . . When people were in trouble, white or black, Jew or Gentile, aristocrat or bureau plebeian, it was "the Rabbi" who was first consulted. He was the Social Service of the community . . . indeed, I might nearly say the Federation. And his wisdom was excelled only by his sympathy and understanding.[3]

Waldman and the rabbi secured the cooperation of B'nai B'rith lodges throughout the Midwest and Southwest to discover what occupations were available in their communities, so that the immigrants' skills could lead to gainful employment.

The first boatload arrived in Galveston on July 1, 1907, from Breman, Germany. Eighty-seven Jews were greeted by Rabbi Cohen and Galveston's mayor, H. A. Landes. The rabbi, speaking in Yiddish, told the immigrants about the United States and its democratic ideals. He introduced the mayor, translating his greeting into Yiddish. The Mayor told the new arrivals, "You have come to a great country. With industry and economy all of you will meet with success. Obey the laws and try to make good citizens." He then shook each immigrant's hand. According to the next day's *Galveston Daily News*, one immigrant, a former school teacher, responded in halting English:

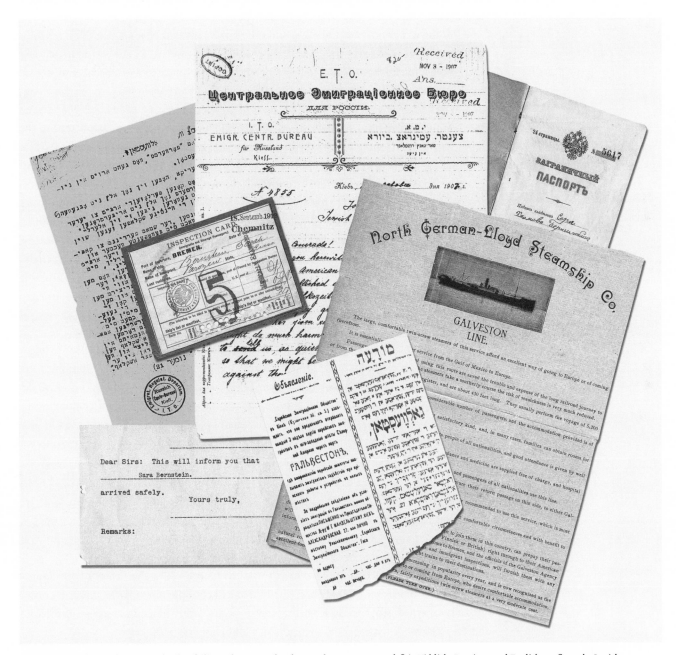

The Galveston Plan with its mounds of multilingual paperwork. The two documents at top left in Yiddish, Russian, and English are from the Jewish Territorial Organization (abbreviated as I.T.O. and E.T.O.). The Russian passport, inspection card, and arrival postcard document the journey of Sarah Bernstein, who reached Galveston on Kol Nidre, 1913. The North German-Lloyd Steamship Co. advertised its Galveston Line as "comfortable" and "excellent." The flyer at center announces in Russian and Yiddish that groups are leaving for Galveston every three weeks. ITO documents courtesy of the Jacob Rader Marcus Center of the American Jewish Archives; Bernstein documents from the collection of David and Binnie Hoffman; North German Lloyd Steamship Co. Galveston Line © American Jewish Historical Society. All rights reserved. American Jewish Historical Society, Newton Centre, Massachusetts and New York, New York; flyer from TJHS Newsletter, spring 1995.

We are overwhelmed that the ruler of the city should greet us. We have never been spoken to by the officials of our country except in terms of harshness, and although we have heard of the great land of freedom, it is very hard to realize that we are permitted to grasp the hand of the great man. We will do all we can to make good citizens.

Cohen recalled the immigrant adding, "There may be a time when the American people will need us, and then we will serve them with our blood."

After the welcome from the rabbi and the mayor came a medical exam. Next, the immigrants were taken to the JIIB, where they received long-awaited mail, bathed, sat down to a wholesome kosher meal, and were given the opportunity to write home and to read Yiddish newspapers. After they were interviewed, they were assigned to go to a community in which their skills were needed, receiving railroad tickets, then supper, followed by an apportionment of food sufficient to last the journey. Telegrams were sent to the communities that would receive the immigrants, so that they could be met at the station.

From July 1907 through September 1914, approximately ten thousand Jewish immigrants entered the United States through Galveston. Of that number, three thousand remained in Texas, including three hundred in Galveston. The majority settled out of state in Missouri, Minnesota, Iowa, Wisconsin, Ohio, Nebraska, Colorado, and Oklahoma. Among them were tailors, carpenters, boot makers, locksmiths, metal workers, bakers, painters, and butchers. Some were admitted as unskilled laborers, others as salesmen, clerks, and bookkeepers.

At the end of 1907, after welcoming 833 immigrants, the Movement was brought to a virtual halt by a national economic depression. As the economy improved, the Movement resumed its previous pace after March 1909. At times the immigrants needed special help, having arrived barefoot and shirtless. Clothing was purchased either by the JIIB or by Rabbi Cohen from his own funds. Twice, couples arrived without legal documents proving that they were married, so Rabbi Cohen performed a marriage ceremony on the spot. According to the memoirs of Rabbi Alexander Ziskind Gurwitz, a Polish immigrant who came through Galveston, Rabbi Cohen intervened on his behalf when immigration officials detained him for questioning. In Yiddish, Gurwitz related to Cohen that he was a certified *shochet* and had previously transferred funds to an American bank. As soon as Rabbi Cohen explained the situation to immigration officials, Gurwitz was allowed to go to the JIIB for a kosher meal. Rabbi Gurwitz settled in San Antonio, where he taught Hebrew and worked as a kosher butcher. He later led High Holiday services in Laredo, where his grown son and grandchildren resided, and he wrote a memoir, reflecting on his life's journey.[4]

As the Movement continued into 1910, nativists opposing the influx of foreigners charged that immigrants were changing "the racial complexion of America" and undercutting American workers by accepting lower wages. These objections stirred Schiff and other American Jewish leaders to organize a lobbying campaign.

The Jewish community was far from united in support of the Galveston Movement. Two influential New York Jewish newspapers, *Yiddishes Taggenblatt* and *Morgen Journal*, ran editorials against the Movement. The Jewish masses, they editorialized, should immigrate to places where they were inclined naturally to settle, rather than be "led" or "transported" to destinations chosen by German Jewish leaders. They warned that immigrants settling in the West would be forced to work on Saturday, the Jewish Sabbath, and would have no place to buy kosher meat. Even in Galveston, where the Movement

Just call me Charlie. Ephraim Zalman Hoffman immigrated to Texas from Poland's Hrubieszow area in 1913 and initially settled in Fort Worth, where this picture was snapped. The face of an Old World acquaintance is projected at right. Because Ephraim's name was difficult to pronounce, co-workers dubbed him "Charlie," the name he formally adopted. From the collection of David and Binnie Hoffman.

was strongly supported by Rabbi Cohen's congregation and the Orthodox YMHA Synagogue, which was made up of Russian Jews, the Bikur Cholim Society, which was composed of Polish Jews from Galicia, objected. Perhaps they feared that many immigrants would remain in Galveston and so become a threat to their livelihood.

In 1911, fourteen hundred immigrants were admitted, the largest number so far. But in October of that year, a seventeen-year-old immigrant girl was raped by another immigrant. The JIIB did not report the assault to authorities, but the victim did. Inspector Alfred Hampton was furious and ruled that immigrants would no longer be sent to the JIIB. Rabbi Cohen, who had been pressing for closer supervision of immigrants by the JIIB, resigned, presumably for a number of reasons: to protest the inspector's ruling, to demonstrate to the JIIB that more supervision was needed, and to indicate that he did not have the funds to help the most needy immigrants. Inspector Hampton, who admired the rabbi, appealed to him to withdraw his resignation, as did Schiff. Rabbi Cohen relented, and he received from Schiff six hundred dollars per year to spend at his discretion. The tension with the immigration inspector was resolved, and the work of the Movement continued.

Then came the infamous "hernia epidemic." Suddenly, in July 1913, a medical inspector diagnosed eight Galveston immigrants with hernias, a condition that barred entry to the United States. Not only were these immigrants deported, but none of their relatives were allowed to come to America. Among Galveston arrivals, hernias were diagnosed at six times the rate that they were found among immigrants disembarking in Philadelphia, and ten times the rate found in New York.

But the fatal blow to the Galveston Movement came when Woodrow Wilson, a Democrat with the ardent support of the labor movement, was elected president. Even though Schiff had voted for Wilson, his Washington contacts were all Republican. So, with a new Democratic administration backed by anti-immigration labor unions, Schiff lost much of his influence. Ironically, these "restrictionists" were gaining power in 1913, the year that saw the largest number of Jewish immigrants come through Galveston—three thousand. In the first quarter of the following year, there was a decline—an average of 162 immigrants per month, down from 217 the previous year, combined with an increasing rate of deportations. Schiff realized that his goal of twenty thousand to twenty-five thousand immigrants per year would not be met. As the Movement's sole benefactor, he concluded that it should come to an end. However, having spent $235,000, he did not regret his efforts. By October 1, 1914, approximately ten thousand Jews had come from Russia through Galveston on one hundred ships. Almost all had settled in the Southwest and Midwest. They would send for their families and attract other Jews. They also would strengthen the Jewish communities where they resided. Historian Bernard Marinbach points out that the Galveston Movement's dispersal of Jews throughout the United States helped make Judaism accepted as one of America's three major religious traditions.[5]

For Rabbi Cohen, success was measured not by numbers but by the impact that the Movement had on each individual who began life anew in a land where there truly was opportunity. Meigs Frost, star reporter for the *Galveston Daily News*, covered the rise and demise of the Movement. Reminiscing years later from his job at the New Orleans *Times-Picayune*, Frost recalled that when Rabbi Cohen met with immigrants, no one would have known that he was a clergyman. He wore "a baggy black alpaca coat, baggier gray striped trousers, a sagging weather-stained hard straw hat." Once thus dressed, he entered the steerage area of a ship and began questioning a broad-shouldered, heavily bearded, giant Jewish immigrant. The man snarled at the rabbi in Yiddish, "What is that to you?"

"I beg your pardon," said the rabbi and moved on to a circle of other immigrants. While discussing with them their problems, the giant of a man who had snarled at the rabbi barged into the crowd, fell to his knees, and kissed the rabbi's feet, beseeching his pardon. He had no idea he had been so rude to the rabbi of Galveston. The rabbi helped the man to his feet and said, "I understand. You were worried. But this is unseemly. Now, let's get you straightened out."[6]

In the December 27, 1914, issue of the *Galveston Daily News*, the tale of the end of the Galveston Movement is told. One headline reads, "Personality of Dr. Henry Cohen Uppermost for Hardly an Immigrant Ship Since 1907 has Touched Galveston Port, but What the Rabbi Was as Familiar a Figure as Immigration Officials."

Toward the end of the Galveston Movement, the oft-repeated tale was told of a stowaway named Demchuk, who was threatened with imminent deportation to Russia, where he would be executed. Rabbi Cohen was not able to persuade local port authorities to let him stay, so the rabbi went to Washington and met with President William Howard Taft.

The President said, "Sorry, I can't help you, but it's wonderful how you Jews do so much to help each other." Rabbi Cohen exclaimed, "This man is not a Jew. He's a Greek-Catholic." The President was stunned: "You came all the way from Galveston for a man not of your faith?" Rabbi Cohen responded, "He's a human being." The President issued an order: "Release Demchuk in the custody of Rabbi Cohen."

There are other versions of this story, which was first reported by Meigs Frost in a 1936 article published in the *Times-Picayune*. Some accounts identify the immigrant as

"Straightening a Tangle." That was the caption under this photo that ran in the Galveston Daily News, September 27, 1914. Rabbi Henry Cohen, center, confers with immigration officials. Photo from the personal collection of Rabbi Henry Cohen II.

"Lemchuk." My cousin David Frisch doubted the veracity of this, among other tales. I believed with perfect faith every word. David became a physicist. I became a rabbi. I decided to go on a quest for the facts, just the facts. My search took me to the Library of Congress, where I found some revealing correspondence between Rabbi Cohen and President Taft. The most significant involved the President's half-brother Charles, on whom the President depended for advice and financial support and who was accused of profiting from a land grab in Alaska because of insider information. The President was viewed by some as benefiting from the transaction. Taft was so stung by this attack on his reputation that on June 17, 1911, he wrote to Rabbi Cohen that he was not involved in any way with the

L'dor v'dor. Rabbi Henry Cohen at the beach in Galveston, 1931, with grandsons David Henry Frisch, fourteen, who became a physicist, and Henry Cohen II, age four, who followed in his grandfather's footsteps to become a rabbi. Photo from the personal collection of Rabbi Henry Cohen II.

transaction. Rabbi Cohen responded to the President's personal secretary that he recognized the accusation as a "canard." He concluded, "We have always felt that the high standard of integrity manifested by Mr. Taft warrants our thorough confidence in his personal unassailability."[7]

I found it noteworthy that the President of the United States would write the rabbi of Galveston defending his own integrity, and that the rabbi would assure the President that he never doubted his moral character. This suggests a strong connection between the two men. This exchange for me is circumstantial evidence that a humane President Taft very well could have facilitated what today we would call political asylum for a Russian refugee—though I have my doubts about the details of the story. A colleague has suggested that my obsession with "the facts" is unwarranted. The deeper meaning of the story is the truth of a rabbi who would take *extraordinary* measures to help a fellow human being, whatever that person's faith.

This "truth" does not depend upon the Taft connection. In 1930, Rabbi William Braude, a younger contemporary, wrote of another instance in which Rabbi Cohen went far out of his way for someone in need. At one time, Galveston had been a stopover point in a brisk white slave traffic. Rabbi Cohen found one unfortunate woman who had been forced into prostitution. He could find no place for her safely to live, so he put her up in his own home, not as a maid or a servant, but as a respectable boarder. She lived there for six months, despite the protests of several shocked congregants.

The rabbi also successfully intervened on behalf of a Roman Catholic woman, an illegal immigrant from Poland who was threatened with deportation, even though she had married an American. A Turkish Jew had been wrongly incarcerated in a mental hospital. Rabbi Cohen facilitated his release to the care of the Jewish community of El Paso. In 1915, he helped a Jewish corporal get discharged from the army in order to marry his pregnant girlfriend and support their baby. When Henry Cohen visited hospitals, he brought comfort and a smile to everyone, whatever one's faith. He was often quoted as saying, "There's no such thing as Episcopalian scarlet fever, Catholic arthritis, or Jewish mumps."

By 1916, Rabbi Cohen had become a role model for the American Reform rabbi. That was the year he spoke to the graduating class of Hebrew Union College (HUC) and expressed the hope that some would be content to remain in smaller cities. There they would be more likely to have an impact on the entire community than they would in large urban areas.

In 1921, Carl Pritz, a board member at HUC, asked Rabbi Cohen if he would allow his name to be submitted as a candidate for the college presidency. The rabbi replied that he appreciated the honor but declined because "among other reasons, I have not the adequate scholarship to be the successor of Dr. (Kaufman) Kohler," the outstanding Reform Jewish theologian of that time. The super-mensch knew his limits.

By 1922, in his address to the Central Conference of American Rabbis, Cohen attached more importance to the rabbi's role as social critic: "[W]here a political or economic situation becomes a moral issue, the pulpit must thunder forth . . . the temple should permit the greatest latitude to its rabbi, it should be 'free' to the discussion of all sociological questions, whether running counter to preconceived opinions or not."[8]

For Henry Cohen, from 1917 to 1930, the moral issue that moved him to action was prison reform in Texas. In 1917, as chairman of the state Committee on the After-care of Prisoners, he wrote,

What chance has a pardoned or released prisoner? He leaves the walls feeling disgraced and dishonored. The state gives him often-times only a second-hand suit of clothes, prison-made shoes that every detective can discern a block away, a ticket to the city or town from which he was convicted, and the munificent sum of $5! How in the name of heaven can he start life all over again?[9]

Rabbi Cohen became an unofficial counselor for ex-convicts, who reported to him weekly. After one year, an ex-convict was expected to be on his own. The rabbi had a remarkable success rate but was not satisfied. The entire prison system had to be changed fundamentally. During the 1920s, Rabbi Cohen led the battle for separation of first offenders, hardened criminals, and the mentally ill. He also championed rehabilitation. Once significant progress had been made, the rabbi resigned from the state prison board but remained active working with ex-convicts by serving on the Galveston County Parole Board.

Among all the cities in Texas, Galveston was unique in that it did not become a center of major Ku Klux Klan activity. A Galveston Klavern was established on November 18, 1920, and William Moody III, son of one of Galveston's most influential families, collected its dues. The Klan did stage an initiation ceremony on September 3, 1922, with two crosses blazing, one on either side of the island. However, because of pressure from Rabbi Cohen and his colleague and friend Father James Kirwin, the City Council would not issue the Klan a permit to march through the city. The *Galveston Tribune*, published by the rabbi's son (my father), vigorously opposed the Klan. Furthermore, the rabbi persuaded the island's Queen Theatre to remove from its schedule "The Birth of a Nation," a film that portrays the KKK as savior of the South. Elsewhere in Texas, Rabbis David Lefkowitz in Dallas, Maurice Faber in Tyler, Samuel Rosinger in Beaumont, and Harry Merfeld in Fort Worth were also vocal or defiant against the Klan.

Rabbi Cohen's stances during the Klan era, as well as his advocacy for prison reform, show him as both a pastor and social activist who looked beyond Texas. He was one of many who advocated a peaceful solution to the world's problems. Each Armistice Day, he composed or quoted a poem that condemned the use of arms. He opposed the introduction of ROTC in Galveston's Ball High School. In his letter of protest to the *Galveston Daily News* he wrote, "Boys in their early teens . . . should be taught the values of peace achievements rather than the glories of war." On Armistice Day, November 11, 1936, he issued a plea for "peace education" and predicted that "it is for the *women* of the world to teach the nations to live on friendly sympathetic terms . . . or cease to exist at all."

Once the horror of Nazism became apparent, Henry Cohen did support the war against Hitler. He would take me along to services at Camp Wallace, where he reminded soldiers of the words of Oliver Cromwell: "Trust in God, but keep your powder dry!" Postwar, I was with him at a Rotary Club meeting at which Dr. James B. Conant, a physicist and educator who played a key role in the development of nuclear weapons, described the potential benefits and dangers of atomic energy. After the program, Rabbi Cohen, all of five-foot-one, stood toe to toe with the professor, who towered well over six feet, and quoted Rashi, the legendary Torah scholar, and his comment about the bee: "I want neither your honey nor your sting."

While Henry Cohen became a Reform Rabbi as the Classical Reform Movement was taking shape, he did not fit neatly into any ideology. He did accept the fundamental principles of Classical Reform: belief in progressive revelation, in adhering to traditions that "elevate and sanctify our lives," in the mission of Israel being a light to the nations. Still, in his personal life, he remained "Biblical kosher" (no pork or shellfish), though he did not object when his family ate crab gumbo. At our Passover Seder, he chanted the Orthodox *Haggadah* (all of it!). After Shabbat eve dinner, he would chant the lengthy *Birkat Hamazon* (the blessing after meals that we called *bentshing*). He made sure that I became a Bar Mitzvah, even though such ceremonies were rare in Reform temples in 1940. He did depart from tradition by having me learn not the *parasha* of the week (Noah), but the Ten Commandments. I guess he figured that I might never read from the Torah again, so at least I would have learned the Decalogue.

Henry Cohen told his colleagues at a Central Conference of American Rabbis lecture in 1902, "All honor to those who follow their convictions in sincerity and in truth, *whether those convictions be Orthodox or Reform.*" His wife Mollie, a Galveston native, was less tolerant of the Orthodox. My cousin David Frisch enjoyed retelling an incident that he witnessed: A prominent Orthodox woman came to call on Mrs. Cohen one Saturday but would not violate the Sabbath by ringing the doorbell. Watching the caller, Mollie refused to answer the door. After the woman had departed, Mollie laughed and said, "If she's too *frum* (pious) to ring a bell on *Shabbos*, I'm certainly too *frum* to answer the door."[10]

The greatest tragedy in the rabbi's life, the death of his daughter, Ruth Frisch, at the age of forty-four, a victim of Hodgkin's disease, apparently led him to return to the Orthodox faith in *t'hiyat ha-maytim*, the (bodily) resurrection of the dead. In a 1940 eulogy, six years after Ruth's death, he referred to her and said,

> There is a time when we were not, and then we are, and if there is a power to call people into life, surely there must be that same power which causes them to live on in any sphere, which the Creator wishes. So I think that in God's own time and in His own way, we shall be brought together again.

Henry Cohen was an unconventional non-Zionist member of the Jewish Agency. He favored Jewish settlement in Palestine. In 1945, when the British restricted Jewish immigration, Cohen wrote the chairman of the American delegation of the Anglo-American Commission on Palestine urging "unlimited immigration to Palestine for those who wish to settle there." However, he did join the anti-Zionist American Council for Judaism. He told me of his fear that the Arabs would never accept a Jewish state in the Middle East. Once Israel was established in 1948, he became a firm supporter. In 1951, he welcomed the *Eilat*, one of the first Israeli vessels to dock in Galveston, and received a letter of gratitude, in Hebrew, from its captain.

However, Henry Cohen was not known for his advocacy of any particular ideology. For the people of Texas and the rabbis of his generation, he transcended ideology because of how far he would go, how much he would do to help a single soul, and because of his pioneering efforts at what today is called *tikkun olam*, repairing the world.

Henry Cohen reminds us of the impact that a single individual may have on other lives and even social institutions. As for those marvelous Rabbi Cohen stories, sure some may be a bit exaggerated, but then what are legends but the tributes paid by generations to those men and women whom they most admire? We do need our moral models. Why was he a model for so many rabbis? Perhaps because he so effectively combined the role of pastor and social activist. Also, he exuded energy, which ended only with his death at our home in Houston, where he had moved after my grandmother passed away in 1951.

Henry Cohen died at the age of eighty-nine on June 12, 1952. Stephen Wise was right:

Rabbi Henry Cohen, circa 1950, reads a children's megillah with an illustrated story of Queen Esther. Center for American History, UT-Austin, CN Number 09919, Texas Jewish Historical Society Collection.

His was a soul that touched and kindled other souls. Three years after his death, Rabbi Cohen's life was dramatized on NBC's weekly radio series *Frontiers of Faith*. The ballad that opened the broadcast included these lyrics:

> In all the state of Texas from Fort Worth to San Antone
> There's not a man who hasn't heard of Rabbi Henry Cohen.
> The sick, the poor, the needy, no matter what their creed
> His heart was always open to his fellow man in need . . .
> And his story bears repeatin' time and time again
> For it teaches us the meanin' of the brotherhood of men.[11]

ACKNOWLEDGEMENTS

Much of this essay is drawn from Henry Cohen II's article, "A Forgotten Tzaddik," *CCAR Journal: A Reform Jewish Quarterly* 53 (Winter 2006), and from Henry Cohen II, *Kindler of Souls: Rabbi Henry Cohen of Texas* (Austin: University of Texas Press, 2007).

NOTES

1. Webb Waldron, "The Busiest Man in Town," *Rotarian*, February 1939, reprinted as "First Citizen of Texas," in *Reader's Digest*, February 1939, 97–98; Anne Nathan and Harry I. Cohen, *The Man Who Stayed in Texas* (New York: Whittlesey House, 1941); *Frontiers of Faith* series, NBC Television, May 15, 1955; Natalie Ornish, *Pioneer Jewish Texans* (Dallas: Texas Heritage Press, 1989), 119–30; Hollace Ava Weiner, *Jewish Stars in Texas*, (College Station: Texas A&M University Press, 1999), 58–79; Henry Cohen, "A Forgotten Tzaddik," *CCAR Journal: A Reform Jewish Quarterly* 53 (Winter 2006); Henry Cohen, *Kindler of Souls: Rabbi Henry Cohen of Texas* (Austin: University of Texas Press, 2007); Jimmy Kessler, *Henry Cohen: The Life of a Frontier Rabbi* (Austin: Eakin Press, 1997).

2. Bernard Marinbach, *Galveston: Ellis Island of the West* (Albany: SUNY Press, 1983), 12.

3. Morris Waldman, "The Galveston Movement," *Jewish Social Service Quarterly* (March 1928): 203.

4. Alexander Ziskind Gurwitz, "Memories of Two Generations," vols. I and II, 1924, typescript, trans. from Yiddish, Box 3A187, TJHS Collection, Center for American History, University of Texas, Austin.

5. Marinbach, "Ellis Island of the West," 104, 114, 181–95.

6. Meigs Frost, *New Orleans Times-Picayune*, December 3, 1936.

7. W. H. Taft Papers, Reel 414, Library of Congress.

8. Henry Cohen, "What Constitutes a Successful Ministry," speech, Central Conference of American Rabbis, Cape May, New Jersey, June 30, 1922, reprinted in *Henry Cohen: Messenger of the Lord*, ed. A. Stanley Dreyfus (New York: Bloch, 1963), 33.

9. "Report of Committee on After Care of Prisoners," p. 3, Henry Cohen Papers, Prison Records, Center for American History, University of Texas.

10. David Frisch, "Some Memories of 1920 Broadway," in Dreyfus, *Henry Cohen*, 45.

11. Irve Tunick, "An American Ballad," *Frontiers of Faith* series, NBC Television, May 15, 1955.

Deep in the Heart of Palestine Zionism in Early Texas

STUART ROCKOFF

As secretary of the Federation of American Zionists, Jacob De Haas traveled around the country building support for the fledgling movement. When he reached Texas in late December of 1904, he did not know what to expect, for the South had lagged behind other parts of the country in fervor for the Zionist cause. While there were a few small Zionist societies in the Lone Star State, there were no coordinated efforts among them. De Haas's first stop was Beaumont. There, his speech inspired the creation of the city's very first Zionist society, with fifty members. Houston already had the Zionist Federation of Houston, and De Haas spoke at a mass meeting presided over by a Reform rabbi, Henry Barnstein of Beth Israel. Barnstein was so interested in the cause that his Jewish study class was reading Theodore Herzl's *Jewish State*, the book that sparked the modern Zionist movement. In Galveston, De Haas credited Rabbi Henry Cohen for the city's strong Jewish sentiment and noted that all the Jews that he encountered there "may be said truly to be Zionists in spirit," though only a minority actually supported the movement. In Waco, De Haas found one of the state's earliest and strongest Zionist enclaves. At the Waco meeting held on Christmas Day, a large crowd turned out to hear the American Zionist leader. He later addressed crowds in San Antonio, a Zionist stronghold, and in Dallas, where he reinvigorated the Zionist organization.

De Haas's successful 1904 tour defies conventional wisdom about Southern views toward Zionism and highlights an often hidden corner of Texas-Jewish history. Zionism has been an important force among Texas Jews since the founding of the modern movement in 1897. While much attention has been given to the opposition of Texas Jews to the quest for a Jewish homeland in Palestine, with a heavy emphasis on the 1943 schism within Houston's Congregation Beth Israel, Zionism flourished in Texas during the first half of the twentieth century. Texas Zionism focused on two goals: to support the small but growing Jewish settlements in Palestine, and to strengthen Jewish identity in Texas during an era of immigration and assimilation. While Texas Jews did their part toward the creation of Israel, the most direct impact of state and local Zionist organizations was to create a community in which Jews could feel comfort and pride in their Jewishness even as they became Texans.

In his published account in the *Maccabaean Magazine*, the official publication of the Federation of American Zionists, De Haas painted a portrait of Texas Zionism in 1904 as a small, undeveloped movement with great potential. His tour proved to be the catalyst for Texas Zionists to organize more effectively and spread their cause.

While in San Antonio, De Haas was amazed to meet Austrian-born Dr. Sigmund Burg, a health officer for the city of San Antonio, who had been among the original members of the Jewish Kadimah Society at the University of Vienna, a hotbed of Jewish national-

Zionist support in Houston. The 1911 Texas Zionist Association convention in Houston paid homage to the Stars and Stripes and to Eretz Yisrael. The group photo appeared in the Houston Post on January 4, 1911, and was taken by professional photographer Joe Litterst. Courtesy of Clayton Library Friends and the Harris County Archives, Houston, Texas.

ism more than a decade before Herzl's founding of modern Zionism. Burg had immigrated to the United States in 1889 and eventually settled in San Antonio, where in 1897 he founded the state's first Zionist group, *Mevasereth Zion*, or Message of Zion. With his strong connection to many of the Zionist pioneers in Europe, Burg was a natural to lead Texas Zionists. Burg also brought his good friend Louis Freed to the cause. Freed, born in Tennessee in 1872, moved to Texas with his family the following year. Although he sold life insurance to earn a living, Freed's passion was Zionism, and he served intermittently as president of the Texas Zionist Association for more than twenty years between 1909 and 1938.

Burg sought to create a statewide confederation of Zionist groups. On December 31, 1905, representatives from six cities gathered at Houston's Adath Yeshurun synagogue to form the Texas Zionist Association. Although nearly all delegates were Orthodox, a Reform rabbi, Joseph Friedlander of Beaumont, was made president of the new organization.

The delegates who gathered at Adath Yeshurun drafted a constitution, proclaiming the object of the TZA to be coordinating the work of Zionist groups around the state and strengthening support in Texas for Jewish nationalism abroad. To spread the Zionist message, they created a monthly magazine, *The Jewish Hope*, with University of Texas Professor C. Pessels as an editor and Nathan Sadovsky of San Antonio as publisher and manager. *The Jewish Hope*, which was published for two years, was at that time the only Jewish periodical published in the state. The TZA held annual conventions in which delegates from Zionist societies across Texas discussed how best to work together to achieve the creation of a Jewish homeland in Palestine. The TZA became a prototype for other states, as Zionists in California, Missouri, New Jersey, Ohio, Maryland, Wisconsin, and Pennsylvania created statewide organizations modeled on the Texas confederation.

Early on, the TZA organized new societies through its Propaganda Committee, which quickly swung into action. During the first year, Freed, Burg, and Friedlander traveled

They Pioneered Zionism in Texas

DR. S. BURG   L. A. FREED

Zionist pioneers. Sigmund Burg, M.D. (left), a "Jewish nationalist" while a student in Vienna, founded Texas's first Zionist group in 1897 in San Antonio. Burg and his American-born cohort Louis Freed, in 1905 spearheaded creation of the Texas Zionist Association, a confederation of societies that served as a model for other states. From the Book of Redemption, Dallas Jewish Historical Society archives.

statewide, giving speeches and organizing local Zionist societies. If a community had at least twenty interested people, the TZA sent a representative to speak and help them organize. The TZA met with success in Tyler, where Freed spoke twice during 1906, helping the city's new Agudath Zion society grow to thirty-five members. Freed also helped launch a Zionist group for young men and women in Fort Worth, a city that emerged as one of the state's strongest Zionist communities. Freed and Burg spoke at Temple Beth Israel, Austin's Reform congregation, where their Zionist views were endorsed by Rabbi Nathan Lublin. Right after Freed and Burg spoke, congregants formed the capitol city's first Zionist society, with fifty members, among them Lydia Littman, who soon became state TZA secretary. Freed hoped that Austin's Zionist organization would reach out to Jewish students at the University of Texas.

Wherever they traveled, Friedlander and Freed spoke before enthusiastic crowds. According to a local newspaper account of an early visit to Fort Worth, Freed spoke to the audience about the harsh conditions under which Jews lived in Russia, stressing the need for a Jewish homeland. Rabbi Friedlander followed with appeals for Jewish unity in support of the Zionist cause. The next day, the pair addressed the local Council of Jewish Women to "thoroughly explain the movement." These speeches portrayed Palestine as a potential homeland for oppressed Jews of Europe, not those who settled in America.

By 1906, Freed reported that almost a thousand Texans belonged to Zionist organizations, an impressive number given that the state's Jewish population was around sixteen thousand. Yet he assured delegates at the second TZA convention in Fort Worth that more effective efforts could easily double the membership. Freed expressed optimism for the future, since increasing Jewish immigration from Eastern Europe was bringing

*Future Zionists. American-born
Lydia Littman, top row second from
left, stands with her eight younger
sisters and her parents, Leopold,
far left, and Harriette, far right.
Lydia (1873–1965) was a charter
member of the Austin Zionist society
and long-time secretary of the Texas
Zionist Association. She helped launch
sections of the Council of Jewish Women
in Austin and Galveston. PICB 05220,
Austin History Center, Austin Public
Library.*

"good Zionist timber" to the state. Indeed, Texas's Jewish population would almost double over the next decade, and Zionists catered to these immigrants with Yiddish programs and speakers. Early on, most Zionist organizations met in Orthodox synagogues, which appealed to the growing number of Eastern European Jews. Yet Freed was not satisfied with the TZA being a predominantly immigrant association. He told fellow delegates, "We must get at the American Jew and show him the greater moral dignity he will secure, and better American citizen he will become when he is a Zionist."

Attracting American-born Jews was difficult. Of thirty-three delegates and officers who attended the 1910 TZA convention in San Antonio, thirty were immigrants, two-thirds of whom came from Russia. For the most part, these were not immigrants just off the boat. Of the twenty-six Zionists who had their immigration information recorded in the 1910 census, the average year of arrival was 1892. Only 12 percent had come to the United States after 1900. Thus, the typical Texas Zionist was an immigrant who had been in the United States for eighteen years. Indeed, most of the proceedings of the annual TZA conventions were in English, with usually only one address in Yiddish. Forty-three percent of delegates were self-employed merchants, mostly in groceries or dry goods. Over a quarter of them were professionals, including three doctors, two teachers, and a rabbi. Twenty percent were manual craftsmen, including four tailors. These Zionists were likely less affluent than the earlier immigrants and the more established German-Jewish elite of Texas. Almost half (49 percent) were renters rather than homeowners. Texas Zionism continued to be a largely immigrant movement. As late as 1930, 76 percent of Waco's Ezrath Zion Society, founded in 1898, was foreign born. These early Texas Zionists were largely part of the rising Jewish immigrant merchant class.

Despite the concentration of Eastern European immigrants, Zionism did appeal to some Reform Jews. At least in its early years, Zionist spokesmen like Freed took pains to assert that being a Zionist was in no way contradictory to being a good American. Apparently, the movement did not seem as controversial to Reform Jews as it would later become. Rabbi Barnstein felt comfortable presiding over the founding mass meeting in

1905, a position he would likely not have taken thirty-five years later when he allied with anti-Zionist forces. In Fort Worth, the young rabbi of Reform Congregation Beth-El, Joseph Jasin, emerged as a leader of Texas Zionism during his short tenure in the state. He served as a co-editor of *The Jewish Hope* and was elected president of the TZA in 1907. He moved to New York in 1908 to become secretary of the Federation of American Zionists. In these early years, Texas Reform leaders seemed open to the movement. Even if someone like Henry Barnstein did not join the cause, he clearly wanted to learn more about it. During the 1909 TZA convention in Waco, Rabbi Isidore Warsaw of that city's Reform congregation, Rodef Sholom, attended and was received warmly. Although he was not willing to commit to the cause, Warsaw described himself as "two-thirds Zionist." One exception to this openness was El Paso's Rabbi Martin Zielonka, who thwarted women's efforts to organize and sustain a local Hadassah chapter.

For many of the state's Reform rabbis, Zionism's main appeal was its efforts to revivify Jewish life in America. Leading Zionists saw the movement as the potential spark of a Jewish renaissance. During his president's report at the 1911 convention in Houston, Freed proclaimed, "There can be no true Jewish culture and advancement without a Jewish land . . . Only then will they feel a pride in their language, traditions, history." George Mayer, writing on the front page of Houston's *Jewish Herald*, described the movement as "a moral awakening, a renaissance, a new birth, so to speak, kindling anew the embers that were fast dying out and turning into ashes." This concept of regeneration was picked up by the mainstream press. In its front-page headline about the 1912 TZA convention, the *Austin Daily Statesman* reported that the "Object of This Organization Is to Perpetuate Customs, Arts, Literature and Nationality of the Race Without a Flag."

Education was an essential part of this strategy. In Houston, Zionists opened a reading room at the Orthodox synagogue Adath Yeshurun, with periodicals in Hebrew, English, German, and Yiddish, as well as books on Zionist subjects. Since the Zionist movement was committed to reestablishing Hebrew as a living language, the TZA encouraged the opening of Hebrew schools under the auspices of local Zionist societies. By 1911, Texas Zionists had formed ten Hebrew schools in seven cities, including Houston, Dallas, Fort Worth, San Antonio, Waco, Galveston, and Brenham, ranging in size from thirty-five to 120 students. Wharton Zionists soon opened their own Hebrew school, enrolling thirty students by the end of 1914. During his 1912 presidential address in Austin, Freed urged convention delegates to continue these efforts to teach Hebrew, declaring, "Our language is one of our most sacred national assets. Every cultured Jew should know something of his own language."

Zionists sought to imbue their communities with Jewish knowledge and self-pride. Several criticized Reform Judaism as being too quick to assimilate into gentile America. Louis Freed told the delegates attending the 1909 TZA convention in Waco, "The old reform school . . . bringing that compromising, apologizing spirit, imitating everything except that which is Jewish, is passing away. The Maccabaen Jew is taking his place." Freed credited Zionism for paving the way for this new, ethnically proud, unapologetic Jew while criticizing the "cringing, assimilated Jew, who would hide his identity." Many Reform Jews did fear the movement, concerned that it would lead others to question the loyalty of Jews to the United States.

Despite the fears of many anti-Zionists that the movement would isolate Jews from the Texas mainstream and lead to charges of dual loyalty and hyphenated Americanism, Zionism seemed to be welcomed by many of the state's opinion makers and political elite. In early January of 1911, the *Houston Daily Post* devoted several pages over three days to cover the TZA convention in the city. The newspaper reprinted the main speeches, including the address "Why I Am a Zionist" given by TZA secretary Lydia Littman. The *Austin Daily Statesman* gave comparable coverage the following January, running a story on its front page. Clearly, leading newspapers editors saw the work of Texas Zionists as newsworthy and mainstream.

Both newspapers mentioned local elected officials who addressed the conventions. In 1911, Houston Mayor H. B. Rice officially welcomed delegates during the convention's evening session. In 1912, the TZA held its convention on the floor of the Texas Senate in Austin, while the state legislature was out of session. The senate chamber was decorated with American, Texas, and Zionist flags. During a public mass meeting, Governor Oscar Colquitt and Austin's Mayor Alexander Wooldridge addressed delegates and supporters. According to the *Austin Daily Statesman*, the mayor and governor "were seldom more in harmony with an occasion." Both extolled the virtues of the Jewish people, with Mayor Wooldridge declaring that if he were a Jew, he too would be an ardent Zionist, and he wished the delegates success in their work. Governor Colquitt also declared himself a friend of the Jews, asserting, "I don't know but four or five Jews in Texas who are not my friend." During his speech, the governor pulled out his personal Bible, citing Psalm 137 with its invocation, "If I forget you, O Jerusalem, let my right hand wither, let my tongue stick to my palate," as proof of the correctness of the Zionist cause.

Governor Colquitt saw no contradiction between being a good Zionist and a good Texan. Indeed, Texas Zionists were proud of their home state and sought to leave its distinctive mark on the Holy Land. At their 1909 convention in Waco, TZA delegates adopted a plan to purchase land in Palestine for a colony called "Texas." They created the Texas Palestine Land Company and set the ambitious goal of raising one hundred thousand dollars. They failed to attract enough financial support, and the TZA chose instead to join with St. Louis Zionists in their efforts to raise money to buy land for Jewish settlement in Palestine.

Yet the dream of creating a Jewish colony that bore the name of the Lone Star State did not die. In 1934, the Texas Zionist Association created *Nachlath* Texas, an effort to purchase property—or *nachlath* in Hebrew—for a Jewish colony in Palestine. Rabbi H. Raphael Gold of Dallas's Congregation Shearith Israel conceived of the project during the buildup toward the centennial celebration of Texas independence. He wrote, "The name of this great commonwealth [Texas] ought to be linked to a living dynamic Jewish movement—the Zionist movement . . . The Texas pioneers founded a city by the name of 'Palestine,' in the northeastern part of the state, thus hallowing the name of the Jewish national homeland."[1] Rabbi Gold called on fellow Zionists "to return the historic compliment" by founding and naming a settlement in Eretz Yisrael "*Nachlath* Texas." The Texas Centennial Commission appreciated this gesture, and its chairman, Cullen F. Thomas, even donated to the cause, writing, "Such an enterprise happily links our beloved Texas to that sacred land." By the end of 1938, they had raised twenty-eight thousand dollars and entered into a formal agreement with the Keren Kayemeth Leisrael (Jewish National Fund) to allot one thousand dunams (around 250 acres) of land in the upper Galilee region for the settlement. While Texas Jews would have first priority for settling in *Nachlath* Texas, this colony was designed for European Jewish refugees. The dream of *Nachlath* Texas apparently did not materialize. Nonetheless, the desire to leave Texas's mark on the Holy Land shows how much Lone Star Zionists loved their home state.

In December 1917, Houston Zionists gathered at the Jewish Literary Society Hall in celebration of Zion Flag Day. The hall was decorated with the colors of both the United States and the Zionist movement. The blue-and-white *Magen David* (Jewish star or shield of David) emblem, which would later appear on the flag of Israel, hung side by side with Old Glory. The meeting opened with the singing of "America," followed by recitation of the Zionist Oath as the audience stood with right hands raised. Miss Lena Mendelsohn, a vocalist, performed two songs. Speeches followed, with Orthodox rabbi Wolf Wilner discussing the Zionist flag and Louis Freed discussing the responsibility of Jews to re-build Zion. Three small Zionist flags were auctioned off, with one audience member pay-ing twenty-five dollars for the privilege of pinning one to his lapel. Flags depicting Zion-ist leaders, such as Theodore Herzl, Louis Brandeis, Stephen Wise, Henrietta Szold, and even Texas's own Louis Freed, sold for a dollar apiece. The meeting came to a close with the Zionist anthem, "Hatikvah."

This mass meeting was typical of those held in other major Texas cities. Zionists used these events to energize their membership and inform them about developments in the movement. Usually coinciding with significant occasions—such as the annual TZA con-vention, the anniversary of Theodore Herzl's death, and the announcement of the 1917 Balfour Declaration—mass meetings were a mix of entertainment, oratory, patriotism, and fundraising. These gatherings encapsulated the diverse activities of local Zionist or-ganizations around the state.

In addition to big-city groups in Houston, Dallas, Fort Worth, Galveston, and San An-tonio, Zionist societies sprouted in small towns such as Corpus Christi, Terrell, Laredo, Kilgore, Corsicana, and Breckenridge. Zionist groups ranged from the socialist Poale Zion and Pioneer Women to Hadassah and various youth groups, such as the Texas Young Zionists Society and the Sons and Daughters of Zion. Another indicator of wide-spread Zionist support is the fact that between 1928 and 1938, Jews in eighty-five different Texas communities donated to the Jewish National Fund, which purchased land for Jewish settlement in Palestine.

Zionist societies engaged in a wide range of activities to meet their twin goals of es-tablishing a Jewish homeland and revitalizing Jewish life in Texas. Local organizations brought a series of leading Zionists to Texas to educate and organize communities and raise money. A list of these speakers is a virtual "who's who" of the world Zionist move-ment, including Louis Lipsky, president of the Zionist Organization of America; Vlad-imir Jabotinsky, the Zionist revisionist leader; Henrietta Szold, founder of Hadassah; Tamar de Sola Poole, three-time Hadassah national president; David Ben-Gurion, Israel's

TWO YIDDISH LECTURES
— BY —
MR. BEN GURRION
The Famous Jewish Orator
Under the Auspices of the Poale Zion of San Antonio

FIRST LECTURE—Sunday, Feb 6, 1916, 8 P M.—
AT MOOSE HALL, COR. CROCKETT AND LOSOYA
Subject—"The Possibility of a Jewish Home in Palestine."

SECOND LECTURE—Monday Feb. 7, 1916, 8 P. M.—
AT REDMEN'S HALL, 112 SOLEDAD ST.
Subject—"The Necessity of a Jewish Congress in America."

|TICKET (admitting holder to the two Lectures), 25c

Two for a quarter. David Ben-Gurion, future Israeli Prime Minister, delivered two lectures in Yiddish when his speaking tour stopped in San Antonio in February 1916. The Socialist organization, Poale Zion, sold tickets to both meetings for twenty-five cents. Files of the Jewish Community of San Antonio Research Project, in the Texana/Genealogy Department, San Antonio Public Library.

History in the making. Chaim Weizmann (1874–1952), second from left, president of the World Zionist Organization, visited Dallas in 1924, drawing followers from Dallas and Fort Worth. From the Book of Redemption, *Dallas Jewish Historical Society archives.*

first prime minister; Itzhak Ben-Zvi, who became Israel's second president; and Chaim Weizmann, president of the World Zionist Organization, who would become Israel's first president.

Szold traveled through the state in 1912, 1914, and 1917 to speak and to organize Hadassah chapters. Initially, she encountered indifference among women in Houston and was encouraged to visit nearby Wharton. There in 1914, she met with seven women and formed the state's first Hadassah chapter. Because a minimum of ten females were required to create a Hadassah "circle," three of the women's young daughters were recruited. "That is how I became a Hadassah member at age six," recalled Mary Mayer Rosenfield. Szold later addressed the TZA's twelfth annual convention in December 1917 and afterward traveled around the state, raising money for the Palestine Restoration Fund. In Dallas, her visit led to creation of the city's Hadassah chapter the following year. In Houston, where a Hadassah chapter finally was organized in 1919, locals reported that Szold's words were "by far the deepest, most logical and inspiring that have so far been presented to a Houston public." The visits of Szold and other international

Young Zionists, circa 1910. Among the charter members of Young Zionists of Dallas were E. L. Doctoroff, left, Charlie Bender (later known as the Texas Cowboy Zionist), and Lew Todes. Courtesy Rabbi Wayne M. Franklin, Providence, RI.

figures played a crucial role linking Texas Zionists to the world movement. Regardless of how far they were from Palestine, Texas Jews could be part of worldwide efforts to establish a Jewish homeland.

Aside from serious meetings, Zionists also staged celebrations for the cause. Most popular were dances and balls that raised money and attracted members. The Young Zionists of Dallas hosted regular dances during the early 1910s, the first of which drew seventy-five couples. In Houston, the Herzl Zionist Society and the Sons and Daughters of Zion held an annual *Simchas Torah* Ball that raised money with its fifty-cent admission and promised a wonderful time "to those who are fond of tripping 'the light fantastic toe.'" Even San Antonio's Poale Zion, the socialist labor Zionist organization, held a gala in 1922 and awarded prizes to the best dancers.

In Houston, the annual Zionist picnic in 1910 attracted aspiring politicians vying for the Jewish vote. According to one account, the candidates' "generosity helped to make the occasion a financial success." In 1938, San Antonio Zionists held a fundraising picnic for the Jewish National Fund at Koehler Park. The big draw was clearly the food, as the organizing committee served traditional picnic fare like hamburgers and hot dogs, as well as hot tamales. Also on the menu were "especially prepared dishes of Gefilte Fish and Belintzes and Strudel."

In 1941, Jacob Levin, the principal of the Hebrew School of Dallas, opened Camp Bonim, designed as an outgrowth of the local Labor Zionist youth group. According to its brochure, the camp sought to "fortify today's youth for Zion's epic struggle" through Jewish educational and cultural programs in addition to such traditional camp activities as swimming, rowing, baseball, and badminton. Campers drawn from cities and small towns across the state learned Hebrew, as well as the history of the Zionist movement. But Camp Bonim was not all serious, judging by the gossip columns of the camper-produced newsletter, the *Blue and White*, which detailed who was courting whom at the camp. The camp closed in 1951 when Levin and other camp leaders moved away.

Labor Zionist summers. This Camp Bonim brochure, picturing a Zionist flag alongside the Stars and Stripes, was mailed to prospective campers in 1946. The camp, which operated near Dallas from 1941 to 1951, supplemented summer activities such as swimming and baseball with Hebrew and the history of Zionism. From the Ginger Chesnick Jacobs Papers, Dallas Jewish Historical Society archives.

One might wonder what summer camps, balls, picnics, and dance contests had to do with creating a Jewish homeland in Palestine. In fact, they helped achieve the other central goal of the movement in Texas, the strengthening of local Jewish life. Social events and educational activities helped Texas Jews, who made up fewer than one percent of the state's population, create a uniquely Jewish world that could withstand pressures of assimilation. Jewish nationalism was a natural response to life as a tiny minority in this far corner of the Diaspora. For many Texas Jews, Zionism was a means to ensure the survival of Judaism in the Lone Star State.

"The Gang," 1945. Camp Bonim's founder, Jacob Levin, stands, back row, second from left, with staff, counselors, and other regulars at the summer Labor Zionist youth camp outside Dallas. Courtesy of Ginger Chesnick Jacobs.

As for the goal of establishing a Jewish homeland, Texas Jews embraced their role as fundraisers. From its earliest founding, the Texas movement understood Zionism as a solution to Europe's Jewish problem, not something that would directly affect their own lives. Most were happy in Texas and had no desire to move to Palestine, but they saw a Jewish homeland as crucial for Jews suffering across Europe. Thus, the practical goal of raising money to support the settlement of Jews in Palestine usually took center stage. In 1912, Jews in Houston founded the Houston Zion Society on the principle "money first, talk next," since "without money, very little can be accomplished in Palestine." The group contributed significant amounts to the Jewish National Fund.

With the challenges and opportunities created by World War I and the 1917 Balfour Declaration, which stated Great Britain's support for a Jewish homeland in Palestine, Zionists began to raise money for the Palestine Restoration Fund. Texas was given a quota of $14,500, with Galveston, Houston, and San Antonio asked to raise the largest sums of three thousand dollars each. Between 1928 and 1938, during the depths of the Depression, Texans donated over sixty-five thousand dollars to the Jewish National Fund. To meet emergencies, Zionists raised additional money. Attacks by Arabs on Jews in Palestine in 1938 led San Antonio's Pioneer Women to raise money to help pay for watchmen to protect Jewish settlements. The women converted their Social Club Fund into a Self Defense Fund. This fundraising work received an official endorsement when Texas Governor James V. Allred declared January 20, 1935, to be Palestine Day in the state, "to pay tribute to the ideals of justice that animated the nations of the earth, including our own, in approving the re-establishment of the Jewish homeland in Palestine."

Later that year, Lily Dow, a twenty-seven-year-old Zionist active in Hadassah, asked to speak at Houston's Congregation Beth Israel on Henrietta Szold's birthday. Rabbi Harry Barnston—who had by then anglicized the spelling of his surname—and temple leaders informed Dow that she could speak only if she avoided presenting "any Zionist propaganda." Indeed, despite support for Zionism from among Texas's political leadership, a number of Jews in the state grew increasingly nervous as Zionism gained momentum around the world. These anti-Zionists were usually Reform Jews who rejected the notion that Jews constituted a separate people who needed their own homeland. They feared that a Jewish state would subject American Jews to charges of dual loyalty and challenge the social and political acceptance that Reform Jews had worked so hard to achieve. Disputes over Zionism came to a head in Houston in the early 1940s, as members of Congregation Beth Israel fought over the issue of Zionism and the meaning of Reform Judaism.

Beth Israel had not always been so hostile toward Zionism. As early as 1909, five of the thirty-seven donors to the Herzl Zion Society for the Jewish National Fund were Beth Israel congregants. Rabbi Barnston, as noted, spoke at early Zionist events and did not openly oppose the movement. In 1926, the TZA and the Texas Federation of Hadassah held a joint convention in Houston, with several sessions convening at Beth Israel. This was likely due to the involvement of Henry Dannenbaum, a past congregational president and ardent Zionist. In 1920, Dannenbaum served as chairman of the National Zionist Convention in Cleveland.

By the end of the 1930s, the darkening situation across the Atlantic led more and more American Jews to support the idea of a Jewish homeland as a haven for Europe's endangered Jewish population. Among the proponents was a new generation of Reform rabbis, including Robert Kahn, associate rabbi at Houston's Beth Israel. Rabbi Kahn en-

Palestine Day in Texas. Governor James Allred officially proclaimed January 20, 1935, as Palestine Day throughout the Lone Star State. From the Book of Redemption, the Dallas Jewish Historical Society archives.

PROCLAMATION
BY THE   NO. ~~____~~ 1471 1
Governor of the State of Texas

Form 2081—G618-921-10M

TO ALL TO WHOM THESE PRESENTS SHALL COME:

January 16 1935

WHEREAS, citizens of this State are planning to memorialize the phenomenal Progress that has been recorded in the modern reconstruction of the Holy Land through the observance on January 20th of Palestine Day, and

WHEREAS, the object of this celebration is to pay tribute to the ideals of justice that animated the nations of the earth, including our own, in approving the re-establishment of the Jewish homeland in Palestine, and to take note of the rebirth of an ancient land that has sacred memories for Christian and Jew alike,

NOW, therefore, I, James V. Allred, Governor of the State of Texas, do set aside and declare Sunday, January 20, 1935, as Palestine Day as an expression of appreciation to an undertaking conceived in nobility and executed in idealism;

And I urge all citizens, regardless of faith, to participate in this celebration by devoting public programs to an exposition of the achievements that have been registered in restoring to modern civilization a land holy to us through centuries of religious sentiment and tradition.

IN TESTIMONY WHEREOF, I, James V. Allred, have hereunto set my hand and caused the official seal to be affirmed hereto this 16th day of January, A. D. 1935.

James V. Allred
Governor of Texas

ATTEST:

Gerald C. Mann
Secretary of State

tered the military chaplaincy during World War II, during which time the long-serving senior rabbi, Henry Barnston, announced his retirement. The leaders of Beth Israel did not wish to make an outspoken Zionist like Rabbi Kahn their new senior rabbi, so they hired New York Rabbi Hyman Judah Schachtel, one of the leaders and charter members of the American Council for Judaism, an organization of rabbis and laity opposed to a

Chaplain's School. Rabbi Robert I. Kahn, with a tallis draped over his uniform, reads from the Torah while attending Army chaplain training sessions at Harvard University in 1942. Collection of Hollace Weiner.

Jewish state. Before Rabbi Schachtel assumed his Houston position, Beth Israel's board took further steps to ensure that the classical Reform and anti-Zionist nature of the congregation would be preserved during a period of tremendous membership growth.

Fearing that newcomers to Houston were more traditional in their religious practice and supported political Zionism, the temple board issued a set of "Basic Principles" that new members would have to endorse in order to obtain full voting rights within the congregation. The Basic Principles asserted, "We consider ourselves no longer a nation but we are a religious community and, therefore, we expect neither a return to Palestine nor a restoration of any of the laws concerning the Jewish state." Other items reasserted classical Reform principles issued in the Pittsburgh Platform of 1885, including a rejection of Talmudic laws concerning food and dress and the endorsement of the religious equality of men and women.

Houston's rival rabbis, Robert I. Kahn, left, and Hyman Judah Schachtel, during a ceremony in Houston. Kahn, in this undated photo, wears his chaplain's tallis. Courtesy Congregation Beth Israel of Houston, est. 1854.

These Basic Principles were the topic of a contentious congregational meeting on November 23, 1943. The pro-Zionist opposition had worked hard to derail the new membership requirements. A group published the *Beth Israel Sentinel*, a four-page broadsheet with detailed arguments against the "Basic Principles." The *Sentinel* accused the temple board of undermining democratic principles by "cramming down the throats of free men, under the threat of possible excommunication, their own anti-Zionism." During the congregational meeting, William Nathan, a one-time temple board member, rose to denounce the current board's actions. Nathan stated that while he was not a Zionist, he opposed any ideological test for membership. Despite this opposition, the principles passed overwhelmingly, 632 to 168.

Not long after this divisive vote, many in the opposition, including William Nathan, resigned from Beth Israel and formed a new Reform congregation, Emanu El, hiring Robert Kahn as their rabbi. This schism within Beth Israel created long-lasting bitterness among friends and families, as well as between Kahn and Schachtel, who both served their congregations for several more decades. While Zionism was an underlying cause of the dispute, it was only one part of a much larger debate over the very nature of Reform Judaism and Jewish identity. Nevertheless, the conflict over the Basic Principles reflected the often-bitter debate between Zionists and anti-Zionists in Texas.

It also marked the last gasp of this debate. Six months after Israel was founded in 1948, Rabbi Schachtel resigned from the American Council for Judaism. Former anti-Zionists saw that the creation of a Jewish state did not lead to charges of disloyalty or an upsurge in American anti-Semitism. The once-controversial issue had been settled, and Beth Israel soon adjusted to the reality of Israel. When Israel's survival was threatened

Nurturing the dream. Families decked out in their finest clothing attended the 1908 Texas Zionist Association convention at Dallas's Shearith Israel. They assembled for a group portrait beneath American and Zionist flags and a Magen David with "Zion" printed at its center. Morris Fair Collection, Dallas Jewish Historical Society archives.

during the Six Day War of 1967, Beth Israel members joined fellow Houston Jews raising money for the besieged country. The Basic Principles were repealed formally without a dissenting vote in 1968, though they had long since fallen into disuse. In 1969, the Zionist Council of Houston celebrated Israel's twenty-first anniversary at the city's Conservative congregation, Beth Yeshurun. The main speaker for the event was Rabbi Schachtel of Beth Israel.

Texas Zionists had witnessed a remarkable chain of events, highlighted by the founding of Israel in 1948. From the creation of the first Zionist organizations in Texas fifty years earlier, Texas Jews worked to make Zionist dreams a reality. And while anti-Zionism grew as the movement progressed, once Zionism had achieved its ultimate goal, Texas Jews united in support of the newborn Jewish state.   ✶

NOTES

1. The East Texas city of Palestine—pronounced "Pal-es-teen"—was founded in 1846, well before the Zionist movement. It had a small, organized Jewish community that peaked in 1900 with around a hundred people, never organized a Zionist association, and dissipated during the Great Depression.

REFERENCES

The best sources for early Texas Zionism are the state's Jewish newspapers, which regularly reported on Zionist activities around the state. These include Houston's *Texas Jewish Herald*, Fort Worth's *Jewish Monitor*, and San Antonio's *San Antonio Jewish Weekly*, *Jewish Record*, and *Texas Jewish Press*. Microfilm copies of these newspapers are at the Center for American History (CAH) at the University of Texas at Austin. Major events and annual conventions were also covered in the state's daily newspapers. An essential source is *The Book of Redemption*, a commemorative volume published by the Southwestern Jewish National Fund in 1939, which contains a tremendous amount of material about the Jewish communities of Texas at the time, in addition to information about Zionist organizations. A trove of Zionist documents is archived in the collection of the Texas Jewish Historical Society at the CAH in Austin. Most notable among these are speeches and letters from longtime TZA President Louis Freed. Also Jacob DeHaas's write-up of his 1904 trip to Texas, originally printed in *Maccabaean Magazine* (vol. 7, pp. 22–31) is here reprinted in the journal *Forum*. Information and photos on the Zionist youth movement in Dallas are best detailed in Ginger Chesnick Jacobs's book *The Levin Years: A Golden Era . . . 1929–1951—Dallas, Texas, Hebrew School of Dallas and its Extended Activities* (Dallas: Ginger C. Jacobs, Dallas Jewish Historical Society, 1989). Founding dates of Hadassah chapters and early documents were provided by Susan Woodland, Hadassah archivist in New York.

The minutes of Waco's Ezrath Zion society are preserved at the American Jewish Archives in Cincinnati. These offer insightful perspective on the work of a local organization. The AJA also has a great deal of material on the Beth Israel schism, including the correspondence file of William Nathan, one of the major figures in the dispute. Congregation Beth Israel's archives has the original copy of a remarkable document, "The History of the Official Adoption of 'The Basic Principles' by Congregation Beth Israel," prepared by board member Israel Friedlander in response to the tremendous criticism that the congregation received. Houston's Temple Emanu El has a collection of oral histories with founding members, as well as additional papers from William Nathan.

I would like to thank Devhra Bennett Jones of the American Jewish Archives, Kerry Hoffman of the Temple Beth Israel Archives, and Myra Lipper of Emanu El for their help with my research.

West Texas oil strike, ca. 1920s, exact location unknown. Courtesy, Jack White Photograph Collection, Special Collections, The University of Texas at Arlington Libraries, Arlington, Texas.

The Entrepreneurial Era Leaving Their Mark

II

West Texas Wildcatters

From Immigrant to Patron Saint Rita

BARRY SHLACHTER

Chance encounters, one aboard a train, the other five days later on a Fort Worth street, set in motion a series of events that turned a Lithuanian-born Jewish dry goods merchant into a successful wildcatter—a term of respect earned by independent oilmen who drilled unproven fields. Haymon Krupp's initial well, the Santa Rita No. 1, opened up West Texas's vast Permian Basin, enriching himself and his partner and helping to transform the impoverished University of Texas from a jumble of wooden shanties into a world-class institution with an endowment second to none among public universities. Krupp, a gray-eyed, self-confident entrepreneur with the heart of a high-stakes gambler, was a Jewish wildcatter of the Roaring Twenties, and he was not alone.

Other Jews seeking riches in the go-for-broke industry as it swept the state during the first third of the last century included hard-drinking Sam Weiner, who sometimes bet the roof over his children's beds and lost, and Fred Fuhrman, an urbane, horseback-riding oilman who ran thoroughbreds at the race track at Ruidoso, New Mexico. Like Krupp, Weiner and Fuhrman were self-educated immigrants who began in far different trades. The Latvian-born Weiner was a haberdasher, a jewelry salesman, a grocer, and a salvage-pipe dealer. The German-born Fuhrman sold Florsheim shoes in Cuba and Mexico. A self-taught oilman who personally oversaw the drilling, Fuhrman would make his mark with the first big strike in West Texas's Andrews County in 1931—with no help from geologists, whom he disdained. The gusher did not bring immediate wealth. Fuhrman waited three long years before a major oil company, Humble, agreed to build a pipeline so the well's output could be sold. He was a private man, and few in Midland, where he made his home, would know he rescued all remaining family members from Germany before Hitler closed the borders to Jews. Married and divorced twice, Fuhrman left no children, but his heirs include offspring of relatives whom he brought out of Europe.

WAITING FOR THE NEXT WELL

A second generation of wildcatters, including Sam Weiner's three sons, grew up in small Texas towns. Formal higher education often was the exception to the rule. Yet there were some radical personal makeovers. Weiner's oldest son Ted, born in 1911, was yanked out of military school after one semester and often pulled out of bed to finish his father's fights. He went from piecing together drilling rigs with cannibalized parts to hobnobbing with movie stars, golf legends, and internationally renowned artists. He also assembled one of the region's finest private collections of modern sculpture.

Striking it rich. The Boner B-2 rig struck oil in March 1935, with Fred Fuhrman among the onlookers at its base. Fuhrman, along with Haymon Krupp and Sam Weiner, sought his fortune in the unpredictable world of Texas oil. Abell-Hanger Foundation Photograph Collection, Courtesy of the Petroleum Museum, Midland, Texas.

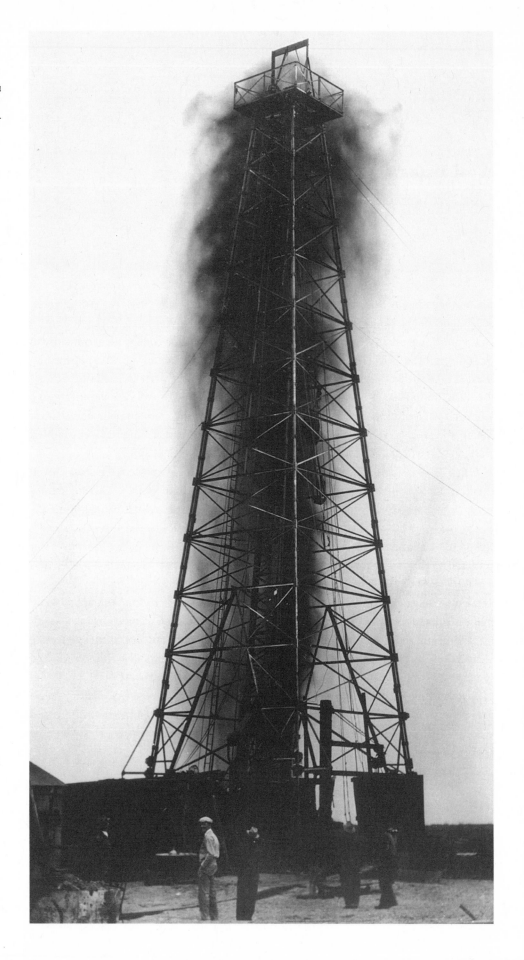

Sam "Skipper" Weiner (1880–1957). A whiskey-drinking wanderer and patriarch of a Texas wildcatting family, Sam Weiner never wore a suit and tie. This photo portrait, made for the Petroleum Museum's Hall of Fame, was created by placing Sam's head on a suited torso. Hall of Fame Photograph Collection, Courtesy of the Petroleum Museum, Midland, Texas.

Sam Weiner lived the classic rags-to-riches immigrant story but with a twist. His childhood had an itinerant Huck Finn quality. Surviving by his wits, he hopped about the country on freight cars without parental supervision. He was born in 1880 near Riga, Latvia, where his father, Tevya Pripic, was a fur trader. Tevya bribed the family's way out of Eastern Europe to join a son already settled in the United States.

Ten-year-old Sam broke both legs jumping a border fence and was left behind to convalesce in Bremen, Germany, and make his own way to America while the rest of the household sailed west. Blessed with an uncanny ability to forge friendships, a skill that would help him throughout his many careers, in 1892 Sam traveled alone to the United States and found a benefactor in a cook on the Cunard liner. He was given better food and berthing for helping lug five-gallon pots of boiled potatoes down to other emigrants in steerage. After he cleared bureaucratic hurdles at Ellis Island, a Jewish immigrant aid society put Sam on a train for western New York state with a ninety-pound sack of needles and notions, a newcomer's barter survival kit.

By then his mother had died. His father, who had borrowed a relative's surname and become known as Theodore Weiner, had remarried a much younger woman whom Sam could not abide. Before turning fourteen, Sam decided to meet up with his oldest sibling, Max, who had become established in Mississippi. Sam worked his way southward, first in coalmines and oil fields in Pennsylvania and West Virginia, where he picked up a working knowledge of the fledgling petroleum industry. "He never saw the inside of a classroom," said a son, Charles Weiner. A butcher's wife in Baltimore taught him how to scribble his signature.

Sam Weiner's childhood included a stint exercising horses at the old Jefferson track in Metairie, Louisiana, and riding the rails, hobo-style, to Memphis and Chicago, receiving several beatings at the hands of railroad detectives. By freight car, he arrived in Corsicana, fifty-five miles south of Dallas, where he peddled jewelry to oilmen and roustabouts. In 1910, he married Lillian "Lili" Blanc, a sixteen-year-old New York native raised in the New Orleans Jewish Children's Home and by then working as a telephone operator at Washer Brothers, a men's clothing store in Fort Worth. Lili had an appreciation for music and could whistle most any song. Lili and "Skipper," as Sam was called, were introduced by a local rabbi, presumably G. George Fox, who married them at Beth-El Congregation. It was to be one of the few times Sam Weiner would find himself in a synagogue.

The couple's first son, Ted, was born in Texas in 1911. A daughter, Ruth, followed in 1914 after the family had moved to California. She died in a streetcar accident at age seven. In California, Weiner sold diamonds on commission, then used his earnings to buy a grocery store in Alameda. There he met a hobo named Jack Dempsey, later to be a famed prizefighter and a lifelong friend. Ready to take risks, Weiner sold his grocery to invest in furs to sell to Montana copper miners. He arrived to find them on strike. His investment lost, Weiner, whose family had grown to include a baby boy, Stanley, born in 1918, moved to Little Rock, Arkansas, where his brother Max had resettled. Starting yet another trade, Sam Weiner peddled civilian clothes to discharged soldiers, reselling their castoff uniforms. In Arkansas, the family grew with two more children—Marjorie born in 1922 and Charles in 1924. Sam opened a Little Rock men's shop, traded in oil leases, and, as always, gambled on cards and cockfights, sometimes grooming his own game roosters. With an old sparring partner of Dempsey's, Bobby Manzel, Weiner raised money for small oil ventures in El Dorado until again losing everything—three small clothing shops, a Cadillac, a Nash, a Chrysler, a number of oil leases, and his home—in a poker game. "The El Dorado oil boom was over and he was gambling more than he was earning," his son Charles was to recall.

Moving yet again, Sam Weiner worked in Pyote, a West Texas town with more rattle-snakes than people, before reuniting his family in nearby Wink, located in Winkler County on the New Mexico state line. There he set up the Westerly Supply Company with a partner, Colonel Lawrence Orlov, in 1927. Each putting up two hundred dollars, they bought used equipment and pipe from major oil companies, repaired the machinery and straightened the pipe, then sold or bartered them to wildcatters. Some wildcatters, like Sid Richardson who became a philanthropist and political insider, later struck it rich. Many others did not settle accounts for years.

Wink was a wild boomtown. Scores of men rented cots by the shift in crude shacks. Violence and graft were common. When a sheriff's deputy arrested a dozen gamblers, a local mobster's enforcers broke into jail, freed the men, and tethered the deputy in chains. Arrests were selective: Out-of-town holdup men were hunted down with a vengeance; locally based bandits, who robbed oil workers on payday, never ended up in jail. Texas Rangers made a few successful raids until corrupt Wink officials began tipping off the crooks. Lawlessness, bootlegging, and prostitution were so out of hand by 1928 that a state judge revoked the city's charter. Several vice lords, including Charles "Heavy" Brackteen, who had the sheriff and then his "reformist" successor on the payroll, controlled the community. Few messed with Brackteen, but Sam Weiner never passed up a good punch. This one ended with the Jewish wildcatter gouged in the head with a broken bottle. "I was embarrassed because Dad lost the fight," recalled Charles Weiner, then a lad of five. "But everyone else was proud because he was the only one who stood up to Heavy. It was a tough town." Another scrap with a burly truck driver was postponed until Weiner's oldest son, Ted, a physical fitness buff and a keen boxer, was pulled from bed as the father's surrogate. After the Wink police cordoned off a section of road, the pair exchanged blows for forty-five minutes until the trucker, frustrated that he could not knock Ted out, pulled a knife and stabbed the teenager in the shoulder, leaving a life-long scar.

At a low point in the late 1920s, Sam Weiner withdrew Ted from the New Mexico Military Institute in Roswell. At first, the family lived in a two-room shack with an outhouse, then moved into a house covered in sheetrock that Sam bought at a sheriff's auction for three hundred dollars. The caliche-soil yard was so hard, his sons used crowbars to break ground for a tree. Another son, named Max, born in 1930, died from scarlet fever in Wink in 1933, a devastating loss for Lili.

Whatever his fortunes at the moment, Sam Weiner dressed the same—leather jacket with gabardine shirt, riding breeches, boots, and Borsalino hat. He stood five-foot-five and was bandy-legged, a result of his childhood injury when he broke his legs jumping the border fence. Sam was never seen or photographed in a coat and tie. Posthumously inducted into the Permian Basin Petroleum Hall of Fame, his portrait was cut out and placed on the shoulders of an anonymous torso dressed more appropriately for the occasion. Sam's favorite thirst quencher was rye whiskey, made in Ochoa, New Mexico, by Brininstool's, the choice of West Texas wildcatters. He once sought legal redress when a man stole a bootleg keg from his private supply.

Like other struggling wildcatters, the Weiners often paid drilling crews in promises—a two thousand dollar bonus if oil was struck. The family's first big strike was Ted's in 1931 when he was twenty. He and a partner brought in neighboring Ward County's second major well. In 1935, Ted drilled the discovery well in the Delaware Basin, also in Ward County. Other successful wells followed, including the Weiner Pool and the Weiner-Floyd Field, both named for the wildcatting family and located in Winkler County.

In 1943, Ted Weiner began the Texas Crude Company in Fort Worth as a partnership with his two brothers, who joined him after their service in the Korean War. (Stanley ran Coral Drilling Company, an arm of Texas Crude that had offshore drilling rigs out of Louisiana. Coral would merge with Fluor Corporation in 1967.) Despite successes in the oil fields, the family was often short of cash during the early postwar years. Ted's daughter, Gwen, recalled that after the family's rented piano was returned because the payments could not be met, her father, who walked to work, surprised her mother with a $250 topaz ring accented with diamonds purchased from a desperate man on the street. A true wildcatter, he always believed in the next well.

Claude W. Brown drilled Ted Weiner's wells but, to his regret, did not always share the wildcatter's optimism. In 1984, Brown wrote: "I personally drilled wells for (Ted Weiner) in the Vaughn field, and he would try to get me to take my pay in acreage (a bonus arrangement), saying he was going to discover the biggest oil play in West Texas . . . I said, 'No, Ted, just pay me cold cash.' So I missed out on the play." The Spraberry Trend area, which Ted's drilling company hit in 1949, turned out to be one of Texas Crude's biggest strikes. Humble Oil offered forty million dollars, but Ted, after talking with his Wall Street partners, refused to sell. It became apparent later that the formation was tightly compacted, notoriously difficult to exploit, taking years to tap economically. It became viable only after Ted's brother Stanley, and others, learned to recover additional oil by flushing out the fractured rock formations with water containing various chemicals. In the end, the sixty-mile-wide and ten-mile-long field in six West Texas counties cleared about twenty million dollars for investors. The Spraberry was still pumping from more than nine thousand wells in 2005.

When the Permian Basin Petroleum Museum inducted Sam and his sons, Ted, Stan, and Charles, into its hall of fame in 1989, it noted that they were the first independents to use the so-called "carried interest concept" of oil field financing, which allowed some

Texas family scrapbook. Ted Weiner (1911–1979), visiting a West Texas drilling site, always believed in the next well. Featured here are gushers in Texas and New Mexico. Courtesy of Gwendolyn Weiner.

taxes to be deferred. After the Internal Revenue Service disallowed the accounting procedure—considered a vital investment tool for the industry—the Weiners took the dispute all the way to the United States Supreme Court, which in 1951 ruled in the oil industry's favor.

The father, who died in 1958, and three sons are also remembered in the Fort Worth Petroleum Club's book, *Oil Legends of Fort Worth*, as a singular family in the West Texas oil patch: Sam, the "rough and tumble guy who loved to gamble and rumble"; Ted, the "guy who did it all, . . . who dragged . . . up" the rest of his family; Stanley, the mechanic and field man, "who built the drilling company into the fifth largest in the world"; and Charles—the lone college graduate—the scientist and scholar with the geology degree. Well into his mid-eighties, Charles, a University of Texas alumnus and the sole-surviving member of the team, was still going to work every morning and making oil investments from his Houston office.

Though not deeply involved in their own faith, the Weiners, no doubt, had their family name invoked in many a Christian's prayer after they dismantled a storage tank for Shell Oil in Wink and donated the wood from the roof to six congregations that used it to build new churches. The Weiners had scant connection to religion. In Fort Worth, Sam's wife, Lili, was a member of the Council of Jewish Women's sewing circle. Although some of the Weiner siblings went to religious school at Beth-El Congregation, daughter Marjorie was the only one to attend regularly and to marry within the faith. Ted Weiner subscribed to Theosophy, a doctrine of thought related to universal brotherhood, harmony with nature, and spiritual and physical evolution in the world.

Ted also dabbled in moviemaking and helped finance several films, including Howard Hawks's *El Dorado*, starring John Wayne and Robert Mitchum. His Hollywood partners brought him into contact with prospective investors for oil ventures, among them Tony Curtis and Janet Leigh. It was in Fort Worth that Ted began collecting art, an interest sparked when he purchased a painting for his parents when he moved them to town. (This followed the loss of Sam Weiner's last Wink home in a poker game.) Ted and his wife Lucile constructed a 6.5-acre sculpture garden with works they collected from around the world, including pieces by Henry Moore, Jacques Lipchitz, Alexander Calder, Pablo Picasso, and Edgar Degas. One art authority called it "probably the finest collection of contemporary sculpture in the Southwest." It was Ted Weiner's desire eventually to give the collection to his hometown. But he withdrew the offer when told that Fort Worth would neither honor his request of turning his estate into a museum nor accept the art without a sizable endowment to cover maintenance. Weiner took his collection with him when he moved to Palm Springs, California, where he served on the Palm Springs Cultural Commission and where he died of cancer in 1979. Today, a number of

With oil came money and glamour. Ted Weiner, far right, helped finance several Hollywood films, and his status as a true wildcatter was a powerful lure to Tinseltown. Elvis Presley, in Army uniform, with movie producer Hal Wallis, Lucille Weiner, and Ted in the late 1950s. Courtesy of Gwendolyn Weiner.

"Texas Gold" refers to the wealth of oil that gushed from barren lands across Texas throughout the twentieth century. The map highlights some of the oil strikes and boomtowns mentioned in the chapters about West Texas wildcatters and East Texas boomtowns. Map by Garry Harman, The Artworks.

pieces from his art collection are on permanent loan to Texas Tech University in Lubbock and the Palm Springs Desert Museum, where the sculpture terrace bears his name.

The Weiners had a lasting impact on the "awl bidness" in Texas. They fought an industry tax issue at the Supreme Court and won. They attached their family name to acres of oil discoveries. But no one brought in a strike as important to Texas as Haymon Krupp's Santa Rita No. 1.

A JEW, AN IRISHMAN, AND A PATRON SAINT

Born in Kovno, Lithuania, in 1874, Haymon Krupp was one of Abraham and Malca Krupp's thirteen children. Like many Eastern European immigrants before them, the Krupps settled in New York, where Haymon learned English and lost his Old World accent in the public schools. At nearly sixteen, he headed west to El Paso to join an older brother, Harris, for whom he would work for twenty years at H. Krupp and Brother, a dry goods store. Indicative of the family's adventurous bent, another brother, Meyer, left El Paso for Nome, Alaska, where he pursued an elusive fortune in mining.

An influx of immigrants from Mexico, just across the Rio Grande, had fueled El Paso's growth from a population of 736 in 1880 to 10,838 by 1890, creating all sorts of business opportunities. Haymon Krupp applied himself to his brother's trade, quickly mastering Spanish as he had English. Nine years later he married a young New Yorker, Leah Silverman. After setting off on his own in 1910, Krupp not only opened retail and wholesale establishments but also manufactured shoes, men's work clothes, women's dresses, and Mexican shawls. At one point, his factories employed five hundred workers and

Haymon Krupp (1874–1949). Lithuanian immigrant Haymon Krupp's gamble to drill in the Permian Basin paid off for the University of Texas, which receives billions in royalties from that vast tract of West Texas land. Hall of Fame Photograph Collection, Courtesy of the Petroleum Museum, Midland, Texas.

filled orders from Texas, New Mexico, Arizona, and northern Mexico. He employed five nephews, all of whom shared the profits. His workers also benefited. His enterprises issued stock, which was given to or purchased by employees, according to Floyd Fierman, the El Paso rabbi and local historian who researched the family history.

Well before becoming a rich wildcatter in the 1920s, the wiry immigrant was civic minded. He joined the volunteer fire department in 1899. Beginning in 1914, he advertised free coal to the poor at Christmas. He donated blankets in 1917 to each soldier in a locally raised Army company upon hearing of the winter cold at their post, Fort Worth's Camp Bowie. And these were not one-time acts of philanthropy. The El Paso Times reported that Krupp continued the Yuletide gift of coal for forty years. Krupp gave generously to El Paso's two synagogues, Congregation B'nai Zion and Temple Mount Sinai, and served as president of the latter. One synagogue posthumously dedicated a hall in his name, the other a chapel. "If there is any truth in the saying that 'He who giveth to the poor leadeth to the Lord and is repaid a hundred fold,' then Haymon Krupp is a striking example of its operations, except that he has been reimbursed many thousand times in place of a mere paltry hundred," New York Times reporter Owen P. White, who grew up in El Paso, wrote on May 3, 1925. "In addition to having recently become excessively prosperous himself, Mr. Krupp has opened up a way whereby the University of Texas bids to become one of the richest institutions of learning in America."

Friendships often led to opportunities. A tenant above Krupp's wholesale dry goods store at 314 South El Paso Street was an earthy, charismatic Mexican named Francisco Villa—"Pancho" to friends, followers, and sworn enemies. Villa became a regular visitor, "shooting the breeze" each morning with the Jewish merchant, a nephew later recalled. One uncorroborated story asserts that Villa was once employed as a truck driver for a Krupp enterprise. Whatever the case, the insurgent general returned to Mexico and, after winning a series of battles, placed an order in 1911 for army uniforms—on the condition that Krupp accept revolutionary "Villa" scrip as payment. Krupp took the risk and, like other border businessmen, covered his bets by selling to the other side. Pancho Villa reportedly made good on most of his debts to Krupp. But 1916 found the merchant unsuccessfully suing the Mexican government in an El Paso court for an $11,900 unpaid bill for overalls for the troops.

No doubt Krupp had been watching the development of the Texas oil industry as it slowly spread westward from the first big strike, Spindletop near Beaumont, in 1901. Black-gold fever swept much of East Texas, the Gulf Coast, then Ranger and Breckenridge in near-west Texas, and Amarillo in the Panhandle. Rough-and-tumble boomtowns sprouted. Fortunes were quickly made, then lost, over the next two decades.

Krupp began organizing a group of friends to buy oil leases. While traveling by train from El Paso to Fort Worth, he ran into Frank Pickrell, an Irishman and a former El Paso bank officer. Both were keen on grabbing a share of the oil boom. Krupp invited Pickrell to join his party, which was en route to Burkburnett, site of a big oil strike. There, Krupp's group bought some non-producing leases.

When his partners headed back to El Paso, Krupp and Pickrell continued on to Fort Worth. While walking down Main Street, Pickrell spotted Rupert P. Ricker, his Army captain during the war. Pickrell had worked in Ricker's intelligence unit as a sergeant. He and Krupp listened intently as Ricker described an oil scheme of his own.

Ricker's eye was on a stretch of West Texas known as the Permian Basin. Little attention had been paid to it except by a Swedish-born geology professor at the University of Texas named Johan A. Udden. Udden contended that there were "natural chances for finding accumulations of gas as well as oil" in a long, underground structure through Pecos, Reagan, Crockett, and Upton counties of the Permian Basin. Ricker, who practiced law in Reagan County, recognized that the University of Texas held enormous tracts of land within the Marathon Fold. A 1917 law allowed them to be secured for test drilling at a bargain price—ten cents an acre. With remarkable prescience, the Republic of Texas and successor-state governments had bequeathed more than 2.2 million acres to endow "a University of the First Class." But the land, much of it poor grazing, was earning a pittance, about three cents per acre annually on what was suitable for cattle—at most one thousand dollars a month. Meanwhile, the university was so poverty stricken, classes in the Austin campus's wooden shacks were sometimes canceled in winter because of the cold.

Ricker was seeking backers to help pay more than forty-three thousand dollars in filing fees that would give him the right to look for oil on more than 431,000 contiguous

Derricks create a new skyline in Burkburnett. Haymon Krupp stopped in Burkburnett with his future partner, Frank Pickrell, and bought some nonproducing leases. Courtesy, Jack White Photograph Collection, Special Collections, The University of Texas at Arlington Libraries, Arlington, Texas.

acres of university land. He had thirty days to produce the cash, but no one in Fort Worth, then an oil-industry center, put much credence in Professor Udden's theory. West Texas was written off as the "oilman's graveyard."

When Ricker learned that Krupp and Pickrell were interested in securing a drilling block, he told them he had the "hottest deal anybody ever heard of." He invited them to the Westbrook Hotel, where his room overflowed with maps, permit applications, and copies of Texas laws pertaining to state land use. When Krupp asked Ricker what he wanted for himself, the lawyer said fifty thousand dollars. That amount, plus the price of the oil leases, would have put the cost at more than ninety-three thousand dollars before a hole in the ground was ever begun. The El Pasoans retreated to another hotel room, where they mulled Ricker's offer for two hours before emerging with a different deal.

They proposed that Krupp advance the cash needed for the filing fees, that Pickrell manage the test well, that Krupp handle the financing, and that Ricker be paid something later. Ricker responded that he would fold his cards and leave the table for fifty thousand dollars, handing over rights to the permit applications. In the end, the pair convinced Ricker to accept just twenty-five hundred dollars, which covered his expenses and left him with some profit but far from the envisioned windfall.

On the long rail trip back to El Paso, Krupp and Pickrell mapped out their strategy: Krupp would raise the funds in New York City while Pickrell would visit each county to ensure the applications were in order. Neither Krupp, age forty-seven and a well-to-do businessman, nor Pickrell, thirty-one, a self-described "bull-headed Irishman," knew the first thing about oil. But they shared similar business hunches and turned out to be well-suited partners. They would work together for eight highly productive years.

But in New York, Krupp found little interest in prospecting for oil in West Texas. Expecting a go-ahead from the Texas Land Commission on the permits, he incorporated the Texon Oil and Land Company in Delaware. Pressed for capital, he arranged to borrow the needed funds from Hanover National Bank. He impressed the bank by packing Texon's board with prominent figures, including the mayor of El Paso, a vice president of the city's biggest bank, a New York furniture manufacturer, and Texas Congressman Claude B. Hudspeth. On March 27, 1919, Krupp put down $43,136 for the permits, which gave Texon two years to start drilling. Then the brokerage that had contracted to sell Texon's two million shares of common stock collapsed. No other firm was interested in representing a non-producing oil company in West Texas. Since he could not find a brokerage to work with, Krupp created one, but Texon shares, which had a one-dollar par value, sold initially at sixty cents, then fell to forty cents during the first year.

To impress prospective investors, Krupp bought leases on three producing wells in Burkburnett, exchanging the investment for Texon stock. The acquisition transformed Texon from a paper enterprise into a real oil company. Then there was Pickrell's flamboyant 1921 sales letter, which quoted geologists predicting an immense discovery and which promised a whopping five-thousand-dollar return on a two-hundred-dollar investment, even with a limited oil discovery. Such fanciful promotion was common in that era of unregulated speculation.

It was during this sales campaign that Santa Rita was selected as the name for Texon's first test well. Pickrell's salesmen had targeted a Roman Catholic ladies' group with cash to invest. The women, the story goes, sought the advice of their priest, a wary clergyman who urged his parishioners to invoke the help of Saint Rita, patron saint of desperate and impossible causes. A company geologist and engineer named Clayton W. Williams, Sr., later a wealthy oilman in his own right, said one of the Catholic women handed him an envelope containing a rose blessed by the priest in the saint's name. She asked Williams to scatter the petals from the top of the derrick and say, "I hereby christen thee Santa Rita." Williams contended that he faithfully executed the request. Another version of the yarn has Pickrell similarly naming the test well several months after drilling had begun, rose petals and all. Another version has Haymon Krupp naming the well after a well-known New Mexico copper mine with the same, sacred moniker.

Another tale, that drilling for Santa Rita began where a wagon hauling the drilling rig became mired in mud, is untrue although often repeated. The site was chosen by a geologist and was an easy distance to a railroad line. June 8, 1919, was the deadline to start operations on the main Texon permit site in Reagan County. A request for more time had been turned down, but Pickrell was told that a water well would suffice since water was needed on an oil-drilling site. Pickrell made the cutoff just hours before midnight, then flagged down a passing motorist to attest that operations had commenced before midnight. By April 1922, deposits of potash were discovered but no oil, and the driller was faced with work stoppages, a high rate of absenteeism by crews (mostly ex-cowhands), and unreliable delivery of supplies. Finally, on May 25, 1923, more than four years since the meeting in the Fort Worth hotel, bubbles of gas rose from the casing head. Santa Rita began to flow on May 28, and it continued uncontrollably for a month. The area was soon covered in black crude. Krupp was upset to see all the oil wasted. Recalled a worker, "One day when the [Santa Rita] No. 1 was flowing by heads [sixty-barrel quantities] before storage tanks were built, Mr. Haymon Krupp was on the derrick floor, and the oil was running down in the cellar and everywhere. Mr. Krupp jumped up and down and excitedly said, 'Boys, boys, my goodness, get some buckets and save this oil, this well has cost a lot of money!'"

Within two years, nine wells were producing 12,800 barrels of oil daily. An audit showed that Texon and its subsidiaries held assets of $9.5 million. Investors, who had paid two hundred dollars for a certificate, later converted to stock, received $1,625 during the last half of the year. The five-thousand-dollar return promised appeared within reach. But the good news brought unexpected problems for Krupp. While most shareholders were satisfied with increasing dividends, dissenters organized to purge Krupp and Pickrell from the board. Among other charges, critics alleged that favored stockbrokers bought stock at a discount. After a 1924 article in *Financial World* alleged that Krupp and Pickrell planned to siphon profits, Texon's stock price plummeted from three dollars to one dollar. Disgruntled shareholders filed two lawsuits against the company in federal court.

One case was dismissed and the other decided in Texon's favor. But then, the company was sued by the geologist who first surveyed Reagan County and by the state of Texas, claiming that it was being shortchanged on royalties. The geologist was paid sixteen thousand dollars in an out-of-court settlement, and Texon paid the state $950,000 to settle the royalty claim.

While Santa Rita No. 1 gained much notoriety, another Texon well on University of Texas land two miles away was to prove an even bigger gusher. The University No. B-1 would produce several thousand barrels of better quality oil per day—after drillers defied Pickrell's order to quit when they hit a depth of more than eight thousand feet. In a 1964 interview, Pickrell said that he and Krupp each received five million dollars and that the other shareholders got a total of sixteen million dollars in 1929 when the company was acquired by what became Continental Oil Company.

Santa Rita No. 1 oil rig. A hallowed Texas monument, the Santa Rita pumping apparatus was reassembled in 1958 in Austin on the University of Texas campus. Santa Rita, patron saint of desperate causes, gets the credit for turning the University of Texas System's endowment fund into the fourth largest in the nation after Harvard, Yale, and Stanford. Photo by Carolyn Cruz.

Krupp called wildcatting "thrilling, romantic work," and he gave numerous interviews around the country to publications ranging from the *Corsicana Daily Sun* to New York's Yiddish-language *Morgen Journal*, apparently in hopes of drumming up investors for his new but largely unsuccessful venture, the Haymon Krupp Oil Company, founded in 1935. At one point, his finances were so low that he borrowed from his second wife, Rebecca Goldstein, but repaid her before his death on February 21, 1949. Krupp would die only modestly comfortable; his partner nearly penniless.

Krupp's greatest legacy would be Santa Rita No. 1. Before the oil strike, the University of Texas was earning about twelve thousand dollars a year from its lands, mostly from cattle grazing. By 2006, the Permanent University Fund, which had expanded to benefit more than fifteen Texas institutions of higher education, held $11.6 billion dollars, all but about one hundred million dollars from Permian Basin oil and gas revenues. In 1958, the Santa Rita rig was moved to the entrance of the University of Texas at Austin at Nineteenth Street and San Jacinto Boulevard where it stands today, a monument to a chance encounter on a train and the unlikely partnership between a Jew and an Irishman. ✱

REFERENCES

El Paso Times, June 15, 1969.

Fierman, Floyd S. "Haymon Krupp, Economic Adventurer in the Southwest." *Password* 26, no. 2 (Summer 1981): 51–77.

Griffin, John Howard. *Land of the High Sky*. Midland: First National Bank of Midland, 1959.

Haigh, Berte. *Land, Oil, and Exploration*. El Paso: Texas Western Press, 1986.

Handbook of Texas Online, s.v. "Krupp, Haymon," www.tsha.utexas.edu/handbook/online/articles/ KK/fkr5.html (accessed November 8, 2005); s.v. "Richardson, Sid Williams," www.tsha.utexas .edu/handbook/online/articles/RR/fri8.html (accessed November 8, 2005).

Myres, Samuel D. *Permian Basin, Petroleum Empire of the Southwest: Era of Discovery, From the Beginning to the Depression*, vol. 1 of 2. El Paso: Permian Press, 1973.

Fort Worth Petroleum Club Historical Committee. *Oil Legends of Fort Worth*. Dallas: Taylor Publishing Co., 1993.

Olien, Roger M., and Diane Davids Olien. *Oil Booms: Social Change in Five Texas Towns.* Lincoln: University of Nebraska Press, 1982.

Permian Basin Petroleum Museum Archives: Claude W. Brown, letter to Permian Basin Petroleum Museum, June 4, 1984; Birdie Krupp Hewitt, letter to Permian Basin Petroleum Museum, n.d.; B. W. Wiseman, Jr., letter to Permian Basin Petroleum Museum, July 30, 1982.

Rundell, Walter, Jr. *Oil in West Texas and New Mexico.* College Station: Texas A&M University Press, 1982.

Schwettmann, Martin W. *Santa Rita: The University of Texas Oil Discovery.* Austin: Texas State Historical Association, 1943, reprinted 1958.

Snider, L. C. *Oil and Gas in the Mid-Continent Fields.* Oklahoma City: Harrow Publishing Co., 1920, reprinted in *Oil in Texas: The Gusher Age 1895–1945,* ed. Roger M. Olien and Diana Davids Olien. Austin: University of Texas Press, 2002.

Weiner, Charles. Telephone interview with author, February 19, 2005.

Weiner, Gwen. Telephone interviews with author and editor, October 2004, December 2005.

White, Owen P. "The University of Texas Strikes Oil," *New York Times Sunday Magazine,* May 3, 1925.

9

East Texas Oil Boom

From New Jersey Farm Boy to Scrap Metal King

JAN STATMAN

Coinciding with the stock market crash of 1929 and the Great Depression, the discovery of oil in East Texas defined a new frontier that brought remarkable prosperity and financial opportunity to a region suddenly flowing with black gold. The stock market crash was only the first shock in a chain reaction of economic disasters that led to business closings, foreclosures, and widespread unemployment. Natural disasters followed, including droughts and dust storms. Farms were lost. Families starved. Breadlines and soup kitchens became the order of the day.

Anyone who wanted to work, however, could find employment in East Texas, where there were jobs to be had and fortunes to be made. The newly discovered East Texas oil field—measuring forty-two miles long and eight miles wide—was the largest, most prolific oil reservoir in the world of the Depression era. Located 130 miles east of Dallas and fewer than sixty miles west of the Louisiana line near Shreveport, it was discovered at a time when the rest of the nation and the world were suffering.

Three discovery wells outlined the boundaries of the great East Texas oil field and marked the beginning of an oil boom heard around the world. Wildcatter C. M. "Dad" Joiner brought in the Daisy Bradford No. 3, the first discovery well, at Turnertown on October 5, 1930. It produced at the remarkable rate of sixty-eight hundred barrels of oil a day. Two months later, on Christmas Day of 1930, Ed Bateman brought in the Lou Della Crim well on the Crim Farm outside Kilgore, producing three times the volume of the Daisy Bradford No. 3. On January 26, 1931, the F. K. Lathrop No. 1 came in eleven miles north and east in Pine Tree, Texas.

News of the oil boom spread like wildfire. Jewish men and women were among the desperate newcomers who flocked into the area by train, mule wagon, and truck. They came by automobile, on horseback, and, when necessary, they simply walked. They overwhelmed once-quiet rural towns, stretching limited resources to the breaking point and beyond.

Although there were plenty of jobs for the newcomers, there was not enough food to feed them or room to shelter them. Families slept in tents, in chicken coops, in barns, and in attics. Joe Riff, a clothier who came from Little Rock, Arkansas, was fortunate to rent a room at one side of the Gregg County Courthouse Square within easy walking distance of his Palais Royal dress shop. As he walked to work each morning, he was obliged to step across the bodies of less-fortunate men and women sleeping on the courthouse lawn, covered with old newspapers and shreds of blankets.

The oil field "frontier" allowed many Jewish families to make their livings by follow-

Oil derricks dominated the landscape
in the early days of the East Texas
oil boom. This postcard of Longview
is titled "World's Largest Oil Field."
From the collection of Jan Statman.

Oil Field at Longview, Texas

World's Largest Oil Fields

ing the discoveries. A definite pattern of chain migration brought Jewish people from the older, deteriorating, played-out oil fields of Arkansas, Louisiana, and Oklahoma to Texas. These "boomers" would "chase the oil fields," moving from one oil boom to the next, then on to the next, and to the one that came after that.

Jews became actively involved in the business of finding and producing oil. Joe Gerson was the brilliant engineer and manager of H. L. Hunt's Parade Refining Company. Phil, Harry, and Jack Berry were University of Oklahoma graduate geologists. Their older brother, Aaron, was also in the oil business. Sonnel J. Felsenthal, nephew of Rabbi Bernhard Felsenthal, an influential early figure in the Reform Movement in the United States, was a large interest owner in the Willow Springs Field near Greggton. Sam Dorfman had property close to the Delta Drilling Company. The Travis and Livingston families came to East Texas from Tulsa, Oklahoma. Ben Balter had been studying law in Pennsylvania. When the Depression interrupted his education, Balter came to Texas where he became an oil field land man. Sam Roosth and Alex Genecov were oilmen from Tyler. Smokey Feldman, Sam Goldman, the Newman brothers, and Dave Isenberg were in the oil business in Gladewater. Izzy Maritsky owned a haberdashery shop in Longview, but he was also deeply involved in the oil business.

Everyone wanted to buy into a well that would make dreams come true. Sometimes they did. More often, they did not. Longview tailor Louis Richkie only bought into proven production. Marshall merchant Louis W. Kariel, Sr. (who would serve as his city's mayor from 1935 to 1947) invested in a number of successful oil wells, as well as some unsuccessful wells, which, he said, "helped define the edges of the field."

Oil would be discovered under a downtown Kilgore bank. A twenty-four-foot section would be sliced off the rear of six downtown businesses, and six successful oil wells would be sunk into the ground with the legs of their derricks touching to form the richest half-acre in the world.

When Sam Krasner and his brother Barney rode into Kilgore with a truckload of seven-inch oil field pipe during the summer of 1930, they found themselves in a boom-

Sisters Adele and Sarah Rutstein pose in front of an oil field fire in Kilgore. Oil field fires were a common occurrence during the oil boom days. Photo courtesy of Mike Joseph.

ing shack town. Although some of the town's original buildings could still be seen, they were often obscured by hastily constructed buildings of tin or sheet metal. Sam later graduated from the University of Oklahoma Class of 1932 with a degree in petroleum geology and twenty hours toward his master's degree. He was actively involved in the East Texas field.

Some Jewish merchants opened small shops to provide the goods and services that made bearable the lives of oil field workers and their families. Phil Hurwitz spent his high school summer vacations helping his older brothers, Sam and Hyman. They opened their Kilgore haberdashery at 6:30 A.M. when drillers and roughnecks were leaving for work. "We would close the store at nine, ten, eleven o'clock, whenever the last man was off the street," Hurwitz said. "Then we would go to Mattie's Ballroom and dance all night, take a shower, lie down for an hour, get up, and go back to work at 6:30 the next the morning. It was an exciting life for a sixteen-year old boy!"

Irving Falk was an awestruck eighteen-year-old when he came to the East Texas oil field. "I didn't know whether to look up, look down, look sideways, or look out for traffic," he recalled. "The oil wells looked like a dense forest. There were oil derricks as far as you could see!"

Irving had come to East Texas to work as one of the "scrap iron men" who went out into the oil fields to buy used oil field pipe and metals. Pipe that was used in an oil or gas well had to be of prime quality so that it would withstand tremendous pressure. During drilling, pipe would become worn out and have to be replaced. There were other uses for such pipe. It might be reconditioned and used as water pipe, or it could be used for construction. If it was in such bad shape that it could not be used for anything at all, it could be cut up and sold for scrap.

"I would go out into the field where the wells were being dug, and I would talk with the oilmen and contract to buy their scrap metal," Falk explained, "They would show me

Irving Falk, born into a family of New Jersey dairy farmers, was among the "scrap-iron men" who scoured Texas oil fields for salvageable scrap metal. They were among the pioneers of recycling. Photo courtesy of Kathy and Irving Falk.

what they had, whether it was pipe, the metal thread protectors used for the ends of pipe, or other metal materials. I would tell them what I was willing to pay for it. I would bid on it, and we would come to an agreement. They couldn't use the scrap metal, so they were happy to part with it, and I was happy to take it away, so it worked out well for us all."

Irving was a shy, frightened young man, fresh off his family's New Jersey farm, and the work he was doing took all his courage. Since he wanted the people he dealt with to take him seriously, when they asked how old he was, he told them he was twenty-one. That sounded like a sophisticated age to someone who was only eighteen, and it buoyed his courage. He was not certain they believed him, but nobody questioned his assertion.

He had grown up on a dairy farm in Passaic County, New Jersey. His parents, Morris and Celia Falk, had emigrated from Russia. Like other immigrants of the time, they worked hard with the hope of becoming part of the American Dream. They eventually purchased a dairy farm where they raised their large family—Louis, Mayer, Fanny, Ada, Anna, Irving, and Betty. Betty was the baby of the family, the youngest child, but Irving was the baby boy, born in 1918.

"We had cows in the pasture and chickens in the pen," he said, "We had a rustic life on our farm, and it was a hard life. We had fifty cows. Those cows had to be milked twice a day every day, with no time off, no matter what. It took the whole family to service the dairy farm. We all worked together, and everyone had his or her own special chores to do."

Irving's chore was to be up before three o'clock in the morning to help with the milk route. Milk deliveries would take about two hours, from three until five o'clock in the morning. When his work was done he would go home to get ready to go to school. "We worked a twenty-four hour day," he said, "We were so busy I didn't even know I was working harder than other people."

In 1926, Irving's oldest brother, Louis Falk, took a vacation to Shreveport, Louisiana, to visit their uncle, Izzie Gelfand, who had become involved in the scrap metal business.

Gelfand encouraged his nephew to remain in Louisiana, convincing him that there were opportunities in Shreveport that simply did not exist on a New Jersey dairy farm. Louis was accustomed to hard work, and he became successful in a short time. Although the opportunities Louis found in Shreveport were excellent, four years later, when oil was discovered in East Texas, far more remarkable opportunities would be created for an enterprising young scrap metal dealer.

Louis took the train back home to New Jersey when his sister Ada married Morris Milstein in a big, beautiful Orthodox wedding in Brooklyn. While there, Louis took an interest in his younger brother, Irving. One day he said, "I want you to think about something that might be a good idea for you. I want you to think about coming to the South. Come to Texas with me!"

Irving had seen the popular cowboy movies of the era, and he had images of Texas as a wild, exotic place populated primarily by cowboys and Indians. As a high school junior, he was not actually considering business opportunities. He knew nothing about oil fields. He was thinking of excitement. He was thinking of adventure. Texas sounded like an exciting adventure, certainly more exciting than life on a dairy farm in East Paterson, New Jersey.

Until that invitation, Irving's greatest adventure had been a train ride to visit his sister, Ada, in Brooklyn. He boarded the train in Passaic, got off at Jersey City, took the ferry across the Hudson River, and then took the subway all the way to Brooklyn. This time he would be traveling halfway across the country on a Pullman train—and it left from Pennsylvania Station! Fortunately, Irving did not have to make the long trip to Louisiana alone. His brother Louis had acquired a business partner, Meyer Weldman. Louis arranged for Irving to travel from New York to Louisiana with Meyer's brother, Sam Weldman. Like their brothers had done before them, Irving and Sam would eventually become business partners. "I was eighteen and Sam was exactly twice my age at thirty-six," Irving said, "He became a mentor to me. I looked up to him. I never would have made it without him."

The older brothers, Louis Falk and Meyer Weldman, had a scrap metal business in Shreveport, as well as in Monroe, Louisiana, where a gas field had been discovered. It was the largest gas field in the world at that time, and the town was in the midst of a gas boom. However, it was never intended that their younger brothers would remain in Monroe because the largest oil field in the world had just been discovered nearby in East Texas. Louis and Meyer wanted to be in business in East Texas, and they wanted the business to be operated by their brothers, people whom they knew they could trust.

"No one could believe there could be so much oil in one oil field." Irving explained, "There had never been a field that large, or with that much production."

Irving and Sam remained in Monroe for two weeks to learn something about the scrap metal business. They then moved on to El Dorado, Arkansas, for their first glimpse of an actual oil field. The El Dorado field was approximately twenty-five years old and had been depleted in that short time. When they arrived, they saw the workmen "pulling the field." The men were taking the field apart and recovering the pipe that had been put down in the wells.

"The first thing we learned in Eldorado was how to tell the difference between what could be salvaged and what should be scrapped," Irving explained.

Sam and Irving spent four weeks in El Dorado before moving to the bustling oil boom-town of Longview, Texas. They erected a warehouse in a scrap yard. Small quarters were built above the warehouse to provide them with a place to live. Their accommodations were not large or glamorous, but the two felt extremely fortunate to have any sort of

The discovery of oil changed the landscape of the quiet East Texas countryside. Oil derricks sprouted in pastures and among the pine and hardwood forests. Photo by Max Statman.

place in which to live. Adequate housing was virtually impossible to find in the oil field towns. "We worked hard," Irving said, "But life on the farm had been much harder than life in the East Texas oil field. I was only working an eight-hour day, so I thought I was on vacation!"

Irving and Sam had arrived in East Texas in June when it was hot. By September and October, it began to rain. It rained for forty days and forty nights. Traffic churned the meager country roads into ribbons of mud.

"These days, when you drive down a highway you see oil wells pumping right at the side of the road. There wasn't any highway there back then, and those wells were back in the middle of the deep woods," Irving said. "It is hard to imagine how crude everything was."

They would see teams of mules pulling trucks, trying to free them from where they had been sunk in the mud. Oilmen would be obliged to hire teamsters with teams of six or twelve mules to pull a wagon or truck through the bad areas where a well was to be located. When it was raining, the teamsters did not dare use their mules because even the mules bogged down in the red clay mud. "The roads were only navigable when it was dry," recalled Irving, describing the muddy conditions in the oil field, "But it was never dry, so the roads were never navigable."

Sam Weldman and Irving Falk made an interesting combination. Sam was the "inside man" who remained in the office, a little room about the size of a small bathroom equipped with a table, a chair, a desk, and a monitor for an outside truck scale. Sam weighed the metal, recorded the weight, flagged it, and kept the books. Irving was the "outside man" who traveled the backcountry roads of East Texas to call on oil companies that had salvage yards within their oil camps. He contracted to buy the used oil field pipe that had been pulled up out of their wells as well as other pieces of used metal equipment. After the metal was taken back to the yard, Sam and Irving decided what it was, whether it was steel, iron, copper, or other metal, and what could be done with it.

Drill pipe was valuable twice. After the well was drilled, the pipe was broken down by joints, cleaned, reused at another location or recycled for construction, fencing, or scrap metal. Photo by Lee Russell, 1939, Detail End of Drilling Pipes, Oil Field, Kilgore, Texas. Library of Congress Prints & Photographs Division, FSA-OWI Collection, LC-USF 33-012175, Lot 0550.

Occasionally, a farmer called to ask if they were interested in buying an oil-storage tank. This aroused their curiosity, and they asked why he happened to have an oil tank on his land. The farmer usually related that someone had paid rent every month to put an oil-storage tank on an isolated area. The rent had not been paid for several years, so he wanted to sell. Falk and Weldman knew the farmer was in possession of a "hot oil" tank used to store illegal oil for a time and then abandoned.

"There were all these derricks in the oil field," Irving explained. "And they were constructed of steel. If the wind blew them over, or if they were abandoned, or if there had been a problem of some kind, we would come in and take them away for scrap. We would cut them up into useful parts and not-so-useful parts. For instance, if someone was building something out of wood, he could reinforce the wood with usable pieces of steel that could be bolted to the wood."

Sometimes they had actual mountains of scrap metal. There is a photograph of Irving standing in front of what appears to be a hillside, but it was actually a mountain of scrap metal. Scrutiny of the photograph shows pots and pans as well as pieces of oil field equipment in the pile.

Falk and Weldman sometimes accumulated enough scrap iron to load a boat. They found someone who was getting up a cargo of scrap to be shipped overseas, or they loaded an ocean-going vessel themselves. Some of the scrap went to Germany or Japan. Irving said, "There was a sad story during World War II about how we sent them all this scrap iron, and the Germans and the Japanese later sent it back to us . . . as bullets!"

A young Irving Falk stands in front of a mountain of cast-off oilrig parts and scrap metal. Photo courtesy of Kathy and Irving Falk.

"Worship services were interrupted when the fire alarm sounded . . . Sunday school was really hot stuff . . ."

Kilgore's Beth Sholom Synagogue.

The new East Texans were determined to maintain their Jewish identity in the oil patch. "At first they met at the different stores," Nathan Waldman explained. "They held Sunday School for the children at Sam Goldman's store, or at Smiley Rabicoff's store. Much of the time it was so hot that they would open the doors, but because of the Blue Laws, the police would make them shut the doors again. Sunday School became really 'hot stuff.'"

Reform Jews attended High Holy Day services at Temple Moses Montefiore in Marshall. Orthodox and Conservative Jews held informal High Holy Day services in the hall above McCarley's Jewelry store in Longview or above the fire station in Kilgore. Services were interrupted when the fire alarm sounded, and it sounded often in the oil field town. The congregation would rush to the windows to see what was on fire and if their help was needed to put the fire out.

"It was during this time that a group of Jewish ladies [in Kilgore] decided to form a Sisterhood" [recalled Adele Daiches]. "The Sisterhood came before the temple. The men got together for minyans in different people's stores here and there, but there was no formal synagogue or temple. Our purpose in forming the Sisterhood was to stimulate interest in building a real synagogue. We called the men together, and they told us that if we would raise fifteen hundred dollars, they would somehow manage the rest. That seemed like an impossible sum of money, but we were determined to do it.

"I don't know how the idea came to me, but I thought we should have a baby contest. It would not be a pretty baby contest, but a contest to select the healthiest baby in town. The prettiest baby was a matter of opinion, but the healthiest baby was something else again altogether. Of course, when I suggested the idea, I was appointed as a committee of one to see about it.

"I went to the Kilgore newspaper and asked the advertising man to give me a two-page sketch. The cost was fairly minimal, as it was for charity. I asked him to mark the page off so that I could sell those two pages for a thousand dollars . . . We went to all the oil companies, the oil equipment companies, the stores, movie houses. We sold fifty-dollar, twenty-five-dollar, ten-dollar, and five-dollar ads. We sold every bit of it.

"Several merchants provided lovely gifts, and the banks opened a little savings account for the winner. By this time there were several doctors in town, and the doctors all cooperated with us. They examined the babies and did the judging. As an added benefit of the contest, many little oil field babies who might never had had health care had the opportunity to be checked by a doctor. I don't know how many health problems were found and corrected . . .

"You won't believe this, but my sister's little girl won! Of course, we would not give the prize to her. We didn't think it would be right, partly because she was a member of the Jewish congregation-to-be . . . It simply would not do. We selected another baby, even though we all knew that it was our little Barbara Ann who really won. It proved to be a successful community project. We developed a lot of good will, and we presented the men with fifteen hundred dollars."

Kilgore's Beth Sholom Synagogue, facing page, was too small to handle the crowd for the annual Purim carnival. The costumed children—including one dressed as Hitler in this 1943 group photo—celebrated the ancient victory over Haman at the American Legion Hall. Synagogue photo courtesy of Mike Joseph; Purim photo courtesy the Sarah and Smiley Rabicoff Family.

. . . The women raised their share, and the men came through with their part of the bargain. Kilgore's Beth Sholom Synagogue was organized in 1936.

"It was not a very big building," Mendy Rabicoff remembered. "When the congregation outgrew the little building, Hyman Hurwitz located an old wood-frame honky-tonk, which was moved to the location and 'reformed' to serve as the community's social hall."

"We had members from Kilgore, Longview, Henderson, Gladewater, Overton, and other towns. We clung together like ducks on a pond," Hyman Laufer said. "We had Sunday school picnics and barbecues, dances, and parties. We had a lot of fun, and we shared a lot of love. This was our home."

—Excerpted from Jan Statman, *Raisins and Almonds . . . and Texas Oil!: Jewish Life in the Great East Texas Oil Field* (Austin: Sunbelt Eakin, 2004), 10–12, 64–65.

If they had a boat coming in, they hauled the scrap metal by horse and buggy or by truck to the railroad siding where it was loaded onto open gondolas. At times they hired up to one hundred men to load the scrap metal. The workers climbed up the huge piles of scrap and threw the material into the gondola. To find enough men to fill these jobs, all that was required was to put the word out that they were hiring. Two hundred or more men would show up looking for work. "What other work could they do?" Irving asked. "They could do farm labor, but that didn't pay nearly as much because there wasn't that much farming still going on in East Texas after the oil came in, and what few farms remained were poor." The scrap-metal loaders were paid a dollar-and-a-half a day, nine dollars a week, and they worked six days a week. "It's hard to imagine," Irving said, "but a person could actually survive on nine dollars a week in those Depression days."

Several other Jewish scrap dealers in the area included the Levinson and Sanov families, who had been in Longview many years before the oil boom. The Applebaums were scrap dealers in Marshall. Sam Dorfman and Sam Sklar were among the successful scrap dealers who later went into the oil business. Scrap dealers from New Orleans or Arkansas were often friends with scrap dealers from East Texas. They attended conventions and meetings together and discussed things they had in common.

When Irving was called to serve his country during World War II, he had to find a reliable person to take care of the business while he was gone. He convinced his sister Ada, her husband, Morris Milstein, and their little daughter, Phyllis, to move to Texas from Brooklyn. "Morris didn't know anything about the scrap business," Falk said, "but

Morris was a very intelligent man and was able to learn it quickly." When World War II ended, Morris moved to Shreveport to work with Louis, but Sam Weldman decided to retire, so Morris returned to Longview.

Now that their sister Ada and her family were settled in Longview, Louis and Irving were determined to bring the rest of the family to the South to go into the scrap metal business. Their sister Fannie and her husband Meyer Crystal, as well as their brother Mayer Falk, went into the scrap business in Jackson, Mississippi. Their sister Anna and her husband Isadore Hoffman were in Hillsboro, Texas. Their youngest sister, Betty, married Mordie Glick and came to Texarkana, Texas.

Louis convinced their parents to sell the New Jersey dairy farm and retire to Shreveport, where he built then a large, comfortable home. It was located near the synagogue, and they were delighted to be able to attend services regularly. When they had lived on the farm in New Jersey, they were unable to attend as regularly as they wished because it was necessary to walk several miles in each direction to attend services.

To make it easier to help their relatives enter the scrap business in the South, Louis and Irving reminded them that a large quantity of industrial steel had became available at the end of World War II when war surplus material was sold for scrap. At one time, Irving even purchased a war-surplus tank, which he kept in the scrap yard. Morris and Ada's son, Howard "Rusty" Milstein, then a small boy, had great fun playing on that tank.

Rusty Milstein grew up in the scrap business. By the time he was twelve years old, he was working in the scrap yard on weekends, weighing scrap metal on the scales. He continued to work in the scrap yard every summer during his college years at the University of Texas in Austin. After college, it became his full-time career.

The scrap dealer's road to success in the East Texas oil patch was not an easy one when these enterprising traders went out into the oil fields to buy and sell used pipe and scrap metals. The Jewish "scrap iron men" were hard-working business people. They were entrepreneurs who were willing to take a chance in doing what they did. What was most important in the oil field, where everyone knew everyone and business was conducted on a handshake, was that they be reliable, responsible, and scrupulously honest. If they agreed to deliver a string of pipe to a certain location at a certain time, everyone knew it would be there. If they described it as a particular quality of oil field pipe, it was exactly what they said it would be. If they agreed to remove a load of scrap on a given day, it would be removed on that day. With diligence, they found success in a time that was like no other time and a place that was like no other place that ever was or ever will be—East Texas in the Boom!   ✳

REFERENCES

This chapter is drawn primarily from the interviews and narratives printed in the author's book *Raisins and Almonds . . . and Texas Oil! Jewish Life in the Great East Texas Oil Field*, published in 2004 by Eakin Press. For this essay, she conducted additional interviews with families in the pipe-and-supply business. Recommended for background reading are Mody Coggan Boatright and William A. Owens, *Tales from the Derrick Floor: A People's History of the Oil Industry* (Garden City, N.Y.: Doubleday, 1970); James Anthony Clark and Michel T. Halbouty, *The Last Boom* (New York: Random House, 1972); Harry Harter, *East Texas Oil Parade* (San Antonio: Naylor, 1934); Carl Coke Rister, *Oil! Titan of the Southwest* (Norman: University of Oklahoma, 1949); Daniel Yergin, *The Prize: The Epic Quest for Oil, Money and Power* (New York: Free Press, 1991); and vertical files, Center for American History, University of Texas at Austin.

10

On the Border A Deck of Cards Led to Del Rio

DOUG BRAUDAWAY

Max Stool, a twenty-two-year-old immigrant living in Chicago, boarded a train in 1904 for California. His journey took him south, then west, avoiding the Rocky Mountains and linking up with the southern transcontinental rail route. Being an avid cardplayer, Max found a game and played away the miles. When the train stopped in Del Rio, Texas, on the Mexican border, a fellow traveler invited Max to layover and play cards—for a while. Max stayed nearly fifty years.[1]

Max Stool had little luggage in hand but carried a good deal of historical baggage. He was many miles from his birthplace and his brethren, although two brothers would follow him to the border town. The enfolding story of the Stool families of Del Rio included textbook elements of Jewish migration to and through the United States. Max Stool took an unexpected detour when he stepped off that Southern Pacific train; his younger brother David Stool would follow via another, more charted path. A third brother, Nathan, full of wanderlust, would come and go. Nevertheless, the brothers found their way to the edge of Texas, to the dusty little town of Del Rio, a place that had never been a magnet for Eastern European migration. Ultimately, two of the brothers and their extended families made their homes and built their lives in a place that was a religious and commercial frontier, and the town is better for their presence.

The Stools lived in Chodorow in eastern Galicia, a region under czarist rule but in dispute between Russia, the Austro-Hungarian Empire, and Prussia. The Stools—a family with eight brothers and sisters—were among the 1.3 million Eastern European Jews who left their homes and immigrated to the United States during the years ending one century and beginning another. Although Russian expansionism and the three partitions of Poland temporarily removed both Ukraine and Poland from the map and put the family under Russian rule, an essential fact was that they were Jewish. Their religion determined their status, limited their options, and defined their identity. Religious persecution intensified in Russia during the late 1800s, with high taxes on kosher foods, bans against Jews living in cities, and the infamous May Laws of 1882. Russian laws basically were designed to limit Jews from becoming part of Russia's economic growth. In sum, "the Russian regime practically forced the Jews to emigrate."[2]

European Jews generally landed on the eastern seaboard at Boston, Philadelphia, or New York City. Some 9.4 percent of immigrants arriving in America from 1881 through 1914 were Jewish; one-fifth of Russian Jewry left their homes to become part of that great immigrant tide. (Only the Irish had left their homes in greater numbers.) Often a husband, a father, or the eldest brother came first—as did Stool brother Morris in 1890. Typ-

Max Stool, the white-collar entrepreneur. He brought chain stores to the border town of Del Rio. Center for American History, UT-Austin, CN Number 12111, Texas Jewish Historical Society.

ically, after saving enough money, that pioneer sent for more family or returned personally to the Old Country to escort relatives to the New World. Stool family members followed this pattern. Eldest son Morris sent for sister Bessie, who came to the United States around 1895. Max immigrated in 1904. Their brother Marx arrived the next year, 1905, and Nathan, the youngest sibling, came in 1911. The brothers pooled their resources and brought most of the rest of the family, including their parents, Eva Sharagrodsky and Menasha Stul, out of Eastern Europe in 1921 with their son, David, his wife, and daughter. Another son, Joseph, came in 1926. According to David Stool's son, who was also named Max, "they transferred from a medieval time, . . . from the Dark Ages to the Modern Ages." In Russia, they had no electric lights or automobiles, nor had they even seen such things until arriving in the United States—a "New World" in many ways. In time, all eight siblings and their parents immigrated to the United States.

In the Old Country, the family surname was spelled in Cyrillic characters, an approximation of which in Roman letters would be *Ctyl*. In English, this was transliterated to *Stul*. It seems that Morris, the first family member to immigrate, anglicized the name further, spelling it *Stool* once he arrived in America.[3] Most of the family followed suit.

Arrival in the United States did not end Jewish migration. Many moved on to secondary locations, sometimes to different neighborhoods, but often to different cities.[4] Once again the Stool family followed the pattern. After arriving on the eastern seaboard, some of the family, like Max, leapfrogged to Chicago, a destination second only to New York City for immigrant Jews, and from there to Texas, Colorado, and eventually to California, where Max Stool finally settled in retirement.

When Max disembarked in Del Rio in 1904, he had no ties to the growing community, but he saw the promise of a town just beginning to mature and connect to the national economy. He was likely conversant in English by the time he arrived in Del Rio. In Europe he had grown up multilingual, speaking Russian, Polish, Ukrainian, German, Yiddish, and Hebrew. Having picked up English, Max soon learned Spanish from his Mexican friends and customers. He became a peddler, as many immigrant Jews did, carrying a pack of goods on his back and sometimes selling old clothes on the border town's dusty streets. With hard work, he traded up to a horse-and-cart operation and eventually to leasing and buying real estate and opening a business at a permanent location.

Max was not the first of his faith to settle in Del Rio. J. Friedlander, an early 1870s Del Rio storeowner, was of German-Jewish background. Herman Mendelsohn Block, a Confederate army veteran, arrived in San Felipe Del Rio (as the community was initially called) in 1874 with his wife, Jane Sampson, formerly of San Antonio. Block worked in Friedlander's store. H. M. Block became a justice of the peace, merchant, and postmaster, and he is credited with giving Del Rio its current, shortened name. Joseph and Ella Hyman moved to Del Rio in the early days from Indianola on the Gulf Coast. The building constructed for the Hyman store still stands on Main Street. San Antonio's Oppenheimers, a banking and ranching family, had a "presence" in town, and the Zlotnik family remained in Del Rio through the 1920s. One may conclude that when Max Stool stepped off the train in 1904, Del Rioans were accustomed to a Jewish presence. Max Stool's arrival, and later that of his brothers, did not generate curiosity or discomfort. Del Rio appeared to be a town where Jews might achieve success and prominence.[5]

San Felipe Del Rio had started as a small farming village near the Rio Grande in 1868. The population remained under two hundred until 1881 when the Galveston, Harrisburg & San Antonio Railroad construction crews arrived. The GH&SA was wholly owned by the Southern Pacific Railroad Company. The passenger service was called "the Sunset Route" and was a popular means for traveling across the country. Rail service from San Antonio began in 1882. Del Rio's ample San Felipe Springs were "a huge fissure in the ground that gushed millions of gallons of crystalline pure water [a day and] allowed for a network of irrigation canals that snaked through the town and on to a rich alluvial plain between the city and the Rio Grande."[6] The Springs motivated the railroad to establish its division headquarters on the north side of town, and that prompted the organization of Val Verde County, with Del Rio the county seat. The rail line was completed in January 1883, creating the southern transcontinental railroad and the "Sunset" route to the western states.

Max's given name at birth was likely Moishe or Moses. Documentation is difficult because early deed records and store advertisements list him as "M. Stool." As he settled into Del Rio, records began to show the name "Max." Clearly he had become American.[7]

"My good name is my protection." Max Stool's advertisement in the Val Verde County Herald, circa 1910. Whitehead Memorial Museum.

Max Stool, center, with employees. This store was a forerunner to Stool's retail store, The Guarantee. Center for American History, UT-Austin, CN Number 12110, Texas Jewish Historical Society.

In Del Rio, The Guarantee is the store most associated with Max Stool. The business began in 1905 with a small storefront and by 1918 had adopted the name that pledged—both in Spanish and English—quality merchandise. The business would be called a department store today, as it carried men's, women's, and children's clothing, shoes, and accessories—"usually the better brand names of the day," according to Michael Stool. The Stool family operated a retail store under that name for ninety-eight years.[8]

Max's biggest impact on Del Rio was his success at bringing national chain stores and significant downtown architecture to Del Rio. Alongside his own store in the 700 block of South Main Street, Max Stool made it possible for four of the country's largest retail chains—Woolworth, Kress, Montgomery Ward, and J.C. Penney—to establish local storefronts.

Max first bought property near the railroad tracks. This was an obvious choice, since much of Del Rio's growth occurred after the railroads arrived. Within a few years, he realized that traditional retail business offered greater opportunities. His later acquisitions were further away from the railroad reserve and warehouse area and at the center of the community's business and residential areas. The Guarantee and the other Max Stool buildings were established at the center of Del Rio's business district.

Six years after settling in Del Rio, Max married his Chicago sweetheart, Anna Ratner. Anna's story is similar to Max's in many ways. She was born in Russia and, according to the *Del Rio Evening News*, "came to America in 1903 to make her home with her parents . . . in Chicago. It was in that city that Mr. Stool met her, bringing her to Del Rio as a bride [in 1910]." Her parents remained in Chicago, but two sisters and a brother, like some of Max's siblings, came to Texas and settled in San Antonio, Hondo, and Crystal City.[9]

In 1916, Max and Anna Stool bought a property at the corner of South Main and Losoya streets, just a block from the courthouse square. By 1922, that investment paid off. Max signed a lease with F. W. Woolworth, "the five and ten pioneer," to build a structure to Woolworth's specifications on that site. In exchange, Woolworth signed a fifteen-year lease. Only six years into the lease, Woolworth contracted to have a two-story extension added to the rear of the building. Max and Anna Stool owned the property until her death in 1934.[10]

Similarly, Max and Anna Stool built Del Rio's S.H. Kress & Company Building at 720 South Main under a 1926 contract. The five-and-dime store was a fixture of Main Street, America, and Samuel Kress was a "pioneer in establishing a company identity by means of a 'signature storefront.'" T. J. Hoffman, the head of the Kress company's architectural division from 1918 to 1928, designed the Del Rio building. "Hoffman's contribution to the development scheme was an elaborate three-story yellow-brick store with a heavy cornice rising above the long, low department store adjacent to it." Construction of the Del Rio Kress Building was completed in 1927. Kress closed its doors in Del Rio about 1996, but the structure remains intact and is an important Del Rio landmark in the heart of the city's Main Street District. While Max did not design it, he built it, and its façade still glows in the sunset.[11]

In 1929, the Stools constructed the building at 753 South Main specifically for Montgomery Ward & Company. The specifications for the structure included the "Spirit of Progress" icon on the building's façade above the front door. The icon was based on a seventeen-foot statue that Ward placed on top of its new Chicago headquarters in 1899, and it appeared on company catalogs in the 1930s. The Del Rio store opened in 1929 as part of the Ward company's transition from a strictly mail-order business to one that sold products out of storefronts.

The Montgomery Ward Building was built to be thoroughly modern in every aspect. Contract clauses about electricity and sidewalks were detailed and required Stool to make certain that the customers had a clean, safe, shopping experience. The completed building was modern and large—three stories tall—and one of Del Rio's largest. (The Ward store was closed by early 1952. The building remained occupied and is currently home to Gabriela's Clothing Store, whose owner is restoring the structure.)

When Max and Anna purchased the property that would house the Montgomery Ward building, they also purchased the site for their new home. The strip of land, exactly one-fifth of the city block, featured storefront property facing South Main Street, residential property facing Griner Street, and the Madre Canal running alongside the south property line. The purchase gave Max the ability to walk from home to business in minutes. Thus an early advertisement in the *Val Verde County Herald* in which Max Stool notes that he gave good prices because, among other things, "My Expenses are light" and "My Habits are not extravagant."[12] Max and Anna ultimately enlarged their home into a two-story structure and "filled it with art, fine furniture and a grand piano. It was a home full of vigor," where people voiced their opinions on everything from the condiments at the table to current events. "There were always additional people staying, . . . ranging from salesmen to landsmen, to relatives. One stayed for two years," according to the family memoir, "Kasha, Kugel, and Pinto Beans."[13]

Having brought three major chains to Del Rio, Max convinced a fourth chain store to relocate to the same 700 block and into a storefront also built by the Stools. J.C. Penney's had opened at another location in Del Rio in the 1920s, but today's Del Rioans remember the store at the 728 South Main location, between the Kress Building and the old Rita Theater. Earlier, an older wooden structure, the Central Hotel, had stood there, but the site was vacant in 1922 when Max built the brick structure that remains in use today.[14]

Fourth of July, 1943, Del Rio. The military band from Laughlin Army Air Field heads the Independence Day parade up Main Street celebrating Val Verde County's Fifth War Loan Drive. The band marches past the block that Max and Anna Stool built. Morrison & Co. was originally Woolworth's. Next door, The Guarantee sign is visible. Between the Kress Building and the Rita Theater is J.C. Penney Co. Whitehead Memorial Museum.

Max is also responsible, at least in part, for the success of Mrs. Crosby's Restaurant, a landmark across the Rio Grande in Del Rio's sister city, Villa Acuña (later renamed Ciudad Acuña). Crosby's Restaurant and Bar started in Del Rio as a small café on the property that is now behind the Woolworth Building. During hard times, Max allowed the proprietor, Esther Crosby, to remain in the property for a token rent payment—coffee or breakfast. Her business survived, thrived, and moved to its present location (which once included a hotel), and became a border icon immortalized in the song "Blame It on Mexico," a George Strait ballad that begins, "In a bar in Acuña called Ma Crosby's, I found myself feeling no pain."[15]

While Max was moving up the business ladder, a second Stool brother, Nathan, arrived in Del Rio. Nathan emigrated in 1911. Although he came to Del Rio, he launched his first business south of the border and learned Spanish before mastering English. When he crossed back over the border, he opened a store in Del Rio—El Remate, a cloth and clothing store. Ten years later, another brother, David, arrived in Del Rio, bringing a third branch of the Stool family to Texas. David was born in 1884 in Chodorow. Like his brothers, he spoke several languages—Russian, German, Hebrew, Yiddish, and several dialects of Polish—for language skills were useful in business. In the Old Country, David had traded agricultural items, particularly sugar beets, so he had entrepreneurial experience before coming to the United States. His only formal schooling was from a live-in Hebrew teacher his parents had hired to teach the children the language of the Torah. In

Del Rio's Main Street in 2003. Mi Jardin, the corner flower shop, occupies the old Woolworth Building. The Guarantee has expanded. The Kress building remains, although its original painted sign has faded. The Dollar Store is in the old J.C. Penney Co. location. David Stool's Star store was in the one-story building, third down from the Dollar Store. Photo by Doug Braudaway.

addition to linguistic skills, David had a good ear and played the violin. Because of poor eyesight, he was not conscripted into the czar's army, but he did work in a shipyard on the Black Sea, painting Russian warships. He married Esther Dlugasch, born in 1894, and they had a daughter, Lisa.

David stayed in the Old Country for a longer time than his siblings because he was successful in business and got along well with the local populace. However, as an employer, he became a target for the Communists. Also, increasing banditry and extortion during and after the Russian revolutions led David and his family to leave for America.[16]

In 1921, David, Esther, and Lisa joined his parents on the SS *Estonia* from the port of Danzig (today's Gdansk) to the New World. Upon arrival, David gave his ultimate destination as Del Rio, Texas, though on his way he visited Boston, Chicago, and Marfa, a West Texas town. David's naturalization papers note two English spellings of the family name: "Stool, formerly Stul."[17]

When David arrived in Del Rio in 1921, his brother Nathan was ready to depart and offered to sell his brother his store on easy terms. The fact that David had no money was irrelevant: "Here is the contents of the store. You owe me $2,750. Pay me when you can." And Nathan was off. David rapidly learned Spanish, picking up enough in six weeks to get to work. He became conversant in English soon after. David officially purchased the "entire stock and furniture and fixtures" from Nathan on the last day of 1921.[18]

A family tragedy marked David and Esther's first year in Del Rio. Their daughter Lisa, their only child at the time, drowned in the Madre Canal, the irrigation waterway that passes through the heart of Del Rio and flowed past the El Remate store. (Perhaps Lisa's death is the source of a Del Rio legend that a child's drowning prompted the canal company to cover the Madre Canal for the several blocks it passes through the downtown area.) After Lisa's death, David and Esther's family grew with the arrival of three sons—Max, Joseph, and Newsom—all born at the family home at 206 West Strickland. In the early 1930s, David upgraded his wooden house, with its upstairs sleeping porch, into a brick-and-masonry structure.

Somewhere along the way, David renamed his store La Estrella—the Star—and this emporium operated for the next eight decades. Some of David's early retail sales came from selling World War I Army surplus bought at auction from nearby Fort Clark, but the business was primarily a "family clothing store." He also carried fabrics and other items: black mantilla, boots, mosquito netting, tarpaulins, white satin for caskets, and white canvas, which was used by sheepshearers for shade and bedrolls and by cotton pickers for cotton sacks. David did more business with Del Rio's Spanish-speakers in the early years. As Las Vacas, an earlier name for the sister city across the border, grew into Ciudad Acuña, his language skills and integrity brought more clientele from across the international boundary. David opened the store at eight in the morning and remained until ten in the evening with Esther bringing him meals. He worked long and hard and had an excellent credit rating. Additionally, for a time in the 1930s, David opened a second shop, on the 500 block of South Main Street; this store was a dress shop, ladies' wear only, of higher quality and cost.[19]

Advertisement for David Stool's Star store. Whitehead Memorial Museum.

Del Rio never had ten Jewish men—enough to form a minyan, the quorum for a prayer service. Although Del Rio had Jewish residents throughout its recorded history, there seem never to have been enough to form a congregation. Both Stool families wanted to be part of an organized religious community. Both families made great efforts (closing their businesses and traveling entire days) to participate in worship services. Max, Anna, David, and Esther attended Sabbath services, religious holidays, and social events in the 150-mile-distant San Antonio. (The highway was not paved until the 1930s.) Their sons had their Bar Mitzvahs there. "I admired my father for making the effort that he did," said David's son, Max. "It was difficult for him."

The younger Max and his wife and children, along with the elder Max's grandson Michael and his family, attended services in Eagle Pass, sixty miles downriver from Del Rio. Eagle Pass, located in nearby Maverick County, had a slightly larger Jewish population than Del Rio, consisting of more than a dozen adults. Combined, Del Rio and Eagle Pass had some ten Jewish families with twenty or so adults. The congregants met on the upstairs floor of the Jewish-owned Riskind Store in Eagle Pass. Michael remembers hearing about a few other Jews who lived in the area during 1920s or 1930s, but the number never grew large.[20]

The Riskind family narrative is similar to the Stool story in several respects. Brothers Abe and Morris Edelstein arrived in Eagle Pass in 1905; a brother-in-law, Michael Riskind, arrived in 1910. The former opened a furniture store; Michael became a peddler then opened the department store that evolved into a men's and women's clothing store. The apartment above the store, where the Riskinds lived, doubled as the Jewish community center. High Holy Day services were conducted there. Some of the Riskinds taught Hebrew. William Munter, a native son of Eagle Pass, recalls in *A History of the Jews of Texas' Middle Corridor* that the Riskind apartment was the setting for fifteen to twenty Bar Mitzvahs.[21]

Despite the dearth of Jewish institutions, neither Max nor David Stool nor their offspring lost their Jewish identity. "None of them kept kosher, which, of course, would be very difficult to do here," Michael Stool observed. But it seems that Max and David and their families always kept an internal Jewish identity that remained in bloom despite desert conditions. Max and Anna joined both the Orthodox and Conservative synagogues in San Antonio. The younger Max Stool subscribed to the *Jerusalem Post* and enjoyed informing people that Del Rio is located on the same latitude as Israel.

The treks to Eagle Pass and San Antonio and the marriages within the faith—the children's and the grandchildren's—offer proof that the family's connection to Judaism did not disappear nor dissipate. Although Del Rio did not have an organized Jewish community, the Stool families went out and found one. The outward rituals of Judaism may not have been practicable with no synagogue nearby, but the families' inward identity remained strong.

Little is known about the more geographically distant members of the family. Morris, the eldest Stool sibling and the one credited with the modern spelling of the name, immigrated to the United States in 1890 but never settled in Texas. Once in the New World, he brought sister Bessie over and continued to help bring other family members. Morris's son Joe played piano at speakeasies in the days when liquor was illegal, and family lore says he even played for another Chicago transplant, Al Capone. Joe later worked for a music-publishing firm, while his brother Jesse became an actor's agent. The two immigrant sisters were Bessie and Rachel. Bessie came to the United States about 1895, married, and settled in Boston. Rachel came to the United States with her parents and remained with them in Chicago. In fact, Rachel and her husband, Morris, their two children, and Rachel's parents, Menasha and Eva, lived in a single, tiny apartment. Some of Rachel's in-laws also settled in Texas.[22]

Brother Marx served in the Russian army during the Russo-Japanese War, but the details are not recorded. Marx arrived in the United States in 1905, went to Colorado and on to California, and back to Chicago. Eventually, in 1914, he came to Texas, first to Marfa, where he opened a store, and then Presidio, where he bought a hotel. He prospered. He continued on to Pecos and Alpine and opened stores in the West Texas oil towns of San Angelo, Monahans, Odessa, and Wink.[23]

Nathan, who had lived in Del Rio from 1914 to 1921, moved even more frequently. Nathan's wanderlust led him to move to a town, buy a store, live there for a few months or a year, and then leave for another town to start over. (He is said to have moved some thirty-two times.) Perhaps he was inspired by the freedom to travel, something taken for granted by Americans but not allowed to Jews in Russia. Whatever the cause, Nathan saw a great portion of the state.

In Lubbock in the 1930s, Nathan made a life-long friend, a local businessman to whom he leased property. The lessee could not pay the rent, but Nathan let him ride with easy terms. Years later, as an octogenarian, Nathan would drive solo down Texas highways all over the state at a high clip. One day, he lost his license for speeding. His children were delighted because they were worried about how safe their elderly father was behind the wheel. Nathan, however, called his old friend, the lessee from Lubbock—Preston Smith, then governor of the state of Texas:

"Preston, you won't believe what those bastard Highway Patrolmen did!" "Nathan, what did they do?!" Governor Smith asked. Nathan told him. The governor replied, "Your license is back. Don't worry about it." And he didn't. Then it happened a second time, and the governor, who served from 1969 to 1973, fixed it again. State troopers eventually gave up. They could not touch Nathan Stool; he was under protection of the governor. While perhaps not the best example of jurisprudence, this incident reflects the

At Sybil June Stool's wedding in Abilene in 1951, she was joined (left to right) by her father, Nathan Stool, his nephew Max Stool, and her uncles Marx Stool and Dave Stool. *Courtesy Max Stool.*

Stool family's fair dealing and generosity as they worked their way across the state, as well as the friendship and respect their colleagues and neighbors conveyed to them.

The last of the eight Stool siblings to reach the New World was Joseph. In Russia, Joseph had attended gymnasium and graduated from college, a rare accomplishment because of Jewish quotas. He was a mathematician, and family lore says that he served as an education official in Ukraine. Joseph survived the communist revolution and attempted to come to the United States, but he could not get a visa because by then the United States was limiting Eastern European immigration. It is unclear exactly why Joseph did not emigrate with the remainder of his family in 1921. Part of the answer seems to have been that, as a teacher, he had a better life and more opportunity than others because educators were held in high regard. It also may have been that "he moved in different circles," protected for a time by politics or academia.

Eventually, Joseph went to Cuba, where he became a college professor. Some time later, he received permission to immigrate into the United States, entering in 1926 from Mexico through Del Rio. He settled in Chicago, where he became a traditional Jewish

religious scholar, studying the Torah, Talmud, and commentaries for the remainder of his long life. He never again used his math degree nor formally taught. He was supported by family and dated the same woman for fifty years, but never married.[24]

The Stool families have strong ties with the University of Texas (UT) at Austin. Education has been important to succeeding generations, as has marrying in the faith. Since Del Rio offered no Jewish community to socialize in and marry from, the university provided opportunities for both. Max's son William, for example, met his wife, Helen, at the Austin campus, where Max's grandson, Michael, also met his wife, Ann. "All of us met our spouses" at UT, said Michael. "It played a very important part of our lives." Grandsons Gerald and Louis also attended the university, and Michael attended the UT law school. The school was important to David's family as well. His son Max began attending UT in 1940, interrupted his schoolwork to serve in England during the Second World War, then returned to Austin and completed degrees in government and law in 1947, marrying Libbie Polsky in between programs. With Max's brothers, Joe and Newsom, also attending the university, all three brothers were at UT together for a time. David and Esther were determined to make educational opportunities available for their children. For younger generations of the families, college was a way out of Del Rio. Like many young Del Rioans, they wanted to see the larger world and to make their mark.

When Max's sight was impaired by cataracts in the mid-1930s, his son William dropped out of school, returned to Del Rio, and managed The Guarantee for a year until his father recuperated from cataract surgery. Max had also lost Anna to leukemia in 1934 and took her death hard. William may have returned to Del Rio to help Max cope with his grief as much as to help manage the store. Ultimately, William operated The Guarantee until 1970, when his son Michael took over. Michael ran it until 2003, when he finally closed

*Max Stool (1882–1972) and
his second wife, Marion Block
(1888–1965). The couple relax in
1956 with his daughter, Goldie, at a
dinner party in California, where they
retired. Courtesy Rosanne Margolis.*

what had become a Del Rio landmark and entrepreneurial tradition. Meanwhile, the younger Max Stool also returned to Del Rio in 1950, working with his father David at La Estrella and, after 1967, operating the store himself until 2001 when this downtown icon, the Star Store, closed.

And Max Stool, the first of the family to arrive in Del Rio, eventually remarried. His new wife was Marion Block, a Waco woman with no known relationship to Del Rio's pioneer Block family. In 1946, Max and Marion sold the home on Griner Street. Max retired and left Del Rio to complete that journey to California.[25] ✹

NOTES

1. "Kasha, Kugel, and Pinto Beans: One Way Tickets from West Ukraine to West Texas," *Texas Jewish Historical Society Newsletter*, June 1999, 10.

2. Lloyd P. Gartner, "Jewish Migrants en Route from Europe to North America: Traditions and Realities," in *Jews of North America*, ed. Moses Rischin (Detroit: Wayne State University, 1987), 27.

3. Lucy S. Dawidowicz, *On Equal Terms: Jews in America 1881–1981* (New York: Holt, Rinehart and Winston, 1982), 7–12; Gartner, "Jewish Migrants en Route from Europe to North America," in *Jews of North America*, 17, 27, 32; Max Stool interview with author, September 21, 2004. Joseph Stuhl, son of David and Esther, has adopted a spelling that is similar to the Old World spelling.

4. Gartner, "Jewish Migrants en Route," in *Jews of North America*, 26, 32.

5. Walter Block (great-grandson of H. M. B.) to author, May 19, 2004; Max Stool interview, September 21, 2004; Michael Stool to author; George O. Perkins, "The Early History of Val Verde County," masters thesis, Sul Ross State College, 1954, 130–130a; "Kasha, Kugel, and Pinto Beans," 11.

6. "Kasha, Kugel, and Pinto Beans," 10.

7. Michael Stool, personal and telephone interviews with author, January to November 2004.

8. Joseph Stuhl, e-mail communication to author, December 2004.

9. "Mrs. Max Stool Dies At Home In Del Rio Monday," *Del Rio Evening News*, March 27, 1934, p. A1.

10. *1872–1972, A Century of Serving Consumers: The Story of Montgomery Ward* (Chicago: Montgomery Ward & Co., Inc., 1972), 69; Val Verde County, Clerk's Office, Deed Records, Vol. 52, pp. 129+; Vol. 70, pp. 4+; Vol. 91, pp. 390+; Vol. 377, pp. 400+; Vol. 684, pp. 424+.

11. Bernice L. Thomas, *America's 5 & 10 Cent Stores: The Kress Legacy* (John Wiley & Sons, Inc., 1997, for the National Building Museum, 1997), vii–5, 32–37; Val Verde County Clerk's Office, Deed Records, Vol. 62, pp. 202+; Vol. 68, pp. 316+; Vol. 75, pp. 261+.

12. Val Verde County Clerk's Office, Deed Records, Vol. 34, pp. 597+; Michael Stool to author; "M. Stool," *Val Verde County Herald*, advertisement, n.d, no page.

13. "Kasha, Kugel, and Pinto Beans," 10.

14. Val Verde County Clerk's Office, Deed Records, Vol. 52, pp. 436+; Vol. 91, pp. 31+; Vol. 109, pp. 252+. The Rita is now known as the Paul Poag Theater.

15. Michael Stool to author. The store was "El Precio Fijo" or "Precio F"—the fixed price. Fixed prices were "a radical departure" from normal haggling over prices common in that day. Max Stool to author; Joseph Stuhl to author.

16. Joseph Stuhl to author.

17. Max Stool to author.

18. Max Stool to author; Val Verde County Clerk's Office, Bill of Sale Record, Vol. 2, p. 449.

19. "Kasha, Kugel, and Pinto Beans," pp. 14-15; Val Verde County, Bill of Sale Record, Vol. 2, p. 449; Deed Record, Vol. 69, pp. 625+; Vol. 84, pp. 635+; Joseph Stuhl to author.

20. Max Stool to author; Michael Stool to author. Many of the Stools are buried in San Antonio at Agudas Achim Cemetery and Agudas Achim Memorial Gardens.

21. William J. Munter, *A History of the Jews of Texas' Middle Corridor* (Laredo: Border Studies Center, n.d.), booklet, 14.

22. Max Stool to author; Joseph Stuhl to author.

23. "Kasha, Kugel, and Pinto Beans," 13–14; Max Stool to author.

24. Michael Stool to author; Max Stool to author.

25. Val Verde County Clerk's Office, Deed Records, Vol. 74, pp. 528+; Vol. 744, pp. 891+; "Kasha, Kugel, and Pinto Beans," 10.

11

The Zale Story Diamonds for the Rough

LAURAINE MILLER

Wichita Falls, Texas. Saturday, March 29, 1924. News of deadly storms around the nation and of strong winds knocking down oil derricks closer to home dominated the front page of the *Wichita Daily Times* that day so long ago. As readers thumbed through the newspaper, perhaps in search of something to brighten their spirits, they could not help but notice an advertisement for a new downtown business. Zale Jewelry Company was opening at Eighth and Ohio streets and offering storewide bargains in fine jewelry. The ad's size, illustrations, and catchy prose practically jumped off the page. It read, in part:

DIAMONDS

WATCHES

JEWELRY

Buy what you please and Pay at your ease!

Iron clad guarantee of satisfaction with every purchase.

This was a bold departure from the discreet announcements typically placed by retail jewelers. Even bolder were the terms of sale: Credit. At cash prices. A dollar down and a dollar a week could buy a $50 diamond ring, a $35 Bulova ladies' wristwatch, or a $37.50 Illinois pocket watch. "Buy them now—Pay later." There were less-expensive items as well. Three-piece sets included an engagement ring, a wedding ring, and a watch, selling for $19.80. Pocket watches for $10. Not junk, but reputable, national brands.

For the oil field roughnecks, farmhands, and railroad engineers fueling Wichita Falls's booming economy, Zale was a new outlet. The Singer sewing machine company had introduced installment buying to America in 1856. By the 1920s, buying on credit was enabling the average income-earner to acquire consumer goods such as automobiles, appliances, and furniture. But not jewelry. Zale's credit policy would make "luxury" available not just to the elite, but to the masses. What's more, customers who paid off an account at Zale had a good chance of establishing credit elsewhere. Zale recognized the dignity of working people, and "dignified credit" would become a catch phrase in the company's advertising.

This was the vision of twenty-three-year-old Morris "M.B." Zale, a Russian-Jewish immigrant who had come to the United States as a child. He was president of the Zale Jewelry Company. Among the company's seven stockholders were his brother William, who was company vice-president, and their uncle, Sam Kruger, who owned a jewelry store a block away that catered to a wealthier clientele. M.B.'s strategy was simple but revolutionary: Sell the best-quality merchandise to the greatest number of people at the lowest possible price—on credit and without interest. "M.B. had great faith in the aver-

age person," said his son Donald. "The other stores were too exclusive for roustabouts in dirty jeans."[1]

Nor did they cater to other working-class whites—or to blacks or Hispanics—all of whom were opening accounts at Zale. Terms as low as a penny down and a quarter a week brought people back into the store, week after week, sometimes for a year or longer, to make payments. Once they paid off one item, they often bought another. If an account was close to being paid in full, an employee in the back office would ring a bell to alert the sales staff, lest the customer leave the store empty-handed. Zale also issued certificates of credit when an account was paid and sent letters inviting customers back. M.B. did everything he could to get and keep their business. "Every customer meant something. Every sale really meant something. I was dying to wait on whoever came into the store. We couldn't let them get out without buying something."[2]

The store's business practices were open. M.B. trained the staff to educate customers about diamonds, watches, and non-jewelry items, including phonographs, a big source of entertainment at the time. "I wouldn't allow anybody to tell a customer a lie because it would come right back. I had to live with these people. I couldn't lie to them. Who the hell else did I have?"[3]

M. B. had studied the credit practices of retail jewelers in Detroit and Chicago and spent time in the Windy City learning the ropes. When he returned to Texas, he gave the concept his own spin. Banking on a large customer base, he could reduce mark-ups to increase sales. The gamble paid off. A year later, Zale was the most successful jewelry store in town, boasting six thousand customers.[4] To celebrate its first anniversary, the store hosted a customer-appreciation party. Souvenirs included Holmes & Edwards teaspoons in the new "Romance" pattern for the ladies, cigars for the men, and music for everyone. An eight-page advertising section—*The Zale Times*—ran in the *Wichita Daily Times* on April 10, 1925, with stories about the business and advertisements for the anniversary sale that would begin the next day: Silver thimbles cost a penny; thirty-two-piece sets of decorated china came free with purchases of fifteen dollars or more. At the time, the section set a record for advertising space in a Texas newspaper.

Before long, Zale was opening stores in other medium-size markets, including Tulsa and Oklahoma City. Like Wichita Falls, where the population grew to more than forty-three thousand in 1930, those cities were prospering from oil, railroads, and agriculture. That formula worked well during Zale's early years of expansion. In time, Zale would become the largest retail jeweler in the world, with headquarters in Dallas, an office in New York, diamond-cutting operations in Israel, and stores in far-away places including Alaska, Europe, Guam, India, and Japan. Call it genius, call it luck, call it vision or simply

M. B. Zale took pains to make this Zale Jewelry store in Wichita Falls, circa 1930, look different than competitors' stores, organizing rings on one side and watches on the other. Courtesy M. B. & Edna Zale Foundation, Dallas, Texas.

intuition and common sense. M. B. Zale recognized the buying power of the emerging middle class. His retailing policies contributed to the great social shift leveling class distinctions in America. By offering customers credit without carrying charges, they could buy silverware, dishes, an Elgin watch—and even diamonds—that otherwise were beyond their reach.

Diamonds for the rough? To M.B., it was just good business.

"The first day we took in $84.75 in cash sales," he told the Zale Corporation NEWS in March 1984. "Contract sales were $368. And I got $26 down . . . We didn't have any fancy customers, you know. The fancy or well-to-do people had a lot of places they could go to shop. So it was just low-priced goods we were selling—trying to sell to the average customer. These customers were trying to make a living just like I was."

The son of an immigrant house painter, M.B. quit school after the seventh grade in Fort Worth to help support the family. Much of his early education came from the school of hard knocks. He might earn three dollars a week, scooping sand, making buttons, or selling chewing gum.[5]

He was born Morris Bernard Zalefsky on September 5, 1901, in Shereshov, a shtetl near Brest on the present Belarus-Poland border. His parents were Samuel and Libby Zalefsky. The family was poor, yet, as is the Jewish custom, Libby kept a *pushke* box in which she deposited coins to help others in need. Shereshov and other Russian shtetls afforded a dreary life for Jews. They were forbidden to attend universities or enter certain occupations or professions. Pogroms targeted Jews and kept them living in fear. With hope, they looked to America. (In 1998, Donald Zale visited Shereshov and took along a map that his father had drawn of the village. Not much had changed.)

First in the extended family to leave Russia for New York was Sam Kruger, Libby Zalefsky's brother. A watchmaker who had operated a small jewelry business near the Russian city of Odessa, he came to America at the turn of the century. Kruger helped Samuel Za-

Libby Zale in 1908 with her "diamonds in the rough," William (left) and Morris B. Courtesy M. B. & Edna Zale Foundation, Dallas, Texas.

lefsky immigrate to New York in 1903. Around 1908, Zalefsky had saved enough money to send for Libby and their sons, Morris and William. In 1911, the Zalefskys moved to Fort Worth. Their train fare was paid by the Industrial Removal Office, an organization that helped resettle Jewish immigrants from the nation's larger cities to smaller communities.[6] Once again, Sam Kruger paved the way. He had settled in Fort Worth several years earlier and opened a jewelry store. Kruger wrote his sister's family, urging them to come west. Texas, he said, provided more opportunities for immigrants than New York. Though "opportunities" eluded his father, M.B. pursued them throughout his career and incorporated the idea of seizing opportunities into his business philosophy.

After school and on weekends, young Morris worked for Kruger, a strict taskmaster who insisted that his nephew polish fingerprints from watches on display. Around 1912, Kruger followed the Texas oil boom to Wichita Falls, where he opened a store. His nephew went to work there in 1919 and in 1922 briefly managed another store for Kruger in Burkburnett, near the Oklahoma border. That is when Morris Bernard Zalefsky reinvented himself as "M. B. Zale," shortening his last name to make it sound more American.

M.B.'s ideas differed from his uncle's, and he was anxious to strike out on his own. In November 1922, he rented space in a drugstore on the square in Graham, another oil boomtown, seventy-five miles southwest of Wichita Falls. With a loan from his uncle, he bought a few display cases and merchandise. M.B. tried to attract both the working class and a more affluent clientele. He placed a large advertisement in the *Graham Leader* announcing the opening of the Zale Jewelry Company, which carried Reed and Barton silver, Seth Thomas clocks, Waltham watches, and Schaeffer fountain pens and pencils. The announcement informed customers about the store's watch repair and optical departments.[7] To help his business grow, M.B. became an authorized dealer of Victrolas. He set up a phonograph outside the store and played a recording of "Turkey in the Straw." The music reverberated across the town square, luring customers inside.

M.B. became involved in civic life in Graham and might have remained. But the Ku Klux Klan was becoming active in the town. In 1923, the Klan held a parade and a rally and also conducted ceremonial cross burnings at the highest point in Graham—across the street from the boarding house where M.B. lived.[8] As the only Jew in town, M.B. decided to move on. He held an auction to pay off his debts, then took his remaining inventory to Wichita Falls, where he rejoined his uncle.

This business try was different. Kruger had moved out of a store at the corner of Eighth and Ohio streets to open a more exclusive business a block away at Eighth and Indiana Avenue. M.B. took over the lease at the first store for $250 per month. Thus Zale Jewelry Company was reborn.

Downtown Wichita Falls bustled in those days with offices, businesses, pedestrians, and automobile traffic. Unlike Graham, the city had a small but active Jewish community with two synagogues. The Ku Klux Klan also had a presence and influence in local government. But the editor of the *Wichita Daily Times*, Ed Howard, editorialized against the white supremacist organization. And on March 24, 1924, a slate of municipal candidates placed a full-page anti-Klan ad in the *Wichita Daily Times*, which read,

> The Ku Klux Klan doctrine of HATE and Private Vengeance Have Brought Their Harvest of Shame. Wichita Falls Stands Disgraced in the Eyes of the Nation. The functions of public office must no longer be prostituted to the ends of secret groups.

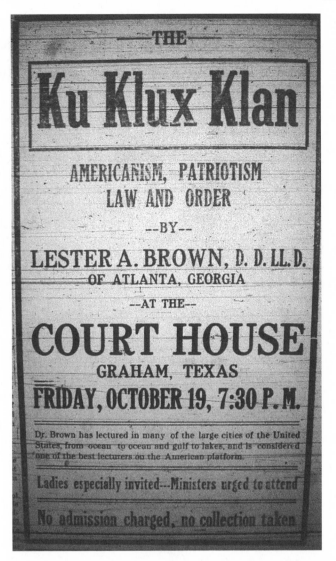

THE

Ku Klux Klan

AMERICANISM, PATRIOTISM
LAW AND ORDER
---BY---
LESTER A. BROWN, D. D. LL. D.
OF ATLANTA, GEORGIA
---AT THE---

COURT HOUSE

GRAHAM, TEXAS

FRIDAY, OCTOBER 19, 7:30 P. M.

Dr. Brown has lectured in many of the large cities of the United
States, from ocean to ocean and gulf to lakes, and is considered
one of the best lecturers on the American platform.

Ladies especially invited---Ministers urged to attend

No admission charged, no collection taken

Activities of the Ku Klux Klan, like the above advertised rally in Graham, led M. B. Zale to move back to Wichita Falls. The Graham Leader, Graham, Texas, Thursday, October 18, 1923.

In Wichita Falls, M.B. was introduced to Edna Lipshy, and they married in 1926. Edna was born in Fort Worth in 1907, one of eight children of Julius and Ethel Lipshy, who had come to the United States from Eastern Europe. Edna moved to Wichita Falls after graduating from high school to be with her sister, Goldie Lipshy Persky, whose husband owned an oil pipe and supply company there.

Early in their marriage, M.B. and Edna experienced tragedy when their oldest child, Herschel, age three, died of diphtheria. The couple donated the proceeds from a family life insurance policy to a Wichita Falls day care center for black children. Today, the successor to that center is named for Herschel Zale. Edna was a mellowing influence on her blunt-spoken husband, particularly when it came to human frailties. The couple was married sixty-nine years, a partnership that also brought Edna's younger brother Ben Lipshy into the business He started working part-time in high school, then full-time when he graduated in 1927.

When the first store opened, M.B. managed the merchandising and William Zale was in charge of advertising. There was a silverware department manager, a credit manager, a collection department manager, and a collector. The watchmaker/optician who had

M. B. Zale, as a young businessman, married Edna Lipshy in 1926, an enduring partnership that spanned sixty-nine years. Courtesy M. B. & Edna Zale Foundation, Dallas, Texas.

worked with M.B. in Graham rejoined him in Wichita Falls. In the early 1930s, Abe Zale, the younger brother of M.B. and William, also joined the business.[9]

M.B. eventually moved the store into Sam Kruger's second location at Eighth Street and Indiana Avenue. Though Zale's clientele continued to be largely blue collar, the displays were as nice as any other jeweler's in town. Risers covered in maroon and ivory velvet showed off sparkling diamond rings and gold watches in the storefront windows. Display themes revolved around holidays, anniversary sales, and June brides. Signs in the window specified terms of credit, including how long it would take to pay off an item. Inside the store, fans suspended from the high ceiling provided a breeze. Shiny linoleum with a black-and-white geometric pattern covered the floor. The innovative M.B. broke with the tradition of arranging display cases in long continuous rows. Instead, he separated cases to better show off merchandise. Watches were on the right-hand side of the store, diamond jewelry on the left. Farther back were the sterling flatware, giftware, and dinnerware.

From the beginning, Zale was a family business. When other kids were playing ball or going to camp, Marvin and Donald Zale, the sons of M.B. and Edna, worked at the store after school, on Saturdays, and in the summertime. Leo Fields, a nephew of both M.B. Zale and Ben Lipshy, also worked in the store as a youngster wrapping china. (As an adult, he became a company executive.)

Young Marvin and Donald would open the door for customers, then "ride" the restraining bar of the door as it closed, most likely when M.B. wasn't looking. As his father had learned from Sam Kruger, Donald Zale learned to wipe fingerprints and smudges off the watches on display and to keep them wound. M.B. challenged his son to learn even more. According to Donald, "M.B. said, in his quiet, inimitable way, 'I could hire a monkey to wind watches. If you do it, turn it over and look at it and see how it's made.' I made up my mind to learn about watches. At age ten, I knew more about watches than anyone in the store. It was a great lesson in merchandising."[10]

In the summer of 1946, the company's New York office needed a delivery boy but could not find one who would work in an office without air conditioning. M.B. sent Donald to do the job. He was thirteen years old. For the young teen, it was a lesson in responsibility and character. Donald lived on his own, first at the Young Men's Hebrew Association, then at the Waldorf-Astoria hotel. "[My parents] always put so much confidence in us as children," he related. "We were always more concerned about ever betraying that confidence than anything else. That's how they raised us." The family belonged to both congregations in Wichita Falls, Temple Israel, the Reform synagogue, and House of Jacob, the Orthodox shul. "Marvin was Bar Mitzvahed at the Reform temple," Donald Zale recalls. "My father's father, Sam Zale, claimed it was a nice Bar Mitzvah—and should have been held in a Baptist Church. When it was my turn, we went to the Orthodox synagogue . . . because M.B. did not want his father to be disappointed again." The Zale children also were close to their maternal grandmother. Donald said he learned to read along with his *bubbe*, Ethel Lipshy. They would read aloud together from *My Weekly Reader*, Ethel with her Yiddish accent.

Zale family life revolved around the business, and the years in Wichita Falls were a special time. In the evenings, M.B. loaded everyone into his yellow Buick convertible and took them out for ice cream. Then they checked on the store. M.B.'s workday started at 6 A.M. On Saturdays, the store remained open until 10 P.M. If people were still on the street after normal closing hours, Zale remained open even later to accommodate shoppers. Customer service, Donald Zale said, always was paramount. "Dad wore a ring in the store. If he was waiting on a customer and saw that another customer needed attention, he would tap his ring on the counter. You'd hear the 'ping,' and someone would help that person."

M.B. also taught his employees to respect all customers, no matter their circumstances. Once, he delivered a silver tea service to a woman who had purchased the set on credit. When he saw that her home had a dirt floor, he asked himself how in good conscience could he sell something so "exotic" to a person who could not afford a floor. But when he placed the tea service on the table, the woman smiled. In later years he told his son, "When I saw the pride in her face I never again sat in judgment of what makes someone happy and how they should spend their money."

The customer always came first, but the business also had to make a profit to survive. Though most customers were honest and paid on time, others had to be pursued with letters or even personal visits. As a young teen, Marvin Zale visited a barbershop to collect on an account. When the barber came after him with a razor, he got out of there—quickly.

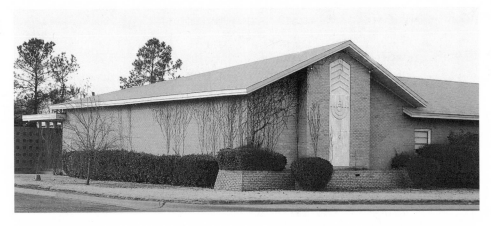

Congregation House of Jacob, where Donald Zale had his Bar Mitzvah, was constructed with wood in 1921 and encased in brick in 1956. © Sandy Wassenmiller.

Bernard "B" Rapoport, a nephew of Sam Kruger's wife, had a similarly harrowing experience as a Zale employee in the chain's Austin store. Rapoport, who later became a multi-millionaire insurance executive and chairman of the University of Texas System Board of Regents, worked his way through UT in the late 1930s, collecting late payments and making repossessions for Zale. Once, a customer behind in payments for a ring punched Rapoport in the face, shattering his glasses, cutting his eye, and requiring stitches.[11]

M.B.'s tenacity and frugality helped the business survive even greater challenges than deadbeat customers. During the Depression, which brought low sales and growing debt to the company, Zale executives did not draw salaries. Instead, they took what they needed for rent and groceries from the wooden cash box in the store. Some employees got pay cuts; others were let go. In 1930, when M.B. tried to borrow ten thousand dollars from a Wichita Falls bank to pay off the company's bills, the bank repeatedly ignored his requests. So he went to Oklahoma City, where he had both a store and an account at a local bank. M.B. asked for a loan and offered to repay it quarterly. The loan officer, J. V. Holt, took M.B. at his word and made the loan. M.B. promised himself then to never again borrow money. He kept that promise until 1957, when the company needed fifteen million dollars for expansion. M.B. later compared the lessons he had learned from the Depression to an Ivy League education at Harvard, Columbia, and Yale.

In 1938, to purchase more goods at lower prices, the Zale Corporation initiated a centralized buying plan. Wichita Falls became the distribution center for what had become a chain of jewelry stores. By 1939, there were twelve stores in three states. M.B. had a knack for finding good locations for his stores by walking around a downtown area, observing competing businesses and pedestrian traffic. Expansion enabled M.B. to promote the most promising employees—family and others, who met his expectations. Zale began opening stores in urban markets, including Austin and San Antonio, as well as competitive Dallas, where other retail shops had begun selling jewelry on installment credit plans.

World War II halted further expansion, and merchandise was hard to come by. Yet Zale obtained fountain pens and cigarette lighters, popular with customers from the Army Air Corps base in Wichita Falls. M.B insisted on charging the fixed price on items rather than high mark-ups. He reasoned that the same people would be his customers after the war, and he did not want to use the shortage of desired goods to profiteer.[12]

"B" Rapoport was working in the Wichita Falls store at the time. He wrote in his memoir that he once sold a diamond ring priced at $49.50 for $40 to a customer who offered cash. After the customer left, Rapoport got a lecture from M.B., who explained that all customers must be treated the same. Rapoport recalled:

Morris . . . was one of the most honorable businessmen I have ever known. He taught me the importance of having high standards. He also taught me that a business must be treated like a child: one does whatever one wants with the profits of the business, but one must never mistreat the business itself. An owner can give away the profits but never cut-rate the product.[13]

There were, however, special giveaways. Zale donated Braille watches to the blind, a program that began in Wichita Falls and later expanded throughout the nation and the world.

In 1944, M.B. took a step in a new direction to expand his client base. That year, Zale bought Corrigan's jewelers of Houston, with the stipulation that the Corrigan name remain. It was the beginning of Zale's Guild Division, which sold higher-quality merchandise. The Guild Division later acquired another upscale jewelry company, Bailey, Banks and Biddle of Philadelphia. Another major change came in 1946: Zale headquarters moved from Wichita Falls to Dallas. The larger city had better rail connections and an airport, Love Field.

M.B.'s travels took him abroad. In 1947 on a diamond-buying trip to Paris, he visited an orphanage for children who had survived the Holocaust. He and Edna "adopted" the orphanage and ensured that the children were relocated to Israel. In 1951, the couple established the M.B. & Edna Zale Foundation. Over the years, the foundation built hospitals and funded day care centers. It has supported a historically African-American college and provided scholarships for black students to attend college and medical school. Zale employment policies also were progressive, including profit sharing, training, and, in later years, a day care center at the corporate headquarters.

Whether in philanthropy, business, or fashion, M.B. was a forward thinker. In 1950, the television show *What's My Line* began a twenty-five-year run, with radio and television personality Arlene Francis as a panelist. Each week, the vivacious Miss Francis wore an open, diamond heart pendant on a chain around her neck. M.B. had a similar item made for Zale—and it became a hot seller.

For all his merchandising brilliance, M.B. always credited his employees, stating that there was no such thing as a self-made man or a one-man company. He recognized and nurtured the talents of his brother-in-law, Ben Lipshy, whose responsibilities grew. When in 1957 M.B. became chairman of the board of directors of Zale, he chose Lipshy to succeed him as president. That same year, the company made a major change in policy, imposing a 10 percent carrying charge on purchases, unless they were paid off in ninety days or less.

In 1958, the company went public with its stock to obtain more capital to open new stores. The Zale Corporation soon operated the largest jewelry chain in the nation, with seventy-four stores in sixteen states, fifteen hundred employees, and thirty-six million dollars in annual sales. That same year, Zale began purchasing diamonds directly from the South African firm, DeBeers. Under the concept of "vertical integration," Zale employees bought, cut, polished, mounted, and marketed diamonds. By eliminating "middlemen," the company lowered its margins and increased profits. The new practices also ensured uniform quality of the diamonds sold at Zale stores. One generation followed another in the Zale leadership. M.B.'s son Donald later would succeed Lipshy as corporation president, with the additional title and duties of chief executive officer. Following in M.B.'s footsteps, Ben Lipshy and Donald Zale each would become Zale chairman.

M.B. expected loyalty and commitment from employees, family and non-family alike. He set the example with his own strong work ethic, which sometimes had a humorous side. As an executive, Donald Zale would brief his father and his uncle, Ben Lipshy, each Monday morning. One Monday he had an abundance of bad news about personnel: An employee in New York broke his arm playing tennis; an employee in Dallas broke his nose when he hit the bottom of a swimming pool, and, tragically, a store supervisor had fallen out of a boat while fishing and drowned. The response was classic M.B. "My father slammed down his fist and said, 'God damn, no one gets hurt at the office. If you bastards would just stay here and work we would not have those problems.'"

Postcard of the Texas Panhandle city of
Amarillo, circa 1960, showcases the
Zale Jewelry store's prime downtown
location at a busy intersection.
Courtesy M. B. & Edna Zale
Foundation, Dallas, Texas.

Donald Zale said his father and uncle were two sides of the same coin. Both were conservative, but also risk takers—M.B. on the merchandising side and Lipshy in business operations. For instance, shortly after he became company president, Lipshy opened the first Zale store outside a downtown business district—at a new shopping mall east of Dallas. M.B. previously had rejected the idea and said he "nearly died" when Lipshy took him to the mall site to see what had been open prairie. It was a good call. Shopping centers became the wave of the future for Zale and other retailers as businesses followed their customers from cities to suburbs.

M.B. and Ben Lipshy differed in their personal styles as well. Lipshy was an impeccably fashionable dresser who looked like he had stepped out of the pages of *Gentleman's Quarterly*. M.B. wore conservative suits and ties. His mannerisms—the way he stood and held his hands—reminded his son Donald of comedian Jack Benny. Give M.B. a prepared speech, and within thirty seconds he would bore the audience. But if he jotted down a few notes on a scratch pad and spoke extemporaneously, he could captivate a room.

After M.B. retired as chairman and chief executive officer of Zale Corporation in 1971, Ben Lipshy and Donald Zale put their own sizzle into the company's advertising and marketing. For example, when Zale opened a store in 1979 at an upscale mall in far North Dallas, the reigning Miss Dallas presided, wearing a strand of pearls more than thirty feet long—reputedly the longest in the world. She also performed the ribbon cutting—with a pair of fourteen-karat gold scissors studded with 234 tiny diamonds.[14]

In the diamond business, negotiations are consummated with a handshake and the Yiddish phrase *mazel und brucha* (or *mazel v'bracha* in Hebrew), meaning "good luck and blessings." Zale Corporation enjoyed its share of luck and blessings and also survived difficult periods in its history. The 1980s, however, brought a new challenge.

In 1981, Peoples Jewellers, Limited, of Canada began buying Zale Corporation stock without informing Zale of its intentions. The companies reached an agreement that prevented Peoples from acquiring more stock without permission from the Zale board of directors. The agreement also gave Peoples three seats—20 percent—on the fifteen-seat board of directors of Zale Corporation. With fifteen hundred stores worldwide, twelve

thousand employees, and annual sales of $1.2 billion, Zale was the dominant player in the retail jewelry industry and many times larger than Peoples. But in 1985, Peoples began expressing disagreements with Zale management and made the first of several offers to acquire the company. In 1986, Peoples brought in another jewelry company, Swarovski International of Austria, as a partner and, thereafter, had the resources to acquire the Zale Corporation in December of that year. The name remained, but the Zale family no longer was part of the business. Five years later, burdened with debt, the company that M.B. had built and others had taken away went into court-supervised bankruptcy. Zale Corporation emerged from bankruptcy in 1993. A year later, the corporation was under new management.

Today, the early players in the Zale story are gone: Sam Kruger, William Zale, Ben Lipshy, and Edna Lipshy Zale. M.B. Zale passed away in 1995 at age ninety-three. His life followed the arc of the twentieth century—its opportunities and its challenges. In the pantheon of Jewish immigrant success stories, M.B. Zale stands apart. He valued ordinary people, and he touched many lives. And he didn't give a damn what others thought of him. In his own words, "I'm just not a conformist."

M.B. and Edna lived comfortably, but not lavishly. They did not drive fancy cars. And they always flew coach class, traveling the world as M.B. sought new opportunities for the company. And though he was more secular than religious, M.B. visited shuls during those trips abroad in Moscow, Budapest, Bombay, and Sidney. He even tried to find one in Shanghai. The couple never forgot the lean years that shaped their lives. When they traveled abroad, Edna saved the dinner rolls from restaurants and toasted them the next day for breakfast. Sometimes the rolls traveled great distances, say, from Europe to Israel.

The M.B. & Edna Zale Foundation is the family's charitable legacy. Donald and Marvin Zale, their sister, Gloria Zale Landsberg, and their cousin, Leo Fields, all remain active with its work. Today, the foundation's assets total $31.5 million, and annual giving

M. B. and Edna Zale left a legacy larger than their international chain of jewelry stores. Beneficiaries of their generosity include formerly segregated facilities, Holocaust orphans relocated to Israel, and an endowed chair in the school of business at Texas A&M University. Courtesy M. B. & Edna Zale Foundation, Dallas, Texas.

Donald Zale at work in his Dallas office, which is decorated with a wall hanging that was needle-pointed by his mother. Photo by Larry L. Rose.

approximates $1.4 million. The M.B. Zale Chair in Retailing and Market Leadership at Texas A&M University, funded by the foundation, keeps M.B.'s business legacy alive. The university also hosts the M.B. Zale Visionary Merchant Lecture series. But for all the huzzahs and hurrahs, "what interested M.B. was to build a solid business," Donald Zale said. "If someone said to him, 'Mr. Zale, you are a legend,' he'd say, 'You know, if I didn't pay my bills I wouldn't be a legend.'" ✱

NOTES

1. Donald Zale, interview with author, Dallas, May 17, 2004.

2. Zale Corp. *News*, March 1984, 2.

3. Ibid.

4. "Many Facets: The Zale Legacy," video (Dallas: Media Projects, Inc., for the Abe Zale Foundation Fund of the Communities Foundation of Texas, 2002).

5. Morris B. Zale, interview with Ginger Jacobs, February 4, 1984, oral history transcript, p. 3, Dallas Jewish Historical Society Archives, Dallas.

6. Hollace Ava Weiner, "Removal Approval: The Industrial Removal Office Experience in Fort Worth, Texas," *Southern Jewish History* 4 (2001): 1, 17–19.

7. Many details about the business history as well as the advertisement in the *Graham Leader* are from Tommy Stringer, "The Zale Corp.: A Texas Success Story," Ph.D. dissertation, North Texas State University, 1984.

8. Dorman Holub, Graham, Texas, e-mail interview, December 17, 2005.

9. Stringer, "The Zale Corp."

10. Donald Zale interview.

11. Bernard Rapoport as told to Don Carleton, *Being Rapoport: Capitalist with a Conscience* (Austin: University of Texas Press, 2002), 46.

12. "Many Facets."

13. *Being Rapoport*, 56.

14. Prestonwood advertising supplement, *Dallas Times Herald*, July 31, 1979.

12

Neiman-Marcus Al Neiman, a Princely Pauper

HOLLACE AVA WEINER

Abraham Lincoln Neiman, the first name in the fabled Neiman-Marcus luxury store chain, died a pauper and lies without an epitaph in Fort Worth's pioneer Hebrew Rest Cemetery. The marketing whiz who supplied nearly two-thirds of the cash to launch the legendary store, Neiman alternated from rags to riches throughout his lifetime and spent his final days in the Home for Aged Masons in Arlington, Texas. "There was a sadness that the Neiman of Neiman-Marcus fame had fallen upon hard times," the late Rabbi Robert Schur, who officiated at Neiman's funeral, once remarked. "How the mighty have fallen."

Born in Chicago on the fourth of July in 1875, Neiman, who was nicknamed "Al," grew up in the Cleveland Jewish Orphans Home. By age twenty-nine, he had become a businessman in Fort Worth, the solo operator of American Salvage, a company that staged sales for local department stores. While selling merchandise at A. Harris & Company in Dallas, he met and fell in love with Carrie Marcus, an elegant assistant buyer touted for her sense of style.

Carrie's background was more stable than his. Born in Louisville, Kentucky, on May 5, 1883, she was the daughter of German immigrants Delia Bloomfield and Jacob Marcus, a cotton broker. She was the youngest of five siblings and was closest to her brother, Herbert, born in 1878. When Herbert was fifteen, he followed another brother, Theo, to the small county seat of Hillsboro, sixty-three miles southwest of Dallas where some cousins, the Rosenbaum brothers, operated a general store. The rest of the Marcus family followed in 1895. Two years later, Herbert set off to Dallas where Sanger Brothers, the city's leading retailer, hired him as a ladies' shoe salesman at fifteen dollars a week. Four years later, Carrie joined her brother in the big city, landing the position at A. Harris & Company where Al Neiman, the freelance pitchman, subsequently swept her off her feet.

Within four months, the pair was married on April 25, 1905. Neiman soon persuaded Carrie and her brother, Herbert, to move to Atlanta to launch an advertising and sales promotion agency. Herbert, smarting because Sanger Brothers had given him a paltry raise, was game. He was confident that he had the potential to earn more money. He also needed extra income because his wife, the former Minnie Lichtenstein, had given birth to a son just five days before the Neiman nuptials.

Six weeks later, the Neiman newlyweds, the Marcuses, and their infant, Stanley, moved to Georgia to start anew. For their Atlanta sales venture, Al Neiman supplied most of the capital, and it multiplied. In less than two years, the foursome had a buyout offer. They could choose to swap their advertising agency for stock in Coca-Cola, then an unknown soft drink, or they could sell for twenty-five thousand dollars. They opted for the cash, because Carrie was homesick for Dallas. She and her brother also shared the dream

Buried in a pauper's grave. Abraham Lincoln "Al" Neiman lived high, dressed well, and died with little more than a cuff link to his name. DeGolyer Library, Southern Methodist University, Dallas, Texas, A1993.1869.

of opening a specialty store that would supplant and surpass Sanger Brothers, the department store that since the 1870s had set the pace in Texas.

Returning to Dallas, the trio used their capital to open a store so choice it would one day become synonymous with *The Quest for the Best*, the title of a subsequent book by Stanley Marcus. Their merchandise concept was novel: Neiman-Marcus specialized in ladies' dresses and millinery. What distinguished it from other stores was that the dresses were ready-to-wear, rather than custom-made by seamstresses. Yet they were beautifully tailored, with deep hems, bias-cut sashes, hand-stitched linings, and expensive buttons. The fabric and styling were de rigueur.

The store's debut was in 1907, a year when women corseted their waists into hourglass figures and topped their outfits with hats decked with flowers. It was also a year rife with typhoid fever. On opening day, Herbert Marcus was sick at home with typhus. Carrie Neiman was in the hospital recovering from a miscarriage. Al and a staff of eight

Carrie Marcus, 1903. A woman with flair and style, Carrie Marcus came of age in an era when women corseted their waists to accentuate hourglass figures. Al Neiman swept her off her feet when they met in the department store where she worked. Four months later they married. DeGolyer Library, Southern Methodist University, Dallas, Texas, A1993.1869.

opened "The Store." He shook each customer's hand and gave each a souvenir tin plate. He promoted the store not as a market for the rich, but rather one that catered to the discriminating customer. The appeal and the merchandise took off. As business multiplied over the next two decades, the store gradually became a local landmark. In 1927, Neiman-Marcus introduced interior decorating ideas into retailing. Instead of merchandising every square foot, the store featured spacious, colorful aisles and even a fountain in the foyer.

The polished décor belied strains within. Disagreements among the partners festered. Al Neiman, often in New York for buying trips, played favorites among manufacturers. Carrie and Herbert looked at styles rather than labels, prices, or friendships. Ambitious employees, sensing Herbert, Carrie, and Al's biases, played one partner against

*Original Neiman-Marcus store at Elm
and Murphy Streets, Dallas, 1913.
DeGolyer Library, Southern Methodist
University, Dallas, Texas,
A1993.1869.*

the other. Complicating these differences was young Stanley, fresh out of Harvard University in 1928 and eager to implement retail ideas of his own. "Stanley was kind of a brash young Harvard graduate at that point," recalled his cousin Norma Harris Mack. He was anxious to put his stamp on the store.

Amid mounting tension and gossip, Neiman admitted to an affair with a buyer. There were rumors of multiple marital indiscretions. Carrie demanded a divorce. The dissolution of the marriage meant the end to the commercial partnership. Neiman's price for surrendering his share of the business was a quarter million dollars. "He left a very sour taste in the family," Stanley Marcus later recalled. "My father had to find the money to buy him out . . . It was a very critical time because my father paid more than the business was worth in order to get rid of Mr. Neiman. It was right at the beginning of the Stock Market break and the Depression."

The buyout stipulated that Neiman not return to Dallas as a retailer for ten years. Nonetheless, in a matter of months, Al Neiman was negotiating to run the women's department at Dreyfus & Company, a rival store across the street. "So my father was forced to sue him," Stanley Marcus recalled. "I remember the judge saying, 'Mr. Neiman, you come to this court with dirty hands.' . . . That was Mr. Neiman's last attempt to come back into the Dallas picture." Despite the divorce, Carrie kept her married name and so did the store.

Notwithstanding his banishment from Dallas, Al Neiman remained high in the affections of his nieces and nephews. "We adored our Uncle Al. We just loved him," said Norma Mack, who grew up in Dallas. "It was a great big blow when we were teenagers. We didn't understand anything."

Leaving Dallas behind, Neiman initially invested his cash in a Kansas City retail outfit, then moved to New York City, where he opened a Fifth Avenue boutique that went

Stanley Marcus (1905–2002).
He recalled that his uncle, Al Nieman,
"left a very sour taste in the family."
DeGolyer Library, Southern Methodist
University, Dallas, Texas,
A1993.1869.

under during the Depression. With little more than business savvy and a thirst for lost luxury, Neiman founded Goldring-Neiman in 1931 and began operating ladies' apparel departments for big-city stores. He emerged as a vice-president of Henry C. Lytton's, a Chicago department store colloquially called "The Hub." By 1938, Neiman was once again a respected retailer and merchant prince enjoying the high life.

A handsome figure with a medium build, about five-feet-eleven-inches tall, blue eyes, and receding brown hair slicked back according to the fashion, Neiman carried himself confidently. And why not? He was a self-made, self-assured gentleman with dapper clothes, manicured nails, and friends throughout the fashion trade. A decade after his ouster from Neiman-Marcus, he also had a new bride, Chicago fashion model Dorothy Squires, a beauty who resembled the Duchess of Kent.

The couple had everything but children. When they learned about the wartime plight of youngsters abroad, they applied to become foster parents of Jewish children being evacuated from England. In 1941, they opened their home and their hearts to Diana and Ursula Woolf, six-year-old identical twins, sent by their parents to the United States for safety. The twins' father was a British soldier and their mother a nurse. In the United States, their "mummy and daddy" were Al and "Dodo" Neiman.

"We were dropped into a fairy land," recalled one of the twins, Diana Woolf Tichner, who eventually became a New Jersey homemaker. "They gave us the finest education— at the Girls Latin School—the finest country clubs and the finest summer camps . . . No one could have had finer lives than we had. For six years they were our parents."

They lived in Chicago at a silk-stocking address near the Drake Hotel off Lake Shore Drive and vacationed in New York, Vermont, and Canada. "We were so fortunate. They obviously loved us, but had to give us up," the twin related. At age thirteen, the girls returned to England. The Neimans visited them often. "It was like having two sets of parents," Tichner recalled. When Ursula married into a prominent Jewish family in Kingston, Jamaica, the Neimans bought her wedding gown, and Al Neiman gave away the bride. When Diana married a New Jersey physician, the Neimans planned and paid for their wedding at New York's Waldorf-Astoria.

Al Neiman, then seventy-three, was operating his own apparel firm, Neiman Associates. From his office at 1441 Broadway, he purchased ready-to-wear fashions and leased apparel departments in medium-priced stores across the country. "Ready to wear is in my blood," he told a New York reporter in a 1949 interview. "I live, eat and breathe it. I have no hobbies. I've tried to retire twice, but I couldn't do it . . . [I am] too young and too active to retire."

The interview was published the year before his ex-business partner, Herbert Marcus, died in Dallas at the age of seventy-two. Carrie Neiman died three years later in 1953. By then, of course, the Dallas store had become part and parcel of the Texas legend, its rise and its reputation paralleling the oil gushers that had come to symbolize the state. When Neiman-Marcus had begun in 1907, Dallas was a cotton-trading center where a great deal of business depended upon farmers and ranchers who paid their bills once a year. The East Texas oil boom, which catapulted the Lone Star State out of the Depression, literally began with a bang in 1930 just one hundred miles east of Dallas.

Now awash in oil, East Texas's nouveau riche were eager to trek to Dallas and buy a wardrobe at Neiman-Marcus, the fashion authority with class and cachet. The once-poor dirt farmers had heard tales of foreigners converting their U.S. currency to jewels at Neiman-Marcus. Now they could afford the same. The exhilaration in the oil patch was aptly summed up in a *New Yorker* cartoon that pictured a wildcatter excitedly telling his spouse he had just hit a gusher. Her response: "How late does Neiman-Marcus stay open?"

The image grew of the rough-hewn cowboy and the sweat-stained oilman lumbering into Neiman-Marcus and counting out hundred dollar bills for fine haberdashery, jewels, and furs, which were scarcely needed in the Texas heat. More and more of the newly rich came to Neiman-Marcus for makeovers. Because they put their trust in Herbert,

Carrie Marcus Neiman (1883–1953). This portrait by artist Douglas Chandor conveys the confidence, style, and imperiousness of "Miss Carrie," an arbiter of tailoring and fashion. DeGolyer Library, Southern Methodist University, Dallas, Texas, A1993.1869.

Carrie, and Stanley, customers were receptive to new fashion trends. Over the years, Neiman-Marcus is credited with helping create, discover, or promote such things as the "step-in" dress, personalized gift-wrapping, and the velvet handbag. When Stanley replaced his father as chairman of the board, he introduced lunchtime fashion shows staged at locations outside the store. He launched foreign country promotions called Fortnights that filled the store from top to bottom with merchandise from France one year and Australia the next. The famous Neiman-Marcus Christmas Catalogues garnered headlines annually. Started in 1926 as a booklet, the Catalogues grew into collectors' items featuring outrageous, Texas-sized gifts, such as His and Hers Beechcraft airplanes, camels, and mummy cases. The annual University of Texas–Oklahoma University football contest, waged at Dallas's Cotton Bowl Stadium, always brought a bonanza of customers. One year, a happy fan walked into Neiman-Marcus and bought a $49,500 blue marquis diamond ring. Although it looked like an engagement announcement was in the offing, marriage was not the motive for the purchase. The customer's wife had every other color diamond but blue, and this completed her set.

In New York, Al Neiman had no regrets. He had glitter aplenty. By all appearances, he was doing well. He and his wife lived in a penthouse apartment on East Fifty-Sixth Street, enjoying full-time help and a first-class travel schedule. Then, in the late 1950s, Al and Dorothy Neiman abruptly moved from upscale Manhattan to moderately priced Morristown, New Jersey. "All of a sudden we found they didn't have the money we thought they did," their foster daughter Diane Tichner said. "We were shocked."

Dorothy Neiman, ailing with cancer, continued to work as an interior decorator. "She had to," Tichner said. "Al had spent all the money his wife set aside in trust funds and savings and even sold the jewelry he had bought her over the years . . . We were told there was a trust fund for us, and he went through the trust fund. We never received any-

Headline news. Neiman-Marcus's expansion beyond Texas was heralded in the Washington Post when a suburban Maryland branch opened in 1977. Clipping and receipts, collection of Hollace Weiner.

thing. Not that I ever expected or wanted anything. Ursula and I could never have had a life if it weren't for them."

Dorothy Neiman died in 1962. Al Neiman, suffering from emphysema, moved to Seventy-Fifth Street in New York, where he subsisted on $135 a month from Social Security. "He lived . . . bed ridden . . . in that apartment," his foster daughter recalled. She phoned daily and three or four days a week visited with food. If he did not answer the phone, she came over to investigate his condition. One day when she arrived, he had collapsed. He was treated at Doctors' Hospital, a private facility in New York. During his recuperation, he moved in with his foster daughter, who by then had two children. The arrangement did not work. Neiman was ill, incontinent, and stubborn. He returned to the solitude and poverty of his apartment.

The foster daughter knew that decades before Neiman had joined Dallas Masonic Lodge #760. As a lifetime member, he was entitled to free respite care in his old age and burial at the Home for Aged Masons in Arlington, a suburb between Dallas and Fort Worth. There he might live and die with dignity. After several years and several more medical emergencies, she persuaded Neiman to move.

In April 1969, three months before his ninety-fourth birthday, Neiman flew back to

Al Neiman's gravestone at Fort Worth's Emanuel Hebrew Rest Cemetery. Photo by Carolyn Cruz.

Al Neiman's gravestone at Fort Worth's Emanuel Hebrew Rest Cemetery. Photo by Carolyn Cruz.

Texas with a ticket paid for by the Masonic home. When he arrived in Arlington and checked in, Neiman had less than $175 to his name. His meager possessions, stored in a shoebox, included one cuff link. And it was not a fancy one.

In Arlington, his first wife's niece Norma Mack visited. "He seemed contented there," she recalled. Stanley Marcus, alerted to his uncle's return, said he "re-established a speaking relationship with him . . . because he was so bereft of friends."

Eighteen months after returning to Texas, on October 21, 1970, ninety-five-year-old Al Neiman died. The Masonic home summoned Fort Worth's Rabbi Robert Schur to conduct the funeral. The rabbi insisted that the famous retailer be laid to rest in a Jewish cemetery rather than the Masonic graveyard. His congregation, which is caretaker of Emanuel Hebrew Rest, a pioneer cemetery deeded to the city's "Israelites" in 1879, arranged for a pauper's plot. Stanley Marcus, then chairman of the board of the luxury store chain, arrived at the funeral in a limousine. He later contributed toward burial costs—on "humanitarian" grounds, he explained. "Not that I had any lingering feeling for the man."

Neiman's rise from rags to riches and back illustrates the opportunity in Texas and in America for a nineteenth-century orphan who began his life with little more than dreams, chutzpah, and charm. His dreams were life long. As his foster daughter summed up his life: "He lived high on memories. He couldn't not live that way. This is the tragedy of it: being many times wealthy, he ended up poor." ✦

REFERENCES

This chapter is based on research and interviews the author conducted over the past twenty years for articles printed in the Fort Worth Star-Telegram, Jewish Women in America, Jewish Stars in Texas, and for freelance assignments. Key sources include:

"Death Takes Mrs. Neiman at Age of 69," Dallas Morning News, March 7, 1953, p. 1.

Feinberg, Samuel, "Al Neiman Now Expanding His Retail Activity," newspaper clipping, ca. 1949, Neiman-Marcus folder, Hollace Weiner papers, Jacob Rader Marcus Center of the American Jewish Archives, Cincinnati.

Harris, Leon. Merchant Princes, An Intimate History of Jewish Families Who Built Great Department Stores. New York: Kodansha International, 1979.

Marcus, Stanley. Telephone interviews, May 2 and 4, 1986, and October 1997. Personal interview, July 28, 1997.

Neiman-Marcus files, Dallas Public Library, Dallas History and Archives Division.

New Yorker. Cartoon by Mischa Richter. October 27, 1956.

Peeler, Tom. "Story of the Store: The Unlikely Marriages of Neiman and Marcus," *D Magazine*, August 1984, 165–71.

Street, James. "Dazzling Dallas," *Holiday*, March 1953, 102–19.

Tolbert, Frank X. *Neiman-Marcus, Texas, the Story of the Proud Dallas Store.* New York: Holt, 1953.

Weiner, Hollace. "'Al' Neiman: The Princely Pauper," *Fort Worth Star-Telegram*, August 24, 1986, pp. 1, 14.

13

West of Neiman's

Best Little Department Store in Sweetwater

JANE BOCK GUZMAN

Abe and Ike Levy operated the best little department store on the six-hundred-mile stretch of sagebrush, tumbleweed, oil wells, and feed lots between Fort Worth and El Paso. A veritable Neiman-Marcus of West Texas, it was the first shop in the region to install electric cash registers and air conditioning, the first to provide live music, and the first to stock irresistible luxury goods.[1]

The Levys were also the magnet for a scattered Jewish community—dozens of men, women, and children who traveled up to forty miles to attend Sunday school in the Levy living room or to break matzo at a community Seder at Sweetwater's Ranch House Hotel. While Sweetwater—a town of ten thousand fueled by cotton, cattle, oil and gas production—never had a synagogue, the Levys nonetheless purchased a Torah for their ad hoc congregation. On Rosh Hashanah and Yom Kippur, when the family closed the store for the High Holidays, the Torah and its portable box with a curtain were moved to a meeting room in the Bluebonnet Hotel. There, seventy-five to eighty-five fellow Jews from isolated places such as Roscoe, Snyder, Stamford, and Colorado City gathered to worship as Abe Levy read from the holy scroll.

The Levys were a blend of business leaders, civic figures, and lay leaders. Like other influential Jewish families that settled in remote Texas towns, such as Eagle Pass and Gonzales, the Levys were immigrant retailers who built businesses from scratch, spurred their towns' development, and forged a Jewish community despite the absence of formal Judaic institutions. Their commercial history is representative of Jewish merchants in many small Texas towns during the first half of the twentieth century before the postwar population began gravitating toward urban areas.

For more than fifty years, from 1910 until 1963, Levy Brothers' Department Store—formerly known as the Sweetwater Dry Goods Company—catered to the elite of West Texas. Many shoppers considered it the epitome of elegance and style. The Levy building on Broadway Street, the main boulevard across from the Nolan County Courthouse, sat on prime real estate. A three-story brick structure, it had a basement used for storage. The first floor contained men's furnishings, shoes for the entire family, gift items, and cosmetics, as well as a large cage of canaries. Customers climbed a wide staircase to the second floor, where they could buy children's and ladies' clothing, piece goods, and sewing notions. The store interior was paneled. Local businesses rented office space on the third floor.

As a child, Sweetwater native Beverly Puckett dreamed of buying clothes from Levy's, which she never could afford when she was growing up. "But when I got my

first job," she recalled, "I bought my first dress at Levy's—a beautiful two-piece white dress."[2]

As early as 1922, the Sweetwater Dry Goods Company proudly advertised in the *Sweetwater Reporter* that it was the only store in the city to sell prestigious Hart, Schaffner, and Marx men's clothing, as well as ladies' Red Cross high-heeled shoes. Partners Abe and Ike Levy decided early on that their business should sell only the finest labels. By 1950, they offered lines such as Charles of the Ritz cosmetics that were advertised in *Vogue* and carried in Dallas exclusively at Neiman-Marcus.[3]

Abe's second wife, Freda, the buyer for the women's department, had an eye for style but little regard for budget or practicality. On a buying trip to New York one season, she fell in love with some pricey angora sweaters and selected forty-eight of them—half that were black and half that were white. For months, they did not sell. On Christmas Eve, a customer from San Angelo, two hours away, drove in to buy gifts for forty-eight friends. As her family was in the oil business, she was flush with cash and scooped up every one of the soft angora sweaters. Needless to say, she received free gift-wrapping. The customer, confident that Levy's would have gifts of the quality and quantity she desired, thought nothing of driving 240 miles round trip for her last-minute holiday shopping. She knew she could depend upon this store.[4]

Sweetwater itself emerged in 1881 when the Texas & Pacific Railroad extended its tracks to a frontier encampment of ranchers and buffalo hunters on Sweetwater Creek, a stream named by a posse of Texas Rangers chasing Indians. With the railroad's arrival, the tent city of Sweetwater, approximately 250 miles west of Dallas, became a county seat. By 1883, it boasted five saloons, a few other businesses, and a courthouse complete with a jail. To encourage growth and train service, in 1898 the town built a small lake to increase its water supply. In 1903, construction began on the Kansas City, Mexico &

Sweetwater, circa 1940s. Levy's Department Store occupied a prominent and sprawling corner location on Broadway Street, Sweetwater's main boulevard. The towering building down the block on the left is the Bluebonnet Hotel, where the Levys hosted High Holy Day services. Pioneer Museum, Sweetwater, TX 79556.

"In time for Christmas." Levy Brothers carried the region's most luxurious clothing. This advertisement of December 3, 1950, in the Sweetwater Reporter, for full-length mink is evidence that furs were popular at Christmastime among West Texans. Pioneer Museum, Sweetwater, TX 76556.

In Time
For Christmas

SAMPLE FURS

Save 1/4, 1/3, 1/2 and MORE   Thur., Dec. 7th

J. I. Zable, Southwest's exclusive Furrier, buys up
$22,500 Worth of Sample Furs from Famous Makers!
All This Season's Favorite Styles.
COATS, JACKETS, CAPES, STOLES, FUR SCARF SETS

Levys'

Orient Railway. The area around the settlement was good for farming and ranching, so the village's population increased. Businesses sprang up selling hardware, piece goods, groceries, meats, and men's clothing. The town had several banks and even a French restaurant. A second lake, constructed in 1914, led to further growth. International Harvester opened a plant in 1920. But it was the discovery of oil in West Texas that turned Sweetwater into a burgeoning county seat with a municipal airport, gypsum plants, meatpacking companies, apparel plants, and a third lake to meet the population's increasing water needs. During World War II, the Army Air Corps leased the airport, renaming it Avenger Field. At the Women's Air Force Service Pilots School, aviatrix Jacqueline Cochran trained women to pilot army planes to relieve men for combat duty. Postwar, the airport returned to civilian status. From the 1910s until the mid-1950s, Sweetwater was a small town on the move, and the Levys moved up with it.[5]

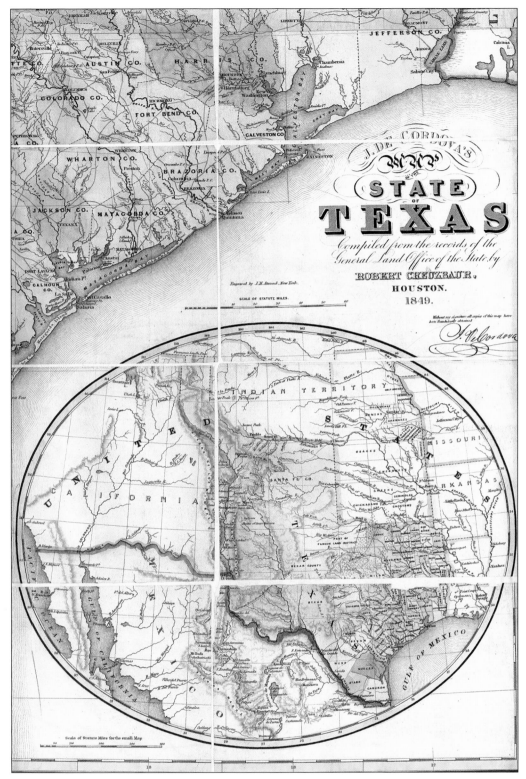

Plate 1. The twenty-eighth state. Three years after Texas was admitted to the Union, surveyor Jacob De Cordova, a Jamaican-born Jew, completed this map of the Lone Star State. Pictured here is the lower corner of the map, which altogether measures 40 by 33 inches. Elsewhere on the 1849 map are signatures of the state's top elected officials (including Senator Sam Houston and Congressman David Kaufman), indicating official endorsement of De Cordova's cartography. Detail courtesy, Special Collections, The University of Texas at Arlington Libraries, Arlington, Texas.

Plate 2. Jefferson's Sinai Hebrew Congregation. Constructed in 1860 as a residence reflecting antebellum tastes, the Greek Revival building was converted to a synagogue in 1873. Today it is home to a garden club and summer theater. Photo by Jenny Solomon. See pp. 186–87.

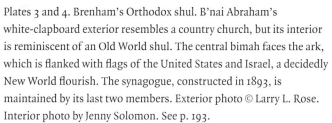

Plates 3 and 4. Brenham's Orthodox shul. B'nai Abraham's white-clapboard exterior resembles a country church, but its interior is reminiscent of an Old World shul. The central bimah faces the ark, which is flanked with flags of the United States and Israel, a decidedly New World flourish. The synagogue, constructed in 1893, is maintained by its last two members. Exterior photo © Larry L. Rose. Interior photo by Jenny Solomon. See p. 193.

Plate 5. Bryan's Temple Freda. Completed in 1913, Temple Freda has served as home for a succession of start-up churches, including Ministerio de Restauracion, which during the winter of 2004 placed a sign above the door advising of services three times a week. Photo by Jenny Solomon. See pp. 190–91.

Plate 6. Victoria's B'nai Israel. Victoria's redbrick synagogue was designed in Classical Revival style in 1923 by the city's most prominent architect Jules C. Leffland. It was one of his last buildings. B'nai Israel remains home to an active, if diminishing, Reform congregation. Photo by Jenny Solomon. See p. 196.

Plate 7. Corpus Christi's Temple Beth El. This Spanish Colonial Revival–style house of worship, designed in 1936 by architect Dexter Hamon, served Temple Beth El until 1982. The arched motif is repeated in porticos, windows, and at the entry, which features a Star of David near the apex and the quote, "Love Thy Neighbor as Thyself." Corpus Christi's Metropolitan Community Church moved into the building in 1991 and obtained a Texas historic medallion for it in 2005. Photo by Davie Lou Solka.

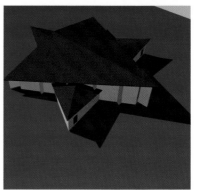

Plates 8 and 9. Wharton's Shearith Israel. Elegantly shaped like a Jewish star, Wharton's sanctuary was designed in 1957 by Houston architect Lenard Gabert. The building was sold in 2002 and remodeled into a Head Start preschool. Photo, Buz Marvins. Overhead of Mogen David Sanctuary, courtesy Texas Jewish Historical Society, Virtual Restoration of Small-town Synagogues, Robert P. Davis, Architect. See pp. 191–92.

Plate 10. Window into Abilene. Temple Mizpah was named for the popular zigzag pendants that resemble a medallion split in half. During World War II, each half was kept by parting sweethearts until they were reunited. The Hebrew word mizpah means watch post. The tradition of the mizpah charm is derived from Genesis 31:49 when Abraham and Laban divide their lands and declare, "May the Lord watch between you and me, when we are out of sight of each other." Photo by Jenny Solomon.

Plate 11. Home away from home. When Abilene's Camp Barkeley expanded into a World War II training center, the army asked the local Jewish community to build a synagogue. Temple Mizpah—with its stone exterior, low-pitched roof, prominent arches, and seating for 250—opened in 1942. The West Texas congregation still conducts monthly worship services, often led by lay cantor Dave Bach, a retired military officer. Photo by Jenny Solomon.

Plate 12. Texas past and present. Beaumont's Temple Emanuel, a modified Byzantine Revival style synagogue, was completed in 1924 at a cost of $110,000. Its architect, Albert S. Gottlieb of New York, advocated incorporating Jewish symbols into the exteriors of synagogues. In an age before microphones, the octagonal copper dome provided excellent acoustics. Atop the dome are a cupola and three-dimensional Star of David. Restoration of the building was completed in 2006. Photo by David Hoffman, FAIA.

Plates 13 and 14. Illumination. Beaumont's dramatic stained-glass windows designed in 1923 by Zeev Raban of Jerusalem's Bezalel School of Art, soar to sixteen feet. The row of three windows depicts the lives of the prophets Jeremiah, Elijah, and Elisha. The Moses window picturing the lawgiver with the Ten Commandments, is surrounded by twelve stained-glass panes, each representing a tribe of Israel. Photos by David Hoffman, FAIA.

Plate 15. Echoes of past and present. Fort Worth's Beth-El Congregation, designed by architect David Stanford, was completed in 2000. The Reform synagogue's limestone blocks, arched copper roofs, and interior courtyards evoke Jerusalem of old. © Photo by Art Lederman.

Plate 16. Houston sunset. Congregation Beth Israel, which dates to 1854 and is the state's oldest Jewish congregation, moved in 1967 to a building so graceful, it was nicknamed "the Taj." The blue tiles, repainted white in 2004, used to glow in the sunset. The architectural firm of Irving R. Klein & Associates designed the building. Congregation Beth Israel, est. 1854.

Plates 17 and 18. Happy Trails. Abe Weinberg (1899–1975), whose family emigrated from Russia around 1900, grew up in Cleburne, the county seat of rural Johnson County. In 1949, he bought seventy acres near Burleson and designed a ranch gate with his name and a shiny Star of David at the apex. The Weinberg Ranch never had more than five or six cattle. Yet the ranch sign— weathered, rusted, bent, and entwined with vines— symbolizes an immigrant American's love of the land and his heritage. Photos by Carolyn Cruz.

Welcome to Sweetwater. By 1939, Sweetwater was a hub of ranching, recreational, and railroad activity. Photo by Lee Russell, 1939. Signboard, Entering Sweetwater, Texas. Library of Congress, Prints & Photographs Division, FSA-OWI Collection, LC-USF35-1326.

The Levys trace their family roots to Rogova in western Russia. Under Czar Alexander III, who came to power in 1881, Abe's father, Max, was imprisoned for eighteen months in Siberia. One relative left for America, then another. Max emigrated in 1888, ending up with a dry goods store in Seguin, thirty-five miles northeast of San Antonio. Abe was born in 1878 and emigrated in 1892. He initially settled in New York. Traveling on horseback, he peddled underwear in the Catskills. He was resourceful, buying odd lots from cotton mills and selling at a good profit.[6]

During the late 1890s, Abe Levy joined his father in Texas and quickly realized that business there was seasonal. When customers had money from the cotton harvest, they paid with cash. The rest of the year, they bartered with chickens and eggs. Resourceful Abe loaded a wagon with goods. According to his daughter Fannie Loeb's memoir, *Sweet and Sour*, Abe ventured to "the more forsaken places" in barren West Texas where people

Retailing roots. Max Levy (far left), father of Abe and Ike Levy, stands behind the counter of his store in Seguin, 1906. Courtesy of the A. and I. Levy family.

"would be so glad to see them that they would buy instead of trade." During three-month forays into West Texas, Abe Levy reveled in his "introduction to cattle, farmers, ranchers, cactus, snakes, mesquite trees, hold-up men, and county lines—all the things that go to color this western part of our great state . . . He managed wagonloads of merchandise over swollen streams and rivers angry with flood waters; he helped the ranchers at roundup time, and he witnessed stampedes and panics."[7] Soon he took his younger brother, Ike, along as chuck wagon cook. Ike had arrived in the United States in 1901 and migrated to Texas in early September.

During one of Abe Levy's layovers in Seguin, he "fell in love with a girl sweeping the sidewalk outside a new store." She was Annie Rosenwasser, a pretty teenager eleven years his junior, whose family had emigrated from Hungary when she was age six. A courtship and lengthy engagement followed. "I was afraid that my wagon-peddling career was not too great an incentive for Annie's happy-home expectation," Abe related in the family memoir. He sought a place to settle down and start a business. In Ballinger, a West Texas county seat near the Colorado River in Runnels County, he formed a partnership with one of Annie's brothers, V. Rosenwasser. Together, they went to New York to buy store fixtures and merchandise.[8]

On a subsequent buying trip to New York, Abe Levy hired "five conscientious and ambitious young men"—all Jewish—"who were willing to adventure in Texas; he equipped them with wagonloads of merchandise from the store and sent them out to the farther region . . . The goods were sold, the bills were paid, and one of the New York gentlemen"—Selig "Zil" Reich—married Abe's sister Tillie. As the family memoir concludes: "The whole venture had not only paid off, but had netted unforeseen dividends."[9]

The West Texas sales route flourished so much that Levy and Rosenwasser soon "took their wagons off the road and established" a chain of stores in Ralls, Colorado City, Sherman, Commerce, Midland, and Fredericksburg. The Sweetwater store opened in 1910. Sweetwater's streets were not yet paved. The sand was knee deep, and the few sidewalks were wooden. Abe felt, however, that Sweetwater would prosper, for it was served by three railroad lines.[10]

In 1918, the Levy Rosenwasser chain split up, with the Levy brothers taking charge of four stores. Annie Levy, who had a heart condition, died in 1920, leaving Abe with three daughters: Fannie, age ten; Hattie, eight, and Helen, five. Two years later, Abe remarried. His new wife, Freda Horowitz Ruttenberg, was a San Antonio divorcee with a six-year-old daughter, Esther. Although Esther was never legally adopted, she became the fourth "Levy Girl." When Abe fell ill in 1923, the brothers sold two of their stores, retaining a Colorado City drug store and the Sweetwater shop, their pride and joy.[11]

From the start, Levy Brother's Department Store was a family business. Abe and Ike were equals. In fact, Ike, a lifelong bachelor, lived with Abe and his family at 501 Broadway. The brothers, who spoke with Russian accents, looked stylishly American, dressed impeccably in tailored suits selected from the stores' merchandise. Both brothers were high-profile civic volunteers from the start. Several years after the Levys' arrival, the *Sweetwater Reporter* of January 28, 1916, profiled Abe and printed his photo. He received high praise from the local press:

> Mr. Levy has been identified with every movement for the betterment of conditions since the day of his arrival. He is a director and an enthusiastic worker in the Chamber of Commerce, contributes as liberally to the support of that organization as any

firm in the city, and always attends the meetings and takes part in the active work . . . A prominent citizen of Sweetwater, in talking to the representative of the *Reporter*, said, "If we had ten men like Levy, in addition to the other live ones, this town would hum. Levy isn't afraid to put a dollar on the trail of development."[12]

The Levys believed in making their customers happy, as well as providing the latest conveniences. They installed Sweetwater's first modern cash registers, which automatically kept a record of each purchase. They hired an orchestra to entertain shoppers during sales. They brought in a representative from the *Ladies Home Journal* Pattern Company to sell and explain the latest fashion designs to local seamstresses. In 1940, Levy Brothers became the first air-conditioned store between Dallas and El Paso. That guaranteed store traffic during the dog days of summer. If customers did not want to leave their homes, they could count on the store's porter, James Garrett, to visit them with merchandise to view, with no obligation to purchase.[13]

During the Depression, when customers were short of cash, the store accepted oil leases as payment or as collateral until better times. Some customers paid with chickens and eggs. Even during the lean years, the Levy family did well enough to drive to Southern California and rent a house for the summer for Freda and the four girls. The family owned a second house on Lake Sweetwater that they opened up for community functions such as 4-H Club meetings.[14]

The larger community always figured into their lives. In 1927, Abe was among "several city dads . . . elected . . . city commissioners," according to his daughter's memoir. The police department came under Abe's purview. He was most embarrassed one evening when the police chief phoned to report that one of his daughters and her friends had removed two watermelons from a back porch of a neighbor's house. The attention the misdemeanor received is an indication of the city's low crime rate and the slow pace of life in a town where just about everybody knew everybody else's business.[15]

Everyone in the Levy family pitched in at the store. Abe and Ike's brother-in-law, Zil Reich, was a floor manager. His son, Maurice, nicknamed Moe, worked a button machine after school. It would stamp out buttons covered with fabric for the convenience of the home seamstress. Moe was paid a quarter per button and claimed he was the richest kid in town. Abe's wife Freda, with her eye for fashion, was the prime buyer. Daughter Hattie grew up working as her father's bookkeeper and personal secretary and ultimately became a ladies millinery buyer. With her sister Fannie, Hattie prepared advertisements for the local newspapers. Esther was a cashier. She met her future husband, Irving I. Bock, a mechanical engineer from Dallas, when his company installed the air-conditioning system in the store in 1940.[16]

Fannie's husband, Irving "Erdie" Loeb, was an electrical engineer with the Texas Electric Service Company in nearby Big Spring. Three years after their 1931 marriage, Erdie began working in the store as office manager and eventually became a partner. He also became a pillar of Sweetwater's community, serving on the school board, chairing the county welfare board and heading up the Red Cross and the United Fund drives. He was also president of the Rotary Club, treasurer of the board of the West Texas Area Girl Scout Council, and president of the Texas Retail Dry Goods Association. He was appointed to the Texas State Board of Corrections. With his father-in-law, he was a charter director of city's First National Bank.[17]

Freda was active in Sweetwater's Creative Art Club, the Sorosis Club, the Book Review

The blended Levy family, circa 1924. In this endearing family portrait, sisters Esther and Helen are seated on floor, Hattie looks over Abe's shoulder, while Fannie stands behind Freda. Courtesy Jane Bock Guzman.

Club, the Sweetwater Garden Club, and the Woman's Forum.[18] Uncle Ike represented the family at home and at conventions abroad in all the men's service organizations including the Elks, Masons, and Rotary.[19] The four daughters did their part in the community. As children, Esther and Helen proudly carried the school banner for the Sweetwater High School football team. Helen, elected Queen of the Carnival, was gowned in a pink ruffled formal for her coronation. Hattie was a "reporter" for two clubs. Fannie was valedictorian of her high school class.[20] Abe also contributed money to schools, churches of all denominations, and livestock shows.

The Levys' involvement with the community was par for the course among successful small-town Jewish merchant families in Texas. Because they arrived on the scene when the town was young, they were integral to its development. What was good for Sweetwater was good for the Levys. Boosterism was part of their local religion, part of who they were, part of the fabric of small-town living. In the day-to-day business world and civic climate, their religion did not matter.

Inwardly, however, Judaism was deeply important. As a minority, they tended to keep an ear alert for Jewish-sounding names in nearby towns. The Levy family became well acquainted with the Shilanskys in Roscoe, the Josephsons in Snyder, and the Bermans in Colorado City. Occasionally, the Strauss family from Stamford came for worship services, and Carl Strauss would sit down in the Levy parlor and charm everyone with his piano playing. Each family fostered and cherished its long-distance relationships with the others and traveled great distances to celebrate Jewish holidays together.

In the early 1920s, Abe traveled to New York to buy a Torah, a purchase reported on October 27, 1922, in the *Jewish Monitor*, a weekly published in Fort Worth.[21] During the High Holy Days, in a conference room at Sweetwater's Bluebonnet Hotel, he would read from the Torah. Some years, he was able to bring in a student rabbi to lead the congregation. At Sunday school, which convened in Abe and Freda's living room from 1933 to 1938, Freda taught young Jewish children hymns such as "Ein Keloheinu," Bible stories, and the importance of the Jewish holidays. Her class was the only Jewish instruction that the handful of local Jewish children received. One student, Harold Berman, recalled that he, his twin brothers, Stanley and Erwin, and his cousins, Phyllis and Joe Berman, came in from Colorado City, thirty miles away, along with Sylvan Landau. Abe's niece and nephew, Harriet and Moe Reich, also attended. Moe recalled being expelled for misbehaving.[22]

Although there were never more than a handful of Jewish families living in Sweetwater, Abe and Freda managed to give their four daughters a sense of Jewish identity. Three of them married Jewish men. Helen wed Morris Siegel of San Antonio, her college sweetheart; Esther married Irving Bock, the air conditioning pioneer from Dallas; Fannie married Erdie Loeb of Big Spring. Only Hattie married a non-Jew, the grandson of the minister of Sweetwater's First Christian Church, despite vehement objections from Abe and Freda as well as the groom's parents. Attempting to please both families, the couple was married by a rabbi and had their union blessed by a minister.[23]

During the build-up to World War II, the Army moved into Abilene, forty miles east of Sweetwater, and opened Camp Barkeley. Once the United States entered the war, the post expanded into a fifty-thousand-man training center. The Army asked the Abilene Jewish community to build a synagogue, which it did, opening Temple Mizpah in 1942. The new congregation had seating for 250 worshippers. With the influx of Jewish military personnel, Abe Levy sometimes invited a serviceman to read from the Torah during High Holy Day worship in Sweetwater. In the late 1940s, worship services ceased in Sweetwater, and Abe and Freda donated their Torah to the new temple in Abilene.[24]

The Levys of Sweetwater continued to hold large family Seders annually. One year, when all the Jews in Colorado City attended, the crowd was so large they celebrated Passover at the Ranch House Motel. Fannie and Erdie Loeb tried to ensure that their daughters, Betty and Ann, would have a strong Jewish background. They joined congregations in Austin, Dallas, Abilene, and San Angelo. Their daughter, Ann Loeb Sikora, carried on the family's tradition of community service, becoming the first woman president of Jewish Federation of Greater Dallas.[25]

Enduring partners. Ike, Freda, and Abe Levy pose outside their home on Broadway in Sweetwater. Ike and Abe were inseparable, and Ike lived with Abe's family. Courtesy Jane Bock Guzman.

Two generations of the Levy family operated the Sweetwater store. Although the business consistently made a profit, by 1963 son-in-law Erdie Loeb wanted to retire. He had been managing the store since Abe's death in 1953 and since Ike's passing in 1956. There were no other family members left in Sweetwater to take over, for by then Moe had opened a shoe-store chain in Sweetwater and four surrounding towns. Levy Brothers' Department Store had always been a family-run business. With no relatives left to operate the store, Levy Brothers' closed its doors. Sweetwater's Hixon's Department Store rented the three-story building, and an era came to an end.   ✶

NOTES

1. Gene Goltz, Levy relative in Abilene, telephone interview, June 10, 2004.

2. Beverly Puckett, interview, June 10, 2004; *Sweetwater Reporter*, December 6, 2002.

3. *Sweetwater Reporter*, July 7, 1922, October 31, 1935, December 3, 1950; *Abilene Reporter-News*, May 21, 1950; *Vogue*, October 15, 1952, p. 6.

4. Maurice Reich, e-mail to author, May 18, 2004; Fannie Loeb, *Sweet and Sour* (San Antonio: Naylor Press, 1947), 30.

5. Nolan County Web Page, www.ladytexian.com/Txnolan/towns/Sweetwater.htm; *Handbook of Texas Online*, s.v. "Sweetwater Texas," www.tsha.utexas.edu/handbook/online/articles/view/SS/hes9 .html (cited May 5, 2005); *Handbook of Texas Online*, s.v. "Sweetwater Army Air Field," www.tsha .utexas.edu/handbook/online/articles/view/SS/qcs1.html (cited May 5, 2005); Hugh Williamson, "Sweetwater: The Crossroads of Texas," *Texas Parade* 33 (April 1953): 32, 34–35; *Sweetwater Weekly Reporter*, July 18, 1903; *Sweetwater Avenger*, September 23, 1943.

6. Loeb, *Sweet and Sour*, 14–15, 17, 20.

7. Ibid., 21–22.

8. Ibid., 23.

9. Ibid., 24.

10. Ibid., 26.

11. *Abilene Reporter-News*, May 21, 1950.

12. *Sweetwater Reporter*, January 28, 1916; Loeb, *Sweet and Sour*, 83.

13. *Sweetwater Reporter*, April 2, 1915, May 19, 1916, June 28, 1917, December 6, 2002; *Nolan County News*, October 17, 1940; Nolan County Historical Commission, *Nolan County: First One Hundred Years, Sesquicentennial Edition* (Dallas: Taylor Pub. Co., 1985), 263.

14. Maurice Reich, e-mails to author, May 5, 6, 2004; Loeb, *Sweet and Sour*, 33; *Sweetwater Reporter*, August 15, 1942.

15. Loeb, *Sweet and Sour*, 73.

16. Ibid., 53; *Sweetwater Reporter*, October 31, 1935; *Nolan County*, 263; Betty Loeb, letter to Mary Franzas Montgomery Cupp, unsent, n.d., Loeb Family Papers, Burlington, Vermont; "Carrier-Bock Company of Dallas was ranked as first distributor in the nation during 1959 in dollar volume of air conditioning for Carrier Corporation." In 1955, it became the first Carrier distributor to pass the million-dollar volume on residential air conditioning. *Dallas Times Herald*, March 15, 1960.

17. *Abilene Reporter-News*, October 28, 1976; *Nolan County*, 263.

18. *Nolan County*, 259; *Sweetwater Reporter*, May 2, 1978.

19. Loeb, *Sweet and Sour*, 89.

20. Ibid., 43, 57; *Yucca Gloriosa*, Sweetwater High School annual, 1926, p. 12; 1927, p. 13; 1930, p. 12; 1931, p. 14.

21. *Jewish Monitor*, October 27, 1922.

22. Harold Berman, telephone interview, January 24, 2004; Danny Sikora, interview, January 4, 2005; Reich e-mail, May 5, 2004; *Jewish Monitor*, May 18, 1928.

23. Loeb, *Sweet and Sour*, 78–79.

24. Temple Mizpah folder, Abilene Public Library, downtown branch.

25. The Dallas Jewish Historical Society established an Ann Loeb Sikora Humanitarian Award. Leslie Wagner, "Ann Loeb Sikora: Her Texas Roots Run Deep—Her Jewish Roots Run Even Deeper," *Journal of Dallas Jewish Historical Society* 15 (Winter 2003): 7.

breaking new ground together

Jewish Federation of Austin

HAPPY

1. having, showing
great joy and pleas
emotion characteri
of well-being and
3. CAUSING ONE

Lynne Dobson/AA-S

Community center groundbreaking

Michael Dell, founder of Austin-based Dell Computers, his wife, Susan, and their twins attend the groundbreaking of the Dell Jewish Community Campus at 7300 Hart Lane on Sunday. The Dells donated 22 acres for the campus, which will include sports fields, nature trails, a swimming pool, park, Holocaust memorial and the Sylvia and Philip Spertus Jewish Community Center.

Dell family scrapbook. Philanthropists Michael and Susan Dell—pictured cradling their newborn twins—placed into their family album a groundbreaking brochure and a clipping from The Austin American-Statesman *that herald the 1996 start of construction at the Dell Jewish Community Campus. Lynne Dobson/The Austin American-Statesman, December 8, 1996; Excerpt Dell family scrapbook.*

Current Events Changing the Texas Landscape

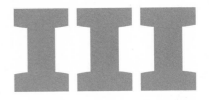

III

14

Little Synagogues across Texas

Baytown, Breckenridge, Brenham, Bryan, Brownsville, Corsicana, Jefferson, Odessa, San Angelo, Schulenburg, Victoria, Wharton

HOLLACE AVA WEINER AND LAURAINE MILLER

The onion-domed synagogue towers in Corsicana, where turn-of-the-century Reform Jews worshipped, is today a community center owned and cherished by the city. In Bryan, Temple Freda, a Classical Revival synagogue within earshot of the railroad tracks, is home to a Hispanic church. In Brenham, a white-clapboard shul, constructed in 1893 with Gothic windows, remains in pristine condition, maintained by a Jewish couple who pray that their sanctuary will find new life as a museum.

Still other Texas synagogues of old are enjoying a Jewish renaissance. In Baytown near sprawling Houston, congregants at Temple Israel enjoy the intimacy of a sanctuary that dates to 1930 when the town was known as Goose Creek. In the Rio Grande Valley, Harlingen's Temple Beth Israel has a bumper crop of congregants, thanks to the impact of the North American Free Trade Agreement. So does McAllen's Mount Sinai Congregation, which proudly compares its synagogue, constructed in 1949, to the birth of Israel the year before.

These small-town synagogues represent Jewish life in Texas, past and present. With their eclectic architecture, they present pleasant surprises to travelers who detour along the state's back roads. Historic preservation medallions affixed to some erstwhile synagogues inform visitors that these landmarks first housed minyans decades ago. In some towns, such as Jefferson where the Greek Revival-style synagogue was converted to a garden club and playhouse, the Jewish population departed more than a century ago. The synagogue in Abilene, with its low-pitched roof, local-stone veneer, and a full arch at the front doors, was built in response to the buildup of Army personnel during World War II and remains in use for monthly services.

Many of these synagogues were once the center of rural Jewish communities that numbered anywhere from thirty to several hundred souls. Historian Lee Shai Weissbach classifies them as "double-digit" and "triple-digit" Jewish communities. They are ideal places for examining Jewish settlement patterns, occupational niches, kinship networks, and relationships between Jews and non-Jews. "The history of small Jewish communities demands attention," Weissbach says, adding that small towns, with their "strong sense of rootedness and intimacy," have been called the "nation's heart and soul."

The very presence of little synagogues across Texas, whether utilized for worship or some other purpose, conveys permanence. These buildings provide testimony that the

*San Angelo's Beth Israel, photo by
Barbara Rosenberg; Corsicana's
onion-domed tower and Jefferson's
historic marker, photos by Jenny
Solomon; Schulenburg's Temple Israel,
Brenham's B'nai Abraham, Baytown's
K'nesseth Israel, © Larry L. Rose;
map by Garry Harman, The Artworks.*

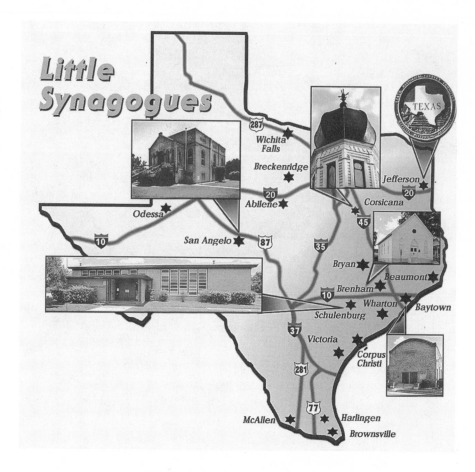

Jewish community was or remains part of the local fabric. Each building's architecture makes a statement about the era—and the place—in which it was constructed and about the status and acceptance of the community's Jews then and now.

ADAPTIVE REUSE

JEFFERSON'S HEBREW SINAI CONGREGATION:
GARDEN CLUB AND SUMMER THEATER

The Jessie Allen Wise Garden Club meticulously maintains the premises of the old Hebrew Sinai Congregation, dusting and polishing the hand-carved ark doors that have remained locked for decades. Jefferson, an antebellum East Texas tourist town, prizes and preserves its past. The city's long-gone Jewish community is part and parcel of that history.

The first Jewish merchant to settle in Jefferson, a tavern keeper, arrived in 1845, just months before Texas statehood. By the Civil War, the Jewish community had grown to 138 households. Jewish leaders in 1862 organized a Hebrew Benevolent Association, purchasing a section of an existing graveyard for Mount Sinai Cemetery.

After the Civil War, migrants from across the defeated South flocked to prosperous Jefferson. Located on Big Cypress Bayou, the city was an inland port and a commercial crossroads for steamboat traffic and horse-drawn wagons. It was also Texas's fourth-largest city, with seventy-three hundred residents. Jews operated just over one-quarter of the city's three hundred businesses. With affluence abounding, the Jewish community chartered Hebrew Sinai Congregation in 1873 and affiliated with the Reform movement. Two years later, the congregation purchased the vacant St. Mary's Catholic School and Convent, a Greek Revival house constructed in 1860 and later used by the Sisters of Charity of Saint Vincent de Paul. The Jewish community remodeled the structure into a synagogue, and in 1876 a social hall designed with neoclassical influences compatible with the original building was completed.

The promise envisioned with the purchase and remodeling of the synagogue was never achieved. Jefferson's commercial trade depended on the bayou, which was connected to the Red River, a tributary to the Mississippi River. A natural barrier in the Red River, called the "Great Raft," diverted water into the bayou. In 1873, the U.S. Army Corps of Engineers dynamited the natural log dam, lowering the water level at Jefferson. Commerce gradually declined. By the end of the decade, all but twenty-six Jewish families had moved to Marshall, Dallas, and other up-and-coming railroad centers.

A comfortable way station for travelers, the city was visited in 1877 by a Jewish gambler, Abe Rothschild, the son of a Cincinnati jeweler, and his paramour, Anne "Diamond Bessie" Moore. She subsequently was found murdered, and Rothschild was apprehended wearing two of her diamond rings. The courtroom drama surrounding her slaying and Rothschild's acquittal is the subject of "The Diamond Bessie Murder Trial," performed annually at the old Hebrew Sinai Synagogue, which doubles as the Jefferson Playhouse during the city's annual springtime pilgrimage of homes.

CORSICANA'S BETH-EL: COMMUNITY CENTERPIECE

Since 1900, Temple Beth-El has captivated Corsicana, an oil, industrial, and agricultural town that was the birthplace of the world-famous Collin Street Bakery fruitcake, Wolf Brand Chili, and country singer Lefty Frizzell. The synagogue exhibits a blend of exotic revival styles. Its twin onion domes, octagonal towers, stained-glass panes, and keyhole windows are straight out of a fairy tale. So is Beth-El's history, complete with a happily-ever-after ending.

Corsicana, fifty-five miles southeast of Dallas, was established in 1848 as the seat of Navarro County. The first Jews came in 1871 when the Houston & Texas Central Railroad extended its tracks to the city. In 1875, they established Hebrew Cemetery. By 1890, about a hundred Jewish families attended worship services at various locations, including City Hall. In 1898, they split into Orthodox and Reform groups, and the Reform Jews organized and chartered Temple Beth-El. When their whimsical building was dedicated two years later, the ceremony included the local rabbi, Christian ministers, an organist, psalm-singing, the lighting of the "eternal flame," girls dressed in white carrying baskets of flowers, and a tribute to the Ladies Hebrew Society president for getting the temple built. High above, light filtered through three windows crafted of Tiffany glass: one, a rose window, depicting a Star of David, and two shaped like tablets inscribed with the Ten Commandments.

Navarro County's oil boom began in 1894 with the first major well drilled west of the Mississippi, and the Jewish community grew along with Corsicana. By the 1940s, an estimated five hundred Jews attended either Beth-El or the Orthodox synagogue, Agudas Achim, which was chartered in 1915. Jews prospered in business, banking, real estate, and law, their presence so pervasive that downtown virtually shut down during the High Holy Days. Jews rose to prominence as fire chief, bank president, Chamber of Commerce president, and mayor.

Corsicana's Temple Beth-El is the crown jewel among Texas' small-town synagogues. Constructed in 1900, the building with its twin onion domes is owned by the city and serves as a community center. Photo © Larry L. Rose.

Temple Beth-El enjoyed a succession of full-time rabbis until the 1960s, when Corsicana's Jews began gravitating to urban areas. In 1980, barely able to form a minyan, the congregation reluctantly disbanded. By then, Beth-El's decaying building needed major repairs and faced demolition. At risk was a beloved Corsicana icon and one of the few onion-domed houses of worship still standing in the Southwest.

That is when the community at large stepped in. Spearheaded by the Navarro County Historical Society, Corsicanans formed a "Save the Temple Committee" and raised more than one hundred thousand dollars from donations, grants, style shows, and musical revues. A prominent Texas restoration architect, Raiford Stripling, stabilized the building's foundation and studied photographs and paint scrapings to bring back the two-story, wood-frame building's original hues—cream-colored clapboard with contrasting white trim.

Today, Beth-El serves as a community-gathering place for meetings, receptions, and weddings. It is administered by the city's parks and recreation department, as is the former Agudas Achim synagogue, a late-1950s building converted into a senior citizens center. Temple Beth-El is a Texas landmark listed on the National Register of Historic Places. In 2005, Rabbi Frank Joseph, a peripatetic rabbi whose motto is "Have Torah. Will Travel," began leading monthly Friday night services at Beth-El for a small group, usually less than a minyan. His father, Ernest Joseph, was rabbi at Corsicana's Agudas Achim from 1966 until his death in 1999 and also conducted services at Beth-El until it closed in 1980. Once again, Corsicana-area Jews can worship under the same roof, in an onion-domed temple, led by a rabbi with the surname Joseph.

BRECKENRIDGE'S BOOMTOWN TEMPLE BETH ISRAEL:
A CHRISTIAN CHURCH

When oil derricks began accenting the Breckenridge skyline in 1920, the West Texas county seat of fifteen hundred people exploded into a boomtown of thirty thousand. More than two hundred derricks sprouted within the city limits. So did tents and shanties that were gradually replaced with permanent buildings constructed of limestone, sandstone, and brick. Merchant Charlie Bender, an ardent Zionist with an expansive personality, a Stetson, and pointy-toed cowboy boots, organized his fellow Jews into Temple Beth Israel.

The congregation's cream-colored-brick structure, with arched windows along the sides, resembled many of the neoclassical churches being erected throughout the town— except the synagogue had Jewish-star medallions embedded into the pilasters framing the façade. The synagogue was completed April 21, 1929. Bender's good friend, Rabbi H. Raphael Gold of Dallas's Shearith Israel Congregation, attended the dedication banquet in the social hall behind the sanctuary.

Beth Israel served Jews living within a twenty-five mile radius, mainly in oil towns and county seats such as Eastland, Cisco, Ranger, and Graham. The style of worship was Conservative Judaism, with the men donning yarmulkes and prayer shawls and taking turns leading Friday evening services. (Saturdays were for business.) Whenever the Breckenridge

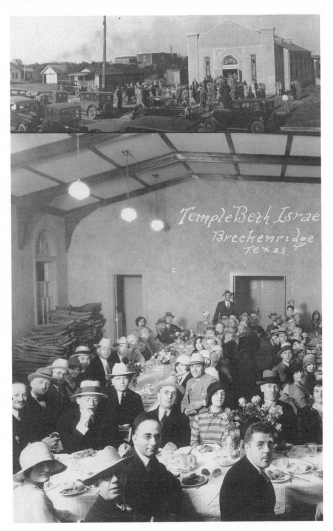

A banquet in the social hall marked the opening of Breckenridge's Beth Israel in 1929. Bertha Bender, far left, Charlie Bender, in his trademark cowboy hat, and Dallas' Rabbi Raphael Gold, far right, are seated at the head table. Basil Clemons Photograph Collection, The University of Texas at Arlington Libraries, Arlington, Texas.

Charlie Bender, "the cowboy Zionist," and wife, Bertha, in Israel. The Benders, ardent Zionists, organized Breckenridge's congregation in 1929 during the city's boomtown era. Center for American History, UT-Austin, CN Number 12115, Texas Jewish Historical Society.

High School Buckaroos hosted a Friday night football game, Beth Israel scheduled services early, so as to finish well before kickoff time. "Oh yes, we took in everything—services and football," recalled Mary Kuperman, who moved to Breckenridge with her husband in 1935.

Kuperman tried to start a Sunday school, but it did not catch on. Instead, she drove her three children to Fort Worth, one hundred miles east, for Bar Mitzvah lessons and Confirmation classes. Charlie Bender and his wife, Bertha, who shared a strong Zionist background, sent two of their four children overseas to Palestine to study Hebrew. During the High Holy Days, when a visiting cantor or rabbi conducted services, the Benders invited the entire congregation to their home for a Rosh Hashanah luncheon. Also on the social calendar were monthly Hadassah meetings for the women, card playing after services for the men—if there was no high school football game to cheer—and monthly Sunday suppers at the synagogue. During worship services, congregants sat on folding chairs.

Because Breckenridge did not have a Jewish cemetery, congregants were often interred in Fort Worth. Gradually, the next generation of Breckenridge Jewry gravitated to Fort Worth, Dallas, and Houston. The older generation followed upon retirement. By 1974, the town no longer had a minyan. A church purchased Beth Israel's building. The cornerstone was removed and placed in the town's Swenson Memorial Museum. At the start of the twenty-first century, the six-pointed stars on the building's front façade no longer represented Judaism per se, but rather the interdenominational nature of the building's occupants, the Abundant Life Family Christian Church.

BRYAN'S TEMPLE FREDA: HISPANIC IGLESIA

Sowing seeds of community cooperation, Jews and Christians together built Bryan's Temple Freda in the years before World War I. Today, the fruits of their labor are a deteriorating landmark and a bumper crop of conflict and bittersweet memories.

Immigrant Jews settled in Texas's fertile Brazos River Valley beginning in 1865. Bryan became the Brazos County seat in 1886, and the economy grew from agriculture, cotton, railroads, and oil. The Jewish community formed a congregation in 1890 and held services in members' homes. In 1912, J. W. English, a non-Jew, donated land for a synagogue but with a caveat: Use the property for religious and benevolent purposes, or it reverts to the English family.

Christians joined their Jewish neighbors, contributing construction funds and materials. Dedicated in 1913, the building is a brick, Classical Revival structure with hardwood floors, a central aisle, and eight pews on either side of the sanctuary. A triangular pediment supported by Corinthian columns forms the "front porch." Above the double doors, the transom window spells out "Temple Freda" in stained glass. According to Temple Freda's listing in the National Register of Historic Places, the congregation's namesake is Ethel Freda Kaczer, who died during its construction, leaving the congregation president a widower. Another account has it that the congregation was named after Freda Tapper, mother of Max Tapper, a Building Committee member whose name is on the cornerstone. His daughter, Lena Tapper Frost, who was born in Bryan in 1915, insists that "the other story is a fabrication." And so, the word *Freda*, which in German means peace, is actually a source of conflict.

In an overwhelmingly Christian community, Jewish observance took commitment. There was no rabbi, so members of the small Reform congregation conducted services, taught religious school and Bar and Bat Mitzvah lessons, and officiated at weddings and funerals. The temple's location near the railroad tracks presented another challenge. The sound of trains whistling by disrupted services. The Jewish Women's Club rode herd over quality-of-life and cultural needs, including a puppet show at Purim. The temple's weekly poker group kept a kitty that paid for the fence around Temple Freda's section of the city cemetery.

During the Korean War, the Jewish community grew when the Bryan Air Base was reactivated. At Passover in 1952, servicemen joined congregants from Temple Freda and students from nearby Texas A&M University in College Station for a Seder at a private home. The National Jewish Welfare Board supplied matzos and *Haggadahs*.

But sometime after 1958, when the Texas A&M Hillel Foundation opened a building of its own, the fabric of the close-knit Jewish community began to unravel. Some congregants left Temple Freda to attend services at Hillel. Controversy arose when break-away congregants discussed taking the Torah with them. In response, a Temple Freda member hid the scroll—according to some accounts, under his bed, and according to others, in the trunk of his car. In 1968, the secessionist group formed a new congregation, Beth Shalom, meeting at Hillel for a while. A few years later, a small group of A&M students and faculty joined die-hard members of Temple Freda for Saturday morning services, which continued until the students graduated and temple members moved or passed away. In 1990, Beth Shalom's congregation bought its own house of worship, a former church in Bryan.

Temple Freda's crumbling Classical Revival building, still owned by the Jewish community of Bryan, has become home to a succession of start-up churches, including the most recent tenant, Ministerio de Restauracion. As for the congregation's coveted Torah, it is in the care of Texas A&M University's Hillel.

WHARTON'S SHEARITH ISRAEL: HEAD START SCHOOL
Shearith Israel's sanctuary, elegantly shaped like a Jewish star, has been remodeled into a Head Start school. For more than half a century, however, the congregation was well known throughout a four-county region for its summer barbecue. At the outdoor fund-

raising feast, the congregation grilled up to six hundred chickens over charcoal. Also popular were homemade kosher dill pickles, made from locally grown gherkins and marinated in crock-pots with dill, vinegar, and secret seasonings. The barbecues ended in the late 1990s as Shearith Israel's aging membership dwindled to around thirty. When the congregation disbanded in 2002, its assets totaled five hundred thousand dollars, which was distributed among Jewish charities and causes. One beneficiary was Houston's Congregation Beth Yeshurun, which agreed to provide lifetime memberships for Shearith Israel's remaining congregants and perpetual care for Wharton's Hebrew Cemetery, established in 1937.

During Shearith Israel's heyday, it had 290 members drawn from a fifty-mile radius. Long-time Rabbi Israel Rosenberg, who served from 1955 to 1978, traveled a hundred-mile circuit from Wharton to Bay City, Palacios, and El Campo, teaching Torah and training dozens of children for Bar and Bat Mitzvahs. Rosenberg was a veritable ambassador to the gentiles, "adept at connecting with the non-Jewish clergy and players of the community," recalled Wayne Franklin, a Rhode Island rabbi who grew up in Wharton. As a youth, Franklin audited the rabbi's conversational Hebrew class, in which the local Episcopal priest was a student.

The congregation began in 1899 and received its charter in 1913. Hadassah founder Henrietta Szold visited Wharton in 1914 and launched the state's first Hadassah circle, recruiting the requisite ten members by drafting three girls, one of them six years old. Affiliated with the Conservative movement for part of its history, at some point the congregation dropped its national affiliation, probably for financial reasons. When Shearith Israel sought to rejoin, Franklin recalled, its application was rejected because it lacked a kosher kitchen. Nonetheless, many Shearith Israel congregants kept kosher, as did the rabbi. During Rosh Hashanah and Yom Kippur, those who refrained from driving on the High Holy Days slept on cots and rollaway beds in the synagogue's community hall.

Congregants were mainly storekeepers, selling to farmers and ranchers who raised cotton, sugarcane, watermelon, rice, corn, and cattle. A county seat, Wharton became the setting for dramas penned by Pulitzer-Prize-winning playwright Horton Foote, son of a local haberdasher. Foote's plays are set in the fictional town of Harrison, a Southeast Texas community that, like Wharton, has one synagogue and is located near the Gulf Coast. He singled out merchant Joe Schwartz, a founder of Shearith Israel, as a prominent Jewish businessman.

Schwartz was present at the dedication of the congregation's first building in 1921, as were mayors from five towns. In 1938, Schwartz donated two acres of land on the outskirts of town for monthly congregational picnics. A community hall was constructed there in 1940 and later a T-shaped education building.

The signature Shield-of-David sanctuary was designed in 1957 by Houston architect Lenard Gabert. Gabert's idea originated a decade earlier when he tried to design Houston's Temple Emanu El in a star shape. The end result bore little resemblance. "It was a matter of scale, more than anything else," said the architect's son and partner, L. M. Gabert, a structural engineer. In Wharton, the ark is housed in the eastern point. To the left is the rabbi's study and to the right a *Kaddish* room with artifacts from the old shul. The remaining points are the entrance and anterooms to either side. The shape gives testimony to the presence, the prominence, and the passing of the once-thriving Jewish community.

LOOKING FOR A MINYAN

BRENHAM'S B'NAI ABRAHAM: TWO CARETAKERS

Leon Toubin, a retired Brenham businessman and raconteur, is all that is left of B'nai Abraham's congregation, and he treats the Orthodox shul like a member of the family. Five generations of Toubin's relatives worshipped here. His grandfather, Joe Levin, was a

Brenham's Orthodox B'nai Abraham, completed in 1893, once supported three minyans a day. © Larry L. Rose.

founder. These days, Toubin and his wife, Mimi, keep the building's paint fresh, the air-conditioning humming, the prayer books stocked, and the door open to requests from civic and church groups for a tour and a talk about the synagogue's history. Occasionally, Toubin exchanges his Stetson for a yarmulke and stops in to say afternoon prayers.

Perched on a rise near the town square, the synagogue resembles a country church, with pitched roof, white-clapboard siding, and pointed arch windows. Until the 1950s, it had an attached *mikveh* and a classroom. Completed in 1893, this synagogue replaced the original 1892 building, which burned. The cornerstone is inscribed in Hebrew; a Texas historical marker stakes B'nai Abraham's claim as one of Texas's oldest Orthodox congregations. Organized in 1885, its twenty charter members first met in the Second Texas Infantry Band Hall.

Though the exterior conjures up images of "American Gothic," the interior is akin to shuls that served shtetls of Eastern Europe. There is a raised *bimah* in the center with a hand-carved banister, an ark on the east wall, and a balcony where women worshipped until the 1950s when they revolted, claiming it was too hot to pray upstairs. Richly varnished woodwork adorns the ceiling, chair rail, and window frames.

Brenham, the seat of Washington County, was incorporated in 1858 and prospered from agriculture, manufacturing, marketing, and railroads. The first Jews came during the 1860s. By the 1880s, there were fourteen families, a B'nai B'rith Lodge, and Hebrew Benevolent Association. The congregation peaked at forty-five families, many who operated businesses around the town square. Toubin said the synagogue once supported three minyans a day and a baseball team, "The Goose Eaters."

There was a full-time rabbi as well as *shochet*, who went door-to-door killing chickens in congregants' backyards. After B'nai Abraham's last rabbi died in 1943, the congregation imported a rabbi, who doubled as a *shochet*, for the High Holy Days. Otherwise, congregants conducted their own services. They hauled their chickens to a kosher butcher in Houston and their cattle to a local slaughterhouse to be killed, kosher style, on a covered countertop.

As older Jews passed on and younger ones left for college and wider horizons, it became harder to gather a minyan. There was a "nice one" during Hurricane Carla in 1960, Toubin said, when Houstonians fleeing the storm attended services. More recently, a Bar Mitzvah and a couple of services were conducted by the youth group from a Houston congregation.

The Brenham area is growing with retirees, weekend residents, and visitors lured by antiques festivals and tours of the Blue Bell ice cream plant. Still, Toubin said, it is doubtful that B'nai Abraham will again serve a congregation. "It has holy scriptures and everything," he said. "The only thing we need is Jewish people."

SAN ANGELO'S CONGREGATION BETH ISRAEL: A HANDFUL OF JEWS

Little has changed at the two-story brick synagogue constructed in 1928 along a major thoroughfare at the corner of Beauregard and Milton streets in San Angelo. Members of the dwindling West Texas congregation have patched the cracks, repainted the interior, and painstakingly replaced the mortar between the bricks. Barbara Cohen Rosenberg, a baby boomer who grew up in San Angelo and moved to the Houston suburb of Sugar Land, enjoys returning. "Because there have been no major additions to this building since it was constructed," she explained, "my childhood memories are comfortable here . . . The stained-glass windows may be painted shut, but in the days before air con-

San Angelo's two-story Temple Beth Israel, completed in 1928, has an upstairs sanctuary. The first floor was apt to flood during heavy desert rains. Photo by Barbara Rosenberg.

ditioning, they were tilted open during services." Passersby could hear voices in responsive readings and Hebrew singing. Initially, the interior was painted with figures, including two fierce lions of Judah on the pillars supporting the ark. All that remains of that artwork is a cloud on the ceiling inside the gold Star of David surrounding the central chandelier.

Approximately forty families belonged to Beth Israel when the twenty-thousand-dollar synagogue was erected a year before the stock market crash. The synagogue's dedication ceremony, broadcast live on a local radio station, began with the singing of "America." The rectangular building was designed with an upstairs sanctuary—possibly to protect the Torahs and worship area from flash floods, common during heavy rains in the desert. The downstairs, which occasionally floods, includes a social hall, kitchen, and classroom. During peak membership in the 1950s and 1960s, the youngest students met in that classroom; a second class convened in the kitchen; two others at opposite ends of the social hall, and another upstairs by the *bimah*. After Sunday school, the children sat on folding chairs in the social hall and together chanted prayers, sang Yiddish folk ballads, and concluded with "Hatikvah."

On weekday afternoons, Rabbi David Schnayerson, who served San Angelo from 1951 until his death in 1971, sat at a wooden table, tutoring Bar and Bat Mitzvah students. Hebrew lessons were optional over the summer, when the rabbi taught in his modest home, and his wife, Gertie, served juice and cookies. Schnayerson continued on the pulpit even as his eyesight failed. "His sermons became more beautiful and heartfelt as he could no longer prepare written sermons," Rosenberg recalled. He is buried in the Jewish section of the city's Lawnhaven Memorial Gardens.

Beth Israel never affiliated with one of the major Jewish movements, possibly due to disagreements between traditionalists and reformers and conflicts over Zionism. "The little community, however, always pulled together with a high percentage of attendance for holiday services and social functions," Rosenberg said.

San Angelo owes its origins to Jewish entrepreneur Marcus Koenigheim, who in 1875 received the town site as collateral for an unpaid fifteen-hundred-dollar debt. Although San Angelo has grown into a ranching, military, and medical center with a population of one hundred thousand, only a handful of Jewish families remain. At Beth Israel, a lay leader still conducts weekly Sabbath evening services, with or without a minyan. Services are often attended by Jewish students from Angelo State University, Jewish personnel stationed at Goodfellow Air Force Base, or an old timer returning out of nostalgia.

VICTORIA'S TEMPLE B'NAI ISRAEL: "WE WILL SUSTAIN IT."

Victoria is home to one of the oldest, continuous, small-town Jewish communities in Texas, with its origins dating to the late 1840s. Shortly after Texas statehood, Jewish entrepreneurs from Alsace began venturing to this Guadalupe River crossing and found business brisk. Located thirty miles from Lavaca Bay on the Gulf of Mexico, antebellum Victoria was a prosperous way station for wagons transporting merchandise to the Texas interior and into Northern Mexico. Six pioneer Jewish families—interrelated through blood, marriage, and business ties—began convening for regular worship services in 1858, praying in private homes. By 1871, the Jewish community was diverse enough to break into factions: one group championing traditional Hebrew worship on the Sabbath and the other favoring less-stringent observance in order to tend to business on Saturdays. The latter group prevailed in 1872 when Temple B'nai Israel was established and subsequently affiliated with the Reform movement.

Among Victoria's Jews were civic figures involved in banking, railroads, ranching, and local government. Many sent their sons to professional schools in the East. Some of Victoria's best and brightest gravitated to Galveston. Among them was Leo N. Levi, an attorney who became international president of B'nai B'rith. Following the Kishineff pogroms in 1903, Levi drafted an international protest petition endorsed by President Theodore Roosevelt, signed by U.S. Secretary of State John Hay, and presented to the Russian czar.

Throughout the twentieth century, Temple B'nai Israel's membership fluctuated from twenty-five to 150 members, depending on the economic fortunes of the city, which is located between Houston, Corpus Christi, and San Antonio. In 1923, the congregation constructed its first and only edifice—a Classical Revival style synagogue on North Main Street. The building, designed by Victoria's most prominent architect, Jules C. Leffland, and built by Joseph Gruy, is red brick and limestone with four brick columns and a Jewish star on the front façade. It has two aisles with ten rows of wooden pews and eight arched windows, originally with green slag-glass panes that were later enhanced with stained glass. During a period of growth, the interior was refurbished in 1989 and paint removed from the brick, a room at the back was converted to a kitchen, and a social hall was added in 1992.

But a decade later, the congregation's membership was dwindling. In 2005, it had twenty-five people among the city's population of seventy thousand. A visiting rabbinical student from Hebrew Union College conducted services monthly and during High Holy Days. The religious school had less than a handful of students. "Things can always change," observed Marjorie Loeb, who grew up in Victoria and raised her daughter during the 1990s when the religious school had thirty youngsters. "The city is working on economic development. If Victoria could grow, things would change at B'nai Israel. We will sustain it as long as we are here. There is something here that people can build on."

POCKETS OF GROWTH

BROWNSVILLE: ON THE BORDER AT TEMPLE BETH-EL

Spanish influence is evident in the white-stucco synagogue that served Brownsville's Temple Beth-El from 1931 to 1989 and that today is home to a Pentecostal church. Constructed with stuccoed masonry and inset clay tiles, the building complex and interior courtyard reflect the cross-cultural nature of this Rio Grande Valley congregation and its international location in a port city along the Mexican border.

Beth-El's cornerstone credits the women of the Sisterhood with providing the money and the drive to erect the congregation's first building, a sanctuary constructed during the Depression at a cost of $4,265. As an afterthought, the women negotiated the inclusion of kitchen and bathroom facilities for forty dollars extra. The sanctuary initially doubled as a religious school. On Sundays, students and teachers gathered among the pews for classes, with the youngest children meeting in the back rows and teenagers sitting up front. By the spring of 1933, the religious school had graduated a Confirmation class of four teenagers. A social hall was added in 1951, and a house next door later served as the religious school.

By 1989, the congregation had outgrown its white-stucco home. Members marched with their Torahs several miles to contemporary new quarters at 24 Coveway Street. En route, church groups served lemonade. The new synagogue has an atrium, rather than a courtyard, and is under one roof. The old synagogue became the home of Shamma Christian Center, a Pentecostal congregation that felt closer to its roots by moving into a formerly Jewish sanctuary.

For more than fifty years, from 1926 to 1977, Beth-El had a lay rabbi—haberdasher Sam Perl, an effervescent civic booster who wore many hats, including a yarmulke. To raise money, Perl organized poker games after Friday worship services. "That was the

Brownsville's lay rabbi, Sam Perl, takes aim, circa 1965, with a pool cue. Photo courtesy Frances Perl Goodman, San Antonio.

only way we could get a minyan to services and to pay off the social hall," long-time Temple board member Ruben Edelstein once remarked.

Today a city of 140,000, Brownsville and Beth-El enjoy a mélange of traditions. Beth-El's members are Ashkenazic, Sephardic, Orthodox, Conservative, Reform, and Reconstructionist. Worship services blend elements of each. In 2006, the congregation's sixty-eight families hailed from Argentina, Austria, Bolivia, Brazil, Canada, Chile, Czech Republic, Cuba, Ecuador, Egypt, France, Germany, Hungary, Iran, Libya, Mexico, Morocco, Poland, Russia, South Africa, Uruguay, and, of course, Texas and elsewhere in the United States. A contingent of Israelis, who opened beach stores on nearby Padre Island, initially worshiped at Beth-El. In 2004, the Israelis started their own prayer group, called Shova Israel, with Orthodox services on Sabbath and holidays.

At Beth-El, the sense of community and continuity remains strong. Some years the congregation has had a full-time rabbi, at other intervals it has not. Attracting rabbis to this remote location has never been easy. With or without a rabbi, Beth-El has vitality. It has a religious school from pre-kindergarten to Confirmation, Sabbath evening worship, Sabbath morning services, holiday celebrations, a morning minyan three times a week, a Hadassah chapter, an annual Israeli Bond drive, and stature in the larger community.

ODESSA'S TEMPLE BETH EL: OASIS IN THE WEST TEXAS DESERT

Odessa—the name evokes Eastern Europe and West Texas, and rightfully so. Located in the arid, oil-rich Permian Basin, the city was named in 1885 by transient railroad workers who hailed from Odessa, Russia. Both Odessa and nearby Midland (so-named because it is mid-way, or 306 miles, between El Paso and Fort Worth) burgeoned during World War II with the demand for oil. Midland became a white-collar, administrative and financial hub of the oil industry. Odessa grew into a blue-collar, petrochemical center. During that era, the white-collar side of the oil business discriminated against Jews. It was the exception, rather than the rule, for Jews to join the corporate ranks or even to be hired as geologists. Jews gravitated to the entrepreneurial pipe-and-supply side of the industry that was centered in Odessa.

Thus, the Jewish congregation established in the Permian Basin in 1946 was located in Odessa—although the impetus for building the first synagogue was to accommodate Jewish troops stationed twenty miles away at the Midland Bombardier Base.

Temple Beth El grew to sixty families by 1961, leading to a larger new building constructed by the local architectural firm of Trainer & Powell. The architects, a Catholic and a Baptist, drew parallels in their design between West Texas and the land of Israel. The eternal light is a tumbleweed of wrought iron; the menorah resembles a mesquite tree; high ceilings evoke the expansive deserts of West Texas and the Middle East, while the roof is scalloped into two rows of six peaks, symbolizing the tents of the Twelve Tribes of Israel. The grounds are planted with fig trees, rose of Sharon, and other vegetation described in the Bible.

Beth El is affiliated with both the Conservative and Reform movements in Judaism. Its bookshelves hold three sets of prayer books—Reform, modern Conservative, and out-of-print Conservative (for those more comfortable with how things used to be). The prayer book used often depends upon the lay leader. The congregation's part-time rabbi, Fort Worth's Sidney Zimelman, who officiates two weekends a month, alternates from one mode to the other.

Odessa and Midland's Jewish population, once largely mercantile, gradually became

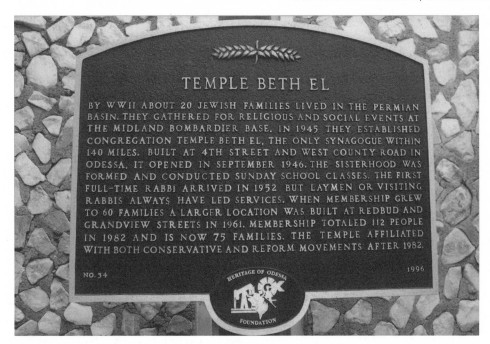

The historic marker at Odessa's Temple Beth El shows an oil field pump and a windmill, emblematic of West Texas. Photo by Jenny Solomon.

professional. The boom-and-bust cycles of the oil industry led the Permian Basin region to diversify. By the close of the twentieth century, a new medical center and university were attracting physicians, professors, and financial analysts who contributed to the growth, diversity, and continuity of Beth El. As the congregation neared its sixtieth anniversary, it had more than one hundred congregants, a school run by volunteer educators, and a youth group. Its calendar—replete with Friday and Saturday services, Purim carnival, Hanukkah festival, Tu-B'shvat Seder, Passover Seder, and Jewish book month—is as full as any big-city congregation's, but on a smaller scale. With a rabbi on staff and weekly services, Beth-El is a magnet for Jews scattered throughout a ninety-mile radius, with congregants driving in from Big Spring, Fort Stockton, and even Hobbs, New Mexico.

SCHULENBURG'S TEMPLE ISRAEL: THE TRI-COUNTIES' STAR

Temple Israel's members boast that they put the "shul" in "Schulenburg," a rural community between San Antonio, Austin, and Houston settled by people of Czech and German ancestry. Since 1946, Schulenburg has been headquarters for Jewish families living in a region of stately courthouses, charming town squares, and painted churches, dubbed the Tri-Counties. At the temple's dedication in 1951, lay leader Hyman Ettlinger, a University of Texas mathematics professor, remarked that some day archaeologists studying the area would discover the Jewish star mounted on Temple Israel's western wall and realize, "Jews were here" too.

They first settled in the region in the late 1850s. In 1880, they were holding Orthodox services in private homes in Columbus, seat of Colorado County. The congregation moved to Hallettsville, seat of Lavaca County, in 1905 and renamed itself Beth Asher, reportedly after the man who put up the most money for expenses in the new location. The community Torah was stored at Hallettsville's Fink Hotel, whose proprietor, Abe Finkelstein, carted it to services at the Odd Fellows Hall. Succeeding generations gradually tilted away from Orthodox traditions and reorganized as a Reform Jewish congregation in 1945.

When the Odd Fellows sold their building in Hallettsville in 1946, members of Beth Asher voted to relocate and erect a synagogue at the geographic center of the area's scattered Jewish community, Schulenburg in Fayette County. They spent thirty-five thousand dollars on a post–World War II modern, red-brick building designed by Houston architect Lenard Gabert. And they took a new name, Temple Israel.

Congregants officiated at services, though visiting rabbis and student rabbis sometimes came for the High Holy Days. Congregant Isyjean Pinchin Korenek, a seventh-generation Texan reared in Schulenburg, studied for her Confirmation by correspondence course with a rabbinical student. As a teenager, she was a one-woman choir on the High Holy Days. Sarah Lippman, who still lives in Schulenburg, was the long-time cantorial soloist and *shammes*, the sexton or caretaker of the synagogue. Friday nights at the temple were reserved for rituals—worship services followed by poker games in the social hall. Each year, the congregation hosted a community Seder.

Temple Israel and its predecessors never boasted large congregations—forty families at most. But members have left their mark on the business, professional, and civic lives of their communities—including former Schulenburg mayors Michael Levey and Hirsh Schwartz. Many are buried at the Jewish cemeteries in Hallettsville, LaGrange, and Columbus.

Today, twenty families participate in annual Seders and High Holy Day services, which can swell with extended family from all over the map. In 2004, about seventy-five people showed up for Passover. "We have an open, welcoming atmosphere," said Temple Israel Secretary-Treasurer Vickie Vogel.

At least one match was made at such an event. Paula Schwartz and Rick Stein met at a Temple Israel Seder in 1973 and married in 1975, settling in Houston. Their son, David Stein, has written about the ease of attending Rosh Hashanah services in Schulenburg, where his father officiates: "No parking problems, no ticket-takers, no rabbis, and you don't have to go early to get a good seat."

BAYTOWN'S K'NESSETH ISRAEL: SUBURBIA APPROACHES

European Jews came to the communities of Goose Creek, Pelly, and Baytown in Southeast Texas, hitching their fortunes to the area's oil-and-gas boom, which began in 1917. Humble Oil and Refining Company, now Exxon, established the Baytown refinery, creating an influx of petroleum-industry workers and opportunities for Jewish merchants to meet their retail needs. By the 1920s, twelve Jewish families were holding services in a rented building on Friday nights and Saturday mornings.

Baytown's K'nesseth Israel, designed in 1930 by architect Lenard Gabert, has a barrel-vaulted ceiling with light fixtures shaped like Jewish stars. © Larry L. Rose.

In 1928, twenty families organized a congregation, K'nesseth Israel. They spent eighteen thousand dollars to buy land and build a synagogue in Goose Creek, and they hired Houston architect Lenard Gabert. It was his first synagogue commission. Later he designed houses of worship in Schulenburg, Wharton, and Houston as well as the Texas A&M University Hillel building in College Station.

Completed in 1930, K'nesseth Israel conveys a hint of the exotic. Its yellow-brick façade soars with a barrel-vault roof, echoed by arched brickwork above the entryway. Light flows into the sanctuary through stained-glass windows and twinkles from tiny light fixtures in the ceiling that are shaped like Jewish stars. In 1992, the synagogue was designated a Recorded Texas Historic Landmark. What's more, it is a repository for memories—of a congregation that celebrated its seventy-fifth anniversary in 2003.

In the beginning, services were Orthodox, though the synagogue had no balcony for women. Some men sat with their wives, others were sticklers for protocol and sat separately. On the High Holy Days, congregant Dave Aron sold *aliyahs* from the *bimah*. Merilee Aron Weiner recalled that her uncle's "distinctive, sing-song chant sales-pitch concluded with a thump on the bible in his hand when the sale went to the highest bidder." Children in the congregation, whether they carried a tune or sang off-key, formed the choir, led by soprano Sophie Keller.

The end of World War II changed the makeup of the area's government and its Jewish population. Goose Creek, Pelly, and unincorporated Baytown consolidated and formed the city of Baytown in 1948. K'nesseth Israel's membership grew to forty-seven families as doctors, chemical engineers, and technicians settled in the community. Five full-time rabbis led the congregation from 1930 to 1953. When attendance shrank as members passed away or moved, visiting rabbis or visiting lay leaders conducted High Holy Day services. Since the late twentieth century, men and women representing K'nesseth Israel's twenty-eight families do it themselves one Friday night a month and on Rosh Hashanah and Yom Kippur. "We use Reform prayer books during the year and Conservative on the High Holy Days," said member Don Teter. "We're 'Conformodox.'"

Teter arrived in the area with a chemical engineering degree from Rice University and a job at the General Tire & Rubber Company plant. He married a local girl, Gertrude Moskowitz, in 1948. Nowadays, he writes about K'nesseth Israel's past and talks about the congregation's future. Some things endure. K'nesseth Israel is the local community's oldest house of worship still used for religious purposes. The synagogue draws members from Houston, thirty miles away, and other surrounding communities. "They say they like the small-town friendliness," Teter said. "One night we had forty people at services—a near record. Besides, we are noted for our receptions afterwards."

TESTAMENTS TO THE PAST

These synagogues of old remain touchstones, starting places for reconstructing stories and patterns of small-town Jewish communities. Each edifice is a metaphorical sermon, articulating ideas and lessons through brick, stone, wood, and stained glass. When the synagogues and congregations are examined collectively, patterns emerge about conflict and cooperation in small towns, about the resiliency and adaptability of Judaism, and about architecture and memory.

Audrey Daniels Kariel, who grew up attending the onion-domed synagogue in Corsicana, has spent her adult life in Marshall, where she has served as mayor. One of the saddest days of her life was May 4, 1973, when Marshall's Temple Moses Montefiore, a Moorish-style synagogue with Romanesque features dedicated in 1900, was razed to make way for a new police station. "The synagogue showed our place in the town," she recalled. Subsequently, she wrote a history of Marshall Jewry, published in the *Western States Jewish Historical Quarterly*. "I didn't want the people who had lived here and made their imprint on Marshall to disappear completely," she explained. "All we've got left in Marshall is a Jewish cemetery. When visitors see how many Jewish people are buried here—more than two hundred graves—they are astounded." A cemetery spells finality. A synagogue conveys vitality.   ✶

Marshall's Temple Moses Montefiore, completed in 1900 by Texas architects J. Riely Gordon and Cornelius G. Lancaster, blended Moorish and Romanesque features. The landmark was razed in 1973 to make way for a new police station. Audrey and Louis Kariel, Jr., Collection, Marshall, TX.

REFERENCES

General

Cohen, Brian. *At Home on the Range: Jewish Life in Texas.* PBS Television Documentary, 1997.

Davis, Robert P. "Virtual Restoration of Small Town Synagogues," www.geocities.com/txsynvr/txsyn.html.

Handbook of Texas Online, www.tsha.utexas.edu/handbook/online.

Hoffman, David, restoration architect, Evant, Texas. Interviews throughout January 2006.

Howe, Jeffery W. *Houses of Worship: An Identification Guide to the History and Styles of American Religious Architecture.* California: Thunder Bay Press, 2003.

Kariel, Audrey. "The Jewish Story and Memories of Marshall, Texas," *Western States Jewish Historical Quarterly* 14, no. 3 (April 1982): 195–206.

Kaufman, David. *Shul with a Pool: The "Synagogue Center" in American Jewish History.* Lebanon, N.H.: University Press of New England, 1998.

Kieckhefer, Richard. *Theology in Stone: Church Architecture from Byzantium to Berkeley.* New York: Oxford University Press, 2004.

Robinson, Willard B. *Reflections of Faith: Houses of Worship in the Lone Star State.* Waco, Texas: Baylor University Press, 1994.

Stolzman, Henry, and Daniel Stolzman. *Synagogue Architecture in America: Faith, Spirit, and Identity.* Victoria, Australia: Images Publishing Group, 2004.

Weissbach, Lee Shai. *Jewish Life in Small-Town America: A History.* New Haven: Yale University Press, 2005.

Zander, Sherry. "Small Synagogues: Synagogues in Small Places Across America," http://smallsynagogues.com/synagogues.htmwebsite.

Baytown

Rosenbaum, Mervin. "K'nesseth Israel Synagogue in Baytown, Texas, Celebrates its 75th Anniversary," *Texas Jewish Historical Society Newsletter* (hereafter, *TJHS Newsletter*), Fall 2004.

Teter, Don. Interview at K'nesseth Israel, June 28, 2005; telephone interview, December 23, 2005.

Texas Historical Commission. Narrative, K'nesseth Israel historical marker and Recorded Texas Historic Landmark, 1992.

Weiner, Merilee Aron. "The Aron Brothers Five in the Tri-Cities Three," *TJHS Newsletter,* February 2002.

Breckenridge

Kuperman, Mary. Telephone interview, October 15, 2005.

Socol, Leon. "Brownsville and Breckenridge: A Tale of Two (Jewish) Cities," *The Jewish Georgian,* November–December 1997, 18, 20.

Teter, Don. "A Visit to Breckenridge," *TJHS Newsletter,* Spring 1994, 9.

Brenham

Kamin, Hortense Yarno. "Growing up in Brenham: Sharing, caring in a small close community," *Jewish Herald-Voice* 78th anniversary—Passover Edition, 1986, 74–79.

National Register of Historic Places Nomination Narrative, http://atlas.thc.state.tx.us/common/viewform.asp?atlas_num=2090000464&site_name=Synagogue%20B'nai%Abraham&class=2001.

Toubin, Leon and Mimi. Interview in Brenham, October 23, 2005.

Brownsville

Temple Beth-El Brownsville Texas, http://betheltx.tripod.com/index.htm.

Weiner, Hollace Ava. "Pearl of the Rio Grande: The Making of a Lay Rabbi, Sam Perl, Brownsville," in *Jewish Stars in Texas: Rabbis and Their Work.* College Station: Texas A&M University, 1999.

Bryan

Alter, Glenda Lauterstein. "The Impact of Judaism on my Life." Yom Kippur Symposium speech. Unpublished. Temple Beth-El, San Antonio, September 25, 2004.

———. Telephone interview, December 30, 2005.

Bassichis, William, Ph.D., Texas A&M University. Telephone interview, January 3, 2006.

Frost, Lena Tapper. Telephone interview, January 25, 2006.

Matcek, Bettye Kahan. Temple Freda and Beth Shalom congregant. Telephone interview, December 30, 2005.

National Register of Historic Places. Nomination Narrative, Temple Freda. Texas Historical Commission web site, http://atlas.thc.state.tx.us/common/viewform.asp?atlas_num =2083003128&site_name+TE....

Parzen, Carol. "A Glimpse of Jewish Life in Bryan: To Celebrate the 125th Birthday of Bryan, Texas (1871–1996)." Bryan: Lang Printing Co., January 1996, 244–47.

Teter, Don. "Bryan's Temple Freda," *TJHS Newsletter*, Fall 1994, 5.

Corsicana

East Texas Historical Association. "1992 Lucille Terry Preservation Award Winner—Temple Beth-El, Corsicana Texas," http://leonardo.sfasu.edu/etha/programs/terry/terry_1992_temple.html.

Joseph, Rabbi Frank. Telephone interviews, December 21–22, 2005.

National Register of Historic Places nomination narrative. www.rootsweb.com/~txnavarr/ religion/temple_beth-el/temple_beth-el_history.htm.

"Rabbi Frank Joseph: Have Torah. Will Travel." www.rabbifrankjoseph.net.

"Rededication of Temple Beth-El, Corsicana," *TJHS Newsletter*, September 1999, 1.

Samuels, Babbette, Corsicana resident and Beth-El congregant. Telephone interviews, December 18–19, 2005.

Jefferson

Tarpley, Fred. *Jefferson: Riverport to the Southwest.* Austin: Eakin Press and Jefferson Carnegie Library, 1983.

Tefteller [Walker], Carol. "The Jewish Community in Frontier Jefferson," *Texas Historian* 35 (September 1974): 2–9.

Odessa

Elsner, Roy. Telephone interview, October 5, 2005.

———. *Temple Beth El Cemetery.* Booklet. Odessa: privately printed, 1999.

"Temple Beth El History," www.geocities.com/templebethel2003/history.html.

Zimelman, Rabbi Sidney. Telephone interview, October 5, 2005.

San Angelo

"Dedication Beth Israel Synagogue," Program. March 24, 1929. Collection Barbara Rosenberg.

"Jewish History of San Angelo." Collection Barbara Rosenberg.

Rosenberg, Barbara. "Beth Israel Synagogue—San Angelo—2005." Typescript.

"Synagogue to be Dedicated on March 24." *San Angelo Standard and Times*, March n.d., 1929. Collection Barbara Rosenberg.

Schulenburg

TJHS *Newsletter.* Fall 2004.

Gabert, L. M. Telephone interview, December 26, 2005.

Hebrew Benevolence Society Cemetery, Columbus, Colorado County, Texas, www.usgennet .org/usa/tx/topic/cemeteries/Etx/Colorado/HM/HebrewBenevolenceHis.txt.

Jewish Cemetery, Hallettsville, LaVaca County, www.rootsweb.com/~txlavaca/jewish_cemetery .htm.

Korenek, Isyjean Pinchin. Telephone interview, December 26, 2005.

LaGrange Jewish Cemetery, LaGrange, Fayette County, www.rootsweb.com/~txfayett/la_grange_jewish_cemetery.htm.

Lake, Amy Schwartz. Recollections. E-mailed by Vickie Vogel, December 22 2005.

Stein, David. "My Schwartz Family History 1835–2001." February 14, 2001

Stein, Paula Schwartz. E-mail, December 29, 2005.

Vogel, David. E-mail, December 22, 2005.

Vogel, Vickie. Telephone interview and e-mail, December 22, 2005

Victoria

Branfman, Gary S. "Life in Victoria, Texas," TJHS *Newsletter*, Summer 1995, 17.

"Congregation B'nai Israel, Victoria Texas," *The Victoria Shofar*, October 21, 2005.

Levi, Godcheaux, L. "Early Jewish Families, Victoria County." Speech to Victoria County Historical Commission, September 1973. Reprinted, "TJHS, Fall Quarterly Weekend & Meeting, October 21–23, 2005, Victoria, Texas."

Shook, Robert W. "Abraham Levi: Father of Victoria Jewry." Reprinted in "Texas Jewish Historical Society, Fall Quarterly Weekend & Meeting, October 21–23, 2005, Victoria, Texas."

Wharton

Dooley, Tara. "Synagogue closes after 100 years: Wharton congregation sees end to small-town Jewry," *Houston Chronicle*, April 27, 2002.

Franklin, Rabbi Wayne. Telephone interview, January 6, 2006.

Holland, Adine. Telephone interview, October 28, 2005.

Milloy, Ross E. "Small-Town Jewry on Wane in Texas," *New York Times*, April 29, 2002, A-17.

Wadler, Larry. Telephone interview, October 28, 2005.

15

Six-Tenths of a Percent of Texas

KENNETH D. ROSEMAN

In the large cities of Houston and Dallas, in mid-sized, regional communities like Port Arthur, Victoria, and Wichita Falls, and in over eighty small towns, Jews spread out widely across Texas. Throughout the twentieth century, they comprised around six-tenths of a percent of Texas's population. By 1940, over 130 cities had Jewish communities of at least ten individuals, and there were many more where individual Jews had taken up residence.

Only ten Texas cities, however, could ever claim Jewish communities of over one thousand people. These communities never represented less than 70 percent of all Texas Jewish residents, and the percentage of Jews in these largest cities began rising in 1960. After 1970, it never fell below 90 percent and it has risen to 97 percent in the population statistics for 2000 (see table 1). There is no more dramatic evidence of the demise of small-town Jewish residence in the state than this fact, which is consistent with national trends toward urban concentration. Many smaller cities that once boasted vibrant Jewish communities are now, effectively, devoid of Jewish population.

Jews moved to Texas for a variety of reasons. The influx of settlers after the Texas Declaration of Independence in 1836 and American statehood in 1846 occasioned new possibilities. Jews, among others, braved this new frontier to build better lives. Expansion of the railroad network across the state following the Civil War and the development of the port of Galveston following the devastating hurricane of 1900 spurred further in-migration. The Galveston Movement, described in chapter 6 of this volume, brought approximately ten thousand Jews to the Southwestern United States, among them three thousand who settled in Texas and subsequently helped their relatives immigrate and join them. The East Texas oil boom of the 1930s and earlier discoveries in the West Texas Permian Basin in the 1920s opened new avenues for corresponding population growth. World War II, with the building of military bases across the state and the growth of related defense industries, spurred migration.

The aggregate Jewish population of Texas has risen steadily during the past century, roughly doubling since 1960. Among factors accounting for this increase are the headquarters relocation of major companies to the state, improved transportation and communication facilities, widespread availability of air conditioning, relatively moderate cost of living, and, by contrast, issues in other states that encouraged out-migration.

Lee Shai Weissbach, a historian who studies Jewish demographics, has described the continual flux of small-town Jewish populations.[1] In a carefully researched book, Weissbach describes the varied, persuasive motivations that drew Jews to smaller towns and the equally powerful motivations that caused them to leave for larger cities.

Jewish mobility in the United States may be divided into three types: immigration

TABLE 1   Texas Jewish Communities that at any time exceeded 1,000 population

City	1918	1927	1940	1950	1960	1970	1980	1990	2000
Austin	300	490	575	750	1,300	860	2,100	5,000	10,000
Beaumont	400	1,150	1,280	n/r	900	900	400	800	500
Corpus Christi	110	200	645	n/r	1,350	1,045	1,040	1,400	1,400
Dallas	8,000	8,000	10,550	10,000	16,500	22,000	20,000	34,000	45,000[1]
El Paso	1,800	2,400	2,250	2,000	3,800	4,500	5,000	4,800	4,900
Fort Worth	2,250	2,100	2,200	1,800	2,800	2,600	3,000	5,000	5,000
Galveston	1,100	1,100	1,200	1,200	n/r	680	620	800	800
Houston	5,000	12,000	13,500	14,000	17,000	20,000	27,000	42,000	42,000[2]
San Antonio	3,000	6,000	6,900	6,250	6,500	6,000	6,900	9,000	10,000
Waco	1,500	1,500	1,150	1,000	1,250	800	750	500	300
Sub-total in large cities	22,250	34,250	40,100	36,250	51,400	59,385	66,810	103,300	119,900
Total Jewish population	30,839	46,648	47,196	52,000	59,500	65,500	71,515	107,300	123,720
Percentage of total in large cities	81.9	73.4	85.0	69.7	86.4	90.7	93.4	96.3	97.0
Texas population	4,663,228	5,824,715	6,414,824	7,711,194	9,579,677	11,196,730	14,229,191	16,986,510	20,851,820[3]
Jewish percentage of Texas population	0.66	0.80	0.74	0.67	0.62	0.58	0.50	0.63	0.59

1. The executive vice-president of the Jewish Federation of Greater Dallas, in conversation with this author, estimated the Jewish population of Greater Dallas in 1999 at between 47,000 and 50,000. This was based on data provided by professional consultants in advance of the Capital Campaign undertaken the following year.

2. The 2001 *Study of the Houston Listed Jewish Community*, conducted and published by the Jewish Federation of Greater Houston, puts the current population at 47,000.

3. Dallas Morning News, *Texas Almanac 2004–2005*, 296.

from other countries, migration from one part of this country to another, and movement within the locale of final settlement. As immigration declined after the passage of the National Origins Act of 1924, the second type of migration became more typical. In recent decades, the shifting of Jewish population of a more local nature has become characteristic.

Jews who settled in small Texas towns first lived close to the central town square. Beginning in the 1950s, as affluence made it possible for Jews (and others) to afford the sprawling ranch houses of newly developed suburbs, Jews relocated. While there were never enough small-town Jewish residents to create an area of Jewish concentration, generally they moved in the same direction and to one or several adjacent subcommunities. Their synagogue, however, often did not follow, mostly because distances were manageable. Only when three conditions were fulfilled did synagogues tend to follow members to new locations: driving distance to the new area of residence increased beyond what was considered acceptable, the old neighborhood was deemed no longer safe, and sufficient wealth allowed building a new structure.

In God We Trust. At the start of the twenty-first century, the most controversial monument on the Texas Capitol grounds in Austin was this set of Ten Commandments tablets. The U.S. Supreme Court ruled in 2005 that the six-foot granite carving is a legitimate part of a larger legal and religious history display. The monument has been on the capitol grounds since 1961. Photo by Carolyn Cruz.

In larger cities, however, the pattern of internal mobility was more complex. The first generation of Jews populated a defined area where they built synagogues and other institutions to provide for their needs. As the community developed, a second area of settlement developed. In Houston, as an example, the initial settlement area was immediately southeast of the downtown. Following World War II, Houston's Jews moved toward the west of the city. The pattern of movement along a single axis from the first area of settlement is similar to what occurred in a number of other large cities. Dallas's Jews moved north along Hillcrest Road; Atlanta's Jewish community developed along Peachtree Avenue; in Baltimore, Park Heights Avenue remained the central axis. In Houston, the movement until recently was further and further to the west of the center city.

Institutions followed population movement, always lagging behind. People moved away from their synagogues and Jewish community centers and then expected, perhaps demanded, that the structures be reinvented in new environs. In Houston, the Jewish Federation and Jewish Community Center eventually relocated in the southwest Houston neighborhood of Bellaire near the new center of Jewish population.

This pattern of unidirectional migration has broken down in recent decades. Houston's Jewish community found three new areas of residence: southwest of the city in Katy, Sugar Land, and Missouri City; north of the city in Spring and other communities surrounding the international airport; and, to a lesser degree, in communities between Houston and Galveston as NASA and other employers established centers in the area. In

Drawing the masses. Goldstein-Migel Co. attracted a mob to its Waco Department Store on April 16, 1916, when it staged an outdoor Easter fashion show on the canopy above the store's sidewalk. The "Panorama of Spring" style show featured frocks of taffeta and crêpe de Chine, Parisian hats and bonnets, and models certain to possess what the store advertised as a "youthful spring silhouette." Photo by Fred Gildersleeve. The Texas Collection, Baylor University, Waco, Texas.

each case, the rapid spread of the Jewish community away from a concentrated center of population strained existing organizations and required the creation of new institutions and outreach programs to provide services to a more diffuse population. This trend is likely to continue. Similar patterns have emerged in Dallas and other Jewish communities around the country.

Kallah of Texas Rabbis, circa 1930s. Founded in 1927, the annual Kallah of Texas Rabbis grew into a social occasion enjoyed by rabbis and their spouses, who formed close, trans-denominational bonds. Courtesy of the Jacob Rader Marcus Center of the American Jewish Archives.

TABLE 2 Texas Jewish Communities with Population of 50 to 999, 1918–2000[1]

City	1918	1927	1940	1960	1970	1980	1990	2000
Abilene			42		110			(60)[2]
Amarillo				350	275			300
Bay Town/Goose Creek			125	300	300			300
Big Spring			64					(1)[2]
Borger			75					
Breckenridge			80	110	110			
Brownsville/Harlingen			50	380	265	160	325	425
Bryan/College Sta.			62					400
Corsicana	200	330	360	210	200			(6)[2]
DeWitt City					150	150		
Ennis			53					
Gonzales			60					
Henderson			53					
Laredo	93	128	175	265	160	420	200	130
Lockhart			50					
Longview/Kilgore				255	270	420	200	100
Lubbock			60	260	230	350	225	230
Marshall	135	170	130					(2)[2]
McAllen		45	45	195	280	295	475	500
Mercedes		250	315					
Midland/Odessa		17	17	210	210	150	150	200
Overton			55					
Palestine	95	120	56					
Pampa			72					
Port Arthur	110	173	250	260	260	260	100	100
Richmond			58					
Rosenberg			58	120				
San Angelo		73	100		125		100	(10)[2]
Sherman/Denison			79					(36)[2]
Texarkana			35	100	100			(30)[2]
Terrell			73					
Tyler	350	650	450	500	750	500	300	
Victoria	120	115		105				(25)[2]
Wharton/Bay City			169	330	270	170	130	(10)[2]
Wichita Falls		505	385	280	260		260	260

[1]Where no population numbers were reported, the space has been left blank.
[2]Numbers gathered independently through interviews.

The population data in the accompanying tables come largely from the *American Jewish Year Book*. The *AJYB* numbers are, by and large, self-reported estimates. There is reason to challenge some figures. Personal conversations with Jews in Wichita Falls, for example, reveal that fewer than fifty people attended recent High Holy Day services and that the reported population of 260 is an overstatement (see table 2). Rather than correct data about which there are questions, the figures are listed as reported in the *AJYB*. Readers are advised to view them with caution. These data, however, represent the most reli-

Kallah of Texas Rabbis, 1976. Texas rabbis gathered in Galveston in 1976 for their annual meeting. Signs of the times are evident in the longish hairstyles, wide ties, colorful shirts, and the leisure suit worn by the rabbi standing fifth from the left. Courtesy, Beth-El Congregation Archives, Fort Worth.

able information, and in many cases the only data, available. The numbers for Dallas and Houston may be modified reliably in light of Jewish population studies conducted by the Jewish federations of those cities, and this updated information is listed at the bottom of table 1. ✺

NOTES

1. Lee Shai Weissbach, *Jewish Life in Small-Town America: A History* (New Haven: Yale University Press, 2005).

16

Most Politics Is Local

STEVE GUTOW AND LAURIE BARKER JAMES

It was a Boston Irishman who said, "All politics is local." For potential Jewish political leaders in Texas, there is more than a grain of truth in this statement. In Texas and the rest of the pioneer West, the lack of stratification by class, religion, occupation, or family meant unprecedented opportunity for Jews in local political affairs. Julius Henry, the first Jew to settle in Corpus Christi after the Civil War, served as postmaster, then alderman. In Weatherford, kitchen merchant Henry Gernsbacher organized the fire department in 1878 and was elected mayor pro-tem in 1883.

There have been a surprising number of Jewish mayors in Texas: Over forty have served twenty-eight different Texas towns, dating from Galveston's Michael Seeligson, a Dutch-born Jew who in 1853 steered the helm of the state's largest port city. Adolph Krakauer was elected El Paso's mayor in 1889 but had to resign when it came to light that he was not yet a U.S. citizen. Maury Meyer served two nonconsecutive terms as Beaumont's mayor, spanning the late 1970s to the late 1980s. Jeffrey Friedman was thirty years old when he was elected "boy mayor" of Austin in 1975. And in Marshall, two Kariel family members served the town as mayor—first Louis Kariel in the 1940s, then his daughter-in-law Audrey Daniels Kariel from 1994 to 2001.

Small Texas towns have had Jewish mayors: Dublin in central Texas, Eagle Pass on the Mexican border, Sherman near the Oklahoma line, and Ysleta in a largely Hispanic region. Jews also have been mayors of larger cities: Galveston (five times), Fort Worth, Waco, and Corpus Christi. Dallas, the state's third-largest city, has boasted three Jewish mayors—all women. Adlene Harrison was actually mayor pro-tem before becoming interim mayor in 1976. Annette Strauss became Dallas's first elected female mayor in 1987 and served through 1991. A Houston native, she married businessman Ted Strauss and carved a volunteer career as a major fundraiser for almost every local arts group, as well as for several universities and hospitals. Her jump to politics capped four decades of civic service, and she easily won in the usually conservative, white-male-dominated city. Strauss led Dallas through an economic downturn, during which high crime and struggles in race relations plagued the city. Her work with the city's African-American and Hispanic constituencies was groundbreaking. Two-term mayor Laura Miller, elected in 2002, was a city council member prior to her run for the mayor's office. Previously, she was a muckraking journalist who spent much of her career railing against the corrupt politics that had plagued Dallas. Despite opposition from the city's outgoing mayor, the daily newspaper, and the "oil elite" (all targets of her investigative journalism), Miller won a tightly contested election with 55 percent of the vote.

Despite their solid presence in local politics, few Jews from Texas have been elected to state or national office. David Kaufman, elected to the U.S. House of Representatives

Michael Seeligson of Holland came to Texas in 1838 and was elected Galveston mayor in 1853. Private collection.

when Texas gained statehood in 1846, was of Jewish descent. He sometimes is identified as a member of the tribe; however, he married a non-Jew, received a Christian burial, and has no known Jewish descendants. Democrat Martin Frost, therefore, claims the distinction of being Texas's first and only Jewish congressman. Elected in 1978, Frost represented Fort Worth, Dallas, and Arlington in the U.S. House until the state's growing Republican majority gerrymandered his district out of existence in 2004. Only one Jewish candidate, Rose Spector, has won statewide elected office, serving on the Texas Supreme Court from 1992 to 1998.

Annette Strauss's volunteer work catapulted her to Dallas City Hall, where she served two terms as mayor from 1987 to 1991. Dallas Municipal Archives, City Secretary's Office, City of Dallas.

BEHIND THE SCENES

Other Jewish politicians, such as Robert S. Strauss, a former chairman of the Democratic National Party who served presidential administrations from LBJ to Bill Clinton, carved out niches in national politics. Billy Goldberg, Houston attorney and businessman, was chairman of the Texas Democratic Party from 1976 to 1980, the only Jew to have headed a major political party in the state. Arthur "Butch" Schechter, a major Democratic Party fundraiser, served as ambassador to the Bahamas during President Bill Clinton's time in the White House. Dallas native Marc Stanley, a Democratic Party mover since the 1980s, is recognized as one of the best grassroots political organizers in the state. Republican counterpart Marjorie Meyer Arsht helped launch George H. W. Bush's political career during a 1963 gathering in her Houston home. Arsht, who became a GOP speechwriter and high-level assistant in the Department of Housing and Urban Development during the Reagan era, worked effectively for forty years to build the Texas Republican Party.

Among others behind the scenes in Texas politics is Bernard "B" Rapoport, whom former Texas governor Ann Richards once introduced as "the only Fabian socialist" she knew worth thirty million dollars. Rapoport subtitled his autobiography *Capitalist with a Conscience*. His capital came from American Income Life Insurance Company, a firm specializing in policies for the union rank-and-file. Rapoport's social conscience came from his parents. His father escaped from exile in Siberia and became a pushcart peddler on San Antonio's Westside. His mother was among the protestors fomenting the 1905 Russian Revolution. "B," his often-used nickname, was born into poverty in San Antonio in 1917. He grew up with proletarian politics that were pro-labor, pro-Zionist, and pro-human rights. At the Rapoports' home in San Antonio, houseguests included Golda Myerson—better known years later as Israeli Prime Minister Golda Meir.

Rapoport, who as a teenager read Tolstoy, Dostoevsky, and Pushkin, aspired to become a lawyer in the mold of Clarence Darrow. Every time the call of an academic career blared forth, a family emergency or economic woe forced him into sales. Rapoport could sell almost anything to almost anyone. He worked his way through the University of

New Orleans, 1988. Future President George W. Bush, far right, celebrates alongside Marjorie Arsht and other Texas Republican stalwarts during the 1988 GOP national convention where his father, George H. W. Bush, was nominated for the presidency. Marjorie Meyer Arsht, All the Way from Yoakum (Texas A&M University Press, 2006), photo from the collection of Marjorie Meyer Arsht.

Powerbroker and political fundraiser Bernard Rapoport periodically visited the White House during President Bill Clinton's administration. Center for American History, UT-Austin, CN Number 10489, Bernard Rapoport Papers (Photograph Component).

Texas with a full-time job at Zale's, the jewelry store chain owned by his mother's brother-in-law's nephew, Morris B. Zale. In 1940, with only his thesis to complete, Rapoport left graduate school to help pay his sister's graduate school tuition at Columbia University. She eventually became chairman of the Psychology Department at San Antonio's St. Mary's University. In a family that placed great store on intellectualism, Rapoport often overheard his mother say, "My daughter, she is a professor." In a much less audible voice she would add, "My son, he has an insurance company, but he is still a very learned boy."

To make ends meet after he married in 1942, Rapoport sold jewelry in Austin, Wichita Falls, and Waco until 1949. By then, he and his wife, Audre, had poured every last penny into a losing populist campaign for gubernatorial candidate Homer P. Rainey in the election of 1946 as he campaigned to keep state government out of university academic affairs. Deeply in debt, Rapoport reluctantly returned to San Antonio to work with his father, collecting rent payments and marketing insurance savings plans. He sold insurance policies so quickly that he attracted the attention of his wife's uncle, an executive with Pioneer American Insurance. Rapoport was offered a job, became Pioneer's top salesman, and was promoted to general agent for Waco.

As Rapoport's fortunes grew, he became a respected philanthropist, devoting his energy and resources to charities and political causes in the United States and Israel. In 1998, *Fortune* magazine named him one of America's forty most generous philanthropists. Education was at the forefront of his philanthropic and volunteer activities. The Bernard and Audre Rapoport Foundation, established in 1989, distributed more than nineteen million dollars during its first twelve years. It endowed Judaic studies chairs at the University of North Texas and the University of Texas in Austin. As a matter of principle, one-sixth of its donations are directed to charities in Israel. Recipients include a Jerusalem day care center for Arab and Jewish children, a high school for the Jewish poor, and a medical center that provides care to Arabs in East Jerusalem.

Rapoport's capital and his conscience give him clout. He is a major fundraiser for Democratic Party candidates and for social institutions from the United Negro College Fund to the Texas Freedom of Information Foundation. On the wall of his Waco office are autographed photos of more than eighty past and present U.S. senators, including Bob Kerry and Ted Kennedy, who once threw him a birthday party in Nantucket. When told that he was on President Richard Nixon's enemies list in the 1970s, Rapoport responded, "It was a real honor." During Bill Clinton's presidency, Rapoport slept in the

White House's Lincoln bedroom, and he was subpoenaed by the Whitewater grand jury that was investigating the President's finances.

Another leading contemporary Texas political fundraiser and philanthropist is Arthur "Butch" Schechter, whose Prussian ancestors arrived in Texas after the Civil War. His great-great grandfather's brother, Chaim Schwarz, was the first ordained rabbi to lead a Texas congregation. Schechter was born in 1939 in Rosenberg, a small town where Jews were a hearty breed of thirty-five to forty families who traveled to Houston to attend religious services and Sunday school. For generations, Schechter's family was part of Houston's Beth Israel Congregation.

Frequent travel between Rosenberg and Houston made Schechter feel like an outsider in both communities. Even being elected "most popular boy" at Rosenberg High School did not ameliorate such feelings. He believes that "not quite belonging" motivated him and other small-town Jews to excel as they searched for a safe harbor. The principal of Rosenberg High School observed that Jewish students excelled more so than others and once asked Schechter, "What do Jews do differently?" Even so, when prayers at high school football games were directed to Jesus, Schechter wondered, "Who was going to take care of me?" Throughout high school and even college at the University of Texas, Schechter encountered plenty of fundamentalists who predicted that he would "rot in hell" because he was not a Christian. "My problem with religious ideologues," Schechter now remarks, "is that I cannot even imagine a God that would condone believers who make a practice of 'condemning, fomenting hatred or holding others in contempt' because of their race, religion or sexual orientation." Schechter graduated from the University of Texas Law School in 1964 and became a successful maritime attorney in Houston. Personally, he experienced little direct anti-Semitism, but he did encounter Houston law firms that would not hire Jews and country clubs that blackballed Jewish applicants.

Schechter has directed much of his time and money to causes that aid the less fortunate. As part of that commitment, he has donated hundreds of thousands of dollars to the Democratic Party and accepted top leadership positions with the Texas Twenty-First Century Democrats and the Washington-based National Jewish Democratic Council. President Clinton appointed him Ambassador to the Bahamas from 1998 to 2001. Israel's vulnerability during the 1973 Yom Kippur War led Schechter to refocus his volunteer efforts toward the Jewish community. He believes that Judaism teaches special sensitivity for the rights of minorities and an appreciation of diversity. His understanding of Judaism compels him to make large contributions of time and money to the poor and downtrodden.

Another younger member of this behind-the-scenes group is Marc Stanley. A grass-roots organizer and fund-raising leader within the Texas and national Democratic parties, one of Stanley's priorities is making sure that Israel's interests remain protected in the minds and voting patterns of Texans. Born in Dallas in 1957, Marc Stanley grew up as a Reform Jew. His British mother and Brooklyn-born father moved to Dallas in 1955. Judaism for them was not filled with ritual. Nonetheless, "being Jewish" was an important part of their identities, not something that the family took lightly. In high school, Stanley became interested in local politics and worked on Adlene Harrison's city council campaign. Later, as an attorney, he became more involved in the political process as a Democratic fundraiser and organizer. In 2004, he was chairman of Congressman Martin Frost's unsuccessful 2004 campaign.

Stanley's connection to Judaism is one of the principal ways that people in the politi-

Marc Stanley, right, jogs along the
Potomac River with President Bill
Clinton and a Secret Service agent.
Courtesy of Marc R. Stanley.

cal arena have come to identify him. In Texas in 1988, there were approximately twenty
Jewish delegates at the state Democratic convention during which anti-Israel Democrats
promoted pro-Palestinian agendas. In 1990, a group called Texans for Justice and Freedom was formed to bring pro-Israel delegates to the state Democratic convention and
strategize a pro-Israel Democratic platform. The political climate at the time reflected an
increased concern about Israel's sometimes harsh treatment of the less-powerful Pales-
tinians under Israeli dominion. Two years later, Stanley was the principal organizer of
Texans for Justice and Freedom. His efforts brought five hundred pro-Israeli delegates to
the Texas Democratic convention in Houston.

Rarely do Democratic political candidates visit Texas without connecting with Stanley
and engaging him in their efforts. Stanley has played important roles raising money for
presidential candidates Michael Dukakis, Bill Clinton, and Al Gore. He makes it clear
that Judaism and his commitment to the security of Israel are part of his ability to deliver.
In this integrated approach, he manages to give the Jewish community significant lever-
age in its dealings with the political forces in the state and nation.

WHY NOT STATEWIDE OFFICE?

To date, there have been no Jewish governors of Texas. Nor have there been Jewish attorneys general, although Martin Frost's grand-uncle Charlie Brachfield ran for the position in 1926, finishing third in the Democratic primary. "The family always concluded
that he lost because he was from a 'dry' county (where alcohol was not sold) and
'wet/dry' was a major issue," Frost recalled.

The dearth of Texas Jews in statewide elected offices and in Congress could simply be
a matter of proportion in relation to the state's total population. Texas's 131,000 Jews are
six-tenths of a percent of Texas's more than twenty-one million residents. Jewish political success on a state or national scale may be undermined by the diversion of potential
politicians into issue-based politics and social causes, such as civil rights, civil liberties,
and Zionism, according to political analysts Gerald M. Pomper and Miles A. Pomper,
who expounded on Jewish party politicians. And of course, there has been the urban/

rural dynamic. To win a general election in Texas, candidates must appeal to both the dense core of urban voters and big-city donors, as well as to rural constituencies and contributors. The majority of Jews have gravitated to urban areas surrounding Houston, San Antonio, Dallas, Austin, and Galveston. It is not surprising, then, that a "candidate from the Big City" would have difficulty establishing a support base in enough small-town locales to carry any statewide election.

Even within the state's large cities, the Jewish population is a small percentage of the electorate. When Houston's Marjorie Arsht ran for the legislature in 1962, her campaign aides assumed the city was home to half a million Jews. They were dismayed to learn that the number was closer to twenty-five thousand, a figure that translated into fewer than ten thousand voters. As a Republican, Arsht could count on few of those votes. "By running as a Republican, I had broken ranks. Jews were supposed to be Democrats—and liberal at that," observed Arsht, who switched to the GOP during the New Deal because Roosevelt took the country off the gold standard. Recalling her unsuccessful bid for elected office, Arsht writes in her memoir, *All the Way from Yoakum*, "The Jewish community, which might have been expected to rally to my candidacy, held back . . . There was not one coffee or gathering among my many Jewish friends. They figuratively walked on the other side of the street . . . I understood completely. Whereas political appointments were sources of pride, at that time Jews simply didn't run for public office for several reasons. Candidates . . . are targets for all kinds of attacks—some true, some false. Also, among Jews there was a fear that if a Jew in elective office did something wrong, all would be held accountable."

Anti-Semitism, either real or perceived, may have played a role in discouraging Jews to run for state wide office. A "pro-Christian bias" has been observed among the general Texas populace. Since the early 1990s, there has been a trend toward church-based power networks, so some political avenues have seemed closed to Jews—the implication being, no mega-church, no statehouse. Despite the fact that Jews have been largely exempt from the blatant racism that has affected Hispanics and African Americans, it was not uncommon for Jews to have been excluded from (or simply not invited to participate in) law firms, social activities, and clubs that might have generated support for more than just a local office.

Martin Frost recalled that his parents joined a short-lived Jewish country club in Fort Worth in a show of solidarity because "we weren't allowed in all the others." He averred that his family never would have joined one of those exclusive country clubs, "even if we could have." Frost doubted, however, that religion is the reason for lack of political participation at a higher level. "Running statewide in Texas is a big deal for anybody," he explained. "I don't care who you are. It's a staggering proposition. Consider the size of the state and the geography. It just costs a lot of money." That may explain why, historically, Texas Jews involved in statewide politics have stayed behind the scenes, fundraising, consulting, and lobbying.

Whether at the local or state level, Jewish candidates and officeholders have contributed significantly to the political culture of the Lone Star State. A few, in particular, have stood out as exemplary. A. R. "Babe" Schwartz of Galveston served three decades in both houses of the legislature. Florence Shapiro is the first Jewish woman in the state senate. Rose Spector was the first Jew elected to the Texas Supreme Court. Martin Frost held a national office for more than two decades. These individuals' contributions to state and national politics straddle party lines and gender barriers.

A. R. "Babe" Schwartz, a Galveston attorney, military veteran, and defender of the average Texan's right to freedom of information, served in the legislature from 1955 to 1981—four years in the house and the rest in the senate. During his tenure, he fought segregation and sponsored numerous bills to regulate nuclear waste disposal. In one session alone, he sponsored ninety-nine bills and major resolutions, of which fifty-three passed. Described in *Texas Monthly* as "an old school Democratic senator," from 1973 through 1979 Schwartz made the mainstream magazine's list of "Ten Best Legislators."

The child of immigrants to Galveston, he was "born on the island" and fondly describes his earliest experiences connecting with nature on the beach. Schwartz was an early champion of environmental causes and credited his respect for nature to his hometown surroundings and to Judaism. He told the Texas Legacy Project that "reading the Talmud . . . leaves you with a feeling that from the earliest times of the nomadic tribes of the Jews, and the earliest settlements, a regard for the land and its productive capabilities was an essential of Judaism." The Texas Surfrider Foundation honored "the dedication of Babe Schwartz, a staunch and vigilant defender of the Texas Open Beaches Act" by naming a scholarship for him.

When first elected to the legislature in 1955, the long, hard road to desegregation was just beginning. Schwartz later told the *Houston Chronicle*, "During the segregation battles, we all got cards in the mail making us honorary members of the Ku Klux Klan. I got up in the House and renounced the membership because one couldn't be an honorary member of a dishonorable organization . . . Threats came by the score, but the best news came in the next mail advising me that I couldn't be a member anyhow because I was ineligible as a Jew. Thank God for little favors."

Across the state and the political aisle, Republican State Senator Florence Shapiro began her political career in Plano, a once-sleepy Dallas suburb that transformed itself into one of Texas's largest cities (population almost three hundred thousand in 2006). She presently chairs the state's Senate Education Committee and serves on Senate committees that focus on finance, administration, transportation, and homeland security. As evidence of her effectiveness and acceptance, Shapiro was elected President Pro Tem of the Texas Senate and served as Governor for a Day when the Texas chief executive was out of state. Shapiro served Plano as a councilwoman in the 1980s and became the city's mayor in 1990.

As the daughter of Holocaust survivors, there can be no doubt about the role that Judaism plays in her life. However, her religion never surfaced as an "issue" in her polit-

State Senator Florence Shapiro discusses a bill from a lectern at her desk in the Texas Senate Chambers. The yellow roses are a birthday bouquet from her colleagues. Texas Senate Media Services.

ical career until she ran for the Texas Senate in 1993. During her years on the Plano City Council, Shapiro sought to eliminate specific references to Jesus Christ during opening prayers at council sessions. Opponents in her 1993 primary election for state senate seized upon her example of tolerance and inclusion and attempted to use this against her. Shapiro's billboards were vandalized with swastikas and other anti-Semitic smears.

"The only thing I could think about was how devastating this was going to be to my parents," she told *Dallas Jewish Life*. "They had escaped Nazi Germany, and for them to see a billboard with my name on it with swastikas and 'Jew' written across it, I knew it was going to be devastating." But devastation turned to resolve, as Shapiro won the primary and then the election. As the only Jewish state senator, Shapiro recalled the legislature's first Holocaust Remembrance Day ceremony in 2003. She had gone to meet some of her Jewish colleagues from the Texas House. As they stood on the capitol steps, non-Jewish legislators from both parties came outdoors to stand with her. At that moment, deep in the heart of Texas, Jews and non-Jews were standing together to say with one voice, "Never again!"

As a Republican in Texas politics, Shapiro encountered other issues that gave her pause. One year, the state's GOP platform announced the party's support of "America as a Christian nation." Despite areas of obvious dissonance, Shapiro has been able to work with fundamentalists by searching for common ground, such as fundamentalist support for Israel. Shapiro recognizes that being a Jew and a Republican is still "a bit unusual" in American politics but notes that the number of Jewish Republicans is growing "every day," as evidenced by the Republican Jewish Coalition, of which she is a board member. She feels that her understanding of Judaism as a religion in which individual strength and commitment to family are paramount led her to the GOP.

Former Texas Supreme Court Justice Rose Birenberg Spector was the first and, as of 2006, the only Jew to hold statewide elective office. In the Texas political world of the 1970s and 1980s, being a woman posed far more challenges than Judaism. Born in San Antonio in 1933, Spector is the daughter of Russian-Jewish immigrants. The Birenbergs were members of Agudas Achim, San Antonio's Conservative synagogue, where Rose was confirmed in the spring of 1948. Spector was accepted to Vassar College, transferred to Barnard, and graduated with the Class of 1954. She was the typical Seven Sisters coed of the Eisenhower era, a smart young woman seemingly content to marry a physician, stay at home, raise her children, and play bridge. In 1962, another physician's wife enrolled at San Antonio's St. Mary's University Law School and encouraged Spector to join her.

That was the impetus for her legal and political career. In 1965, after graduating magna cum laude from St. Mary's, Spector began a dual career as a lawyer and a municipal judge, an appointed position. She assisted another San Antonio attorney with a landmark public school case that challenged the fairness of relying on property taxes to finance public education. When that case, *Rodriguez v. San Antonio Independent School District*, was appealed to the U.S. Supreme Court in 1973, Spector missed the oral arguments because the timing coincided with preparations for her son's Bar Mitzvah.

Inspired by the campaign of Frances "Sissy" Farenthold, a liberal Democrat who came in second in the 1972 Texas Democratic Party's gubernatorial primary, Spector ran for County Court at Law in 1974 and became one of the first women to hold judicial office in Bexar County. Six years later, she was elected judge for the state's 131st Judicial District, a position that she held until 1992. "When I ran for district judge," she told the *Texas Lawyer* of January 24, 2005, "Ronald Reagan overwhelmingly won Bexar County, and

Judge Rose Spector, the first woman elected to the Texas Supreme Court, is the only Jew in Texas to win a statewide office. State Bar of Texas Archives.

[despite the Republican tide] I overwhelmingly won my district bench." In 1992, she successfully ran for the Texas Supreme Court. Her reputation for fairness and independence swayed people otherwise voting a straight Republican ticket. "Once you got elected, you were for everybody," she told the San Antonio Express-News.

The Texas high court, one of ten state supreme courts to which judges are elected on a party ticket, reviews only civil cases. According to the Texas Lawyer, Spector "often [went] against the grain." When reviewing insurance appeals, she tried to persuade her colleagues to uphold consumers' rights. When the court refused to review a challenge to the state's anti-sodomy statute in 1994, Spector dissented and accused the majority of "shirking its equitable duty." In a 1993 divorce case, her dissenting opinion accused the chief justice of "adopting the medieval view of marital relations." She noted, "In the judicial system dominated by men, emotional distress claims have historically been marginalized."

Spector served for six years before being swept off the bench in a 1998 Republican tidal wave. While on Texas's highest judicial body, she gained a reputation as a consensus builder and an even-handed jurist, despite dissents articulating women's rights. Spector was the Texas Supreme Court's lone woman justice until January 1995, when Priscilla Owen, a Republican branded a "conservative activist" and later appointed to the federal bench, joined her. Following Owen's first year on the Texas high court, Spector said of her colleague, "Although we don't necessarily agree on everything, it is good to have another woman." Spector joked that the high court's gender lineup reminded her of a cartoon showing a boardroom filled with two women and the rest men. The pair of women is reflecting, "Only two women." The men are thinking, "Oh, we're surrounded."

FROST: A CAREER OF FIRSTS

It took more than 130 years from the time that Texas became the twenty-eighth state for Martin Frost to begin his twenty-six-year stint as the state's first Jew elected to Congress. From deep roots in rural politics to power politics on Capitol Hill, former congressman Martin Frost set precedents for Jews who followed his lead.

He was the first Jew in the U.S. Congress to hold an elected party leadership position, becoming chairman of the House Democratic Caucus in 1999. He was the first Jewish chairman of the Democratic Congressional Campaign Committee, a post since awarded to two other Jews. Although many Jews had served in Congress before Frost, most hailed from New York, California, and other states with larger Jewish constituencies. "When you get elected from an area like Texas," he observed, "by necessity . . . you are more equipped to build coalitions across philosophical and regional lines."

The Frost family's political involvement began more than a century ago. Unlike Schwartz, Shapiro, and Spector, Frost is not the child of immigrants. His grand-uncle, Charlie Brachfield, was county judge of Rusk County from 1898 to 1902, a state senator from East Texas from 1903 to 1911, and president pro tem of the Texas Senate in 1909. During the 1930s, his maternal grandfather, M. H. Marwil, was two-term mayor of Henderson, the oil-rich county seat of Rusk County.

Frost's first taste of campaigning came at age fifteen when, as a representative of his Fort Worth synagogue, Beth-El Congregation, he was elected regional reporter of the Texas Federation of Temple Youth. He became president of the local chapter and national treasurer. At Paschal High School in Fort Worth, Frost was president of the National Honor Society and co-editor of the newspaper.

Martin Frost, caricatured in a 1959 Texas-Oklahoma newsletter, got his first taste of the campaign trail when he ran for office in his synagogue youth group. Courtesy, Beth-El Congregation Archives, Fort Worth.

Day or night Martin is on call
As FWFTY Prexy, he gives his all.
Frost loves to travel and make friends,
Invite him to your town any week-end.

Martin

Martin Frost has deep roots in Texas, as evidenced by his campaign appearance in a Stetson, cowboy shirt, and ostrich-skin belt. Courtesy, Special Collections, The University of Texas at Arlington Libraries, Arlington, Texas.

After high school, Frost earned a Bachelor's Degree in History and Journalism from the University of Missouri in 1964 and graduated from Georgetown University Law Center, where he made law review, in 1970. By then, he had decided upon a political career and moved to Dallas. "I was comfortable in Texas," he recalled. "I felt I understood the people and the politics."

His first job after law school was clerking for Federal District Judge Sarah T. Hughes, the Dallas jurist who swore in President Lyndon Johnson following the Kennedy assassination. Frost contacted Robert Strauss, the political strategist and future chairman of the Democratic National Party. Strauss had gone to college with Frost's parents at the University of Texas and was a friend of the family. "Bob was an anomaly, the only Jewish politician on a national level at that time," Frost recalled. "He helped me get that clerkship."

Following the clerkship, Frost became a legal commentator for Dallas public television, working with anchorman Jim Lehrer, who later became a PBS icon. He began practicing law at Carrington, Coleman, Sloman, Johnson, and Blumenthal—one of the few Dallas law firms at that time with a Jewish named partner, Robert Blumenthal. Frost ran for Congress in 1974 and lost to a TV weatherman. Four years later, Frost won in a rematch.

"Religion has never been a factor in any of my congressional races, although I'm not sure that would have been true everywhere in the state," the former congressman said. "In Dallas, Jews have been so much a part of the civic establishment of the city. There was Fred Florence in banking, Neiman-Marcus, Bob Strauss, and three Jewish mayors . . . Religion was irrelevant."

During his years on Capitol Hill, Frost became the ranking Democrat on the House Rules Committee and the senior Southern Democrat in the House. Conservative pundit George Will praised Frost as a skillful "political mechanic." Frost authored the Amber

Hagerman Child Protection Act, which established a nationwide alert in response to child kidnappings. He shaped legislation involving defense spending, healthcare, and campaign finance. He was ousted from office in 2004 when redistricting forced him to run against a popular Republican incumbent in a newly minted Republican-majority district, though he felt vindicated by a series of appeals court rulings questioning the validity of the mid-decade redistricting.

POPULISM, DEEP IN THE HEART OF TEXAS

As for the Jewish governor question, could a state sometimes described as the "buckle of the Bible Belt," ever elect a Jewish governor? The question became relevant in 2006 when a long-shot independent candidate, Richard "Kinky" Friedman, a former Peace Corps volunteer, songwriter, humorist, and mystery novelist, attracted national publicity in his bid for the governor's mansion. Kinky's platform was straightforward—"Texas Politics Stinks."

Texas voters are prone to independence. Lack of traditional political experience is not necessarily a liability in the Lone Star State. In 1994, for example, Ann Richards, a seemingly popular governor, was defeated by a Texas businessman with no previous political experience. He was George W. Bush—not just anyone, of course, but the son of a past president and a man with the charisma to become president himself. Sometimes in Texas, the popular politician is the novice—the inexperienced politician or the "anti-politician." Kinky Friedman revels in the fact that he is of the latter category. "The professionals gave us the *Titanic*," he has said, "but the amateurs gave us the Ark."

A Chicago native, Kinky was two years old when his family moved to Texas in 1946. His father, who later became an educational psychologist, went to work as the first executive director of Houston's Jewish Community Council. His mother was one of the city's

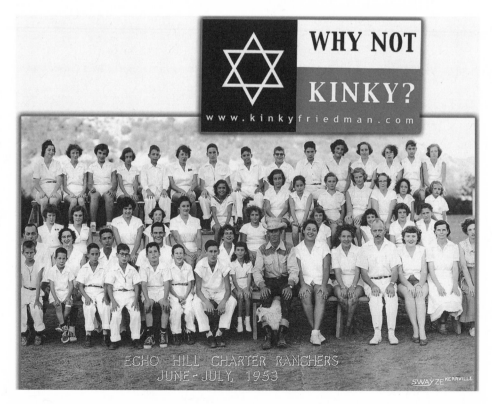

Echo Hill Ranch, Texas's oldest camp for Jewish youngsters, opened in 1953 on 400 acres in the Texas Hill Country. Camp founders Tom Friedman, an educational psychologist, and Minnie Friedman, a speech therapist, are seated in the second row, far left. Their son, Roger, sits in the front row, second from left, with a band-aid on his knee. Son Kinky, who became a songwriter, mystery writer, and populist candidate for governor in 2006, is sixth from left with a big smile. The cowboy in the front row is Clarence Buckelew, a rancher who helped out for the first few years of the camp. Photo provided by the Friedman Family and Echo Hill Ranch.

first public school speech therapists. In 1953 "Uncle Tom" and "Aunt Min" Friedman converted a four-hundred-acre Boy Scout camp into Echo Hill Ranch, a rustic, non-competitive summer camp for Jewish youngsters in the Texas Hill Country. The concept of *tikkun olam*, repairing the world, resonates at Echo Hill, which has influenced three generations of Jewish youth and is the oldest Jewish camp in the state.

Friedman's gubernatorial campaign made much of his Jewishness—not in the "parenthetically, he's Jewish" kind of reference, but in the "he's Jewish and proud of it" way. His bumper stickers featured a *Magen David* on the Lone Star flag and asserted, "My Governor is a Jewish Cowboy." His candor regarding religion and political office hearkens back to comments made by nineteenth-century Galveston Mayor Michael Seeligson. Seeligson declared in the *Occident*, a Jewish journal published in Philadelphia, that his primary intention in running for mayor was to show that a Jew could achieve the office. "There is certainly an Evidence," wrote Seeligson, "[that] if our people would only sustain their rights and privileges . . . they can be elevated to any office they aspire."   ✳

REFERENCES

Annette Strauss Institute for Civic Participation, University of Texas at Austin, http://communication.utexas.edu/strauss/.

Arsht, Marjorie Meyer. *All the Way from Yoakum: The Personal Journey of a Political Insider.* College Station: Texas A&M University Press, 2006.

Burka, Paul. "Senator A. R. Babe Schwartz: Where Are They Now? Politics." *Texas Monthly,* September 2001. www.texasmonthly.com/mag/issues/2001-09-01/politics6.php.

Casstevens, David. "Rick Perry, Meet Your Nightmare," *Fort Worth Star-Telegram,* January 30, 2005, 1-G, 11-G.

"From Muckraker to Mayor," *The Nation,* February 18, 2002, www.thenation.com/blogs/thebeat?bid=1&pid=18.

Frost, Martin. Telephone interview with Hollace Weiner, December 12, 2005.

Green, Linda. "Florence and Howard Shapiro: This Couple Makes Marriage and Politics Compatible," *Dallas Jewish Life,* reprinted in *Texas Jewish Historical Society Newsletter,* September 1996, 13–15.

Guzman, Jane. "Southern Jewish Friends of Bill," *TJHS Newsletter,* March 1998, 19.

Harrington, James C. "Court Shows Insensitivity to Women," *Texas Lawyer,* May 24, 1993, 12.

Houston Chronicle, June 22, 1986, sec. 3, p. 6. Reprinted in Ruthe Winegarten, and Cathy Schechter, *Deep in the Heart: The Lives and Legends of Texas Jews, A Photographic History.* Austin: Eakin, 1989, 180.

Institute of Southern Jewish Life. "A Comprehensive Listing of Southern Jewish Mayors Throughout History," www.msje.org/history/archive_mayors.htm.

Jaffee, Robert David. "A Different Brand of Governor," *Jewish Journal of Greater Los Angeles,* November 11, 2005, www.jewishjournal.com/home/searchview.php?id=14930.

M. Seeligson to Isaac Leeser, June 19, 1853. American Jewish Archives, MS 197, reprinted in *Occident* 11 (June 1853): 188.

Pomper, Gerald M., and Miles A. Pomper. "Jewish Party Politicians," www.rci.rutgers.edu/~gpomper/JewishPartyPoliticians.htm.

"Profiles of Success: Bernard Rapoport," *TJHS Newsletter,* Fall 2001.

Rapoport, Bernard, with Don Carleton. *Being Rapoport: Capitalist with a Conscience.* Austin: University of Texas Press, 2002.

Recio, Maria. "Ruling may spur Frost to run again," *Fort Worth Star-Telegram,* December 26, 2005, 1.

Shapiro, Florence, to Ken Roseman, telephone conversations and e-mail, December 2005 through January 2006.

Spurr, Gary. "Martin Frost Congressional Papers at University of Texas at Arlington," *Southwestern Archivist* (April 2005): 18.

State v. Morales, 826 SW2d (Sup. Ct. Texas 1992).

Texas [San Antonio] Jewish Press, 26 (June 1948).

Texas Legacy Project. A. R. Babe Schwartz interview with David Todd, June 20, 1997, www .texaslegacy.org/bb/transcripts/schwartzbabetxt.html; Sharron Stewart, interview with David Todd and David Weisman, October 23, 2003, www.texaslegacy.org/bb/transcripts/stewartsharrontxt .html.

"Texas Insurance Cases in the Supreme Court, 1991–1999: A Report from Court Watch," www .kraftlaw.com/Articles/InsuranceCases.htm.

Twyman v. Twyman, 855 SW 2d, 642–44 (Sup. Ct. Texas 1993).

Weiner, Hollace. "A Case When Women Reigned Supreme," *Texas Bar Journal*, October 1996, 890–91.

Will, George. "Put your money on Martin Frost," *Fort Worth Star-Telegram*, January 23, 2005, 3E.

Winegarten, Ruthe, and Cathy Schechter, *Deep in the Heart: The Lives and Legends of Texas Jews*. Austin: Eakin, 1989.

17

Minority Report

Dr. Ray K. Daily Battles the Houston School Board

LYNWOOD ABRAM

Shortly before her death in 1975, Dr. Ray K. Daily, a pioneering ophthalmologist who served twenty-four years on the Houston school board, told her son she hoped that one day a school in Houston would be named for her. Thirty years later, a naming committee granted that wish: a new elementary school in west Houston would bear her name. "At long last," said her son, Dr. Louis Daily, Jr., also an ophthalmologist. The honor was indeed a long time in arriving. In politically conservative Houston, it had taken more than half a century for Ray K. Daily to be viewed as a visionary rather than a radical. The fulfillment of Ray Daily's ambition is another chapter in a story that is, by any standard, remarkable.

Dr. Ray, as she was called, had a host of distinctions. In 1913, she became the first Jewish woman to earn a degree from the University of Texas Medical Branch, graduating second in a class of forty-four. She was the first woman president of the board of the Houston Independent School District (HISD). An advocate for improving educational opportunities for women and minorities, Daily took part in developing Houston College for Negroes, the forerunner of Texas Southern University, the alma mater of the late Congresswoman Barbara Jordan. In 1934, Dr. Ray made the motion at an HISD board meeting to create what became the University of Houston, a state university that has expanded into four campuses with thirty-five thousand students. She turned the first spade of dirt at the site of the first campus building. In 1970, Ray Daily became the first woman to receive the Ashbel Smith Distinguished Alumni Award from the University of Texas Medical Branch, an honor recognizing service to the medical profession and to humanity. Dr. Ray also was the first woman president of the medical staff at Houston's Memorial Hospital and headed the medical staff at Houston's former charity hospital, Jefferson Davis Hospital. With her husband, Dr. Louis Daily (1884–1952), an ear, nose, and throat specialist whom she met while both attended medical school, Ray Daily formed one of Houston's best-known husband-and-wife medical teams.

In attaining these distinctions and goals, Ray Daily overcame prejudice against women and Jews in medicine, politics, and education.

Ray Karchmer Daily's background was, to put it mildly, unusual among those who attained professional and political success in Houston. Born in 1891 in Vilna, the capital of Lithuania, then part of the Russian Empire, Ray Karchmer and her family fled persecution and came to the United States, landing in Galveston in 1907. At the time, the Russian empire was rife with pogroms, raids by murderous Cossacks against the Jews with government connivance.

Her father, Kalman Karchmer, had been a caretaker for a wealthy nobleman in Poland whose home, according to Louis Daily, Jr., "was a grand affair, painted white." Young Ray

yearned to live there, and, years later when she became a successful physician, she and her husband bought a large white house on Houston's fashionable North Boulevard. At last, she had the spacious home of her dreams. Dr. Ray's son still owns the house.

"The first duty of an immigrant from (czarist) Russia," Dr. Ray wrote in an essay published while she was in medical school,

> is his departure from Russia. Russia . . . hates her freedom-loving subjects, and at the same time she keeps her gates closed and will not let the freedom-seekers out. One desiring to pass the boundaries of the country has to obtain special permission to do so; but one suspected of the love of freedom will never be granted this request. The thing left to do is to smuggle away. Since the number of immigrants is enormous, there are people who make it their profession to transport whole companies of these freedom-seekers to Germany. [They are] unscrupulous men who will rob the immigrant of almost all the money he has.

The arrival of the Karchmers in Texas was part of the Galveston Plan, an immigration movement, underwritten largely by New York philanthropist Jacob Schiff, to encourage and help Jews from Eastern Europe settle west of the Mississippi. The sponsors, most of them well educated, prosperous, and with Western European roots, feared that the continuing flood of poor and uneducated Jews from Eastern Europe to the crowded cities of the Northeast United States would fan anti-Semitism. Rabbi Henry Cohen of Galveston joined in this effort and helped find suitable locations for the immigrants in Texas and elsewhere.

Accordingly, the Karchmers proceeded from Galveston to Denison, seventy-five miles north of Dallas and four miles below the Oklahoma state line. There, Ray's father became a junk dealer whom Louis Daily, Jr., described as "the poorest man in Denison." Ray graduated from high school in 1909 at age eighteen as valedictorian of her class.

Because Dr. Ray seldom discussed her early life, how she became interested in medicine in general and ophthalmology in particular is unknown. Then as now, admission to medical school was not easy. At that time, however, aspiring physicians in Texas were admitted to medical school without previous college training. In the year after Ray Karchmer earned a scholarship at the University of Texas Medical Branch in Galveston, admission rules were changed to require previous college credits.

An article published in the *Galveston Daily News* upon her graduation from medical school noted that Dr. Ray was "a Russian maid who six years ago was unable to speak English, and who has completed eight years of scholastic work in that six years." The article described the graduating class of 1913 as being "in many respects, the most remarkable senior class known to the institution." The honor roll was composed of fourteen graduates, about one-third of the graduating students.

"It was difficult enough, when I was young, for a woman to get a medical education, and when I graduated in 1913, it was not easy to get an internship and impossible to get a residency," Dr. Ray recalled in a 1970 interview with the *Houston Chronicle*. As in many things, however, Ray Karchmer overcame the obstacles in her path and was accepted for internships at several hospitals. Unable to afford off-campus housing, she chose Woman's Hospital in Philadelphia because it had a dormitory for females.

Upon completion of her internship, Ray Karchmer returned to Texas. She and Louis Daily, also an immigrant from Lithuania, were married in 1914 and opened their joint practice in Houston, specializing in the eye, ear, nose, and throat. During World War I, Louis Daily served in the Navy. After his return, the Dailys took turns maintaining their practice while they alternately traveled to Europe to further their medical studies. Dr. Ray spent much of 1923 and 1924 in Vienna, at that time a premier place for medical training, studying ophthalmology.

Over the years, Dr. Ray gained national fame in her chosen profession. She was a pioneer in developing techniques for cataract surgery. She produced films of many of her surgical procedures, and these were used to teach medical students at schools such as Harvard University. One of the films was reproduced in microfilm and placed in the Crypt of Civilization at Oglethorpe University in Georgia, to be opened in A.D. 8113. Dr. Ray was a clinical professor of ophthalmology at Baylor College of Medicine in Houston, and in 1948 she was elected a vice-president of the American Academy of Ophthalmology and Otolaryngology, the first woman to hold that office. Fluent in five languages, she contributed numerous articles to professional journals in the United States and elsewhere and translated articles published in European journals. She was a founder of the

Houston Academy of Medicine. With her son, she wrote the section on the lens in the two-volume set *Ophthalmology in the War Years*.

Shortly after opening her medical practice, Dr. Ray joined the Woman's Club of Houston in fighting for women's suffrage. "That got me started,'" she later reflected, "because the next project the club tackled was raising teachers' salaries, and I've been interested in schools ever since."

One of her causes was the Houston Open Forum, which flourished for twelve years in the 1920s and 1930s. Serving on the forum's council with Daily were heiress Nina Cullinan, lawyer Captain James A. Baker, Houston School Superintendent E. E. Oberholtzer, and Houston cultural leader and philanthropist Ima Hogg. The organization brought to Houston such speakers as muckraker Lincoln Steffens, frequent Socialist presidential candidate Norman Thomas, Margaret Sanger, founder of the birth control movement, and historian Will Durant.

In 1926, Daily used her influential friends to secure the appointment of a woman, Blanche Goldman, to fill a vacancy on the Houston school board. After Goldman completed two terms, she decided against running again. Dr. Ray tossed her own hat into the ring and in the election of 1928 won a seat on the school board.

In politics, Daily's progress was smoothed with the help of her friends—long-time Houston Mayor Oscar Holcombe and Marcellus E. "Mefo" Foster, founding editor of the *Houston Chronicle* and later editor of the *Houston Press*, a Scripps-Howard newspaper. Holcombe appointed Dr. Ray to the city's Board of Health. Because of his brave and successful fight against the Ku Klux Klan in Houston in the early 1920s, Dr. Ray regarded Foster as a role model and the greatest man she had known. "For a year, he could go nowhere without a guard, yet he never faltered," she would recall.

As a progressive school board member during the Red Scare era, Dr. Ray inevitably made enemies among political reactionaries who did not hesitate to play political hardball. In 1943, for example, opponents distributed a circular that labeled her a "Russian born Red Jewess" and charged that she had been "investigated by the FBI and they no doubt have their eyes on her now." In the election of that year, she won handily as did Ima Hogg, her cohort from the Houston Open Forum. Hogg and Dr. Ray were often in the minority as they battled to raise female teacher salaries to the same level as men's. They advocated hiring teachers on merit, rather than gender or social class. During the Depression, Dr. Ray also had fought the board's tendency to fire married women, who were perceived as taking jobs from men.

Later, Daily was the loser in a heated controversy over the acceptance of federal funds for a free-lunch program for needy children in the Houston schools. Although Daily fought valiantly for acceptance, in 1948 the school board turned down the proposal, convinced that federal aid was evidence of "creeping socialism." (Nearly twenty years later, in 1967, the HISD board changed course and finally joined the national program.) In 1952, at the height of the McCarthy Era, Daily's opponents attacked her for favoring the free-lunch program and finally defeated her bid for re-election. The candidate who ousted Daily, Dallas Dyer, a member of the right-wing Minute Women of the U.S.A., became a leader among those opposing racial integration of the Houston schools.

Charming, gregarious, and fond of stimulating conversation, Dr. Ray also could be imperious and tough. A former employee at her office said she ran a tight ship and could be hard on those who failed to measure up to her high standards of professional service. She made numerous trips to Europe, often taking young Louis with her.

How did Dr. Ray manage to handle the roles of wife, mother, physician, school board member, and civic leader? Her son observed, "She was very disciplined and was a perfectionist." Once, when he was writing an article for a medical journal, she made him rewrite it five times. "Every word had to be correct, every sentence had to be perfect. Everything had to be perfect."

Louis Daily and I have known each other most of our lives, as my parents were friends of Dr. Ray's. Once I asked if I might borrow a book from her library, The Autobiography of Alice B. Toklas by Gertrude Stein. "No," she replied, "but you can have it. It's yours." When I took the book home, I discovered that Stein had autographed it. Fearing that Dr. Ray had forgotten about that, I called her and said I would be happy to return the book. She laughed and told me to keep it. I still have it, one of my cherished possessions.

Born and brought up in a Jewish home, Dr. Ray was active early in her career in the National Council of Jewish Women, which advocated many of the social causes she championed. She and her husband were members of the city's Reform congregation, Beth Israel, and later left to join Temple Emanu El, the more liberal congregation that broke off from Beth Israel. Dr. Ray embraced humanism, which has been called many things but perhaps is best described as a philosophy for those who think for themselves.

In the 1960s, Ray Daily, the friend of the young, was appalled by student rebellions, one of them at Texas Southern University, but hoped that in the future such impulses would be tamed by reason. "Of course, I have hope for the future; of course, I see a constantly improving world. Nothing comes easily; nothing comes without the leveling influence of time," she said.

Dr. Ray continued to practice medicine until she was eighty-three. Louis Daily, Jr., said his mother "just wasted away" from various ailments, including osteoporosis. She died in Houston on November 28, 1975. Dr. Ray asked that no obituary notice be published. Nonetheless, the Houston Chronicle printed a short article about her life, and the Houston Post eulogized her in an editorial as a "lively and courageous warrior" who "fought without rancor" for high principles. The newspaper added, "She slipped out of this life so quietly over the Thanksgiving weekend that her death went unnoticed by the public." The new elementary school bearing her name and recognizing the contributions she made to her community, her profession, and her family bears witness that her work within the Houston school district is at long last widely accepted and applauded. ✱

REFERENCES

Carleton, Don E. Red Scare! Right-wing Hysteria, Fifties Fanaticism, and Their Legacy in Texas. Austin: Texas Monthly Press, 1985.

Daily, Louis, Jr., M.D. Interviews with the author.

Galveston Daily News, May 30, 1913.

Handbook of Texas Online, s.v. "Daily, Ray Karchmer," www.tsha.utexas.edu/handbook/online/articles/DD/fda85.html.

Houston Chronicle clipping files.

Houston Post, November 1975.

Karchmer, Ray. "The Trial of the Russian Immigrant," San Jose Mercury, n.d.

Mulvany, Tom. "Dr. Ray K. Daily Reflects on a Full Life as She Nears her 80th Year," Houston Chronicle, May 31, 1970.

Ornish, Natalie. *Pioneer Jewish Texans: Their Impact on Texas and American History for Four Hundred Years, 1590–1990*. Dallas: Texas Heritage Press, 1989.

Silverthorne, Elizabeth, and Geneva Fulgham. *Women Pioneers in Texas Medicine*. College Station: Texas A&M University, 1997.

Winegarten, Ruthe, and Cathy Schechter. *Deep in the Heart: The Lives and Legends of Texas Jews*. Austin: Eakin Press, 1990.

18

Opening Legal Doors for Women

Hermine Tobolowsky

GLADYS R. LEFF

Until 1972, when a woman married in Texas, her husband assumed control of her separate prenuptial assets. This included her earnings, her real estate, and even her clothing. A husband could drain his wife's bank accounts, dispose of her property, collect rents from her real estate, and spend the proceeds as he chose—except for their homestead. If the wife worked outside the home, the husband could collect all of her wages. Even if a husband deserted his wife, leaving her penniless, state law failed to require him to support her. If the woman was destitute as a result of her husband's desertion, she might be allowed to sell some of their community property.[1]

Mistreatment and disregard toward married women went far beyond community property. A husband who caught his wife with a lover could kill the culprit and receive no punishment. Such behavior was deemed justifiable homicide. If a wife killed her husband's mistress, she could be tried for murder.

Married businesswomen suffered additional indignities. Dun & Bradstreet, the national credit-rating service, rarely listed a woman with a solvent credit rating. In Texas, a married woman could not go into business unless a state court first declared her *femme sole*, the legal term for an unmarried woman. The husband had to consent to this action. *Femme sole* status was limited to a married woman's mercantile activities.[2] Without her husband's agreement, she was still restricted from purchasing an automobile or obtaining a credit card.

The legal status of married women in Texas loomed as a major concern for many wives who realized that they suffered discrimination and prejudice because of gender. Despite the fact that Texas women had complained for years about inequitable treatment codified in more than forty statutes, the Texas legislature saw little reason to alter or amend the status quo until the late 1950s, when Hermine Dalkowitz Tobolowsky became a champion of women's rights in Texas.

Born in 1921 in San Antonio, Tobolowsky was the first of two children of Maurice and Nora Brown Dalkowitz. Her parents taught her to be independent and self-sufficient. Her father was a Lithuanian immigrant who arrived in America at age fifteen. Her mother, born in Belton, Texas, showed an independent streak when, as a teenager, she went to work against her father's wishes. Tobolowsky attended San Antonio public schools, then matriculated at Incarnate Word College and the University of San Antonio (now Trinity University). She had an extremely close and protective relationship with her younger brother Marcus "Tommy" Dalkowitz. Now a retired general surgeon in San Antonio, Marcus recalled that his sister fought his battles in school if he needed her help. The siblings remained close throughout her life.[3] The brother and sister grew up in a large two-story house in which eleven relatives shared one bathroom. Every member of the extended family worked in Maurice Dalkowitz's dry goods business, a chain of twenty-eight general stores across South Texas.

For entertainment when Hermine was little, her parents took her and her brother to political rallies long before they were old enough to understand the politicians' remarks. Hermine was a serious child. Rather than being interested in dating and parties, she was more troubled by political developments in pre–World War II Germany and America's anti-communist, red-baiting campaigns.[4] Her family worshipped at San Antonio's Temple Beth-El in the 1920s and 1930s when controversial Rabbi Ephraim Frisch was in the pulpit. The rabbi, a social activist, championed many of the same political causes as the Dalkowitzes and warned of Hitler's rise to power. Hermine's religious life revolved around Temple Beth-El, where she was confirmed, taught Sunday School, and sang in the choir.[5]

From the time Hermine was a youngster working in the family store, her father encouraged her to attend law school because of her talent for persuasive argument. Hermine's initiation to discrimination against women occurred her first day of law school at the University of Texas in Austin. She was called into the office of a dean, who gave her a list of eligible bachelors to help her find a husband instead of forging a legal career. Another professor told her that he took ten points off each female student's grades because women should not be lawyers.[6] During Hermine's freshman year, she learned that Texas law is derived from both English common law and ancient Spanish rules. Both sets of law treat women as chattel.[7] Despite the discrimination against female students, Hermine was one of two women—out of eleven who initially enrolled—to graduate from the University of Texas School of Law in 1943. She was among the top ten in her class and on the editorial board of the *Texas Law Review.*

The young lawyer's academic rank did not assure her a job. Law firms also discriminated against women. When Hermine interviewed with a top Houston law firm, she was told that, if hired, she would never deal directly with clients. Her activities would be limited to legal research. When she interviewed with Texas Supreme Court Justice James P. Alexander, he contended that no woman had the ability to serve at his court. Hermine retorted that both women and men paid his salary. Hermine accepted a position with the San Antonio law firm of Lang, Byrd, Cross and Labon, where she worked for four years before entering private practice. In 1951, Hermine married Hyman Tobolowsky, an executive with Dallas retailer E. M. Kahn. Moving to Dallas, she set up her legal office in the couple's new home.[8]

As a law student and a young attorney, Tobolowsky was active in her quest for social justice, especially for women. At that time, the strategy of women like Tobolowsky was to seek repeal, one by one, of discriminatory statutes. For example, until 1953 Texas women could not sit on juries. That year, a coalition of organizations in which Tobolowsky was active successfully campaigned for a constitutional amendment that allowed women to serve as jurors.

It was four years later, in March 1957, that Tobolowsky began in earnest her drive to repeal all of Texas's discriminatory laws against women. Representing the Texas Federation of Business and Professional Women (BPW), she traveled to Austin with several others to testify for a bill giving married women control of property that they owned before marriage or acquired afterward by gift or inheritance. Rather than listening to the women's arguments, members of the Senate Affairs Committee responded with amusement. One lawmaker handed Tobolowsky a cigar, challenging her to smoke it because

The Texas ERA. The Equal Legal Rights Amendment, which Hermine Tobolowsky drafted in 1959, was put to a statewide vote in 1972 and passed by a four-to-one margin. The campaign button, a collector's item, is in Tobolowsky's papers at Texas Tech University. Photo courtesy of Southwest Collection/Special Collections Library, Texas Tech University, Lubbock, Texas.

she acted like a man. Tobolowsky left the hearing "convinced that it would take too long to tackle the discriminatory laws one by one." [9]

Later that year at the annual convention of the state BPW, Tobolowsky proposed researching the state legal code, documenting every statute that discriminated against women, and drafting one amendment to invalidate them. The Texas federation voted to back her with a statewide educational campaign and with funding to lobby the legislature. Tobolowsky's research identified forty-four such laws and culminated in her writing the Texas Equal Legal Rights Amendment. The proposed amendment stated that equality under the law shall not be denied nor abridged because of sex, race, creed, or color.[10] She believed that because the amendment was framed in terms of legal rights for all, people understood its meaning. The amendment was introduced in the Texas legislature in 1959, but did not come to a vote in either house. The Texas BPW pledged continuation of the fight for its passage.

"The more people who opposed me, the more determined I got," recalled Tobolowsky, who served as Dallas BPW president from 1958 to 1959, state president from 1959 to 1960, and state legislative chairman for fifteen years. "I told the legislators that had they passed the anti-discrimination bills, I would not have been determined to go all the way to get the Equal Legal Rights Amendment in Texas passed."[11]

Among the politicians with whom Tobolowsky tangled was State Senator Wardlow Lane, an East Texas Democrat who said, "If you think the stupid little women in my district would listen to you, come here and see."[12] Tobolowsky took him up on his challenge, organized the women in Lane's district, and helped end his twenty years of service in the Texas senate. He was defeated for re-election in 1964. Tobolowsky remarked that the senator realized too late the power of determined women.

Another state senator told Tobolowsky that no woman had the ability to sign a deed and handle shares of stock. Some lawmakers accused her of having trouble with her husband. In response to their ridicule, Tobolowsky often left lawmakers with a brief that she had prepared lecturing them about government and reminding them that they represented all Texans, and that more than one-half were women.[13]

In 1958, Tobolowsky sent long-time Dallas legislator George Parkhouse information about equal legal rights concerns and asked him to introduce the amendment to the state senate, which he did in the next legislative session.[14]

Tobolowsky kept a close watch on many candidates for the Texas legislature. In 1961, she notified BPW members of her concern that San Antonio legislator Franklin Spears,

Hermine Tobolowsky. Tobolowsky, sporting a "Support ERA" badge, speaks at an ERA hearing at the Austin Statehouse in June of 1977. The inscription—"To Hermine—With lasting gratitude for your leadership & example"—is from Sarah Weddington, the attorney who successfully argued the historic Roe v. Wade pro-choice abortion ruling before the U.S. Supreme Court. Photo courtesy of Southwest Collection/Special Collections Library, Texas Tech University, Lubbock, Texas, Hermine Tobolowsky Collection.

one of the most vocal opponents of the Equal Legal Rights Amendment, planned to run for the state senate to replace Henry B. Gonzalez, a liberal ally who had moved on to a career in the U.S. Congress. Tobolowsky asked club members to contact Spears's opponents to learn their positions on the amendment.[15] Despite Tobolowsky's opposition, Spears won and served in the Texas senate the next six years. Tobolowsky paid particular attention to legislators who promised to support the amendment, then voted against it. During the 1965 session, she informed BPW members of those politicians who had reneged. She urged club members to write to those legislators immediately.

With each election, the amendment gained adherents but still failed to pass. More lawmakers argued that women needed protective legislation. In the mid-1960s, the State Bar of Texas endorsed a new Family Code and a separate law that would allow women to own and manage property. Despite passage in 1967 of the Family Code, Tobolowsky and the Texas Business and Professional Women kept pressing for the equal rights amendment. In 1967, it passed in the senate but lost in the house in a close vote.[16] Four years later, in 1971, the Texas ERA passed both the state house and senate. On November 7, 1972, Texans voted by a four-to-one margin to ratify the Equal Legal Rights Amendment.

While the Texas legislature had been arguing the merits of a state equal rights amendment, a similar debate was taking place in the United States Congress. Tobolowsky contacted Texas Senators Lloyd Bentson, a Democrat, and John Tower, a Republican, and urged them to support the federal measure. Both Texas senators voted for the ERA, along with most members of the House of Representatives. Some expressed concern regarding the removal of protective legislation for women, but eventually they supported the measure without change. On March 22, 1972, during a special session of the state legislature, Texas became the eighth state to ratify the prospective federal amendment. Tobolowsky wanted to see the federal amendment pass, and she traveled around the country as legal council to the national BPW, lobbying state legislatures for ratification. Here she was unsuccessful. The proposed amendment died in 1982, failing to receive the requisite support before the ratification deadline.

Tobolowsky continued to practice law in Dallas, to advocate women's issues, and to participate in community organizations. She was legislative action chairman for the Dallas section of the National Council of Jewish Women. As a member of Hadassah, the women's Zionist organization, she participated in a number of educational panels. She was a life member of the Women's Foundation of Texas, American Bar Association, National Association of Women Lawyers, Kappa Beta Pi Legal Society, and the Dallas Women's Political Caucus. The *Dallas Times Herald* named Tobolowsky a "news shaper" in 1972 and 1974. The Texas Women's Political Caucus named her Woman of the Year in 1975, and the Texas Business and Women's Club selected her Texas Woman in History in 1976. At her Dallas synagogue, Temple Emanu-el, the Sisterhood successfully nominated her for the Texas Women's Hall of Fame in 1986. She also received the Woman Helping Woman award from several Soroptomist groups. The Women's Law Caucus of the University of Texas School of Law established the Hermine Tobolowsky Award in honor of her work. She also was listed in a half a dozen Who's Who directories that spotlight women, lawyers, and American Jews of distinction.

Hermine Dalkowitz Tobolowsky died July 25, 1995, of complications from diabetes. She was seventy-four. Her husband had died in 1968. The couple had no children. Her colleagues mourned her as the "Mother of the Texas ERA." Former Texas Governor Ann Richards told the *Dallas Morning News* that Tobolowsky's fight for legal justice was unparalleled. The Dallas newspaper also eulogized her as a "mighty oak."[17] Congressman Henry B. Gonzalez, her former ally in the Texas legislature, wrote Tobolowsky's brother, Marcus Dalkowitz, "It was with pride and admiration that I observed her as she fought against great obstacles to obtain favorable consideration of bills, which would provide the most basic equality under law. I was proud to have the opportunity to work with her."[18] A front-page tribute in the September/October publication of the Texas Federation of Business and Professional Women outlined the twenty-five-year struggle for the Texas Equal Legal Rights Amendment and described Tobolowsky as a "lawyer, leader, mentor, advisor or simply friend." The tribute added: "When you think of equality, the state of Texas is a better place to live for both men and women because of Hermine Tobolowsky."[19] ✡

NOTES

1. "The Legal Status of Married Women in Texas," pamphlet, Texas Federation of Women's Clubs, Fort Worth, Texas, November 18–22, 1912.

2. Peter Wyden, "The Revolt of Texas Women," *Saturday Evening Post* 241 (January 11, 1961): 25, 55–56.

3. Dr. Marcus Dalkowitz, interview with author, November 25, 2004.

4. Jennifer Lenoir, "Hermine Dalkowitz Tobolowsky: Mother of the Texas ERA," *Lubbock Magazine*, October 10, 1998, 6–9.

5. Gertrude Miller, "Chai Profile," *Dallas Jewish Life*, March 1994.

6. Lenoir, "Hermine Dalkowitz Tobolowsky," 9.

7. Wyden, "The Revolt of Texas Women," 55.

8. Miller, "Chai Profile."

9. Carolyn Lesh, "High Profile: Hermine Tobolowsky," *Dallas Morning News*, October 19, 1986, E1–E2.

10. Miller, "Chai Profile."

11. Ibid.; *Handbook of Texas Online*, s.v. "Tobolowsky, Hermine Dalkowitz," http://tsha.www.lib .utexas.edu/handbook/online/articles/TT/fto49.html (accessed June 6, 2005).

12. Miller, "Chai Profile."

13. Lesh, "High Profile."

14. Hermine Tobolowky letters to George Parkhouse, June 1958, Hermine Tobolowsky Collection, Woman's Collection, Texas Woman's University (Hereafter TWU), Denton, Texas.

15. Hermine Tobolowsky letter to Texas Federation of Business and Professional Women's Clubs, November 27, 1961, Tobolowsky Collection, TWU.

16. *Handbook of Texas Online*, s.v. "Texas Equal Rights Amendment."

17. *Dallas Morning News*, July 27, 1995, Tobolowsky Collection, TWU.

18. Henry B. Gonzalez to Marcus Dalkowitz, July 28, 1995, Marcus Dalkowitz papers, San Antonio.

19. *Texas Woman* 63, no. 2 (September–October 1995): 1.

El Paso The Wild West Welcomes Holocaust Survivors

MIMI REISEL GLADSTEIN AND SYLVIA DEENER COHEN

El Paso, the international city that borders two countries and two states, has long been a crossroads of people and cultures, from nomadic Indians and migrating Mexicans to Jews who came as frontier merchants and later as Holocaust-era refugees. Both haven and highway, this city at the southernmost point of the Rocky Mountains is a natural passageway that diverse groups have traversed for centuries. Through this mountain pass, Spanish explorers journeyed from the Chihuahuan Desert to Santa Fe. The first Anglo settlers arrived shortly after the Texas Revolution in 1836, and Jewish entrepreneurs began setting up shop in 1849 after the U.S. Army constructed an adobe outpost named Fort Bliss. Outlaws hid in El Paso in the 1880s, the decade during which two Jewish merchants were elected mayor. Throughout the Mexican Revolution, from 1910 to 1920, El Paso served as a center of intrigue. Exiled leaders sought refuge there. Revolutionary general Pancho Villa—bandit to some, folk hero to others—contacted Jewish merchants and tailors to outfit his troops. One of those merchants, Rubin Cohen, recalled: "Whatever Villa wanted, Villa got!"

Since World War II, El Paso's Jewish population has held steady at around five thousand people. While the Jewish numbers remained stable, the city's total population nearly tripled to seven hundred thousand at the end of the century, making El Paso the largest American city along the Mexican border. Despite the Jewish community's shrinking proportion to the whole, El Paso's Jewish families maintained a high profile. Ever since the city's first rabbi arrived in 1898, Jewish religious leaders—along with a priest and a minister—have presided at civic occasions as if they represented a third of the populace. The city's long-time Reform rabbi, Martin Zielonka, who served from 1900 until his death in 1938, was among the founders of the College of the City of El Paso. Conservative Rabbi Joseph Roth, who served Congregation B'nai Zion from 1923 to 1953, headed the Philosophy Department at the Texas College of Mines, forerunner of the University of Texas as El Paso. A post–World War II rabbi, Floyd S. Fierman, wrote a series of colorfully titled history books—*Roots and Boots* and *Guts and Ruts*—that record experiences of the region's Jewish pioneers and demonstrate the degree to which Jews were among the mix of people that settled the Southwest.

When the Chamizal National Monument, celebrating the end of a century-old border dispute, opened in 1967 on an island in the Rio Grande, it evolved into a multicultural center with programs illuminating race and ethnicity. Chamizal became an avenue for understanding among Mexicans, Hispanics, native tribes, blacks, Anglos, and Jews. Logically, the Chamizal Memorial Theatre hosted the region's first Holocaust remembrance observance in 1976 produced by Sally Gilbert and Norma Geller—a standing-room-only multimedia production. The production closed in silence with survivors

Ernst Kohlberg (1857–1910). A hearty immigrant from Westphalia, Kohlberg was among the first European entrepreneurs to settle in the frontier pass between the mountains. He became the Southwest's first cigar manufacturer and was shot to death in 1910 by a drunken gambler he had sued for unpaid debts. University of Texas at El Paso Library, Special Collections Department, Kohlberg Collection.

lighting memorial candles. Survivors were not yet ready to pour out their stories; however, the Chamizal Memorial programs, four in all, ignited a spark among the survivors and wakened the curiosity of the El Paso community to the *Shoah*—the Hebrew word, meaning "catastrophic upheaval," that is used to describe the Holocaust.

El Paso remained a sleepy town until after World War II, when many of the soldiers—both Jew and non-Jew—who had passed through Fort Bliss elected to settle in West Texas. A large number of soldiers had married local girls. Others chose to return to the Southwest after a cold winter or two in the North. In addition to the warm and arid weather in the foothills of the Franklin Mountains, what drew veterans to El Paso was the low cost of living and the abundant, affordable household help. Even lower-middle-class families could employ live-in Mexican housekeepers. Because everyone had a "maid," social life and entertaining in homes was quite active. Jewish women were freed from

Pancho Villa, Mexican revolutionary general, outlaw, and folk hero. Villa ordered supplies from merchants in El Paso Del Norte. "Whatever Villa wanted, Villa got!" University of Texas at El Paso Library, Special Collections Department, Mexican Revolution Collection, Photo 15-2-021.

many household duties and often became active in social service organizations, in card-playing circles, and even in family businesses. The El Paso section of the National Council of Jewish Women, which served the community from 1917 until 2003, was instrumental in founding the El Paso Lighthouse for the Blind, the El Paso School for Emotionally Disturbed Children, and many other key community institutions.

Two of the newcomers to El Paso in the late 1930s were Emil and Regina Reisel, who had the foresight to leave Stanislav, Poland, in 1935 as Hitler was rising to power. They reached the United States in 1938 via Nicaragua and lived in Las Cruces, New Mexico, until 1945 when Emil began operating a wholesale warehouse in El Paso. Although a

South of the Border. Ciudad Juarez served as El Paso's playground and source of hired help. Texans routinely crossed the border to visit Mexico's colorful plazas for an inexpensive lunch or dinner with drinks. University of Texas at El Paso Library, Special Collections Department, Mexican Revolution Collection, photo 15-2-1-07.

recent arrival, he headed up the El Paso Jewish Community Council's committee that re-settled Holocaust survivors. Nationwide, approximately two hundred thousand Jewish refugees entered the United States from Europe between 1933 and 1945. Another one hundred thousand immigrated during the postwar period from 1945 to 1950. Of the latter group, around seventy-five ended up in El Paso—a small number percentagewise, yet a group that would have significant impact.

For many of the Jewish refugees who moved to El Paso, the city was an alien environment. Some survivors came to El Paso because they had relatives in the city. A few were recruited directly by Emil Reisel, who met them in New York when he visited the Hebrew Immigrant Aid Society (HIAS) offices. Other survivors decided to move to far West Texas after a brief experience with big cities and cold climates in other parts of the country. El Paso, with its 364 days a year of sunshine, felt like a more hospitable environment. It was an international city with manageable traffic, a low crime rate, and a small-town atmosphere.

Reisel's main task was to find employment for the men among the refugees. When he could not place an immigrant in a job, he put him to work in his own wholesale dry goods business, Rio Grande Sales Company. He gave many newcomers a start and then provided them with merchandise on credit to begin their own businesses. While Emil Reisel took charge of job placement for the men, an impromptu women's auxiliary—made up of his wife, Regina, her sister-in-law, Sally Rosen, and a friend, Ida Bendalin—oriented the women to their new environment. This entailed securing housing, furnishing homes, and showing them the ins and outs of shopping. After her first trip to the grocery store,

Emil Reisel, he made things happen. Reisel, a follower of Zionist revolutionary Vladimir Jabotinsky, emigrated in 1935 as Hitler's shadow crossed Europe. In El Paso, he spearheaded the resettlement of Holocaust refugees. El Paso, Holocaust Museum and Study Center.

one woman expressed confusion: "How do you know what to choose?" The array of soaps overwhelmed her. On the other hand, El Paso groceries did not have all the products the immigrants were used to. Bagels were unknown. One woman asked the store manager for sour cream, which was not then generally available in the region. The grocer haughtily replied, "Madam, all our cream is fresh." On another occasion, as a woman was leaving a store, a checker said, "Thank you. Y'all come back." So the shopper walked back and heard the checker ask, "Can I help you?" She replied in her heavily accented English, "You told me to come back."

While Emil Reisel was finding jobs for the men and his wife was taking women shopping, the couple's two daughters got involved. "Here, teach them English," the girls were instructed. A refugee's age or country of origin did not matter. The sisters taught them English. There was no bilingual education in those days, yet the children of survivors felt driven to achieve and often became top students.

The Holocaust survivors who came to El Paso had varied backgrounds. Most exotic was Sarah Hauptman, a lion tamer active in the Belgian underground. Henry Kellen of Poland had studied textile engineering in Paris. Eva and Sigmund Weiser were pharmacists educated in Italy. Nathan Weiselman was a Polish tailor. Most built new lives, seldom continuing in their earlier professions. Many had a facility for language and quickly picked up conversational English and Spanish, enabling them to work among the border's bilingual clientele.

One of the most romantic stories is that of Rudy Burgheim (1891–1983), a diminutive man, about five feet tall, who escaped from Germany and spent the war years in Shanghai. By the time he arrived in the United States, he was close to sixty and had never married. When no work could be found for him in El Paso, he became a stock boy at Rio Grande Sales Company. Once established in Texas, he visited relatives in Chicago, where he met Beatrice, also never married and also diminutive, measuring all of four feet ten inches. It was a love match. The couple opened a small store in downtown El Paso, prospered, and bought a home. Their devotion to each other was legendary.

Ben Kandel, a Polish accountant, survived the Krakow ghetto, the Plaszow penal labor camp, and the Mauthausen Concentration Camp. He met Emil Reisel at the HIAS office in New York. Reisel offered him a job as a traveling salesman in the Southwest. After four years of life on the road and several attempts at operating businesses in Las Cruces, New Mexico, and Laredo, Texas, he settled in El Paso, where he successfully developed Ben's Men's Store downtown.

Drs. Sigmund and Eva Weiser received doctorates in pharmacy from Italy's University of Modena. Returning to their native Poland in 1939 to attend her father's funeral, they were trapped when Hitler invaded. Through connections in Italy—among them the Grand Duke, nephew of King Vittorio Emanuel—they escaped on the last Italian Red Cross train leaving Poland. They hid in Genoa until an informer told police their whereabouts. Eva Weiser often retold the story of sitting at Genoa police headquarters, crying. The police captain told her not to weep, that she would be grateful later because he was sending the couple to the Ferramonti De Tarsia internment camp near Cosenza in the south of Italy. It was one of fifteen internment camps Mussolini established in the summer of 1940. What she did not realize then was that the Nazis were demanding that some inmates in northern Italy be sent to death camps. Being in the south saved the couple's lives. After the war, both Weisers became active with the Haganah, procuring boats to smuggle Jews into Palestine. They also returned to their work as pharmacists. However,

Survivors of the Nazi Holocaust Who Settled in the El Paso–Las Cruces Area

Peter Biro, Hungary

Sarah Biro, Hungary

Olga Bowman, Pacin, Hungary

Hannah Burstein, Tarnow, Poland

Cecilia Camp, Czechoslovakia

Julius Dula, Ubrez, Slovakia

Ruth Dula, Pakastoy, Slovakia

Thomas Dula, Michalovce, Slovakia

Albert Eger, Presoy, Slovakia

Edith Eger, Kosice, Slovakia

Hedwig Eichwald, Germany

Yolanda Engel, Trevisov, Slovakia

Zoltan Engel, Velky Ruskov, Slovakia

Larry Gladstone, Munkacx, Hungary

Alex Gluck, Visne Reviste, Slovakia

Helen Gluck, Tegena, Slovakia

Morris Gluck, Visne Reviste, Slovakia

Monique Hauptman, Belgium

Nathan Hauptman, Poland

Sara Hauptman, Belgium

Guy Hauptman, Belgium

Edith Hecker, Frankfurt, Germany

Karl Hochman, Cernowitz, Romania

Gertrud Hofbauer, Germany

Freddy Kahn, Giessen, Germany

Edith Kallman, Visne Reviste, Slovakia

Ben Kandel, Lvov, Poland

David Kaplan, Kovno, Lithuania

Henry Kellen, Lodz, Poland

Jerry Kellen, Lodz, Poland

Julia Kellen, Kybarty, Lithuania

Erna Kerner, Vienna, Austria

Frank Klein, Hajduboszormeny, Hungary

Itzhak Kotkowski, Warsaw, Poland

Thelma Krugman, Koloszyce, Poland,

Mark Kupfer, Novy Korczyn, Poland

Elias Kurtz, Wysoki, Brzerg, Poland,

Dave Lantos, Hungary

Mike Levinter, Hungary

Lucie Liebman, Vienna, Austria

Rachel Lipson, Saudinal, Lithuania

Zundel Lipson, Kovno, Lithuania

Hilde Mason, Frankfurt, Germany

Lee Mason, Kassel, Germany

Ruth Metzger, Germany

Irma Oppenheim, Falkenberg, Germany

Irene Osborne, Germany

Arlene Pergricht, Budapest

Bernard Pergricht, Sosnowiec, Poland

Bluma Piciotto, Germany

Albert Rosenberg, Germany

Nathan Ryback, Radan, Poland

Eric Saks, Vienna, Austria

Agnes Schaechner, Debrecen, Hungary

Tibor Schaechner, Budapest, Hungary

Mike Schkoll, Germany

Albert Schuller, Cologne, Germany

Rose Schuller, Brussels, Belgium

Yvonne Schuller, Paris France

Gertrud Schweitzer, Vienna, Austria

Lee Schweitzer, Vienna, Austria

Richard Selig, Poland

Peter Shugart, Budapest, Hungary

Ilonka Stockl, Berlin, Germany

Juergen Strauss, Dortmund, Germany

Elizabeth Vorenberg, Worms, Germany

Manfred Vorenberg, Kassel, Germany

Nathan Weiselman, Radom, Poland

Lea Weiselman, Zemosc, Poland

Eva Weiser, Lvov, Poland

Sigmund Weiser, Kolomyja, Poland

Helen Zurio, Ubrez, Slovakia

Irvin Zurio, Michalovce, Slovakia

when they moved to El Paso to join Sigmund's cousins (Marcus, Paul, Sigmund, Leo, and Oscar Rosen), he went to work in one of the Rosens' retail stores, and Eva Weiser became a full-time housewife.

Dr. Larry Gladstone—the family name was originally Glattstein—enlisted in the Hungarian armed forces in 1941. Jewish soldiers were discharged quickly and put into labor battalions. Gladstone survived typhus, near starvation, and two death marches in Austria, first to Mauthausen and then to Gunskirchen, the site of mass graves. In 1946, with assistance from El Paso relatives, he resettled in West Texas, graduated from the College of Mines, then enrolled in Southwestern Medical School in Dallas, where he met his bride, Beatrice "Bitty" Marcus. He served at the U.S. Army Medical Corps' William Beaumont Medical Center in El Paso and then went into private practice, from which he retired in 1992.

Siblings Agnes and Ferenc "Frank" Klein arrived in El Paso in 1949 with help from their cousins, the Schwartz family, owners of the Popular Dry Goods Company. The

Kleins survived Auschwitz, where their mother and aunt had been selected upon arrival for extermination. Ferenc and his twin brother, Otto, were taken to Dr. Josef Mengele, whose infamous experiments on human subjects are well documented. Otto survived and resettled in Switzerland. Agnes married Tibor Schaechner, also a survivor, whom she met in Brooklyn and brought to El Paso. Tibor had survived the war in safe houses in Hungary, ending up in the Budapest ghetto months before the Russian Army liberated it. In El Paso, he worked at the Popular Dry Goods Company from 1960 until it closed in 1995. Agnes earned her Master's Degree in social work and worked for the Texas Department of Human Services for twenty-two years.

A number of survivors who settled in El Paso have written memoirs about their experiences, replete with impressions of the Texas-Mexico border region. Among the published authors is Itzhak "Isaac" Kotkowski, who, as a teenager, served in the Polish Army, spent time in a Soviet prison camp, and wound up in a displaced persons camp in France. He immigrated to Israel, to Mexico City, and from there relocated to El Paso to go into an automotive business. Kotkowski's autobiography, *The Wiles of Destiny: Memoirs of Itzhak Kotkowski*, was published in English, Spanish, and Polish. He wrote that he adjusted quickly to Mexico because he had studied Spanish in Warsaw. His "interest in Mexican history and geography sparked an ability to quickly assimilate into the local cultural and business communities."

Mark Kupfer, who fled a Polish ghetto after the 1939 German invasion and survived the war in bunkers, attics, farms, and a forced labor camp, did not live to see his memoir published. His children completed *From Darkness to Sunshine: A Young Boy's Odyssey.* Initially, Kupfer resettled in Chicago, then Detroit and New York, where he met his wife, Rose Eisenberg. Together they moved to El Paso, his wife's hometown. He wrote that El Paso, with its small park in the center of town, reminded him of Europe. Describing his first day in El Paso, he recalled, "In the morning, the sun woke me up, and I couldn't believe what I saw . . . It was December 25 . . . yet there was no snow or ice. The weather there was glorious compared to the eastern cities . . . I said, 'This is beautiful, it's heaven on earth.'"

Among the Holocaust survivors who worked for Emil Reisel was Jake Beilinson. He and his wife Frieda came to El Paso because her uncle, Joe Ravel, lived there. Later, Jake and Frieda divorced and left El Paso, both resettling in California. Frieda's memoir, *Some Dare to Dream: Frieda Frome's Escape from Lithuania*, was published in 1988 under her new married name, Frieda Frome. In her book, she remarked that El Paso was interesting to her because so much of the population was of Mexican descent and spoke Spanish. "They seemed more like the natives of the Baltic countries than any of the people I had yet seen in America." Although her ex-husband was known in El Paso as Jake Beilinson, in her book Frieda identified him as Koba Yanovitch. His original name was dropped in the transition from Europe to the United States.

Among the most unforgettable refugees was Henry Kellen—whose original surname was Kacenelenbogen. A native of Lodz, Poland, Henry, his wife Julia, and nephew, Jerry, survived the Holocaust due to the kindness of a Lithuanian farmer, Andrius Urbanos, who hid them during the war years. In El Paso, Emil Reisel gave Henry Kellen two sample cases, a car, and a sales route that sent him out to remote towns such as Lovington, New Mexico (pop. 9,400) and Safford, Arizona, (pop. 9,000). Although he arrived speaking few words of English, Kellen became a top-notch salesman—evidence of the charm and persistence that would characterize his later endeavors.

Typical of refugees from Nazi Europe, Kellen and other survivors spoke little about

Julia and Henry Kellen, in Berlin, bound for the United States. After the war, Henry went to work in Berlin translating French into German. When President Harry Truman authorized five hundred visas for Holocaust survivors, the Kellen family was among the recipients and immigrated to El Paso. El Paso Holocaust Museum and Study Center. Prewar memories.

their Holocaust experiences. They applied themselves to building new lives and community ties. Holocaust survivors the world over were slow to dredge up their experiences, although many, like Isaac Kotkowski and Elizabeth Vorenberg, quietly had begun compiling memoirs. They shared little of their past with their children, much less with strangers. Rabbi Floyd Fierman, who was adept at taking oral histories, attempted to interview the local Holocaust refugees. In the introduction to his 1983 book, *Insights and Hindsights of some El Paso Jewish Families*, he wrote that the survivors were polite but unwilling to respond to queries. In his opinion, "they failed to cooperate because they did not want to leave any records for future Gestapo—secret police—who might conceivably seek them out to finish what the Hitlers of the world started. This is a psychological withdrawal with which I sympathize."

Throughout the fifties and sixties, popular culture paid little attention to the Holocaust, except for occasional productions such as Playhouse 90's *Judgment at Nuremberg*, telecast in 1959, and Sidney Lumet's film, *The Pawnbroker*, produced in 1965. The latter focused on memories of a survivor. The catalyst for transforming the *Shoah* into a topic of conversation across America was the NBC miniseries, *Holocaust*, televised in April 1978. In conjunction with its airing, journalists scoured their circulation areas for survivors who could put a local face on the highly rated television show, which attracted 120 million viewers. Writer Eli Wiesel, a Holocaust survivor and future Nobel Peace Prize laureate, criticized the miniseries for trivializing the deaths of six million Jews. He encouraged survivors to tell what had really occurred. Immigrants began to pour out their experiences. They were glad for the sympathy this evoked.

Prewar memories. Henry Kellen, first row far right, with family in Palanga, Lithuania, before World War II. A native of Lodz, Poland, Kellen was with his family in Kovno when the war broke out. He, his wife Julia, and a nephew, Jerry, escaped the Kovno Ghetto and were hidden by a Lithuanian farmer. The rest of the family perished. El Paso Holocaust Museum and Study Center.

Seven months before the NBC miniseries, a group of Dallas survivors who worshipped at Shearith Israel had started to meet regularly. They called themselves Holocaust Survivors in Dallas. Their organizer was former physical fitness instructor Mike Jacobs, a native of the Polish town of Konin. He had survived five years in ghettos and concentration camps and emerged with optimism to start a new life. His group grew to include spouses and children who shared his dream, which he described in his memoir, *Holocaust Survivor: Mike Jacobs' Triumph Over Tragedy*, as a "place where we Holocaust Survivors could gather and memorialize our loved ones as . . . we had no cemetery to go to." Jacobs's vision of a Dallas Holocaust Center was so vivid, he had blueprints made as well as a mock-up model of the proposed museum.

In April of 1983, a national Holocaust Survivors Gathering convened in Washington, D.C. Jacobs brought his architectural model with him and was interviewed by camera crews from ABC Television's *Nightline*. The publicity inspired others to follow his example. It also spurred contributions to fulfill Jacobs's dream. In 1984, he became the founder of the Dallas Holocaust Museum and Study Center, which opened in the basement of the Dallas Jewish Community Center. It featured a fifteen-ton railroad boxcar that the Nazis had used to transport Jews to the ghettos and death camps. The Dallas Holocaust Center became a model for other grassroots museums across the country that would start through the efforts of one survivor and then gather momentum.

El Paso's Henry Kellen contacted Mike Jacobs in 1984, brainstormed, and developed a warm friendship. Soon, Kellen began collecting wartime artifacts and memorabilia that would become the core of a collection for an El Paso Holocaust museum. He returned to his native Poland to gather more materials. To exhibit them, he "shnorred" a display case from the Popular Dry Goods Company, courtesy of Albert Schwartz, one of the department store's owners and a descendant of a pioneer El Paso family.

Kellen asked the El Paso Jewish Federation, the successor to the Jewish Community

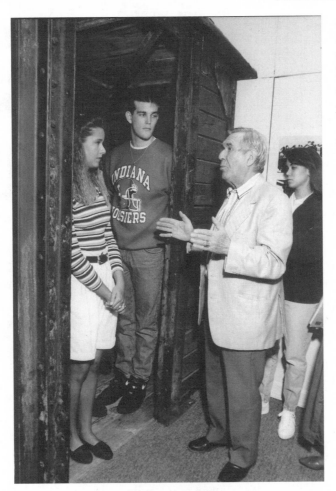

Mike Jacobs, founder, Dallas Holocaust Museum. Jacobs takes teenagers on a museum tour that begins in a railroad boxcar that transported Jews to concentration camps. Jacobs provided the inspiration for El Paso's Holocaust museum and spoke at the dedication of the museum's first display case in 1984. Dallas Holocaust Museum.

Council, to provide space for his display. At first, Federation directors allotted him one wall in a conference room, which Kellen filled with pictures and maps. Slowly, he began encroaching into other areas of the room. When the Union Fashion, a Jewish-owned men's store, gave Kellen a mannequin, he dressed it in an authentic concentration-camp-inmate uniform, bandaging and bloodying it for realistic effect. Another Holocaust survivor, Bernard Peregricht of Budapest, came upon the mannequin suddenly one day and was taken aback. "That's me," he said, pointing his finger. "That is what I looked like."

Kellen's quest for artifacts, memorabilia, and display cases grew. So did visitors to his Holocaust exhibit. Shortly after the first display was installed, Kellen began booking tours to the conference room. He invited schools, churches, and units from the Army's Fort Bliss. They came. Visitors sat on chairs, on the floor, and even on the conference table. Innocently, Kellen allowed children to handle the artifacts. A heavy Nazi helmet was passed around, and the children tried it on.

Needing clerical help, Kellen pulled in Sylvia Deener Cohen, the senior adult director at the Jewish Community Center. Cohen and Kellen had become acquainted years before when both worked at Emil Reisel's Rio Grande Sales Company. "Sylvia," he would often ask her, "could you write this letter for me?" She did. When a photographer from the nearby White Sands Missile Range in New Mexico arrived one day to photograph artifacts on display, Kellen steered him to Cohen. "Sylvia," he said, "you take care of it." She did. One day, when Kellen was hanging posters on a second wall of the conference room,

Small but meaningful. El Paso's first Holocaust museum consisted of one display case filled with artifacts from survivors, memorabilia from military personnel, and items that Henry Kellen brought back from visits to Europe and Israel. El Paso Holocaust Museum and Study Center.

Cohen admonished him that he had only been given permission to fill one surface. "Who cares?" he responded. Gradually, Holocaust materials engulfed the room. There were complaints from some Federation board members that the conference room, often utilized to plan recreational activities, was incompatible with pictures of death and devastation. Henry Kellen was unfazed.

His collection grew as retired military personnel who had fought in the European theater donated Nazi memorabilia. Among the donors was former El Paso Mayor Peter de Wetter, whose Army unit had liberated concentration camps. Another liberator, Major General Raymond L. Shoemaker, former commandant of Fort Bliss, donated artifacts and spoke at events. Unfortunately, Nazi memorabilia attracts a certain type of thief. In 1987, the conference room was broken into. A Nazi saber was stolen. An investigation concluded that the motive was greed, not anti-Semitism, for such a saber could bring twenty thousand dollars on the open market.

With the theft and the burgeoning number of visitors, the need for a separate, independent Holocaust museum became obvious. There was no space to expand in the JCC building. More and more groups booked tours. A new organization, headed by Beth and Meyer Lipson, formed with the goal of constructing a local Holocaust museum and study center. Albert Schwartz, who had given Kellen his first display case, became president. He and the board continued to fundraise for a permanent space. Sylvia Cohen, by then drafted as a tour guide and lecturer, was spending so much time with Henry Kellen's Holocaust display that the fund-raising board picked up one-fourth of her salary. In 1988, the board assumed half her pay, and the exhibits consumed half her time. Once the museum was under construction in 1992, it consumed three-fourths of her working day as she conducted oral history interviews with survivors and trained docents from across the community. By the time the El Paso Museum and Holocaust Center moved from its single conference room into a free-standing building in 1994, Sylvia Cohen had become its executive director.

The modest, one-story building was designed with fifteen hundred square feet for the museum and another fifteen hundred square feet for the offices of Jewish Family Service, the social service arm of the Federation. Prominent local businessman Louis Rosenbaum and his wife Miriam donated the bulk of the funds for the $310,000 building, located on land in the Jewish Federation's parking lot. On opening day, the keynote speaker was Sister Rose Thering, the Dominican nun whose research led the Catholic Church's Vatican II Council in 1965 to reverse its historic doctrine holding Jews responsible for the death of Jesus. "The Holocaust was the culmination of the teaching of contempt," she often said. Her keynote address in El Paso signaled the focus of the museum. It would not only be a setting to learn about the Nazi era, but also a space for people of all religions and backgrounds to reflect upon the impact of intolerance.

When the tiny El Paso Holocaust Museum opened its doors in 1994, it was the only such museum between Dallas and Los Angeles. Two years later, the Holocaust Museum Houston opened. In 1998, Albuquerque launched the New Mexico Holocaust and Intolerance Museum and Study Center, with assistance from the El Paso Holocaust Museum. Also in 1998, San Antonio's Mazal Library, the largest private collection of books and records on the Holocaust, opened to the public by appointment. Two years later, San Antonio's Jewish Federation opened a Holocaust Education Center and Memorial Museum. By the beginning of the century, there were more than a score of Holocaust museums across the nation, including the U.S. Holocaust Memorial Museum in Washington, D.C., that had opened in 1993.

The proliferation of Holocaust museums, particularly in places like El Paso with relatively few Jews, is evidence of their relevance as a community resource for teaching tolerance. The local response to the El Paso museum demonstrates a hunger for knowledge in a region scarcely touched by the Holocaust. During the El Paso museum's first year, five thousand students toured the facility along with hundreds of drop-ins. By 2001, twenty-five thousand students a year were visiting the museum, and there was a waiting list. The museum became a component in the educational program of the public schools. At Fort Bliss, the Office of Equal Opportunity and the U.S. Army Sergeant's Major Academy incorporated tours and workshops into their curricula.

El Paso Holocaust Museum and Study Center, a modest building in a natural setting framed by the Franklin Mountains, opened in 1994 and was destroyed by fire in 2001. El Paso Holocaust Museum and Study Center.

A larger museum necessitated more complex interior designs and displays than a single room with one showcase. Lucie Liebman, a Holocaust-era survivor who had fled from Vienna, stepped in as volunteer curator. She worked side by side with Richard Glass, a local artist. He put into artistic form her ideas for museum exhibits. Together, they maximized the use of educational tools. Professional librarian Mary Ann Plaut volunteered to arrange scholarly materials. Sylvia Cohen recruited a score of docents and speakers from the wider community. Among them were Sol Lederman, a former prisoner of war, and Ernesto Martinez and Gonzalo LaFarrell, two military veterans who witnessed the liberation of the camps. Eileen Licht, Toni Harris, Norman Farb, Phyllis Saltzstein, and Trish Belbel were mainstay docents. Giving tours in Spanish was Dottie Grodin. Former U.S. Army photographer Neal Axelrod, who documented the liberation of concentration camps, gave tours. Professors from the El Paso branch of the University of Texas signed on as tour guides. They included humanities professor Robert Wren, who incorporated Holocaust studies into his classes; Robin Scofield, who assigned freshman English students to research the topic; Ilsa Irwin, who conducted many a tour in German; and David Hackett. Hackett is the Holocaust scholar who translated and annotated *The Buchenwald Report*, a volume filled with transcriptions of Allied Forces' interviews with concentration camp inmates.

One of the most unusual aspects of the El Paso museum is its relationship with the German military. Fort Bliss is home to the German Air Force Air Defense Artillery Center and School, which has 130 staff members and trains around six hundred soldiers a year. When the El Paso Holocaust Museum opened, German Brigadier General Eckart Wienss mandated that every soldier under his command tour the museum. One of Wienss's successors, Brigadier General Peter Merklinghaus, continued the policy. At museum workshops, he spoke about Germany's postwar efforts to come to terms with the Holocaust. Often, the general's driver would pick up Kellen, and the pair would travel to Cochise Community College in Arizona or to Western New Mexico University in Silver City to present seminars. The story of General Merklinghaus and Henry Kellen's friendship was featured in the El Paso Times on April 29, 2002.

The museum's second president, David Marcus, launched a series of high-profile dinners. New York Governor Mario Cuomo was the first big-name speaker. Subsequently, the museum hosted Mikhail Gorbachev, the former Soviet Union premier; General Colin Powell, former chairman of the Joint Chiefs of Staff and future U.S. Secretary of State; General Norman Schwartzkopf, commander in chief of U.S. forces in Operation Desert Shield; Christopher Reeve, the actor paralyzed in a horseback riding accident; and New York Mayor Rudolph Guiliani.

In early October 2001, seven years after the museum opened and a few weeks after the toppling of the World Trade Center towers, the El Paso Holocaust Museum was destroyed by fire. Former President Bill Clinton, scheduled to address the annual fundraising dinner, visited the charred ruins. The fire destroyed 80 percent of the exhibits and artifacts. Because of the tense times, people could not help but wonder about the cause of the blaze. The fire department ruled it an electrical malfunction.

Although the original building was gone, the educational program continued. Shortly after the fire, the museum's new executive director, Leslie Novick, flew to Berlin at her own expense, along with a native Berliner who used her influence to gain access to the Topography of Terror Museum, the Resistance Museum, and the villa in Wannsee where the Final Solution was planned. Novick selected exhibit materials that were flown

Colin Powell, former U.S. Secretary of State, spoke in El Paso during the 1990s when the museum hosted a succession of high-profile speakers. His guide is Sylvia Cohen. El Paso Holocaust Museum and Study Center.

back to El Paso for display in a downtown bank. The Junior League of El Paso took on Holocaust training as a project, developing PowerPoint presentations, which its members took to the schools. One schoolteacher, Christina Vasquez, developed such expertise that she went to work at Holocaust Museum Houston heading its education program.

The big-name speaker program waned. Although bringing in world leaders focused the public spotlight on the museum, there was disagreement among the board of directors as to whether it was worth the considerable expense. In recent years, speakers have not been quite as high profile but have a closer connection to the Holocaust. They have included the chairman of the U.S. Holocaust Museum and the Danish ambassador to the United States, honored for his country's rescue of seventy-five hundred Jews during the Holocaust.

Even when the El Paso Holocaust Center became a museum-without-walls, it continued its mission. Three years after the fire, two El Pasoans—Sam Legate and Jim Scherr—donated downtown space at 101 Kansas Street for a temporary museum location. The space opened in October 2004 and began booking school tours and workshops.

Henry Kellen, in business attire, shortly after his arrival in El Paso, and (below) as elder statesman, museum organizer, and community speaker in the 1990s. El Paso Holocaust Museum and Study Center.

There are plans for a new, permanent El Paso Holocaust Museum in an existing eighty-seven-hundred-square-foot building that will be gutted and renovated, with completion slated for the end of 2006. Henry Kellen, who was eighty-six when the museum burned, remains the driving force at the El Paso Holocaust center. He continues scheduling half-day, full-day, and two-day workshops for schools, community groups, and colleges in Texas, New Mexico, and Arizona. His calendar is full. He hopes to live to see the opening of the new museum. His original display on one wall in the Jewish Community Center has expanded into schools and colleges and inside the gates at Fort Bliss. The El Paso experience demonstrates that there is a need, an interest, and an audience for Holocaust studies not only in Washington, D.C., and New York, which have tens of thousands of Jews, but also in the American Southwest, at a cultural crossroads with relatively few Jews, in a remote corner of the Diaspora. ✳

REFERENCES

Eger, Edith Eva. *Coping With Growth*. New York: Irvington Publishers, 1990.

Fierman, Floyd. *Insights and Hindsights of Some El Paso Jewish Families*, vol. I. El Paso: El Paso Jewish Historical Society, 1983.

Frome, Frieda. *Some Dare to Dream: Frieda Frome's Escape from Lithuania*. Ames: Iowa State University Press, 1988.

Hackett, David. *The Buchenwald Report*. Boulder, Colo: Westview Press, 1995. (Another El Pasoan, Albert G. Rosenberg, was part of the intelligence team from the Psychological Warfare Division that prepared the initial Buchenwald Report. Rosenberg taught in the Department of Social Work at the University of Texas at El Paso.)

Jacobs, Mike. *Holocaust Survivor: Mike Jacobs' Triumph Over Tragedy*. Austin: Eakin Press, 2001. The Dallas museum that Mike Jacobs founded in 1984 moved in 2005 to a temporary downtown location, launched plans for larger, new quarters, and changed its name to the Dallas Holocaust Museum, Center for Education and Tolerance.

Kotkowski, Itzhak. *The Wiles of Destiny: The Memoirs of Itzhak Kotkowski*. El Paso: Kotkowski, 1995.

Kupfer, Mark Bernard. *From Darkness to Sunshine: A Young Boy's Odyssey, Twentieth Century Miracle*. Pittsburgh: Dorrance Publishing Co., 2002.

Llorente, Jeany, "Faithful Friends," *El Paso Times*, April 29, 2002, D-3.

Martinez, Leonard. "Mending relations: Nun's work helped heal Jewish-Catholic rift," *El Paso Times*, February 18, 2005, D-1.

Weiner, Hollace Ava. "The Mexican Connection: Rabbi Martin Zielonka, El Paso." In *Jewish Stars in Texas: Rabbis and Their Work*. College Station: Texas A&M University Press, 1999, 102–19.

20

Forty Acres and a Shul "It's Easy as Dell"

CATHY SCHECHTER

We regret to say that we are unable to record the existence of a handsome temple, as our Israelitish brethren, although having purchased a lot sometime ago for the purpose of erecting a synagogue, has as yet neglected it, or perhaps did not feel themselves strong enough to enter into such an undertaking; but we hope that ere long a gorgeous and handsome edifice erected by the Israelites of Austin, wherein the voice of an eloquent and able minister will be heard for the elevation of Judaism, will beautify and adorn some street of the Capital.
—Charles Wessolowsky, in a letter to Rabbi Edward B. M. Browne, May 1879

Hitchhiker: "I may live badly, but at least I don't have to 'work' to do it."
—Richard Linklater's 1991 film, Slacker

In the 112 years between the time B'nai B'rith circuit rider Charles Wessolowsky wrote his politely scathing criticism of Austin's Jewish community to the screening of *Slacker*, the seminal film about a day in the life of Austin, little changed. The pokey college town and state capital with a landscape of lakes and hills had ever been a perfect place for thinkers and tinkerers, poets, potheads, and sun-and-water aficionados to live a mellow life, and Jews who came to Austin originally to conduct some business, politics, or teach have been no different. The Jewish population always had been large enough and diverse enough to support a "temple and a shul"—Southern parlance for a Reform and a Conservative congregation—but Austin's preponderance of professors made the capital city fairly transient. Some Jews faded into the landscape, their numbers a wispy guess. The sort of person who stayed in this place eventually would acquire the mindset that it is okay to wear Birkenstocks to synagogue. No one asks very much of you. Lay back, man, it's Austin.

How ironic is it, then, that around the same year *Slacker* codified life in Austin that the Jewish landscape changed dramatically? How on earth did that happen? As the television commercial says, "It's easy as Dell."

A NEW-AGE *KEHILLAH*

In the medieval European *kehillah*—the Hebrew word for "community" and the name given to a Jewish communal organization that had quasi-governmental authority—there arose an Enlightenment, freeing Jews from the confines of parochial life to pursue education, work, and culture outside the community. Aware of the medieval experience of enlightenment, not a few of the early Jewish Texans brought this sense of possibility to the Lone Star State. If, therefore, a nineteenth-century soothsayer of Jewish communal fates had surveyed Austin, Texas, in the 1870s, the capital city would have seemed an

The State Capitol. Its dome rises above downtown Austin, the self-proclaimed "music capital of the world," home to over thirteen thousand Jews. Photo by Carolyn Cruz.

unlikely place for a new-age *kehillah*, except that among Texas Jewish communities, Austin always marched to the beat of its own drum.

Despite the city's laissez-faire style of being and growing, and even though it has not ever seemed to care what the rest of the Jewish world thought, Austin unwittingly became a model, twenty-first-century new-age *kehillah*: a self-determining Jewish community. But this *kehillah* was not designed for self-protection from Cossacks, kings, anti-Semites, or the czar's army. For donors, the rationale for the new *kehillah* was an economy of scale and monetary savings, eliminating repeated solicitations for construction of new buildings scattered around town. For dreamers, it was the chance of a lifetime to build something for everyone, where all would pray and play in the same space, where Jewish children could meet, date, and, hopefully, marry other Jewish children.

The center of this new *kehillah* is the Dell Jewish Community Campus, a wooded, forty-acre plot of land in northwest central Austin. The property, the last remnant of the Hart Ranch, had for years been an oasis in the center of Austin. Since the 1970s, schools, shopping centers, apartment complexes, and neighborhoods to which Jewish families gravitated had grown to surround the property. Patti Edelman Leonard, an East Texas native from Tyler, lived on the other side of the fence from the Hart ranch. When the land went on the market in 1992, she contacted Keith Zimmerman, a commercial real estate broker and former vice-president of the Greater Austin Chamber of Commerce, whom she knew was shopping for land for a JCC—a Jewish community center.

Slacker image. A worshipper wearing a yarmulke and prayer shawl with blue jeans and tennis shoes is not unusual at Austin's Congregation Agudas Achim. The carved lions, capitals, and Ten Commandments on the polished wooden ark are among the historic possessions the congregation refurbished and moved to its new synagogue on the Dell Community Campus. Photo by Carolyn Cruz.

After a quiet but feverish bidding war against a local parochial school, Michael Dell, founder of Dell Computer Corporation, and his wife Susan, a longtime board member of the Jewish Federation of Austin, were prevailed upon by Zimmerman and the Jewish community's leadership to make an eleventh-hour bid of eight million dollars, slightly more than the asking price. With the land in the hands of the Dells and the Jewish community, many plans were envisioned and shared, a communal controversy erupted, and all hell broke loose—not a little of it generated by Patti Leonard, whose hope for a traditional JCC soured when she learned of plans not only for a Jewish community *center*, but of a *campus*, with a JCC and multiple synagogues.

HYMIE'S TOWN

For years, the Jewish Federation of Austin (JFA) had been housed peacefully on Jollyville Road in far north Austin in a one-story building, lovingly purchased by Hymie Samuelson and other community activists. Hymie, a haberdasher and diarist who has authored fifteen books, ranging from the autobiographical to the metaphysical, embodied the homespun quality of the community during the years 1950 to 1985.

The squat Jollyville building served the community well through placid years of slow but steady growth that characterized most of the twentieth century. Though far from the center of town where most Jews lived, it offered a neutral place—away from the city's two competing synagogues, the Reform Beth Israel, founded in 1876, and Conservative

Hymie Samuelson. Renaissance man and patron saint of the Jewish Federation of Austin, Samuelson relaxes with a young friend playing video games in the education wing at the Dell Jewish Community Campus in Austin. David Finkel photography— www.davidfinkel.com.

Agudas Achim, chartered in 1924. As the community spread its wings through the 1980s, the Jollyville complex acquired a veritable trailer park of portable buildings and housed a preschool, a small library, offices, and a community hall for the annual Austin Jewish Book Fair. Old timers often characterize the place and the times as friendly, a space where everyone involved either knew or was related to everyone else.

That spirit was illustrated by the way Hymie and some fellow congregants at Beth Israel constructed the two large Ten Commandment tablets for the temple sanctuary. With a dedication ceremony approaching in February 1967, temporary décor was needed to adorn the ark. Hymie and his extended family cut plywood and covered it with wallpaper in a decoupage style reminiscent of a fifties ranch house. Hymie sat on his bedroom floor several nights in a row and painstakingly painted calligraphic Hebrew letters on the tablets so that they would be ready for the dedication. The Ten Commandments still grace the sanctuary.

The same communal involvement was evident at the Jollyville campus.

The growth of Austin's Jewish population had always paralleled that of the general community, remaining at roughly one percent of the overall populace. No one expected things to change dramatically. But the "slacker" mentality changed to "slicker" when the city dubbed itself "Music Capital of the World," and the youthful executives of new high tech and Internet companies flocked to the beautiful and relaxed environment of a growing city. From 1980 to 1990, Austin's Jewish-affiliated population more than doubled, from twenty-one hundred to five thousand. By the end of the century, it had redoubled to more than ten thousand, and by 2002, the *American Jewish Year Book* estimated the city's Jewish population at 13,500, making it the nation's third-fastest-growing Jewish community after Las Vegas, Nevada, and Portland, Oregon. The appearance of young "Dellionaire" Jews who made millions in the brave new world of high technology took the mellow Austin Jewish community completely by surprise.

LAND, POLITICS, AND ACADEMIA: NOT A PLACE FOR MERCHANT PRINCES

From Austin's inception as the Texas capital in 1839, settlers were drawn to the town for its physical beauty. Austin's first notable permanent Jewish resident, who moved to the capital in 1850, was Phineas De Cordova (1819–1905). He and his half brother, the well-known surveyor and land promoter Jacob De Cordova, ran a land agency and newspaper

Phineas De Cordova (1819–1905).
A land agent and notary public,
Phineas De Cordova was Austin's first
notable Jewish resident and a founding
officer in 1879 of Temple Beth Israel.
This advertisement for his General Land
Agent office is part of the frontispiece in
his brother Jacob's 1858 book, Texas:
Her Resources and her Public
Men. DeCordova photo, Center for
American History, UT-Austin, CN
Number 03505, Texas Jewish
Historical Society Collection.

publishing business. Another Jewish pioneer, Henry Hirshfeld (1834–1911), immigrated to Texas in 1859 from Prussia seeking adventure and mercantile pursuits. After serving in the Confederate Army, Hirschfeld became a founder and vice-president of Austin National Bank, retired early, and invested in real estate. He was the founding president of Temple Beth Israel, with Phineas De Cordova his vice-president.

That Austin is the capital of Texas has always provided members of the Jewish community with access to politicians and state government. Phineas De Cordova himself was a protégé of governors P. H. Bell and E. M. Pease, for whom he served as business manager. The Texas senate named him its official secretary for three terms from 1859 to 1865. Other Jews undoubtedly touched circles of power, but for the most part, Austin Jews have been on the periphery or quietly influenced political life from the back room. Austin has had one Jewish mayor, Jeff Friedman, also known as "the hippie mayor," who served from 1975 to 1977. More recently, there have been occasional Jewish legislators representing Austin, among them Sherri Greenberg (1990–2000) and Elliot Naishtat (1990 to the present), but neither their numbers nor their contributions have been significant over time.

The University of Texas also has seen many brilliant Jewish professors come and go. Professors Harry Joshua Leon and Ernestine Phelps Leon taught in the Classics Depart-

VIP Guests. Jim Novy, left, bows his head alongside Lady Bird Johnson, and President Lyndon Johnson at the dedication of Agudas Achim's refurbished sanctuary, December 30, 1963. Novy had invited his friend LBJ to speak at a previously scheduled dedication November 24 that was postponed in the wake of the Kennedy assassination. Johnson kept his promise and visited when the ceremony was reset a month later. In 1938, LBJ arranged for Novy to help forty-two Jews emigrate from Poland to the United States. LBJ Library Photos by Yoichi Okamoto.

ment, and Harry was the first to teach Hebrew at the university for credit. He also served on the board of directors for Congregation Beth Israel. Mathematician and athlete Hyman Ettlinger, who taught at the university from 1911 to 1969 and chaired the Mathematics Department for twenty-five years, in 1913 organized Hillel's predecessor, the Menorah Society for Jewish Students. Ettlinger served as secretary at Congregation Beth Israel for twenty-five years. Thanks to the Charles and Lynn Schusterman Family Foundation of Tulsa, Oklahoma, the Austin campus has a new Center for Jewish Studies. In recent years, the university has made a number of impressive acquisitions, such as the Isaac Bashevis Singer papers housed at the Harry Ransom Humanities Research Center.

While these contributions have enhanced the intellectual life of the Austin Jewish community (as well as the estimated five thousand Jewish students who attend the university from all over the world), the long-term contributions to the growth and development of the community by university faculty have remained largely in the realm of the mind. Brilliant minds subsisting on professor salaries build programs but generally contribute little for bricks and mortar.

Academia and politics aside, Austin's Jewish community never had a genuine merchant prince as Houston did with its Westheimers and Levys, Dallas with its Zales and Sangers, or San Antonio, which had Frosts and Freemans. Those families made fortunes and generously gave back to their hometowns, where walls and halls in synagogues, universities, rodeo coliseums, and hospitals honor their names. While some of Austin's Jewish merchants made small fortunes, the city had no towering arts complexes or public libraries named for them. If Austin benefited from the largesse of out-of-town Jewish families, it was because they attended or sent their children to the University of Texas. Just as in 2005 the fortunes largely earned elsewhere in Texas helped build a six-million dollar Hillel Center for Jewish Student Life and a five-million dollar Hillel endowment, in the early 1900s the Jewish congregations around the state were solicited by Beth Israel's president, Joe Koen, to help pay the Austin rabbi's salary, since he tended to so many of the out-of-town Jewish students.

THE ULTIMATE SLACKER

How unlikely is it, then, that a dentist's son from Houston who came to Austin in 1983 to go to UT, *dropped out*, then became not only Austin's first real merchant prince, but also the world's first high-tech mail order maven?

In his autobiography, *Direct from Dell: Strategies that Revolutionized an Industry*, Michael Dell describes himself as a modern-day newspaper-boy-turned-mogul. Propelled by his parents' work ethic and a discerning knack for eliminating the middleman, he expanded his paper route by targeting a mailing list of new homeowners. He launched his mail-order computer business in the University of Texas's Dobie Dormitory, skipping class to work on his home-built computers. His wife, Susan Lieberman, was born and raised in Dallas, where she spent many hours at the Jewish Community Center. The marriage of these two children of affluent Jewish families brought a new style of philanthropy to Austin and to its Jewish community.

For one thing, the sheer number of dollars available to donate eclipsed anything that anyone in Austin had ever seen. Austin's long-time Jewish philanthropists, Milton and Helen Smith, had given thousands of dollars to B'nai B'rith and Congregation Beth Israel. So had benefactors at Congregation Agudas Achim, such as Shirley and Jarrell "Tank" Rubinett. But no one, especially not fresh-faced newcomers like Michael and Susan Dell, had ever offered to give *millions*. Nor did the Dells intend to do so without community support. The Dells proposed a *community match*. This concept of philanthropy, a new style for Austin's Jews, stipulated that the Dells would not build anything unless the community paid its share. Even then, the Dell name would have to adorn the entry gate.

A sputtering and surprised reaction ensued among those who had built the community with their blood, sweat, and tears. On the one hand, there were those who fumed, "How dare they try to ghettoize us! All it would take is one bomb on Rosh Hashanah, and boom, the whole community would be gone! It's just another marketing opportunity, that's why they want their name there." On the other hand, there were those who viewed the proposal as a once-in-a-lifetime deal. "How could we afford this land otherwise? It is in the middle of the 78731 zip code, the largest stack in every synagogue's bulk mail. This could become a showcase, not just for us, but for all of Austin."

Thus, the lines were drawn in a battle that would forever alter the Austin Jewish community into one that within ten years would be changed beyond recognition.

KEEPING UP WITH THE CHRISTIANS

Historical records and contemporary anecdotal evidence demonstrate a pattern within Austin's Jewish community in which it takes its largest leaps forward under pressure from gentile neighbors. As Charles Wessolowsky noted in his letter to Rabbi Browne, there was a congregation in Austin in 1879, but no Jewish edifice. What Wessolowsky may have learned, but omitted, was that the Jews of Austin had been struggling for seven years to form some sort of communal organization. A Hebrew Benevolent Association, typically a Jewish community's first endeavor, formed the first Sunday of December 1872 in the mayor's office. With eleven hundred dollars in pledges, a motion passed to purchase land for a synagogue, and a committee was organized to find a site and negotiate a price. When a follow-up meeting failed to attract more than five people, the effort disintegrated.

By February 1874, still no congregation existed. Outside lecturers were invited to coax the community to organize. Once again, a group went to the mayor's office to negotiate, and once again, money was raised, $1,320, toward the purchase of land for a synagogue, to be named Congregation B'nai Shalom. The effort, however, again dissipated. Perhaps because the principals involved were comfortable in secular organizations like the Masons and Odd Fellows, the effort to form a congregation was replaced with a B'nai B'rith fraternal lodge, which took hold in 1875 with twenty-eight male members from among the eighty adult Jewish men living in Austin.

The failure to form a congregation meant there was no formal religious instruction for children. The Austin *Daily Democratic Statesman* of September 24, 1876, noted that while local Jews were "an intelligent class of people," all other Texas cities of similar size had synagogues. "We can see no reason why Austin should not keep company with them," the newspaper editorialized.

Thus shamed, the Jews of Austin met that very day at two o'clock in the afternoon at the Odd Fellows Hall and organized Congregation Beth Israel. In a close vote, thirteen for and twelve against, they decided not to solicit money from the gentile community to construct a synagogue. They would be self-supporting and not a burden on the community.

By the time Wessolowsky arrived three years later, Mr. Sigmund Philipson, the religious school superintendent, and Mrs. D. Friedman, the principal, had been engaged to teach the children and lead the choir. Contrary to patterns in other Texas Jewish communities, there was no Ladies Hebrew Benevolent Society to support these religious efforts. Once again, Wessolowsky lamented with a light lash: "We are deprived of the pleasure of not being able to chronicle the existence of a Hebrew Ladies Society of any kind. Our Jewish ladies in Austin, no doubt, fully understand their duties and all they would need perhaps, is a 'reminder.'" Ultimately, a synagogue was dedicated in 1884; funds were solicited from non-Jewish "capitalists," and a Ladies Auxiliary Society began in 1892.

History sometimes has a way of repeating itself, and when it comes time maturely to take care of its needs, the Austin Jewish community sometimes reacted only in the face of public scrutiny. In 1995, IBM wanted to move a division of high-level innovators to Austin from south Florida. Among them were a number of Orthodox Jewish families. According to a front-page article in the November 20, 1995, *Austin American-Statesman*, the families balked at the move to Austin because there was no kosher butcher and no Jewish day school. Within a month of the article, the H.E.B., a Texas supermarket chain, opened a kosher butcher counter at one of its Austin stores. Within a year, educator Dana Baruch founded the Austin Jewish Community Day School.

FORTY ACRES AND A SHUL: BIRTH OF THE CAMPUS CONCEPT

By 1992, with the Hart property purchased as the site of a Jewish Community Center, a confluence of events led a group of large donors to explore other uses for this generous expanse of land. The sudden Jewish population boom made it clear that Congregation Beth Israel was outgrowing its building, constructed in the 1950s and early 1960s. Agudas Achim's building, though newer, suffered untenable foundation problems. The Jollyville building and surrounding trailers lacked a swimming pool and community hall. The growing community needed a lot all at once.

Besides the Dells, other high-tech success stories had burst on the scene, most no-

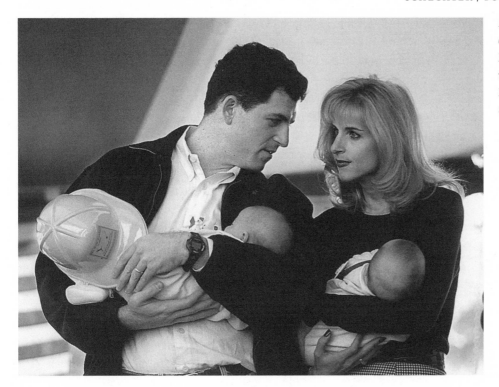

Michael and Susan Dell and the couple's newborn twins attended the December 1996 groundbreaking for the Dell Jewish Community Campus. Lynne Dobson/The Austin American-Statesman, December 8, 1996.

tably Marc Seriff, a hometown boy who returned after starting America Online, and Mort and Angela Topfer, one of several "Dellionaires" spawned by Dell's fabulous success. They and others with deep pockets realized they were about to be asked for large donations from all sides for capital campaigns. Under the leadership of investment consultant Phil Spertus, of Chicago's Spertus family fame, and land developer Sandy Gottesman, the buzz developed into the realization that economies would be realized if both congregations moved to the forty-acre Hart tract and joined the new Jewish Community Association of Austin (JCAA) to form a consortium and build a campus. The JCAA, representing the marriage of the Jewish Federation of Austin, the old Jollyville JCC, and Jewish Family Service, was organized using a corporate model, with a CEO overseeing the four branches while streamlining support functions such as accounting, marketing, fundraising, and maintenance.

Michael and Susan Dell offered both Agudas Achim and Beth Israel a generous ten-thousand-dollar, ninety-nine-year lease if they would construct new synagogues on the proposed campus. The congregations would own and manage their buildings, but the land would remain in the hands of the community. Footprints were set aside for matching educational buildings, which congregations could share with the JCAA or other organizations. There was talk of potential savings, such as a community library and a print shop. A Campus Committee formed with three representatives from each entity, including Beth Israel, Agudas Achim, the JCAA, and the major donor families. To negotiate arrangements, the Campus Committee met under the leadership of Angela Topfer.

Topfer, who was not Jewish, was born in England and raised in London and Cambridge. She earned a business degree from the Cambridge College of Arts and Technology and owned a business that bought and remodeled homes. She had met and married Mort Topfer, a Jew, when both worked for Motorola in Chicago. The Topfers relocated to Austin in 1984 when Mort became vice-chairman of the Dell Corporation.

Topfer, charged with overseeing construction of a controversial campus in a divided Jewish community, presented vision and determination that no headstrong parochial leaders could stop. Initially the only female on the Campus Committee, she conveyed her determination during the first meeting to get the task completed by placing on the table two brass balls, a masculine metaphor that communicated her strength. No one ever challenged her, at least not to her face. Before Angela Topfer's untimely death from cancer in June 2003, she had, by the sheer force of will, brought the campus to life.

THE NEO-*SHTADLAN*

During the Middle Ages, when Jewish communities existed unto themselves and were largely self-governing, there existed an official called the *shtadlan*, or diplomatic spokesman. This diplomat to outside rulers spoke the language of the court and served as the intercessor for coreligionists in matters of taxation, protection, and conscription.

The obvious differences between medieval European ghettoes and the twentieth-century Austin Jewish community notwithstanding, the creation of a Jewish community campus demanded a similar degree of communal cohesion. Austin needed a local collaborative governing structure as well as a *shtadlan* to navigate through the maze of city permits, neighborhood protests, and emotional City Council meetings it would take to build the new campus.

Austin's political landscape in the late twentieth century was divided into two distinct camps: developers and neighborhood activists. Protecting the Edwards Aquifer watershed and preserving habitat of golden-cheeked warblers, salamanders, and other local flora and fauna was often the focus of the battles symptomatic of the larger, more fundamental fight about the character of the growing city. Not surprisingly, Jews were on both sides of the ongoing disputes. The Campus Committee sought substantial land development on a forty-acre urban tract that provided habitat for deer, foxes, and other wildlife and would be located among homes and apartment complexes. Developer Sandy Gottesman, a Jew who spoke the language of City Hall, became the liaison or *shtadlan*. Under his

Austin's Conservative Congregation Agudas Achim constructed its synagogue on the Dell Jewish Community Campus in 2000. Photo by Carolyn Cruz.

guidance and tutelage, a lobbyist was engaged to ameliorate concerns arising from Austin's signature fears of traffic, noise, harm to wildlife, and unseemly lights at night.

The opposition—centered in the local neighborhood's Northwest Austin Civic Association—sought Jews to lead the chorus against the Dell campus. The protestors found a vocal partner in Patti Edelman Leonard, whose original vision of a Jewish Community Center conflicted with the new vision of a Dell Jewish Community Campus. Leonard and a Jewish newcomer, Allen Tannenbaum, became magnets for anti-development neighborhood activists who put up orange yard signs that declared, "Downsize Dell Campus." The pair also became popular spokespeople when the media came calling.

AUSTIN'S YOM KIPPUR WAR

Meanwhile, another strain of opposition was growing among congregants at the Reform synagogue, Beth Israel. By 1991, Beth Israel had increased its membership, thanks to the opening in 1989 of a full-time day-care center (with a waiting list, no less) and the arrival of a dynamic young rabbi, Steven Folberg. Some among the older generation complained about the unholy smell of dirty diapers and wear and tear on the hardwood floors. Such issues symbolized in microcosm a generational conflict about the roles the congregation should fulfill. The dissension, however, was voiced mostly during late-night parking-lot whispers after long and tedious meetings. The combination of new families who joined Beth Israel for day care, coupled with the new rabbi's charisma and the high-tech population growth, led the congregation to explosive growth.

Moving a congregation from one part of town to another is generally a once-in-a-lifetime experience. The older generation at Beth Israel loved the Shoal Creek temple; Hymie Samuelson was not the only congregant who had worked with his hands to decorate it. Still, the congregation was running out of space. After the purchase of the Hart ranch by the Dells, Beth Israel voted twice, by wide margins, two years in a row, to move to the campus. But many of the older generation's movers and shakers vehemently opposed selling their centrally located synagogue at Shoal Creek to move to a campus with the

Austin's Reform Temple Beth Israel remains at its Shoal Creek location. Photo by Carolyn Cruz.

name of a newcomer to Austin. Toward the mid-1990s, the congregation appointed two committees to study whether to expand at Shoal Creek or move to Hart Lane. The congregation's proximity to a creek and changing permit rules about building in the flood plain complicated previous expansion plans and limited options for growth. With roughly the same amount of money, a new, larger facility could be built on the Hart tract.

The decision to move or not to move, however, was ultimately about much more than dollars and cents. In the final analysis, there was a conflict of priorities—those who wanted to be Reform Jews in their own space versus those who wanted to be Jews among other Jews, yet still pray in a Reform synagogue.

Three Beth Israel representatives served on the Campus Committee. Two favored the move. One did not. The opposing representative and the congregation's president were both attorneys, who parsed the campus agreement to its death. The negotiations collapsed completely in 1999 when the president of the Beth Israel shocked the congregation with a Yom Kippur announcement that, despite two congregational votes to the contrary, there would be no move to the Dell Campus.

REBIRTH OR STATUS QUO?

Those who wanted to be part of something larger than Congregation Beth Israel spearheaded the formation of a new Reform congregation, Beth Shalom, whose initial mission was to be the Reform presence on the Dell Campus. Its name, Beth Shalom, meaning house of peace, hearkened back to the unsuccessful attempt in the 1870s to form a congregation called B'nai Shalom. Beth Shalom's founder was Donald Coplin, one of Beth Israel's representatives to the Campus Committee. Other disaffected Reform Jews joined Coplin. When Congregation Agudas Achim carried its Torahs to the Dell Campus the next year, Coplin and others from Beth Shalom joined the Torah march and shared in carrying of the sacred scrolls.

In 2003, three years after Agudas Achim moved to its new facilities at the Dell Jewish Community Campus, Beth Israel finally expanded its educational and social hall space at the Shoal Creek site. Among the benefactors was Sandy Gottesman, the only donor who made substantial contributions of both time and money to build both the Dell Campus and Beth Israel's new education building.

When the dust settled, the Dell Jewish Community Campus opened in the year 2000 with a community center, an education building, and Congregation Agudas Achim's new sanctuary, which features natural lighting, textured limestone, and a communal feel that has received accolades from architecture critics. In addition to the activities of the Conservative synagogue and JCAA, the campus housed the Early Childhood Program, the Austin Jewish Academy (grades K–8), a swimming pool, and a variety of congregations without walls, including Beth Shalom and the trans-denominational Kol Halev. Jewish Family Service and the Austin Jewish Community Relations Council, while part of the Association, were located off-campus because there was not adequate privacy to house the former and no space left for the latter. The JCAA had grown that fast.

The footprint reserved for Congregation Beth Israel remains undeveloped. Forces within the Jewish Community jockey for that land. It could become a home for Temple Beth Shalom, or a home for the aged, or another educational center. It could become a multi-purpose cultural center, with prayer space for Beth Shalom, as well as other congregations that the campus has spawned, including Kol Halev and a few Orthodox minyans. Austin's growing Jewish community will debate this within its new framework.

In retrospect, fears of blurred lines among denominations were largely baseless. The formation of a strong sports or *Maccabi* program in 2005 drew children from Beth Israel onto campus. There were occasions when Beth Israel became an extension of the campus. Since 2003, the entire Jewish community has collaborated to present an annual Tapestry of Learning, an inter-organizational education effort. For one week, adults select classes as if they are in a university. Some seminars meet on the Dell campus, others in the new classrooms of Beth Israel.

At Beth Israel, the sepia photographs of founder Henry Hirshfeld and of Joe Koen, president for forty-four years from 1899 to 1944, adorn the library walls of the Shoal Creek building, their legacy intact. Their congregation stayed put and continues to stand alone. B'nai Shalom came back to life, while the community's collective future moved north to a campus where deer and foxes still roam at night and committee members stand in the parking lot, rehashing it all.   ✳

REFERENCES

Austin American Statesman, 1995–present.

Austin Chronicle, 1997–1998.

Building for the Future, Congregation Agudas Achim, Austin, Texas, May 5–7, 1969. Austin: Congregation Agudas Achim, 1969.

Dell, Michael, and Catherine Fredman. *Direct from Dell: Strategies that Revolutionized an Industry.* New York: Collins, 2000.

Fishkin, Joseph. "40 Acres and a Pool: Letter from Austin." *Forward*, July 24, 1998, 1, 4.

Gross, Harriet P. "Texas Hillel Prepares to Move into Stunning New Center," *Texas Jewish Post*, September 29, 2005, 14.

Linklater, Richard. *Slacker.* Detour Film Production, 1991.

Of Celebration, of Memory, and Hope, 125 "Plus" Years Anniversary Celebration, April 4–6, 2004. Booklet. Austin: Congregation Beth Israel, 2003.

Schmier, Louis, ed. "Letter Number Thirteen." In *Reflections of Southern Jewry: The Letters of Charles Wessolowsky, 1878–1879.* Macon, Ga.: Mercer University Press, 1982.

Silberberg, Jay. *Austin Jewish Community, 1850–1950.* Senior thesis. University of Texas at Austin, August 1974.

"Slacker," http://merlin.alleg.edu/employee/a/acarr/fs/slacker.html.

Turner, Carolyn, Milton Turner, and Eddie Baum. *The First One Hundred Years of Temple Beth Israel, Austin, Texas.* Austin: Temple Beth Israel, 1950.

Winegarten, Ruthe, and Cathy Schechter, *Deep in the Heart, the Lives and Legends of Texas Jews, A Photographic History.* Austin: Eakin Press, 1990.

21

Comfort and Discomfort Being Jewish in Fort Worth

RALPH D. MECKLENBURGER

In the 1920s, when the Ku Klux Klan rose to prominence in Fort Worth, Jewish attorney Theodore Mack began avoiding court appearances for fear that Klan-influenced juries would be prejudiced against clients represented by a Jew. At the same time, Jewish merchant Leon Gross, owner of Washer Brothers, a large downtown men's wear store, was actually invited to join the Klan! Was Theo Mack, in town since 1894 and Fort Worth's first Jewish attorney, paranoid? Not likely. The Klan was a racist, anti-Catholic, and anti-Semitic brotherhood whose rallies of white-hooded members and burning crosses struck fear in hearts across the South. These Jewish experiences with the KKK were emblematic of the Fort Worth Jewish community's status. Jews had plenty of friends in the community at large, but as Jews they kept their eyes peeled for danger. Leon Gross, it should be noted, politely declined to become a Klansman, but he promoted a store employee who was in the Klan to company "vice-president" because Klan members were known to boycott non-Klan establishments.[1]

By some measures, Jews always have felt at home in Fort Worth, Texas. At the same time, even if some might have liked to do so, Jews have never forgotten that they are a minority. They have worried about hostility from neighbors—even if many never experienced hostility. In a Bible Belt city in the Southwest where "what church do you go to?" is regarded not as an invasion of privacy but a routine question to greet new neighbors, Jews are keenly aware of their difference.

When Fort Worth was still a military post, founded in 1849 to protect the region against Comanches, its first few Jews arrived and became cotton buyers, cattle traders, and small merchants. The fort disappeared early on as the frontier moved westward, but the settlement that had formed around it grew, for the city was a prominent stop on the famed Chisholm Trail cattle drives. The Jewish middle class grew with it, and when the railroad arrived in 1876 and cattle could be slaughtered and meat processed for shipping back East, Jewish-owned businesses and workers shared the prosperity and growth. Fort Worth was a city on the make, its leaders anxious for further expansion. By the turn of the twentieth century, the city had six hundred Jews among its twenty-six thousand residents. An Orthodox synagogue, Ahavath Sholom, had been founded in 1892, and a Reform synagogue, Beth-El, was organized in 1902.

How comfortable were Jews in this first half-century or so of the city's existence? That they felt little need to organize in the early years may indicate simply that they all knew one another, anyway. It clearly means that the pioneering souls who headed off to the frontier were not, on the whole, people to whom regular worship, kosher food, or other Jewish amenities were priorities. A B'nai B'rith lodge, chartered in 1876, lasted only a few years. (Another started in 1901 and survived). A Sabbath school for children petered

Leon Gross (1866–1945). Haberdasher Leon Gross declined an invitation to join the Ku Klux Klan. To insure against a KKK boycott of his shop, he promoted an employee who was in the Klan to store vice-president. Courtesy, Beth-El Congregation Archives, Fort Worth.

out shortly after it started in 1879. What the early Jews did feel the need for, apparently, was a cemetery. So John Peter Smith, one of the city's prominent leaders, *gave* the Jews an acre of land for that purpose just south of downtown in 1879. That same year, he also gave land for Protestant and Catholic cemeteries, an indication that Jews were part of the city's religious mosaic. Smith would serve six terms as mayor beginning in 1882, and to this day the public hospital is named for him. The founding of Emanuel Hebrew Rest Cemetery demonstrated both that the Jewish pioneers had sufficient Jewish consciousness to want their own cemetery and that the city fathers wanted them to feel at home and bring more coreligionists to town.

No doubt local Jews also felt affirmed by their neighbors in 1903 when the infamous Kishineff pogrom captured headlines around the world. With the complicity of the czarist government, thousands of Jewish homes and businesses were destroyed, hundreds of Jews beaten or raped, and forty-nine killed. Among the many protest meetings held in America was one in Fort Worth, organized by Ahavath Sholom leaders and held at the City Hall Auditorium. Attended by a crowd of three hundred, the forum, reported in the next day's *Fort Worth Telegram*, began with an invocation from a minister followed by speeches from the mayor, a judge, and a congressman. Local Jewish historian Hollace Weiner concludes, "The venue and the lineup of dignitaries demonstrate the degree to which the Jewish community had integrated into the mainstream."[2]

Not that anti-Semitism was entirely absent. Researching locally written credit reports on nineteenth-century Fort Worth businesses to R.G. Dun & Company (forerunner of

Ku Klux Klan weekly. The American Citizen, a KKK newspaper published in Fort Worth from around 1921 to 1926, reported events at home and around the nation. This headline was printed on July 20, 1923. Center for American History, UT-Austin, DI Number 02277, Texas Newspapers.

Emanuel Hebrew Rest Cemetery in 2006 (this page) and in 1898 (facing page). The cemetery sits on an acre of land given to the "Israelites" in 1879. Contemporary photo by Carolyn Cruz; archival photo, courtesy, Beth-El Congregation Archives, Fort Worth.

today's Dun & Bradstreet), Weiner also found that reports to the commercial credit service identified many people by ethnicity—German, Swiss, Italian, and, likewise, Hebrew, Israelite, or Jew. Occasionally, a pejorative is added for Jews. A July 27, 1866, report on Fort Worth Jewish merchant Jacob Samuels and his firm, for instance, states, "They are slippery Jews & may as well be watched."[3]

Fort Worth's synagogues slowly followed their members out of downtown, first to the south side, Beth-El in 1920 and Ahavath Sholom in 1950, then further out to the southwest, Ahavath Sholom in 1980 and Beth-El in 2000. While at any given time in the twentieth and now twenty-first centuries several Jewish residences could have been found elsewhere in the city, Jews mostly have clustered together, moving with the city's middle and upper-middle classes to the south and southwest, and to a lesser extent to the somewhat more affluent west side. Yet there has never been a predominantly Jewish neighborhood, as is common in larger eastern and Midwestern cities. This suggests strongly that while Jews wished to be near other Jews and relatively near Jewish community institutions, they never felt the need to huddle together against a hostile environment. Parents may have wanted their children to go to neighborhood schools where they would not be the only Jews, but they never concentrated Jewish residential patterns sufficiently to create anything remotely like a mostly Jewish school. Even in 2005, the Jewish community (according to Jewish Federation of Fort Worth and Tarrant County records) consisted of only slightly more than a thousand Jewish households, with another nine hundred in surrounding Tarrant County communities. This represents fewer than three thousand Jews in a city of over half a million people, and perhaps five thousand in a

Mourners arrive by horse and buggy for the burial of merchant David Linsky, a member of Woodmen of the World, who died in 1879. Courtesy, Beth-El Congregation Archives, Fort Worth.

county of over a million and a half. Fort Worth Jews always have been integrated, a minority sprinkled amongst the Christian majority.

As a rabbi who has served in Fort Worth for twenty-one years and has spoken with many septuagenarians and octogenarians whose experiences covered most of the twentieth century, I have found stories of blatant anti-Semitism few and far between. Still, the significant tolerance—at least for anyone with white skin—of the nineteenth century did not survive World War I and the Great Depression. T. R. Fehrenbach's *Lone Star: a History of Texas and the Texans*, reports, "The 1917–1918 war suddenly made the nation aware of vast numbers of so-called hyphenated Americans." There were not many resident "foreigners" for Texans to lash out against, "but this did not prevent a great upsurge of the Klan in the rural areas, with much of the old Populist rhetoric against the Jews." Oriented, Fehrenbach reports, towards fundamentalist Protestantism, KKK rhetoric also lashed Roman Catholics, and African-Americans took the brunt of actual attacks. Fort Worth was a major Klan center. A weekly Klan newspaper, *The American Citizen*, published in Fort Worth, boasted twenty-five thousand readers. Marion Weil, who moved to Fort Worth at age fourteen in 1921 and thus came of age as the Klan rose to power, reported that the Klan controlled the police and District Attorney's office (and, others add, the City Council). He recalled a Jewish insurance man "run out of town" by the Klan for having a relationship with the daughter of a Klan member and another Jewish man, son of a storeowner, who was tarred and feathered. (The latter incident was reported in the daily newspapers.) Weil himself, however, never had any problems nor felt the least bit in danger. There was "a lynching tree" for blacks; but for Jews, incidents were few and—at least by contrast with lynchings—mild.[4]

When Miriam "Ma" Ferguson was elected governor of Texas against a KKK candidate in 1924, the Klan, in Fort Worth as elsewhere, fell from prominence as quickly as it had risen. Lingering Klan influence, however, may have played a part in 1927 when Jewish plumbing contractor Morris Strauss was kidnapped, tied up, and blindfolded by men in police uniforms, driven out of town to where other conspirators helped drag him from the car and flogged him with ropes and sticks. The overwhelming majority of Fort Worth Jews were never hurt or even directly threatened by the KKK. Still, Jews found good reason to be nervous, and the feeling lingered.[5]

Even the most assimilated Jews were well aware of being regarded as part of a distinctly different group. Washer Brothers' owner Leon Gross, mentioned above, was reputedly not much interested in Jewish observance. Recollections of Marion Weil, his nephew and employee, and of Etta Brachman, who moved to Fort Worth in 1921, agree on this. But the Grosses, according to Brachman, "knew they were Jewish because the Christians let 'em know, such remarks as 'Well, I don't have anything against buying from Jews.'"[6]

Many Fort Worth Jews of the first half of the twentieth century believed that W. C. Stripling of Stripling's Department Store, founded in 1890, and Amon G. Carter, Sr., who in the 1910s and 1920s consolidated Fort Worth's newspapers into one paper, the *Fort Worth Star-Telegram*, and became a hugely influential community leader for decades, did not hire Jews. Stripling's, however, had a Jewish tailor at one point and paid to run Jewish New Year greetings in the *Jewish Monitor*, a weekly published in Fort Worth. Carter retained first one Jewish attorney (Sidney Samuels) and then a second (Abe Herman). Jews' perceptions of prejudice in the business sphere may or may not have been exaggerated but were certainly not entirely unfounded. One local business leader, George W. Armstrong (1866–1954), founder of the Texas Steel Company, unsuccessful candidate for Congress in 1902 and for the Texas Democratic gubernatorial nomination in 1932, published books and bankrolled periodicals that echoed Henry Ford's *Dearborn Independent*, which spoke of international Jewish conspiracies. Such blatant bigotry, though the exception rather than the norm, could not have done anything to ease Jewish psychic insecurity.[7]

Fort Worth Jews, then, lived comfortably enough in the pre–World War II era. But even if bigotry was mild in Fort Worth compared to some places "back East," Jews had reason to worry that beneath the surface in this mostly comfortable environment, hostility lurked.

Members of the Fort Worth National Council of Jewish Women (NCJW) initiated numerous pioneering civic and philanthropic projects throughout the twentieth century, sometimes on their own as Jewish women, such as an Americanization School to teach English and survival skills to newly arrived immigrants, Jewish and gentile, from 1907 to 1973, and sometimes as partners with other groups. With the local Junior League, for instance, they began the Bluff Street Child Care Center downtown, and with United Cerebral Palsy operated a sheltered workshop for the mentally and physically handicapped.

Dual Identity. The Jewish Monitor, which circulated in North Texas, Oklahoma, and parts of Arkansas and Louisiana from 1913 to the late-1930s, featured a masthead rich with ethnicity, replete with Magen David and menorah. The headline advising readers to attend the annual Fat Stock Show demonstrates Jewish support of western cultural events. Courtesy, Beth-El Congregation Archives, Fort Worth.

Fort Worth Live Stock Exchange building, a landmark emblematic of the city's nickname, Cowtown. Photo by Lee Russell, 1939. Library of Congress Prints & Photographs Division, FSA-OWI Collection, LC-USF34-033184-D.

Idealism was the prime motivation in all these projects, but occasional comments of participants are also a valuable window into their psyches. Bernice "Beanie" Weil, for instance, recalling her countless volunteer hours, said, "We wanted to be seen as American!" Why would a woman born in Oklahoma in 1910, raised in Kansas, and a Fort Worth resident since her marriage in 1934 think she could be seen as anything else? We should

New American citizen. Holocaust-era refugee Annie Rutlader proudly shows her citizenship papers at the NCJW Americanization School, where she studied English and civics. Courtesy, Fort Worth Star-Telegram Photograph Collection, Special Collections, The University of Texas at Arlington Libraries, Arlington, Texas.

remember that when she was a young adult during the Great Depression, Henry Ford was serializing "The International Jew" in the *Dearborn Independent*, and Father Charles E. Coughlin was spewing anti-Semitism on the radio. Historian Jonathan Sarna quotes a 1938 poll showing that twenty percent of Americans at that time thought Jews should be deported. A Fort Worth NCJW leader of the next generation, Dorothy Winston (president from 1971 to 1973), observed in like vein, "We can never be equal until they know us." Council members wanted to do good works and to be seen doing so as Jews.[8]

In 1977, the NCJW proposed and offered to fund a neighborhood playground in southwest Fort Worth's Tanglewood Park, an area where many Jews lived. The city parks department agreed. According to the *Star-Telegram*, neighbors worried that a playground would attract "pot-smokers," "hoodlums," and minority children from high-crime neighborhoods. Despite tense, angry community meetings, the playground was built. The real issue, many recognized, was fear of integration, of which Jews locally as well as nationally had been outspoken supporters. (In 1965, Beth-El's Rabbi Robert Schur paraded up Main Street with the Reverend Dr. Martin Luther King, Jr.) While the opposition to so benign a project as a playground surprised NCJW members, what the newspaper reported as "threatening phone calls containing anti-Semitic and racist remarks," deeply shocked them. This was the 1970s, not the KKK 1920s! Yet anti-Semitism had not, after all, disappeared.

When I ask Fort Worth Jews of the post–World War II generation about anti-Semitism when they were growing up, they generally respond that overt acts of hostility against Jews largely ceased to be an issue. The 1940s and 1950s appear to have been a transition period. Paschal High School basketball coach Charlie Turner made clear that he knew which young men in his gym classes were Jews, and he regularly called one "rabbi." Some loved him, and others were intimidated. The coach was a legend who took Paschal teams to state championships in 1945 and 1949, and few dared challenge him. On a more positive note, when fire gutted Beth-El in 1946, neighboring Broadway Baptist Church immediately offered its sanctuary for Jewish worship until the temple was rebuilt, and public school authorities made Lilly B. Clayton Elementary School available for Jewish Sunday school.

America, and Fort Worth, were changing. Historian Jonathan Sarna points out that Americans of all ethnicities, people who rarely encountered one another earlier in their lives, were thrown together in the military to fight World War II. They returned home at least partially disabused of their stereotypes and prejudices. Awareness of the Holocaust, the positive image of Jews created by the birth of Israel in 1948, the postwar emergence of Jews in many fields—authors, entertainers, even beauty queen Bess Meyerson and sports hero Hank Greenberg—and a conscious move on the part of American society to teach tolerance, led to a significant diminution of anti-Semitism nationally. A Fort Worth Jewish businessman told me that anti-Semitic slander ceased to be acceptable in polite society once most people knew of the Holocaust. All this was supplemented by the civil rights revolution of the 1960s and 1970s and the homogenizing impact of television on American culture, which brought "the other" into people's living rooms. American pluralism became the norm as the twentieth century continued. Fort Worth Jews who came of age in this period may recall an occasional incident of being called a "Jewboy" or the like, but many insist that they experienced no anti-Semitism at all in Fort Worth.[9]

On the other hand, discussion often turns to a more difficult and complex matter— restricted city and country clubs and evidence of the so-called "five o'clock curtain." By the 1920s, and perhaps earlier, several Jews—Theodore Mack, Leon Gross, investor Dan Levy, attorney Max K. Mayer, builder Harry B. Friedman—were members of the Fort Worth Club, which was founded as the Commercial Club in 1885 (the name changed in 1906). Subsequently, there have always been at least a few Jewish members, and today there are many. A very few Jews have been admitted to the city's oldest country club, River Crest, founded in 1911, which many in the Jewish community regard as restricted even today. Leon Gross was an early member, and the club lists a few Jews on its current roster. Colonial Country Club opened as gentile businessman Marvin Leonard's private venture in 1936 and was turned over to a board of directors—including, significantly, Jewish coin dealer B. Max Mehl—in 1942. Post–World War II country clubs—Ridglea (1955) and Shady Oaks (1958)—have been perceived by Jews as far more welcoming, though some think that Ridglea, too, was overly "selective" at first. Theodore Mack, a third-generation Fort Worth attorney and grandson of the Theodore Mack above, speaks of his family being well aware that Jews were not welcome in the clubs. Long-time Jewish members remained on the roster, Mack suggests, but in the Klan era of the 1920s the city and country clubs became restricted. Even after World War II, it was one thing to do business with Jews or accept them as neighbors, and quite another—at the rarified, affluent level of such clubs—to accept more than a few as social peers. Moreover, the blackball system, which enables current members to veto new members, and to do so without it becoming widely known who did, enabled this subtle brand of prejudice to flourish. Yet there were times when many Jews entered this or that club. Mack reported that when he wanted to join Colonial Country Club in 1966, one professional colleague surprised him by refusing to be a sponsor. Colonial Country Club General Manager Vergal Bourland said that he would be happy to present the application if Mack would allow him to hold it for however long it took for a certain anti-Semitic board member to miss a meeting, at which point he was sure the Macks would be accepted, as indeed they were. This calls for a bit of interpretation. Setting aside a certain inherent snobbery in the club mentality and system, many and, especially postwar, perhaps most members at the Fort Worth Club, Colonial, or any of the others, readily would have admitted any otherwise qualified Jewish applicant. Still, there were enough bigots to be contended with that at various times any of the clubs, and certainly the older ones, probably have been restricted.

Even with the Texas "good ol' boy" mentality, in which much business is done over lunch or on the golf course, one can live quite decently without country or city clubs. Many could not afford one even if membership were wide open. Yet the knowledge (even if, as we have seen, in some periods it may have been erroneous "knowledge") that the clubs frequented by the city's elite were not open to Jews clearly left Jews with the sense that prejudice lingered. In many cities, Houston and Dallas among them, Jewish country clubs owe their origins to Jews feeling excluded from established clubs. In the mid-1950s, a group of Fort Worth Jews bought a large house on Oak Grove Road in south Fort Worth, fixed it up nicely with a pool and other amenities, and hired a chef and staff. While Oak Grove Country Club got off to a promising start, such institutions are expensive to maintain and there were not enough Jews sufficiently desirous of a club to keep it going more than about two years. By the mid-1970s, the perception was that all but River Crest were largely open to Jews. River Crest today has fewer Jews than the other clubs, but Jewish members—and Bar and Bat Mitzvah parties at the club—are not the rarity they once were.

Jews were more and more visibly accepted as the twentieth century continued. Jewish attorney and banker Bayard Friedman was elected mayor, serving from 1963 to 1965.

On the links. When posh Shady Oaks opened in 1958, it was perceived as the first Fort Worth country club that welcomed Jews who could afford the initiation fee. Oilman Ted Weiner, fourth from left, a charter member, poses with his celebrity foursome and the club pro. Pictured are golfing legend Ben Hogan, comedian Jack Benny, club pro Dick Metz, Weiner, and Hollywood producer Hal Wallis, whose credits include Little Caesar *(1931),* The Maltese Falcon *(1941), and* Casablanca *(1942). Courtesy of Gwendolyn Weiner.*

Friedman's vision was instrumental in the development of Dallas–Fort Worth Airport, and when he died in 1998 his funeral was held at the symphony hall downtown. Similarly, there have been Jewish elected officeholders in recent decades, including thirteen-term Congressman Martin Frost, and many Jews playing leadership roles supporting the arts, reflecting acceptance of Jews.

Equally telling, legendary entrepreneur Charles Tandy added Boston's Radio Shack to his corporate portfolio in 1963 and Chicago's Allied Radio in 1970. In 1970, Tandy decided to consolidate management in Fort Worth and brought to town many Jewish executives from Boston and Chicago. When Bernard Appel (later Radio Shack president from 1984 to 1992) hesitated to commit to a move without checking out the local synagogues, Tandy replied, "Bernie, if you don't like the synagogue we've got here, I'll build you your own."[10] Tandy went to great lengths to make sure his newly arrived executives acclimated to Fort Worth, so when a Jewish friend reported the false rumor that he did not like Jews, a shocked Tandy replied with characteristic bluntness, "What else can I do? I brought the whole goddamn tribe down here from Boston!" While the local synagogues were adequate for the new arrivals, Appel remembered Tandy's initial promise. When Ahavath Sholom planned to build a new synagogue in the late 1970s, Tandy helped, both by aiding All Saints Hospital to buy the old synagogue and by contributing to the new one, which has a "Charles Tandy President's Office."

By 1998, no one seemed to find it incongruous that Texas Christian University would be establishing a chair of Jewish Studies and arranging for an annual Gates of Chai Lectureship. Gentiles as well as Jews contributed to make these possible, though the lead gifts were from Jewish families—Rosalyn and Manny Rosenthal for the endowed professorship and Stanley and Marcia Kornbleet Kurtz for the Gates of Chai headline speakers, who have included Nobel Peace Laureate Eli Weisel, novelist Chaim Potok, and Rabbi Harold Kushner.

Radio Shack President Charles Tandy, whose portrait includes his trademark cigar. Tandy recruited many Jewish executives to town, including Bernie Appel, who asked his boss if Fort Worth had a synagogue. Tandy replied, "If you don't like the synagogue . . . I'll build you your own." The metal plaque (inset) from Congregation Ahavath Sholom is a testament to Tandy's generosity toward the shul. Photo by Ellen Appel.

This author came to Fort Worth in 1984. I have conversed with two decades of Jewish teenagers about anti-Semitism. Unlike their elders who speak of restricted clubs, teens frequently turn the conversation to their Christian friends who worry that, as nonbelievers, Jews will go to hell. Young Jews struggle with a sense of alienation when Protestant para-church organizations such as Young Life and the Fellowship of Christian Athletes run programs, even in schools, which their Christian friends enjoy but which their Jewish parents do not want them attending. By and large this seems not anti-Semitism at all but simply the price of living as a small religious minority, particularly since the 1980s when Evangelical Christianity in America became far more assertive than previously.

When a deranged man went berserk at Wedgewood Baptist Church on September 15, 1999, shooting fifteen people, eight of them (including himself) fatally, an interfaith fiasco ensued. Mayor Kenneth Barr called for a public observance to help the community mourn. City leaders, determined that all the citizens participate, moved the tentative date back a day to avoid Yom Kippur. At a planning meeting, I urged that the event be kept reasonably nondenominational. A church having been the target, Jesus' name need not go unmentioned, but the goal should be communal solidarity, not a Baptist prayer meeting. The planners, including the head of the county Baptist association, agreed. Governor George W. Bush, who was likely to attend, should be the major speaker, I urged. To that they did not agree. The major addresses would be from the minister of Wedgewood Baptist Church and the president of Fort Worth's Southwest Baptist Theological Seminary. The governor attended but did not speak from the podium, telling us beforehand that that he did not want to exploit the situation for political gain. That the ministers were told of the agreement not to make this a revival meeting was clear from what Wedgwood's Pastor Al Meredith declared during the service, namely that he knew he was not supposed to preach, "but if you had the cure for cancer, would it be responsible not to

"Talking to the rabbi." The Rev. Dr. Bailey Smith, incoming president of the Southern Baptist Convention, asserted in September 1980 that God does not hear the prayers of Jews. The Fort Worth Star-Telegram responded with a cartoon in which an angel manning a switchboard puts Rev. Smith on hold because God is "on another line, talking to a rabbi." Etta Hulme, Fort Worth Star-Telegram.

FORT WORTH STAR-TELEGRAM   TUESDAY EVENING, SEPTEMBER 23, 1980

Opinions

ETTA FORT WORTH STAR-TELEGRAM
HULME   N.E.A. 80

CELESTIAL BELL

"WOULD YOU MIND HOLDING, DR. SMITH? AT THE MOMENT, HE'S ON ANOTHER LINE, TALKING TO A RABBI"

share it?!" The crowd at Texas Christian University's Amon G. Carter Stadium and a national television audience were too great a temptation to resist. Soon the Baptist preachers literally had people waving their arms, shouting "Hallelujah" to God and Jesus. That night, as I arrived at Beth-El for Erev Yom Kippur services, a Southwest Baptist Seminary professor awaited me in the parking lot. He had to let me know, he said, how embarrassed he and many others were for Baptists. Other Protestant clergy friends expressed similar sentiments in days following. Quite a number of Jewish congregants, who had watched the service on television, asked of Meredith's sermon, "Was he saying we are a cancer?!" He was not saying that, of course, merely that his brand of faith was the sole and exclusive path to societal as well as personal salvation.

Not all Evangelicals, to be sure, are aggressive and triumphalist. Fort Worth Jews and Christians of all stripes maintain personal friendships. Though the Southern Baptist Convention periodically issues national calls for missionary efforts to convert Jews, little seems to happen locally. After one such national proclamation, the Reverend Dr. Steven Shoemaker, senior minister of Broadway Baptist Church, readily accepted an invitation to cross the parking lot to neighboring Temple Beth-El to discuss the matter. He declared from the *bimah* that he and his church had great respect for Jews and Judaism. The national Church did not speak for them.

More remarkable is the story of Monica "Posy" McMillen, a member of the large, nondenominational McKinney Memorial Bible Church. McMillen, who grew up in Indiana,

Interfaith pilgrimage. Posy McMillen, right, Fort Worth's equivalent of the Righteous Gentile, dances a hora with rebbetzin Graciela Zeilicovich on a nighttime Sea of Galilee Cruise, part of a tour McMillen led to Israel in 2005. Courtesy Fort Worth Star-Telegram columnist Jim Jones.

thinks of herself as a third-generation Christian Zionist and has had some involvement in Hadassah, the women's Zionist organization. In 1990, she was shocked when an Israeli friend in Fort Worth asked her why Christians hate Jews? She began to explore the history of that stereotype and to learn and teach about what Jules Isaac has called the Christian "teaching of contempt" over the ages. When efforts to bring a traveling Anne Frank exhibit to Fort Worth were floundering in 1997, the international Anne Frank organization contacted McMillen for help. She raised money and volunteers from both the gentile and Jewish communities to bring the exhibition to town, and back again in 2002. Twenty thousand visitors, including busloads of children, saw the first show, and more the second. In 1998, the local Jewish Federation honored her with a trip to Yad Vashem in Jerusalem for further studies. Her classes on the history of anti-Semitism continued, both at McKinney Memorial Bible Church, where there was initial resistance to allowing a woman to teach men, and at many local churches and synagogues. During the first Anne Frank exhibition, McMillen learned of a Christian Women's Zionist organization in Albuquerque, *Yad B'Yad* (hand in hand), and started a chapter in Fort Worth. That group was designed for Christians, so when Jewish women began joining ("We never charge them dues," McMillen says), it was reorganized under the name *Hashomer* (the guardian). By 2005, *Hashomer* had grown to 150 members, some Jewish but the majority Christian. McMillen has led three trips to Israel with a local Orthodox Jewish woman, Etta Korenman, and a fourth with Rabbi Alberto Zeilicovich of Ahavath Sholom. McMillen says of the Christian women who participate in *Hashomer*, some of them "grew up never hearing the word 'Jew' used without 'damn' attached. But after the Holocaust that became politically incorrect." She resents being lumped together with premillennialist Christians whose motivation for supporting Israel is the return of Christ and the conversion of the Jews. She and her group are mindful of God's promise to Abraham. "If God loves the Jews, we certainly should," she says.

In the 1920 edition of the *Lasso*, yearbook of Fort Worth's North Side High School, beneath the picture of each varsity baseball player is a personal write-up. Several have nicknames—"Cockie," "Hex," and "Tunt." The only Jew in the school was Joel Rosen, the team's first baseman and son of Sam Rosen, who was developing Rosen Heights as working-class housing for employees in north side meat-packing plants and raising his own family there. The blurb beneath Joel's photograph begins, "'Jew' started the season looking like a rookie, but soon developed into a real star." Close to a century later, we cannot hear the tone of voice as we imagine teammates yelling, "Catch it, Jew!" "Hit it out of the park, Jew!" Yet we might surmise that "Jew" was uttered with a smile, not a sneer, else it would not have ended up beneath Rosen's yearbook picture. Ask Fort Worth Jews, today or at any point in its history, if they find the city a comfortable place to live, and the overwhelming majority would say "yes." Jews have thrived in Fort Worth. They have made friends, made a living, and made a home for themselves. Yet they have never forgotten, or been allowed to forget, that in at least one important aspect of identity, they are different.   ✱

NOTES

1. Hollace Ava Weiner, *Jewish Stars in Texas: Rabbis and Their Work* (College Station: Texas A&M University, 1999), 97; Marion Weil, interview with Hollace Weiner, July 31, 1994, tape recording, Beth-El Congregation Archives, Fort Worth; Hollace Weiner, *Beth-El Congregation Centennial* (Fort Worth: Beth-El Congregation, 2002).

2. "Liberal Donations to Kishineff Fund," *Fort Worth Telegram*, June 5, 1903, 2; Hollace Ava Weiner, "The Jewish Junior League: The Rise and Demise of the Fort Worth Council of Jewish Women, 1901–2002," Master's thesis, University of Texas at Arlington, 2004, 67.

3. Texas, Vol. 28 [Tarrant County], p. 202C, R.G. Dun & Co. Collection, Baker Library, Harvard Business School, Boston, Massachusetts.

4. T. R. Fehrenbach, *Lone Star, a History of Texas and the Texans*, updated edition (Cambridge, Mass.: Da Capo Press, 2000), 644–45; Marion Weil oral history tapes, Beth-El Archives.

5. Tom Kellam, "The Mind of an Anti-Semite: George W. Armstrong and the Ku Klux Klan in Texas," *Chronicles: A Publication of the Texas Jewish Historical Society* 1, no. 1 (1994): 13–39.

6. Weil, oral history tape, Beth-El Archives; Etta Brachman, interview with Ron Stocker, December 17, 1985, transcript, Beth-El Archives.

7. Kellam, "The Mind of an Anti-Semite," 32n4; *Handbook of Texas Online*, s.v. "Armstrong, George Washington," (cited July 30, 2005); See also Memoirs of George W. Armstrong (Austin: Stack Co., privately printed, 1958), 189–99.

8. Jonathan Sarna, *American Judaism* (New Haven and London: Yale University Press, 2004), 261; Weiner, "The Jewish Junior League," 117, 144, 148–49.

9. Sarna, *American Judaism*, 266–67, 272–74.

10. Irvin Farman, *Tandy's Money Machine* (Chicago: Mobium Press, 1992), 295.

Afterword

This anthology has presented a slice of Texas ethnic history and a segment of Diasporic Jewish history, largely through anecdotal narrative—documented accounts of people making their way in a still-developing state. It also has presented vignettes of small-town Jewish communities and synagogues, demonstrating Jews' physical presence and social place in the Lone Star mosaic. There has been a paucity of scholarship on Texas Jewry. This volume lays the groundwork for further study by delineating primary and secondary source materials, by documenting trends, and by interpreting the significance or insignificance of a Jewish presence during the state's formative years.

Some contributors to this anthology perceive Texas Jews as more assimilated than not. Others portray Jews as proudly showing their distinctiveness. Still other essays describe secular, assimilated Jews whose lives nonetheless demonstrate stereotypical Jewish immigrant drive and *tikkun olam*, the prophetic admonition to repair the world.

The historiographic debates and cultural arguments will continue: Is the Texas brand of Judaism and pattern of Jewish accomplishment any different than in comparable regions? Does the Lone Star flag infuse a special identity and create a hybrid Jew indigenous to Texas? Surely the Holocaust museum in El Paso is part of a nationwide pattern with a local stamp. Certainly the Texas Zionist Association, founded in 1905, demonstrates that a significant segment of Texas Jewry was and is connected publicly to an international movement. The niches Jews have filled elsewhere—as junk dealers, jewelers, and reformers—they also filled in Texas, but in the oil field, as recyclers of pipe; in the diamond business, popularizing consumer-credit policies; in the political-action arena, overturning more than a century of discriminatory laws.

Similar or singular? These Lone Stars of David are both similar to Jews elsewhere yet singular in the ways they adapted and impacted the largest state among the lower forty-eight. ✺

Contributors

LYNWOOD ABRAM has been with the *Houston Chronicle* for over forty years as a reporter, assistant city editor, and the paper's Voter's Guide editor. A native Houstonian, he is a 1949 graduate of the University of Texas at Austin.

DOUG BRAUDAWAY, an instructor of government and history at Southwest Texas Junior College, Del Rio, is the author of *Del Rio: Queen City of the Rio Grande* (Arcadia, 2002); *Railroads of Western Texas: San Antonio to El Paso* (Arcadia, 2000); *Val Verde County* (Arcadia, 1999), and several journal articles and historical marker applications.

HENRY COHEN II, grandson of the legendary Rabbi Henry Cohen of Galveston, was born in Houston, graduated from the University of Texas, and was ordained at Hebrew Union College in 1953. He was an Army chaplain in Korea, assistant rabbi in Great Neck, New York, where he met his wife, Edna, and rabbi at a "town and gown" congregation in Champaign-Urbana where he earned a Master's in Philosophy of Education. He is rabbi emeritus at Beth David Reform Congregation in Gladwynne, Pennsylvania, and was its fulltime rabbi from 1964 to 1993 when it was located in Philadelphia. He is the author or *Justice, Justice: A Jewish View of the Black Revolution* (UAHC Press, 1968), *Why Judaism?* (UAHC Press, 1973), *What's Special about Judaism?* (Xlibris Corp., 2002), and *Kindler of Souls: Rabbi Henry Cohen of Texas* (University of Texas Press, Spring, 2007).

SYLVIA DEENER COHEN was the first Executive Director of the El Paso Holocaust Museum and Study Center and continues to serve on its Advisory Board and Content Committee. In 1986, she toured concentration camps as part of the March of the Living and conducted survivor interviews through Steven Spielberg's Shoah Foundation. Although retired, she works with survivors through Jewish Family and Children's Services. When she moved to El Paso from the Bronx, she became aware of the resettlement of Holocaust survivors in her role as administrative assistant to Emil Reisel at the Rio Grande Sales Company.

CAROLYN BAUMAN CRUZ, an award-winning photojournalist, is a freelance photographer based in Fort Worth. During more than a decade with the *Fort Worth Star-Telegram*, she covered tornados, rodeos, Super Bowl XXX, and news events across Texas. She has been active in the Association for Women Journalists and formerly worked for the Wilkes-Barre *Times Leader* and as a stringer for the *Associated Press*. Her avocation is sailing, and she and her husband, Vince, compete in regattas.

PATRICK DEAREN, a former award-winning journalist, is the author of eight novels and six nonfiction books, including a biography of Mayer Halff, *Halff of Texas* (Eakin, 2001). In 1995, he was a finalist for the Spur Award of Western Writers of America for his novel, *When Cowboys Die* (M. Evans & Co., 1994). Among his four young adult novels is *When the Sky Rained Dust* (Eakin, 2005), set in Texas during the 1930s drought. He lives with his wife and son in Midland, Texas.

MIMI REISEL GLADSTEIN has served the University of Texas at El Paso in many administrative capacities: She has chaired the English and Philosophy departments twice; been Associate Dean for Liberal Arts; directed the Women's Studies Program; and chaired the Department of Theatre, Dance, and Film. She directed El Paso's first Holocaust Remembrance Program, serves on the board of the El Paso Holocaust Museum and Study Center, and was its vice-president of education. Gladstein is the author of five books and numerous articles. She is recognized internationally for her John Steinbeck scholarship and teaching. In 2003, she received UTEP's award for Outstanding Faculty Achievement in the College of Liberal Arts.

STEVE GUTOW, a rabbi, lawyer, and political organizer, is executive director of the Jewish Council for Public Affairs in New York City. He graduated college and law school from the University of Texas in Austin. He launched the Southwest chapter of the American Israeli Public Affairs Committee, was founding executive director of the National Jewish Democratic Council, organized the Twenty-first Century Democrats, and in 1996 ran the Texas Democratic Party Coordinated Campaign. Ordained in 2003 from Philadelphia's Reconstructionist Rabbinical College, Gutow served as rabbi of the Reconstructionist Minyan of St. Louis until August 2005.

JANE BOCK GUZMAN, a native Texan, is an adjunct professor in history and government at Richland College in Dallas. She has a Ph.D. in American history and her dissertation was on David Lefkowitz, rabbi at Dallas's Temple Emanu-El, 1920–1949. Guzman lectures at Southern Methodist University's Informal Adult Education courses in Jewish American history. Her articles have been published in *Legacies: A Journal for Dallas and North Central Texas* and in the *East Texas Historical Journal*. She has written entries for *Del Norte de Tejas: Mexican Americans in North Texas* and *Jewish Women in America: A Historical Encyclopedia*. She is the granddaughter of Freda Levy, about whom she writes in this anthology.

GARRY HARMAN, a freelance graphic designer, received a Bachelor of Fine Arts in Advertising Design from the University of North Texas. A Texas native raised in Fort Worth, he has worked for Harcourt College Publishers, KTVT-Channel 11, and for numerous advertising agencies. He was the graphic designer for *Beth-El Congregation Centennial*, published in 2002 by Fort Worth's Reform congregation.

LAURIE BARKER JAMES cannot claim to be a native Texan, but considers herself blessed to have spent almost three decades in North Texas. A 1989 graduate of Austin College, she has worked for local and state government and nonprofit social service agencies for over sixteen years. She is currently a freelance grant writer and fund development consultant. This is her first published work of nonfiction.

GLADYS R. LEFF, professor emeritus of the Dallas County Community College District, retired in 1995 from Richland College after twenty-nine years with the district and passed away in 2006. She earned her B.A. and M.A. from New York University and Ph.D. from the University of North Texas. She had written for *Legacies: A Journal for Dallas and North Central Texas*.

RALPH D. MECKLENBURGER, rabbi at Fort Worth's Beth-El Congregation since 1984, is involved in communal and ecumenical affairs at the local, state, and national level. He is the Jewish co-chair of the Jewish-Christian Forum of the Texas Conference of Churches and is adjunct faculty at Brite Divinity School at Texas Christian University. His articles and sermons have been published widely. He was ordained at Hebrew Union College–Jewish Institute of Religion and has held pulpits in San Francisco and Ann Arbor.

LAURAINE MILLER is an award-winning journalist, radio producer, and media consultant. She has been an editor, reporter, and editorial writer at *U.S. News & World Report*, the *Dallas Morning News*, *Fort Worth Star-Telegram*, *Washington Star*, and *Dallas Times Herald*. She produces *The Shape of Texas*, a public radio show about architecture. She is a diversity trainer for the Robert C. Maynard Institute for Journalism Education in Oakland, California, and a consultant to CorpusBeat, a web-based magazine written by high school and college students in the Corpus Christi area. A New York native, she is a graduate of Barnard College and a Texas resident since 1981.

STUART ROCKOFF, raised in Houston, received a Ph.D. in U.S. history from the University of Texas at Austin with emphasis on immigration and American Jewish history. Since June 2002, he has been director of the history department at the Goldring/Woldenberg Institute of Southern Jewish Life and the Museum of the Southern Jewish Experience in Mississippi, where he works to preserve and document the history of Southern Jews.

LARRY L. ROSE is a retired newspaper editor and publisher working as an art and architectural photographer and media consultant. During a forty-one-year newspaper career, he was editor and publisher of the *Corpus Christi Caller-Times* and held editing positions at the *Dallas Morning News*, *Washington Star*, *Miami Herald*, and *Sun-Sentinel* in Ft. Lauderdale, Florida. He was a visiting professor of journalism at Texas A&M University-Kingsville, and, as a student at Kent State University, worked for James Michener on the book, *Kent State, What Happened and Why.*

KENNETH D. ROSEMAN, anthology coeditor, is the rabbi of Congregation Beth Israel in Corpus Christi. He has authored numerous Jewish history books, including a prize-winning series for juvenile readers, and a long list of academic articles. He has taught Jewish history at Southern Methodist University and holds a Ph.D. in Jewish history from Hebrew Union College–Jewish Institute of Religion.

CATHY SCHECHTER, an award-winning writer, co-authored the Texas Jewish Historical Society's first book, *Deep in the Heart: The Lives and Legends of Texas Jews* (Eakin Press, 1990). In 1995, she founded Orchard Communications, Inc., a social marketing consultancy that develops awareness and education campaigns for governmental and nonprofit agencies. A fifth-generation Texan and native of Waco, Schechter lives in Austin and is vice-president of the Jewish Community Association of Austin.

BARRY SHLACHTER, a prize-winning journalist, was formerly the *Associated Press* bureau chief in Pakistan. He also reported for the AP in Japan, India, and East Africa. Following his years as a foreign correspondent, he was a Neiman fellow at Harvard University. After 9/11, on special assignment with Knight Ridder Newspapers, he covered New York City, the Middle East, and the Tora Bora front in Afghanistan. He currently covers business for the *Fort Worth Star-Telegram*, for which he also writes a weekly beer column.

JENNY SOLOMON is an accomplished photographer from Tennessee now living in Fort Worth. She has spent the last twelve years documenting historic religious landmarks of the southwestern United States through the lens of her camera and photographing the native flora of the region along the way. She is a graduate of the University of Georgia.

JAN STATMAN, a New York native who lives in Longview, is author of *Raisins and Almonds and Texas Oil! Jewish Life in the Great East Texas Oil Field* (Eakin, 2004), *The Battered Woman's Survival Guide* (Taylor, 1995), and is co-author of *Living with Environmental Illness* (Taylor, 1998). She wrote the Final Word column for the *Dallas Morning News*, the Arts column for the *Longview News*, and Artist's World column for the *Longview Post*. Statman is a graduate of Hunter College, New York City.

BRYAN EDWARD STONE, a fifth-generation Texan, is an Assistant Professor of History at Del Mar College in Corpus Christi. He completed a Ph.D. in American Studies from the University of Texas at Austin in 2003, and his dissertation, "West of Center: Jews on the Real and Imagined Frontiers of Texas," is under advance contract with the University of Texas Press.

ROBERT S. STRAUSS, a diplomat and popular lecturer, has occupied the Lloyd Bentsen Chair at the LBJ School of Public Affairs at the University of Texas. He was chairman of the Democratic National Committee from 1973 to 1976, chairman of Jimmy Carter's presidential election campaigns, a cabinet-level trade representative, and Carter's personal representative to the Middle East peace negotiations. He was awarded the Presidential Medal of Freedom in 1981 and was George H. W. Bush's Ambassador to Moscow in 1991 and 1992. Strauss founded the law firm that became Akin Gump Strauss Hauer & Feld, which has offices in fifteen cities around the globe.

HOLLACE AVA WEINER, anthology editor, is a Texas transplant born in Washington, D.C. A former reporter at the *Fort Worth Star-Telegram*, she wrote *Jewish Stars in Texas* (TAMU Press, 1999) and has contributed articles on Texas Jewry to anthologies and journals. She is a past president of the

Southern Jewish Historical Society, received a Master's in history from the University of Texas at Arlington, and has won research fellowships from the American Jewish Archives and the Jewish Women's Archive.

GARY P. WHITFIELD, a 1966 graduate of Austin College and a retired Fort Worth middle-school teacher, was born near the central Texas town of Dublin and fondly recalls the years when his hometown had a Jewish mayor. Whitfield is president-elect of the Tarrant County Historical Commission, a member of the Texas Lodge of Research A.F. & A.M., and camp historian for the Tarrant County Robert E. Lee Sons of Confederate Veterans. Whitfield's avocation, documenting Texas graves of Civil War veterans and masons, has led to articles in historical magazines and speeches to historical societies.

Index

Page numbers given in **bold italics** refer to illustrations contained within the text or material contained in their captions. Color plates, or material contained in their captions, are indicated in **bold**.

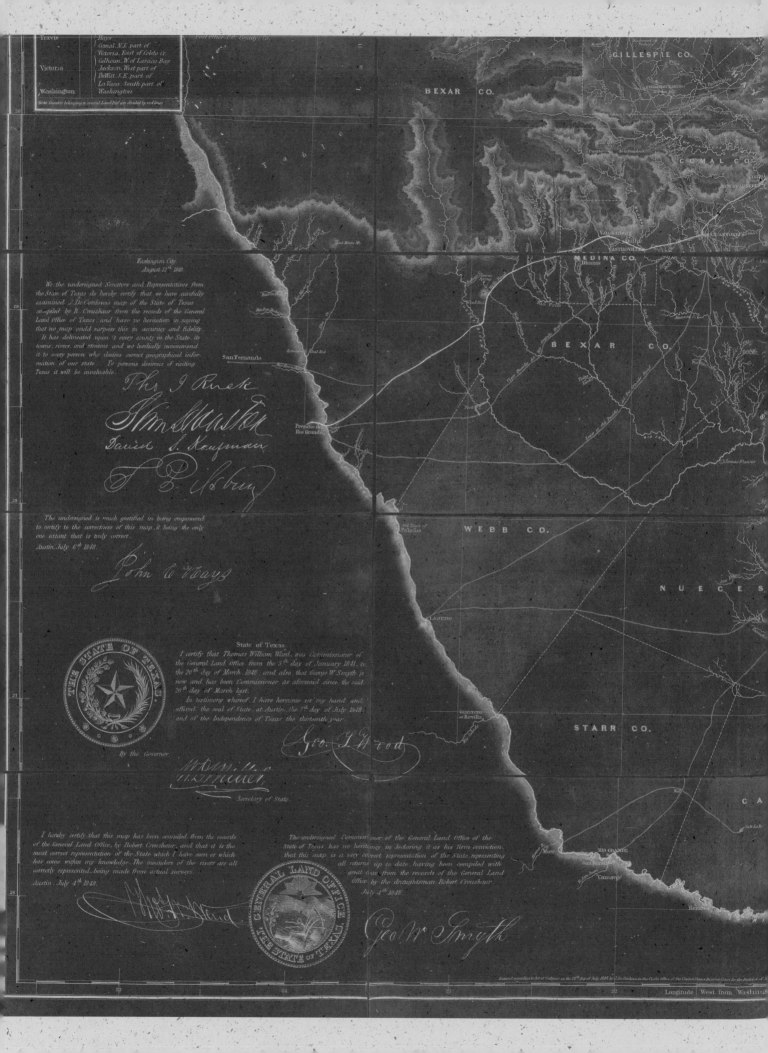